# How to Do *Everything* with

# HTML

## James H. Pence

Osborne/**McGraw-Hill**

New York   Chicago   San Francisco   Lisbon
London   Madrid   Mexico City   Milan   New Delhi
San Juan   Seoul   Singapore   Sydney   Toronto

W9-BKD-985

Osborne/**McGraw-Hill**
2600 Tenth Street
Berkeley, California 94710
U.S.A.

To arrange bulk purchase discounts for sales promotions, premiums, or fund-raisers, please contact Osborne/**McGraw-Hill** at the above address. For information on translations or book distributors outside the U.S.A., please see the International Contact Information page immediately following the index of this book.

## How to Do Everything with HTML

Copyright © 2001 by The McGraw-Hill Companies. All rights reserved. Printed in the United States of America. Except as permitted under the Copyright Act of 1976, no part of this publication may be reproduced or distributed in any form or by any means, or stored in a database or retrieval system, without the prior written permission of the publisher, with the exception that the program listings may be entered, stored, and executed in a computer system, but they may not be reproduced for publication.

1234567890 CUS CUS 01987654321

ISBN 0-07-213273-6

| | |
|---|---|
| **Publisher:** | Brandon A. Nordin |
| **Vice President &** | |
| **Associate Publisher:** | Scott Rogers |
| **Acquisitions Editor:** | Megg Bonar |
| **Project Editor:** | Pamela Woolf |
| **Acquisitions Coordinator:** | Alissa Larson |
| **Technical Editor:** | George Semerenko |
| **Copy Editor:** | Rachel Lopez |
| **Indexer:** | Karin Arrigoni |
| **Computer Designers:** | Tara A. Davis, Lucie Ericksen |
| **Illustrators:** | Michael Mueller, Lyssa Sieben-Wald |
| **Cover Series Design:** | Dodie Shoemaker |
| **Cover Design:** | Greg Scott |
| **Cover Illustration:** | Mel Lindstrom, Tom Willis |

This book was composed with Corel VENTURA™ Publisher.

Information has been obtained by Osborne/**McGraw-Hill** from sources believed to be reliable. However, because of the possibility of human or mechanical error by our sources, Osborne/**McGraw-Hill**, or others, Osborne/**McGraw-Hill** does not guarantee the accuracy, adequacy, or completeness of any information and is not responsible for any errors or omissions or the results obtained from use of such information.
Screen shots of CoffeeCup GIF Animator, ©2001 CoffeeCup Software. Used by permission.
Screen shot of CSS Validator Page, ©2001, Liam Quinn and The Web Design Group. Used by permission.
Screen shots of Cute FTP and CuteMAP, ©2001 Globalscape, Inc. Used by permission.
Screen shot of Mapedit Software, ©2001, Boutell.Com, Inc. Used by permission.
Screen shot(s) reprinted by permission from Microsoft Corporation.
Netscape Communicator browser window ©1999 Netscape Communications Corporation. Used by permission. Netscape Communications has not authorized, sponsored, endorsed, or approved this publication and is not responsible for its content.
Screen shot of W3C® HTML Validator Page ©2001 W3C (http://validator.w3.org). Used by permission.
The images in this book were created with PaintShop Pro and Microsoft Photo Draw.

# Dedication

This book is lovingly dedicated to

My Lord and Savior, Jesus Christ. He gave everything for me, that I might have everything in Him (2 Corinthians 5:21).

My wife, and the love of my life, Laurel. You believed in me, even when I refused to believe in myself.

Robert Key. I write to support my outreach into the Texas prison system, and humanly speaking, you are why I am doing that. Thank you for inviting me in, brother.

# About the Author

**James H. Pence**, and his wife Laurel live near Dallas, Texas, where he directs Tuppence Creative Ministries, an outreach that promotes excellence in the arts for the glory of God. James turned to writing as a helpful means of expression after the death of his infant daughter, Michelle. Nearly 10 years later, "A Road not Chosen," James's narrative account of his and Laurel's experience was published in Dallas Theological Seminary's *Kindred Spirit* magazine.

A full-time freelance writer with a broad diversity of writing experience, James strives for excellence in all his work. He has contributed op-ed pieces to the *Dallas Morning News* and has been published in *Writer* magazine and the 2001 edition of *The Writer's Handbook.* Also a fiction writer, James's first novel, a suspense-thriller titled *Friendly Revenge,* was released in October 1999 (Hard Shell Word Factory). A second novel, *The Osmosis Project*, is currently under consideration by a major publisher. He also is beginning work on a second book for Osborne/McGraw-Hill, *CSS: A Beginner's Guide.*

James trained in creative writing and journalism at Dallas Theological Seminary, where he is currently completing work on a master's degree. He is an accomplished speaker and teacher, having served as an ordained minister for more than 20 years. James is also a gospel chalk artist and vocalist. He uses these talents in reaching out to inmates in the Texas prison system.

James offers 1-, 3-, and 5-day Web authoring seminars: *E-Z HTML Workshop: Web Authoring for Non-Techies.* For booking information for these seminars or his creative writing seminar, visit his Web sites: www.tuppence.org and www.jamespence.com, or e-mail him at: jim@tuppence.org.

# Contents

# Acknowledgments

John Donne wrote: "no man is an island unto himself." That is certainly true when it comes to writing a book. Many more have played a part in this book than space will allow me to mention, but some deserve special recognition.

Megg Bonar, my acquisitions editor, gave me the opportunity of a lifetime. Thank you for all your help and encouragement as we've seen this book become a reality.

Alissa Larson and Pamela Woolf, my acquisitions and project coordinators have been incredibly patient with me as I "learned the ropes." I deeply appreciate your gracious instruction and guidance through the editing and rewrite process, not to mention your tireless work in helping to craft this book.

Rachel Lopez did a superb job as my copy editor. I observed your edits and tried to learn with each chapter, so that your job might become easier as the book progressed. Thank you.

My good friend and technical editor, George Semerenko, deserves a big "thank you." Sorry about some of those late nights you spent debugging my code. Thanks for being honest in your critiques and adding your expertise.

Finally, my agent, Michael Rosenberg, deserves credit for negotiating a great contract. Thanks, Michael, I'm looking forward to many more projects.

By the way, thank you Sherry and John for suggesting I develop a seminar in HTML. If it hadn't been for you, I'd have never written this book.

# Introduction

The title *How to Do Everything with HTML* is an ambitious one indeed. It is something akin to titling a book, *How to Do Everything with English.* Better yet, how about *How to Do Everything with Algebra?* The obvious question is: How do you know when you can do *everything* with any of the above?

HTML is a language, and there are different ways to learn languages. Have you ever seen a book that promises to teach you Japanese in 30 days? Generally, what you get with those books are some basic phrases you can use if you travel to those places. You don't generally learn a whole lot about the language. Although you might be able to order in a restaurant or ask directions, you definitely can't do "everything" with it. On the other hand, you could buy a hefty book on Japanese grammar that expounds the language to the smallest detail. If you make it all the way through one of these reference books, you might have read everything "about" the language. However, you still probably will not know how to do everything "with" it.

HTML books work about the same way. You can buy books that are great for figuring out how to do specific things with HTML—kind of like those "learn Japanese in 30 days" books. In these books you'll find instructions that are so focused and pointed that you can practically cut and paste the code into your own pages. Other HTML books are large, intimidating tomes that literally tell you "everything" about HTML. However, these are not the kind of books a beginner will find helpful.

You see, doing "everything" with Japanese, Algebra, English—or HTML— doesn't mean learning a few stock phrases, formulas, or lines of code. Neither does it mean you must digest an entire reference book of material. It doesn't necessarily even mean that you are fluent. Doing "everything" in this context means you are functional and competent. That is, you understand how the language works, and you know how to use it without pulling a handbook out every five minutes. That's what this book is all about. *How to Do Everything with HTML* is aimed at teaching you how to do Web pages by helping you understand HTML and how it works. While this book won't bring you to a point where you never need reference books, it can help you to gain a strong enough command of HTML so that you don't need to design Web sites with a reference book open the whole time, or cut and paste someone else's code into your site. *How to Do Everything with HTML* can give you the satisfaction of being able to develop your own site and know that it is *yours!*

## Who Should Read this Book

This book is designed for anybody who has ever wanted to do a Web site, but just hasn't got an idea of where to start. You're not a "techie" and definitely wouldn't consider yourself a computer expert, but you're comfortable with your PC. You know how to find your way around your computer, transfer files, change directories, install software, create and save files, and so on. In other words, you're past the stage of being afraid that your system might self-destruct if you do something wrong. You're also willing to learn and not afraid of trying something new. Most important, you *really* want to be able to design and build your own Web pages. If the "want to" is strong enough, you'll be willing to work through the examples and teach yourself this new skill of Web authoring.

## How to Read this Book

If you already have worked with HTML and done some Web authoring, you should have no problem plugging in to any chapter at random and working with that chapter's subject matter. However, if you have never worked with HTML before, you might want to keep some things in mind as you work through this book. While many HTML books are reference-oriented (you already know what you want to do, and find out how to do it by looking it up in the index), this one is tutorial-oriented. The goal of *How to Do Everything with HTML* is to help you write Web pages by understanding how they work. Therefore, you might keep in mind some of the following suggestions as you read:

- **Each chapter builds on the preceding one**    Work through the book chapter by chapter. That way you'll be able to use what you learned in earlier chapters as you develop new skills progressively through the book.

- **Work through the examples; don't just read them**    With any skill, you need to practice. Web authoring with HTML is no different. If you only read about it, you'll never learn it.

- **Modify the examples for your own use**    You'll learn faster and have a better understanding of how HTML works if you experiment with the examples rather than just typing them in "as is." As you play with the code and see the results of your "experiments," go back to the text and try to think through why you got the results you did.

- **Make use of the offline "mini" Web site**    Most HTML books make the code from the book available to the readers as an added bonus. With this book, we decided to actually assemble the examples into a "mini" Web site that you can download and set up on your own computer. This offline site enables you to find the code you need quickly (and gives you some additional pages not provided in the book). It also provides you with all the images created for this book. Most important, you will be able to "dissect" a Web site and hopefully gain an understanding of how to put your own site together. At the end of each chapter you'll find a list of code and images from that chapter and where to find the files.

■ **Take note of the Web design principles**   In most of the chapters, you will find a Web design principle relating to the chapter's subject. While the focus of this book is HTML, following the Web design principles help you to avoid some of the most common mistakes made by beginning Web authors.

## Help You'll Find in this Book

As you read through *How to Do Everything with HTML*, you'll find some helpful resources mixed in with the regular text. These special icons and text boxes give you additional information related to the topic at hand. These helpful conventions and their names are as follows:

### Did you know?   What Boxes Are For

Did You Know boxes give you interesting and helpful background information that is related to the topic at hand.

### How to ...   Utilize These Boxes

How To text boxes add special tips and tricks and other fun things you can do.

*Notes provide additional information related to the particular discussion, but are not necessarily action-oriented.*

*Tips contain additional tidbits of information that will make things easier—how to make the best use of software features, and so on.*

**SHORTCUT**   *Shortcuts offer time-saving steps and suggestions for easier ways to perform particular tasks.*

**CAUTION**   *Look to Cautions for information about pitfalls to avoid, workarounds to employ, and "gotchas" to be aware of.*

## How this Book Is Organized

*How to Do Everything with HTML* is organized into three main sections. Each section focuses on a different aspect of HTML and Web design.

- **Part I**   Chapters 1–7 take you through the basics of HTML and how to build a Web site. These chapters show you everything you need to know to get a site up and running.

- **Part II**   Chapters 8–10 focus on style, how to structure your pages, and how to make them look good. Beginning with tables and then moving to frames and Cascading Style Sheets, you'll learn to craft your site and make it distinctively "yours."

- **Part III**   Chapters 11–18 and the appendixes show you how to add "bells and whistles" to your pages. With audio and video, animations, forms, JavaScript, and even such "advanced" as Dynamic HTML and XML, you can learn how to make your pages "fly." The four appendixes provide practical reference guides that are designed to help you put into practice some of the things you learn—without having to reread the text.

One final recommendation for working through this book and developing your own Web site: Have a great time!

# Part I

# HTML Basics— Everything You Need to Build a Web Site

# Chapter 1

# Get Your Feet Wet with HTML

## How to...

- Understand HTML
- Create and Display a Simple Web Page
- Create a Working Template
- Convert Text to HTML
- Add Comments to HTML
- Create a Home Page for a Web Site

The World Wide Web—you've just got to be a part of it. You've surfed the Net for years and have always wondered what it would be like to put up your own site, but you've got a nagging fear that doing Web pages is too difficult for you. After all, you're not a programmer or a "techie." Relax. You don't need to be a techie to learn how to do Web pages. If you can create and save a text file, know how to use a Web browser, and have some basic experience with the Internet, you have all the skills you need to create Web pages.

So, if you want to do your own Web pages, where do you start? You begin with HTML, the language of the World Wide Web.

# Understand HTML

HTML stands for *Hypertext Markup Language*, and it is the language in which virtually all Web pages are written. Now, don't break out in hives when you hear the word "language." You don't need complex logical or mathematical formulas to work with HTML, and you don't need to think like a programmer to use it. Computer programmers must think through the tasks that they want their programs to perform, and then develop an elaborate (and usually complicated) series of instructions to tell the computer what to do. Although you do need to do some thinking and planning when you use HTML, it is not nearly that difficult. So, how *does* Hypertext Markup Language work?

*Hypertext* refers to the way in which Web pages (HTML documents) are linked together. When you click a link in a Web page, you are using hypertext. It is this system of linking documents that has made the World Wide Web the global phenomenon it has become.

*Markup Language* describes how HTML works. With a markup language, you simply "mark up" a text document with tags that tell a Web browser how to structure and display it. HTML originally was developed with the intent of defining the structure of documents (headings, paragraphs, lists, and so forth) to facilitate the sharing of scientific information between researchers. All you need to do to use HTML is to learn what type of markup to use to get the results you want.

## Markup 101: Four Key Concepts

The first step toward understanding and working with HTML is learning the basic terms that describe most of the functions of this language. You will come across these terms repeatedly as you use HTML and, if you understand them, you will have progressed a long way toward comprehending HTML itself.

### Elements

All HTML pages are made up of *elements*. Think of an element as a container in which a portion of a page is placed. Whatever is contained inside the element will take on the characteristics of that element. For example, if you want to put a large heading on a page, you would enclose it in a *heading* element <h1> </h1>. If you want to create a table, you put the table information inside the *table* element <table> </table>. To construct a form, you need the *form* element <form> </form>.

### Tags

Often, you'll find the terms *element* and *tag* used interchangeably. It's fairly common, but not strictly accurate. An element is made up of two tags: an opening tag and a closing tag. Although it might seem somewhat picky to make this distinction, when XML (*eXtensible markup language*) becomes the big boy of the Web, it will be a very important difference to remember. So, get in the habit of distinguishing between elements and tags, and you'll save yourself some confusion down the line.

## Did you know?

## HTML Uses

You can use HTML for more than Web pages. Once you have a grasp of HTML, you can use it to develop a wide range of applications, including interactive texts, tutorials, e-books, presentations, and more.

Did you
know?

## SGML

HTML is not the only markup language; in fact, it's not even the first. HTML is a subset of a very complicated language called SGML (Standard Generalized Markup Language). SGML is not only a markup language in its own right; it's also sort of a master language from which many other markup languages have been developed. HTML is just one of those languages. XML is a new language developed from SGML, and it is expected to eventually replace HTML as the "language" of Web browsers. During the transition, XHTML (sort of an HTML and XML hybrid) is the preferred method for writing Web pages.

All tags are constructed the same way. The tag begins with a "less than" sign (<), then the element name, followed by a "greater than" sign (>). For example, an opening tag for the *paragraph* element would look like this: <p>. The only difference in a closing tag is that the closing tag includes a slash (/) before the element name: </p>. Your content goes between the tags. A simple paragraph might look like this:

```
<p>This is an HTML paragraph.</p>
```

TIP
*Some HTML elements do not use closing tags. These are called empty elements. For example, the line break element <br> does not require a closing tag. Whereas HTML is flexible where some closing tags are concerned, XHTML and XML are not. The best way to be prepared for the future is by getting in the habit of always using opening and closing tags. In the case of empty elements, write them like this: <br />. When a browser sees the slash, it will recognize the element as one that does not need a separate, closing tag.*

### Attributes and Values

*Attributes* are another important part of HTML markup. An attribute is used to define the characteristics of an element and is placed inside the element's opening tag. For example, to set a paragraph's alignment, you would use the *align* attribute:

```
<p align=" ">This is an HTML paragraph.</p>
```

Be sure to notice that an equals sign and a set of quotation marks follow the align attribute. That's because an attribute needs a *value* to go with it.

*Values* work together with attributes to complete the definition of an element's characteristics. An easy way to think of how attributes and values work together is to compare them with nouns and adjectives. A noun names something; an adjective describes it. An attribute names a characteristic; a value describes it. If *color* is an attribute, *red* could be a value. To instruct a browser to display red text, you would write it as follows:

```
<font color="red">This text will be red.</font>
```

If you wanted to center a paragraph, you could write it with this attribute-value combination:

```
<p align="center">This paragraph is now centered.</p>
```

 *Not all attributes and values work with all elements. If you include a color attribute in the paragraph <p> element above, the browser will ignore it.*

 *Always enclose your values in quotation marks. Although this is not always necessary in HTML, XHTML, and XML demand it.*

## Nesting

Often you will want to apply more than one element to a portion of your page. An essential concept to understand is *nesting*. Nesting simply means that elements must never overlap. For example, because the paragraph <p> element does not accept a color attribute, if you want to center it and have it display in red text you might use <p> and <font> together:

```
<p align="center"><font color="red">Centered, Red text.</font></p>
```

These elements, on the other hand, are overlapping:

```
<p align="center"><font color="red">Incorrect</p></font>
```

Although HTML can be pretty forgiving if your elements are not properly nested, if you overlap elements when you are working on more complicated constructions such as frames or tables, your page might not display properly.

Now that you have a handle on the basic concepts behind HTML, it's time to roll up your sleeves and create your first Web page.

# Create and Display a Web Page

Creating a Web page is so easy, you'll wonder why you waited this long to learn how to do it. All you need are a simple text editor, such as Windows Notepad, and a Web browser to view the page—and you're off and running.

## Create a Web Page in Notepad

To create your first Web page, use Windows Notepad or another text editor. Although you could use Word, WordPerfect, or any other word processor to create HTML documents, it's easier to start with a simple text editor. (For more about HTML authoring tools, see Chapter 17.)

### Understand Document Elements

The elements listed in the following could be called *document* elements because they describe and define your HTML document. You won't use all of these right now, but it's good to know them and understand what they do.

- **<html> </html>**   Defines the beginning and end of the document.
- **<head> </head>**   This is the document header. It works like a storehouse of important information about the document. This information generally is not displayed in the document.
- **<title> </title>**   The title element is nested inside the header. It displays a page title in the title bar at the top of the browser.
- **<body> </body>**   The main body of the Web page goes inside this element.
- **<meta> </meta>**   Goes inside the <head> element and is used to contain even more detailed information about a document.
- **<link> </link>**   This element can be used to link the page to other documents, such as a style sheet or a JavaScript file.
- **<style> </style>**   Allows you to embed style information in the document.
- **<frameset> </frameset>**   Used in place of the <head> element when you want to create a "frames" page.

■ **\<isindex /\>**   Tells a browser that a searchable index of the page resides on the server.

■ **\<!doctype\>**   Describes what version of HTML the document conforms to.

TIP

*Choose your \<title\> carefully. One way search engines find, categorize, and list your page is by its title. So, if you want people to find you, be sure that every page on your Web site has a title that concisely and accurately describes that page's contents. The better your title choice, the more likely your page will come up high on a search engine's results.*

At this point, you need to concern yourself with only the first four elements: \<html\>, \<head\>, \<title\>, and \<body\>. These are the elements you will find in virtually all HTML pages. Strictly speaking, you can get away without using any of them. To see for yourself, just open Notepad and type "This is an HTML page." Then save the document as test.htm. When you display it in a browser, you'll discover that the browser recognizes and displays the page just fine. So, why use HTML?

HTML enables you to define the structure of your page. Although you could display pure text using the method described earlier, you couldn't do much more. So you add the necessary elements to create the Web page you want.

## Create an HTML Template

An HTML *template* is simply a file that has all the basic elements for a Web page already written. It's a good starting place to learn how to create an HTML document. An added benefit is that it saves you the trouble of typing these elements every time you want to create a new page. To create an HTML template, follow these steps:

1.  Open Notepad or another text editor.

2.  In the File menu, choose Save As.

3.  Save the file as template.htm.

4.  At the top of the page type **\<html\>**.

5.  Now add the header element: **\<head\> \</head\>**.

6.  Inside the header, type **\<title\> \</title\>**.

7.  On the next line, type **\<body\> \</body\>**.

8.  Finally, type **\</html\>**.

9.  Click the Save icon.

You have created a template that you can use whenever you want to make a new Web page. Your HTML code should look something like this:

```
<html>
<head><title></title></head>
<body></body>
</html>
```

Incidentally, you could just have easily written each of the tags on a separate line or all on one line for that matter. Web browsers don't really care. It's a lot easier, though, if you try to write your code so that you can understand what the different elements are doing. If it's all jumbled together, you might find yourself confused when you go back in and modify your page.

SHORTCUT    *Creating different templates for your Web pages will speed up your work considerably. Once you have designed a page, save it as a template. Then you can perfectly reproduce the layout every time you want to use that design.*

## Create a Web Page

Now that you have a template to work with, it's time to see just how easy it is to create your own Web page.

1. Open template.htm in Notepad.

2. In between the <title> tags, type **First Web Page**.

3. In between the <body> tags, type **This is my very first Web page!**

4. Save the document as page1.htm.

CAUTION    *Always save the file with either an .htm or .html extension. If you allow Notepad to save your file as a text (.txt) file, a Web browser will not be able to read it.*

Your finished HTML code should look something like Figure 1-1.

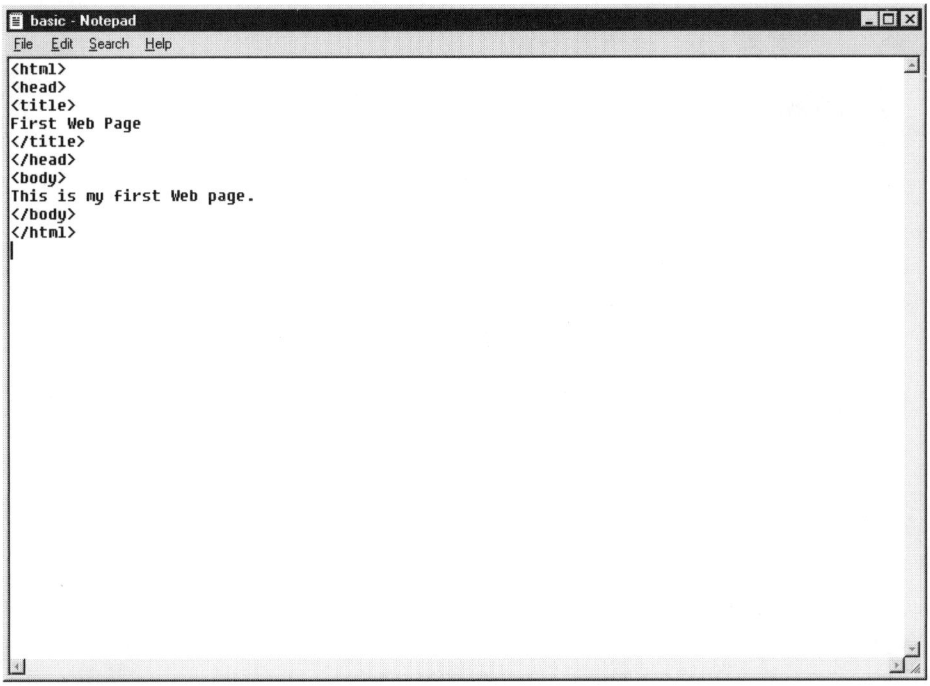

```
basic - Notepad
File  Edit  Search  Help
<html>
<head>
<title>
First Web Page
</title>
</head>
<body>
This is my first Web page.
</body>
</html>
```

**FIGURE 1-1**    A basic HTML page in Notepad

NOTE

*If you are using Windows 95 or higher, you are free to use the longer .html extension. But because your files might end up on a UNIX server, which recognizes only three-letter extensions, it is good practice to save your files with the shorter .htm extension.*

## View Your Page in a Web Browser

Once you have saved your page, it's time to see what it looks like. To display your page, follow these steps:

**1.** Open your favorite Web browser and click the File menu.

2. In Netscape, choose the Open Page option. Internet Explorer users should choose the Open option. If you're using another browser, it will have a similar choice.

3. If you're using Internet Explorer, click the Browse button. Netscape users should click the Choose File button in the Open Page dialog box:

4. Navigate to the directory where you saved the file and click it.

5. IE users click OK; Netscape users click Open. Your file should be displayed in the browser and should look like the sample in Figure 1-2.

You've created your very first Web page! It's as simple as that. As you progress through the rest of the book, you will learn to build on that simple skeleton, creating Web pages that you will be proud to display for the world.

# Convert Text to HTML

As you begin to think about what you would like to put on your Web site, you might be wondering about material that you already have written but that is not "Web ready" yet. Maybe you have some recipes or short stories you've written. Or you might want to put your company's employee manual online. Will you have to retype all that information? Not if you learn how to convert it to HTML. Although it's possible to have a word processor save a file in HTML format, it's not a great idea. Word processors tend to generate messy HTML. Besides, it's quite easy to convert text to HTML.

## Import Text into an HTML Page

Importing text into your HTML document is as easy as using the cut and paste options in Windows.

1. Open template.htm in Notepad.

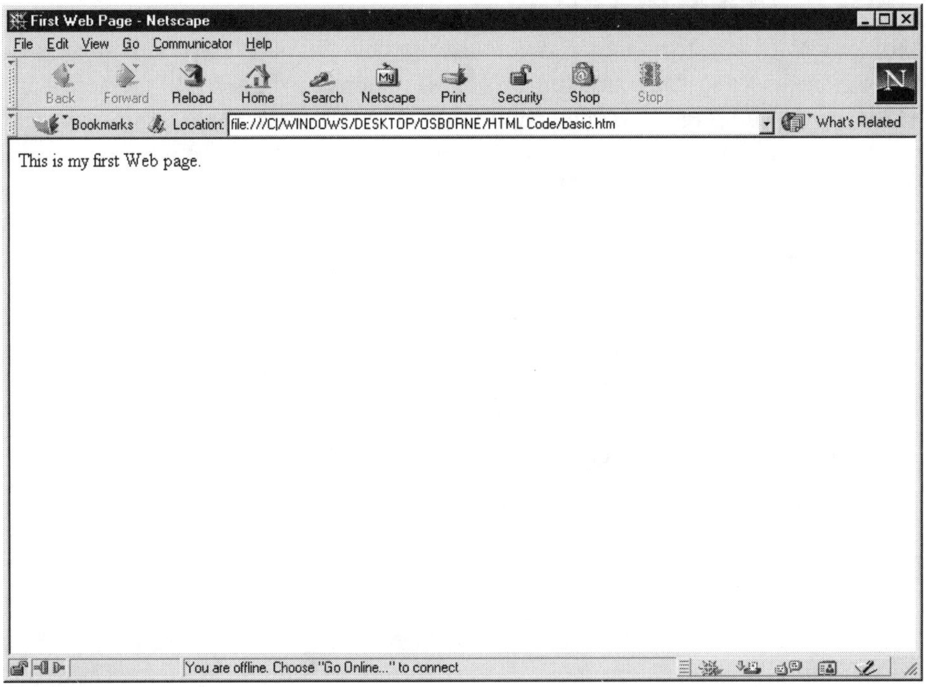

**FIGURE 1-2**    Your first Web page

**2.** Open the document you want to import in your word processing program.

**3.** Select the text you want to import and copy it to the clipboard.

**4.** In Notepad, paste the text in between the <body> tags and then save the document under a different file name (so you don't ruin your template).

**5.** Now, display the page in your browser.

When you import text into an HTML document, it loses any formatting it originally had. It will simply appear as a solid block of text. If you want the material you imported to be organized or formatted in some way, you'll have to do it with HTML elements. In the next couple of chapters, you'll learn how to take your text and shape it up with text elements.

## Convert a Page of Text to HTML

Another way to transform material you already have into a Web page is to simply save the file as a text file (but using an HTML extension). Then add the necessary HTML tags (see Figure 1-3). The main thing to remember is that you must save the file as a pure text file, not as a word processor file. Otherwise, the word processor's codes will interfere with your HTML.

1. Open the file you want to convert to HTML.

2. At the top of the document, type **<html><head><title></title></head><body>**.

3. At the end of the document, type **</body></html>**.

4. From the File menu, choose Save As.

5. Choose Save As Text, and name the file convert.htm.

6. Open the file in your browser.

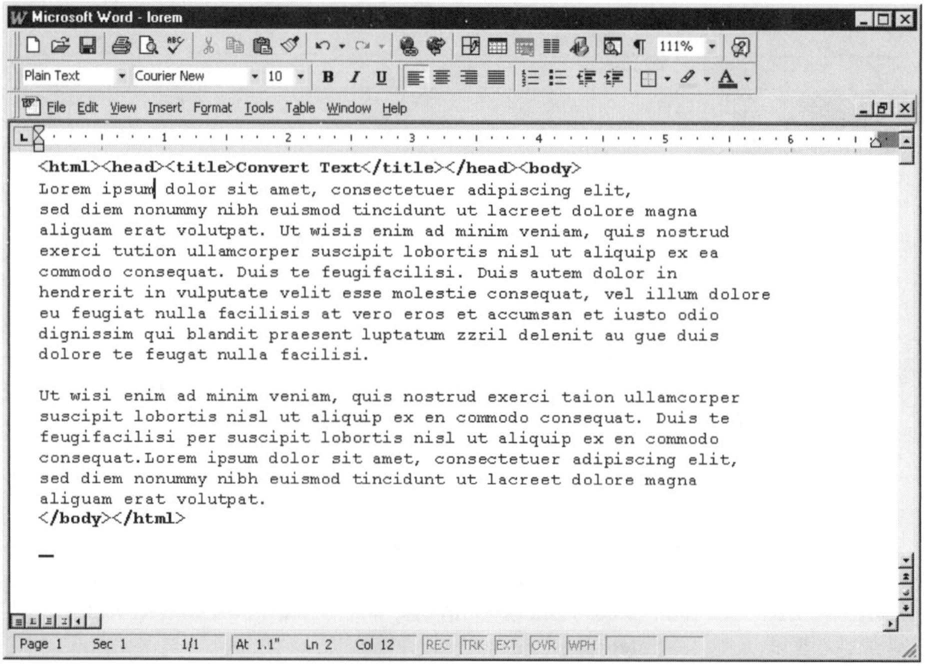

FIGURE 1-3    A word processor document with HTML tags added

# Add Comments to Your HTML Document

Although the first HTML pages you write will be fairly simple, they can get complicated in a hurry. As your pages become more detailed and complex, you might find it difficult to remember what a particular section of code is supposed to do. The easiest solution is to add comments to your HTML source code. Comments function as little notes to yourself (see Figure 1-4). Web browsers will ignore the comments completely, but they will come in very handy if you are writing a complex page with many lines of HTML.

Adding comments to your HTML is easy. Just enclose your comment between comment tags: **<!--** *Add your comment here* **-- >**.

To add a comment to the Web page you just created, follow these steps:

**1.** Open page1.htm in Notepad.

**2.** In between the <body> </body> tags, type the first comment tag:  **<! --** (a "less than" sign, followed by an exclamation point and two dashes).

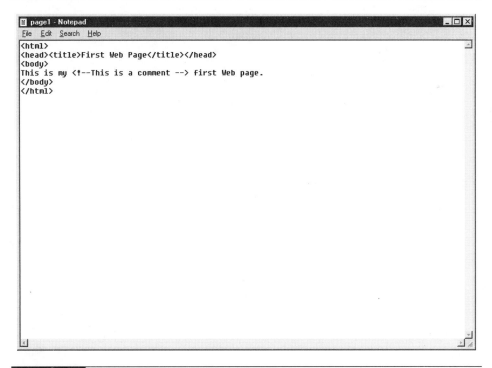

```
<html>
<head><title>First Web Page</title></head>
<body>
This is my <!--This is a comment --> first Web page.
</body>
</html>
```

**FIGURE 1-4**    HTML code with a comment added

**3.** Type: **This is a comment.**

**4.** Type the closing comment tag: **-->** (two dashes followed by a "greater than" sign).

**5.** Your completed comment should look like this:

```
<! -- This is a comment -->
```

If you display the page in a browser, the comment should not display (see Figure 1-5). If you see it, check your comment tags to make sure you wrote them correctly.

TIP *Comment tags are useful for more than putting little notes in your code. When you want to use JavaScript to add some special effects to your page, you can hide the script in comment tags to hide it from older browsers that can't use JavaScript. Older browsers then will ignore your script, whereas JavaScript-enabled browsers will execute it.*

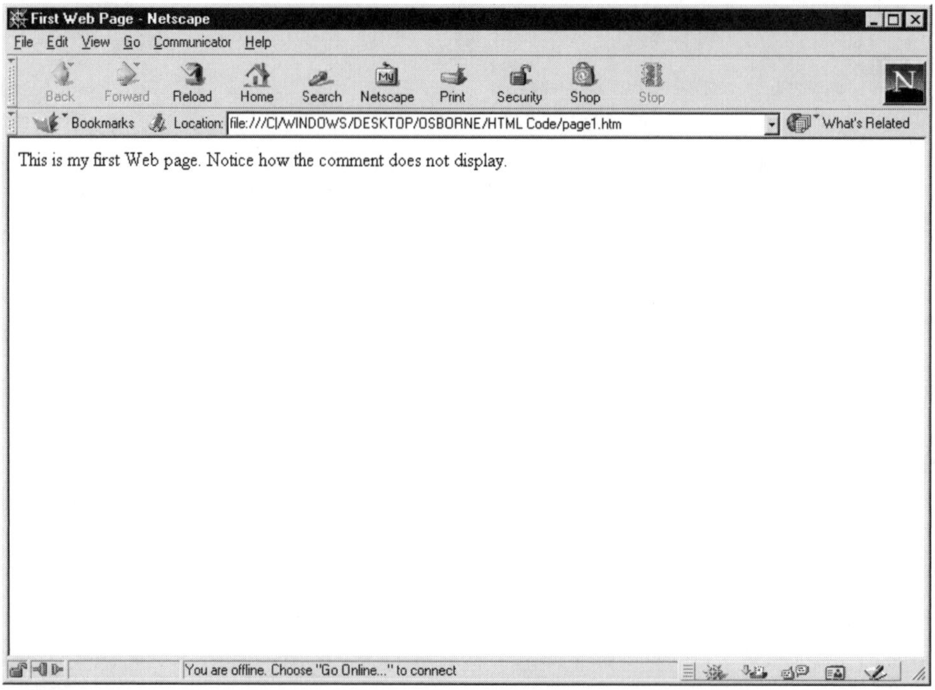

**FIGURE 1-5**    Comments do not display when your page is viewed

# Learn Good Web Design

Writing Web pages is one thing. Designing Web sites is another matter altogether. It is possible to learn the technical aspects of creating HTML documents without gaining an understanding of what makes a good Web site and what makes a poor one. This book is designed to teach you HTML and good Web design principles. At the end of each chapter you will find a brief section on Web design with some principles to keep in mind as you learn HTML.

## Web Design Principle: Plan Your Site Before You Build It

It might seem that this principle is stating the obvious, but you'd be surprised how many Web sites are built on the fly. Someone gets the idea to put up a site, and then simply adds pages without much thought or planning. The site that results usually is a confusing jumble of Web pages that is virtually impossible to navigate. So, before you build your site, try a few of these planning ideas:

- **Clearly define your site's purpose**    Is it a personal site? A business or e-commerce site? Is your site informational in nature? Your design will be influenced by the reason for your site's existence.

- **Consider your audience**    Who do you want to visit your site? What are their needs and interests? Why will your site attract them?

- **Decide what your site needs to be a success**    Many sites add a lot of the "bells and whistles," such as animation, video, audio, and response forms. But if you are merely adding things because they look cool, you might be detracting from your site rather than enhancing it. Decide what you really need to have before including it on your pages.

- **Study sites of similar purpose**    Once you've nailed down your site's purpose, do a little searching to find sites that are similar. Learn from their good design and from their mistakes.

- **Storyboard your site before you construct it**    To a Web designer, a storyboard is like a blueprint. It gives you some sort of idea how your site will work when it actually is constructed. A storyboard can be as simple as a flowchart on paper, with a box representing each page. Or you can use 3×5 cards for your design, taking advantage of the ability to rearrange the cards into different layouts before you develop your site. (For more on storyboarding, see Chapter 7.)

The more planning and preparation you put into your Web site, the better it will be. It also will be easier to add to it and modify it, because you'll have an overall picture of where you are going and what you want to accomplish.

## Practice, Practice, Practice

The best way to learn good Web design (not to mention HTML) is by doing it. The temptation with a book like this is to use it merely as a reference guide, pulling out the snippets of code you need to solve certain problems or create certain effects. But if it is your goal to learn HTML and Web design, you'll do better if you actually develop a Web site as you work through the book. The examples and exercises in this book are designed with that purpose in mind.

To take full advantage of the exercises in this book, try developing your own personal HTML reference site. You'll build it page by page with the examples and suggestions you find in this section.

To get started, follow these steps:

1.  Create a directory on your computer's hard drive that is titled "HTML Reference."

2.  Copy template.htm to that directory.

3.  Rename template.htm to index.htm or default.htm.

NOTE    *Most Web servers require you to name your "home" page either index.htm or default.htm.*

Now you've created a "home" page for your HTML reference site. Granted, right now it is nothing more than a blank page. But beginning in Chapter 2, all that will change.

# Chapter 2

# Work with Text and Lists

## How to...

- Designate Headings
- Format Text
- Create Bulleted Lists
- Build Numbered Lists
- Create Definition Lists

In Chapter 1, you learned how to create a basic Web page. In this chapter you'll have the chance to put something more than raw text on your page. You'll also learn to use lists to provide order and structure for your content.

Working with simple text elements and lists is a great way to begin learning HTML. Text formatting elements are simple, straightforward, and uncomplicated, but they give you good practice for working with tags. Working with lists will allow you to experiment with the concept of nesting that was covered in the last chapter. Nesting (placing HTML elements inside one another) is an important practice that will become essential in the coming years with XML's growth.

# Designate Headings with <h#> </h#>

The purpose of the heading element is to indicate different heading levels in a document. The tags are made up of an *h* with a number following it. For example, to specify a level one heading, you would write:

```
<h1>This is a level one heading.</h1>
```

A level two heading would look like this:

```
<h2>This is a level two heading.</h2>
```

HTML includes six heading levels: <h1>, <h2>, <h3>, <h4>, <h5>, and <h6>. Although the primary function of the <h#> element is to specify headings, it also often is used as a quick way to tell a Web browser to display different sizes of text. Try typing the following HTML code to see how the six heading levels will display on a Web browser:

2

```
<html>
<head><title>The Heading Element</title></head>
<body>
<h1>This is a level one heading.</h1>
<h2>This is a level two heading.</h2>
<h3>This is a level three heading.</h3>
<h4>This is a level four heading.</h4>
<h5>This is a level five heading.</h5>
<h6>This is a level six heading.</h6>
</body>
</html>
```

Now, save this file as headings.htm and open it in your Web browser. Figure 2-1 shows you what you should see when you display your page.

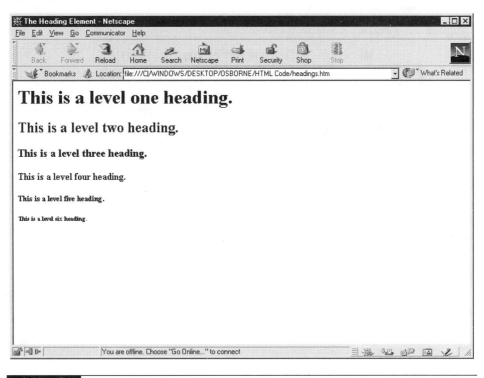

**FIGURE 2-1**    Six heading levels

To experiment further, try adding the align attribute to some of the headings and then check your results. Change the level one heading to read:

```
<h1 align="center">This is a centered level one heading.</h1>
```

Now, modify the level three line to read this way:

```
<h3 align="right">This is a right-justified, level three heading.</h3>
```

Save the file and display it in your browser. It should look like Figure 2-2.

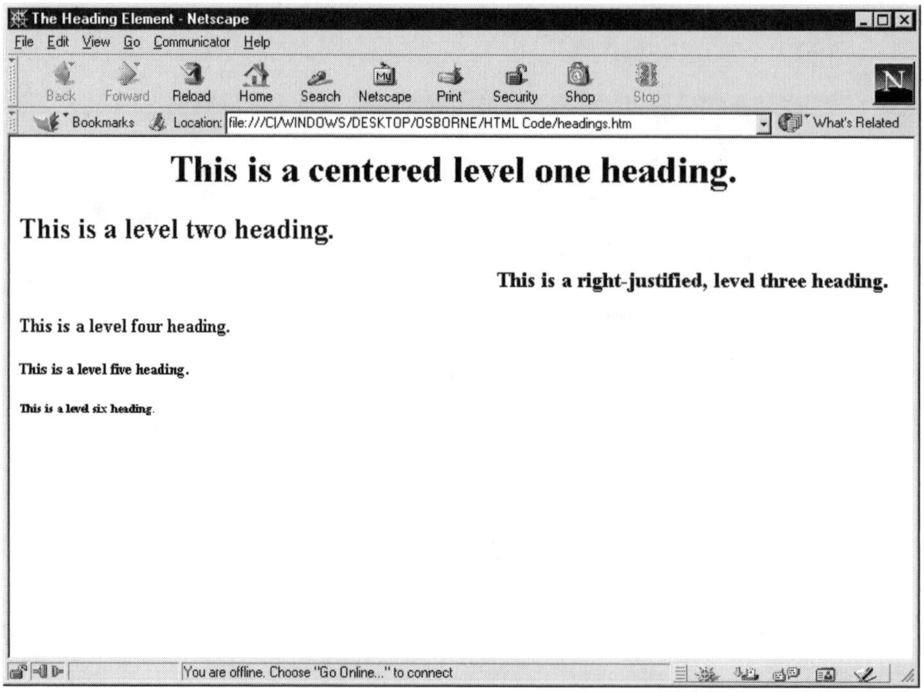

**FIGURE 2-2**    Heading levels with <h1> and <h3> repositioned

2

# Control Text with Character Elements

The character elements give you some basic controls over how text will display on a Web browser. There's nothing fancy here—just meat-and-potatoes text control. As you work with these elements, you will notice that some of them are named for how a character actually will look when it appears on a browser (for example, the bold <b> element for bold text). These are called *physical* elements because they describe the physical appearance of the characters. Other text elements derive their names from the intended function or purpose of the text (for example, the <strong> element also will display bold typeface, but the element's name stands for strongly emphasized text). When a character element is named this way, it is called a *logical* element because it describes the logical function of the text.

## Display Italicized Text

If you want to display text in italic, you have no less than six different elements to choose from. Interestingly, each has its own distinct purpose:

- **<i> </i>**   The *italics* element is a physical element for displaying italicized text.

- **<em> </em>**   The *emphasis* element is a logical element for emphasizing important portions of a document. It generally displays italicized text.

- **<cite> </cite>**   The *citation* element identifies a portion of your document as a reference to an outside source.

- **<var> </var>**   This logical element indicates a *variable*, as might be used in computer code.

- **<dfn> </dfn>**   This logical element identifies a portion of text as a *defining instance* of a term. It also generally displays in italic.

- **<address> </address>**   You might use this logical element (which also renders your text in italics) to set apart your address or personal information at the bottom of a Web page. This element also generally adds a line break before and after the address.

To see each of these elements in action, use your template to create a new HTML document, and save it as text.htm. Then add the following lines in the <body> </body> portion of the page to get the results shown in the following illustration:

```
<i>The italics element renders text in italics.</i><br />
<em>The emphasis element also produces italicized text.</em><br />
<cite>The cite element identifies a citation.</cite><br />
<var>The var element marks a variable.</var><br />
<dfn>The dfn element stands for a defining instance.</dfn><br />
<address>The address element marks off address or author
information.</address><br />
```

> *The italics element renders text in italics.*
> *The emphasis element also produces italicized text.*
> *The cite element identifies a citation.*
> *The var element marks a variable.*
> *The dfn element stands for a defining instance.*
> *The address element marks off address or author information.*

Why are there so many different ways to generate your text in italic? Because HTML is not only concerned with what someone sees when they view a Web page. Hypertext Markup Language is aimed at defining the "nuts and bolts" of a document; not simply its appearance.

Do you have to use all of these different elements? No. But keep in mind that the World Wide Web didn't get that name for nothing. As your knowledge of HTML grows and you become more concerned with making your pages accessible to as many people as possible, you might develop an appreciation for these logical elements.

## Display Bold Text

Two different elements allow you to display boldface text:

- **<b> </b>**    The *bold* element is a physical element that allows you to render boldface text.

- **<strong> </strong>**    The *strong* element also displays in bold. Strictly speaking, this logical element indicates a heavier or stronger emphasis than does <b>, but there is usually no difference in how the two look in a browser.

Try this line for a side-by-side comparison, like the one shown in the following illustration:

```
The <b>bold</b> element and the
<strong>strong</strong> element are the same.<br />
```

> The **bold** element and the **strong** element are the same.

## Display Big and Small Text

If you want a portion of text to appear slightly larger or smaller than the surrounding characters, you can use the following elements:

- **\<big> \</big>**   This element displays text one font size larger than the surrounding text (for more on font sizes, see Chapter 3).

- **\<small> \</small>**   This element reduces text by one font size.

To see the difference, put this line in your page. The following illustration shows what you should see on your screen:

```
The <big>big</big> element and
the <small>small</small> element are useful tools.<br>
```

> The **big** element and the small element are useful tools.

## Create Superscripts and Subscripts

Sometimes you might have a need to add a superscript to your text. Maybe you'll be documenting a source and want to insert a footnote reference at the end of a quotation. Or perhaps you're a science nut and want to describe the molecular structure of water or carbon dioxide. Then you'll need to know how to do a subscript.

- **\<sup> \</sup>**   This element creates a superscript.

- **\<sub> \</sub>**   This element forces text to display as a subscript.

To see these elements in action, insert the following line into your page. It will create a line with both superscripts and subscripts, as in the following illustration:

```
The <sup>superscript</sup> and <sub>subscript</sub> elements
raise and lower text.<br />
```

The <sup>superscript</sup> and <sub>subscript</sub> elements raise and lower text.

## Display Monospaced Text

If you ever need to have your text display in a fixed-width or monospaced font, you have several options available:

- **\<tt> \</tt>**   The "tt" in this case stands for *teletype*. It is a physical element that forces text to display in a "typewriter," or courier style font. It derives its name, obviously, from teletype machines.

- **\<code> \</code>**   This logical element not only displays in a courier, fixed-width font, but also indicates that the text is a portion of computer code.

- **\<kbd> \</kbd>**   Standing for *keyboard*, this logical element identifies its contents as keyboard input. Generally, it displays as a monospaced font. Some browsers also might display it as bold.

- **\<samp> \</samp>**   This is another logical element. It describes its contents as *sample output*, most often rendering text in a monospaced font.

These elements all produce basically the same results. Add the following lines to your page to see for yourself, and then compare your results with the following illustration.

```
The elements <tt>teletype,</tt> <code>code,</code>
<kbd>keyboard,</kbd> and <samp>sample</samp>
all produce the same results.<br />
```

The elements teletype, code, keyboard, and sample all produce the same results.

# Display Strikethroughs

If you want your text to display with a horizontal line drawn through it, you again have more than one element to choose from:

- **<s> </s>**   This *physical* element will display text as "strikethrough."

- **<strike> </strike>**   The *strike* element is another physical element for producing strikethrough text.

- **<del> </del>**   The *deleted* element is a logical element that indicates (by a strikethrough) that the text has been deleted but left in the page.

Try this sample line to see how these three elements compare. Your screen should resemble the following illustration.

```
To display <s>strikethrough</s> text, use the <strike>strike
</strike> or the <del>deleted</del> elements.<br />
```

To display ~~strikethrough~~ text, use the ~~strike~~ or the ~~deleted~~ elements.

# Display Underlined Text

If you want text to display underlined, you again have more than one option:

- **<u> </u>**   The *underline* element will render text with a line underneath.

- **<ins> </ins>**   The *inserted text* element is a logical element that indicates text that has been inserted since the document was written.

Although either one of these elements will produce underlined text, the <ins> element is supported only by Internet Explorer 4 and higher. If you want your text underlined, you are better off using the <u> element. The following illustration reflects the results you will get with these elements:

```
Use the <ins>inserted text</ins> element or the
<u>underline</u> element for underlining text.
```

Use the <u>inserted text</u> element or the <u>underline</u> element for underlining text.

## Retain Text Formatting with <pre>

Even if you haven't been working with HTML for very long, you probably have noticed that any special formatting, spacing, and line and paragraph divisions are lost when you bring text into an HTML document. As you'll see in the next chapter, elements are provided that will allow you to re-create that formatting. But what if you don't want to go to all that trouble? By using the *preformatted text* element, you can tell a browser to display your text exactly as you entered it. Simply enclose the text between the <pre> </pre> tags, and the browser will leave it "as is." The downside of this element is that the browser will display the text in a typewriter-style monospaced font. However, in the next chapter you'll learn how to override this and instruct the browser to use a different font.

To see how <pre> works, try adding the following lines to your sample page. As you see in the illustration that follows, the browser retains whatever spacing you gave the characters:

```
<pre>This is a sample of preformatted text:
Thirty days hath September,
     April, June, and November.
          All the rest have thirty one,
Save February and it has twenty eight.</pre><br />
```

```
This is a sample of preformatted text:
Thirty days hath September,
     April, June, and November.
          All the rest have thirty one,
Save February and it has twenty eight.
```

The text formatting elements give you limited influence over how your text is displayed. In the next chapter you will expand that influence. But before moving into that arena, it will be helpful for you to learn a simple way to structure the information you put on your Web pages.

# Organize Your Material with Lists

HTML lists are a great way to organize material on your Web site. Whether you want to list the ingredients of your favorite recipe, create a page of links with their descriptions, or offer step-by-step instructions for washing a dog, you can use list elements to put your material in order.

## Create a Bulleted List

You need two elements to create a bulleted (or unordered) list:

- **<ul> </ul>**   The *unordered list* element enables you to create the list.

- **<li> </li>**   You specify individual items on the list with the *list item* element.

Use your template to create a new HTML document. Save it in your HTML reference directory as ulist.htm. Then, in between the <body> </body> tags:

1. Type an opening *unordered list* tag: **<ul>**.

2. Next, add a set of *list item* tags: **<li> </li>**.

3. For each new list item, add another set of <li> </li> tags.

4. When the list is complete, type a closing **</ul>** tag.

The code for a simple unordered list might look something like what you see here:

```
<html>
<head><title>Unordered Lists</title><head>
<body>
<ul>
<li>This is the first item</li>
```

```
<li>This is the second item</li>
<li>This is the third item</li>
<li>This is the fourth item</li>
</ul>
</body>
</html>
```

When you display your page in a browser, it will produce a bulleted list, like the one in the illustration here:

- This is the first item
- This is the second item
- This is the third item
- This is the fourth item

You'll notice when you display the list that your browser supplies a solid disc as the bullet for each item. If you would prefer a circle or a square, you can specify it by using the type=" " attribute. To specify the type of bullet for the entire list, put the attribute inside the opening <ul> tag:

- ■ To specify a square: **<ul type="square">**

- ■ To specify a circle: **<ul type="circle">**

- ■ To specify a disc: **<ul type="disc">**

You also can control the type of bullet for each separate item by putting the attribute inside the <li> tag. For example, the following code will supply a different bullet for each item, as reflected in the illustration that follows:

```
<ul>
<li type="square">This supplies a square.</li>
<li type="circle">This supplies a circle.</li>
<li type="disc">This supplies a disc.</li>
</ul>
```

- ■ This supplies a square.
- o This supplies a circle.
- • This supplies a disc.

## Create a Multi-Level List

To create a list with multiple levels, you simply nest one or more unordered lists inside each other. Save ulist.htm with the new name: ulist2.htm. Now make a multi-level list from it:

**1.** Inside the first set of <li> tags, type **<ul>**.

**2.** Add a line that says **<li>This is a sub point.</li>**.

**3.** Add another line that reads: **<li>This is another sub point.</li>**.

**4.** Close out the sub list with **</ul>**.

Your list should look like this:

```
<html>
<head><title>Unordered Lists</title><head>
<body>
<ul>
<li>This is the first item
    <ul>
        <li>This is a sub point</li>
        <li>This is another sub point</li>
    </ul></li>
<li>This is the second item
    <ul>
        <li>This is a sub point</li>
        <li>This is another sub point</li>
    </ul></li>
<li>This is the third item
    <ul>
        <li>This is a sub point</li>
        <li>This is another sub point</li>
    </ul></li>
</ul>
</body>
</html>
```

If you want to add another level of sub points, you can do it by nesting another complete list inside each <li> </li> element where you want the next level. A multi-level list such as the one rendered here will resemble Figure 2-3.

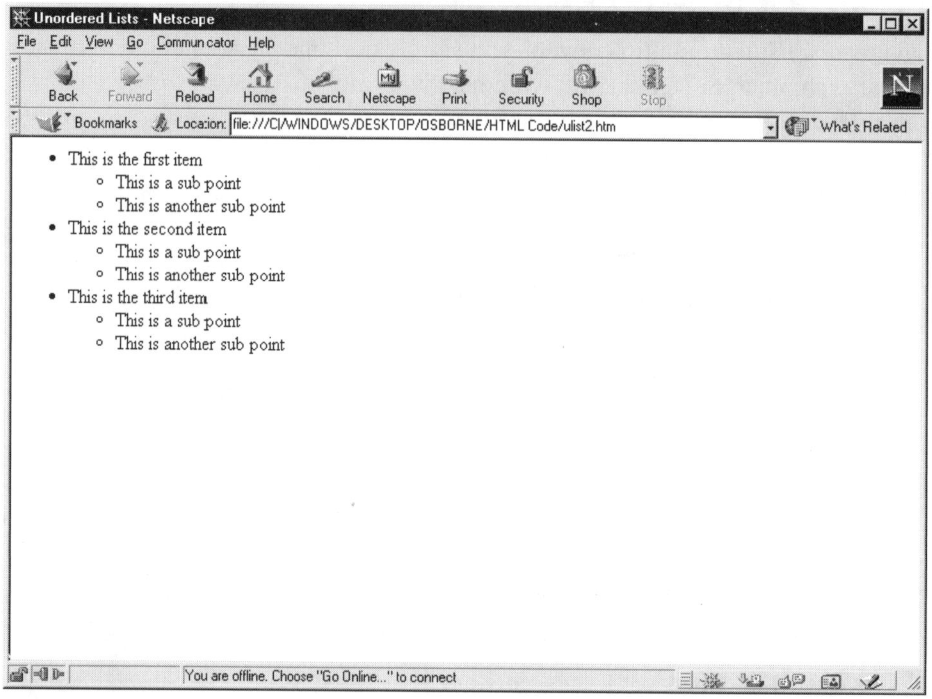

**FIGURE 2-3**    A multi-level list depends on the proper nesting of elements

NOTE    *You can get away with putting your sublist below the list item to which it applies instead of inside the tags. Most browsers will still display it properly. However, it's sloppy HTML and will not meet the more stringent standards of the future.*

TIP    *It isn't necessary to indent the different lines of your code, but it makes it easier to read and distinguish the various outline portions from one another. Indenting and adding comments will make your HTML easier to understand.*

## Create Ordered Lists

What if you want to display an outline with numbers and letters delineating the various points? Or perhaps you want to create a list of instructions in numbered sequence. Lists that arrange items in sequence by number or letter are called *ordered lists* in HTML and are quite similar in their structure to unordered lists. To create an ordered list, you need the following:

- ■ **<ol> </ol>**   The ordered list element

- ■ **<li> </li>**   The list item element

## Use <ol> to Create a Numbered List

You can create a simple numbered list by enclosing a series of list items inside the ordered list element, as in the following sample page. Use your template to open a new HTML page and save it as olist.htm. Then type in this code:

```
<html>
<head><title>Ordered Lists</title></head>
<body>
<ol>
     <li>Ordered lists display items with numbers.</li>
     <li>But HTML doesn't sort the items.</li>
     <li>It only numbers them.</li>
     <li>You have to do the arranging yourself.</li>
</ol>
</body>
</html>
```

After you save your page, display it in your browser. You should see a numbered list like this:

> 1.  Ordered lists display items with numbers.
> 2.  But HTML doesn't sort the items.
> 3.  It only numbers them.
> 4.  You have to do the arranging yourself.

When you display this in a browser, you will notice that the list is numbered in sequence. The actual format depends on the browser you use, but normally it is simply a numbered list. One important difference with numbered lists is that if you nest the lists to create multiple levels, the browser uses the same numbering system throughout; it does not automatically change to a different one with each level. You must use the type attribute to specify any changes you want.

## Use the type Attribute to Specify Numbers or Letters

Just as you can instruct the browser to use different types of bullets in an unordered list, you can tell the browser what types of letters or numbers to use. This is very useful if you want to produce an outline in HTML, as you have a nice range of choices available. You specify numbers or letters with the type=" " attribute, just as you did for unordered lists. To produce this:

- **<ul type="I">**   Capitalized Roman numerals

- **<ul type="i">**   Lowercase Roman numerals

- **<ul type="1">**   Numbers (default)

- **<ul type="A">**   Capital letters

- **<ul type="a">**   Lowercase letters

As in unordered lists, if you place the type attribute inside the <ol> tag, you can specify your preferences for the entire list. If you place the attribute inside a <li> tag, it will change only that particular list item.

## Use the start Attribute to Choose a Starting Number

What if you want to begin a list at a point other than *1* or *A*? All you need to do is include the start=" " attribute at the point where you want to change the number or letter. The browser will start the list at the number you choose and continue numbering from that point. For example, if you want to start a list at the number 23, you might do it this way:

```
<ol type="1" start="23">
```

Create a new HTML document and save it as olist2. htm. Now, try typing the following code and displaying it in your browser to see what a list like this might look like if you did it with Roman numerals, starting at number 10:

```
<html>
<head><title>Ordered Lists</title></head>
<body>
<ol type="I" start="10">
     <li>This is the tenth list item.</li>
     <li>This is the eleventh list item.</li>
     <li>This is the twelfth list item.</li>
     <li>This is the thirteenth list item.</li>
```

```
</ol>
</body>
</html>
```

When you display this in your browser, the list will begin with the Roman numeral "X," as in the following:

```
 X.   This is the tenth list item.
 XI.   This is the eleventh list item.
 XII.   This is the twelfth list item.
XIII.   This is the thirteenth list item.
```

 *Beware of a little quirk with the start attribute. It makes no difference whether you are using numbers, letters, or Roman numerals in your list. To specify a starting point, you always do it with Arabic numbers (1, 2, 3); not the characters that will display in the outline. If you modify the preceding code to use the Roman numeral for 10, start="X", you'll find the browser ignores the instruction entirely.*

## Create an Outline with <ol>

To present material in outline format in HTML takes a bit more thought and planning than it does with an average word processor, but it will produce satisfying results. The following sample HTML code will produce a 3-point Roman numeral outline with lettered sub points:

```
<html>
<head><title>A Sample Outline</title></head>
<body>
<ol type="I">
    <li>First Main Point
        <ol type="A">
            <li>First Sub point</li>
            <li>Second Sub point</li>
        </ol></li>
    <li>Second Main Point</li>
    <li>Third Main Point</li>
</ol>
</body>
</html>
```

The following illustration shows how an outline would look on your Web browser:

```
    I.  First Main Point
        A.  First Subpoint
        B.  Second Subpoint
   II.  Second Main Point
  III.  Third Main Point
```

CAUTION  *Make sure you have properly nested your tags. Your sub point list should be placed in between the list item tag it relates to. If you overlap them or leave out a closing </ol> tag, your outline will not display the way you want it to.*

## Create Definition Lists with <dl>

Perhaps the most versatile type of list is the definition list. Originally developed as a means of creating glossaries in a document, this type of list lends itself most readily to use on Web sites. You will use a different set of elements to create this type of list:

- **<dl> </dl>**   The *definition list* element creates the list.
- **<dt> </dt>**   The *definition term* element identifies the term to be defined.
- **<dd> </dd>**   The *definition description* element sets off the definition.

To see how a definition list works, try typing in the following code and displaying it in your browser. Save the file as dlist.htm. Notice that the code also includes some of the text formatting elements covered earlier in this chapter:

```
<html>
<head><title>Definition Lists</title></head>
<body>
<h1>HTML Terms Defined</h1>
<dl>
<dt>HTML</dt>
<dd>HTML stands for HyperText Markup Language</dd>
<dt>Element</dt>
<dd>An <u>element</u> is made up of two tags.</dd>
<dt>Attribute</dt>
<dd>An <I>attribute</I> describes an element's characteristics</dd>
```

```
<dt>Value</dt>
<dd>A <b>value</b> identifies a specific characteristic</dd>
</dl>
</body>
</html>
```

Displayed in a browser, a definition list will look similar to the one in the following illustration:

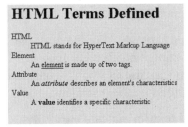

As you can see, this type of list can be very useful; you could use it to provide a page of links, with a special paragraph explaining each link. It also might be used to create a directory of your Web site. The possible uses of the definition list are limited only by your imagination.

# Learn Good Web Design

In this chapter you have learned a host of ways to control how text displays on your Web page. As you develop your ability to create Web pages, keep the following design principles in mind.

## Design Principle: Don't Overload Your Pages with Text

Have you ever visited a Web site where the entire site was made up of pages and pages of text? If you have, you probably have found it tedious to wade through all the material before you on the screen. If you've never experienced what this is like, try visiting one of the many sites that display books that have been "digitized" and put on the Web. How would you like to try reading *War and Peace* on a 12-inch monitor? Not a pretty picture? Neither is trying to labor through a Web site that is straight text; yet you would be surprised how many sites offer their content precisely that way. If you think your material is important enough to put on the

Web, it also is important enough to present it in a format that will encourage people to actually read it. If you plan on displaying a lot of text on your site:

- **Learn to make use of white space**   If you can avoid it, never have a page that is simply a solid block of text. In the chapters that follow, you'll be learning different ways to use white space (space unoccupied by text or pictures) to enhance your presentation.

- **Break your text up into smaller bits**   Go through your content and edit it. Try breaking things up into smaller, bite-size paragraphs.

- **Use lists to your advantage**   For the most part, the trend in Web design is away from the simpler structural elements of HTML, such as lists. But the HTML lists are very useful when it comes to organizing and presenting material. Don't dismiss them—use them.

- **Use headings and text formatting carefully**   Headings and the text formatting conventions you learned in this chapter can be very useful in drawing attention to the portions of your page you want visitors to notice; but be careful how you use them. Think of them as you would salt: Used sparingly, it enhances; too much makes things unpalatable.

## Practice, Practice, Practice

You can read every HTML book in print, but if you don't actually work with the language, you'll never master it. Reading about HTML without doing it is like reading 50 different books on how to fly an airplane, and then expecting to be able to hop into the pilot's chair and fly a Cessna. Even with all that information in your head, you aren't likely to be successful. The more you practice the things you learn in each chapter, the better your command of HTML will become.

In Chapter 1 you created an HTML file and named it default.htm or index.htm. That will be your "home page." In this chapter you created several new Web pages with the following names: headings.htm, text.htm, ulist.htm, ulist2.htm, olist.htm, olist2.htm, olist3.htm, and dlist.htm. As you work through this book, you will take these pages, and others you develop, and build them into an HTML reference manual. You also will put into practice most of the skills you learn.

In this exercise, you will begin developing your home page into a directory for the entire site:

**1.** Open your default or index file.

**2.** Create a level one heading that reads "My HTML reference guide."

**3.** Begin a definition list by inserting a **<dl>** tag below your heading.

**4.** Choose a name or title for each of the preceding files (pages) . Some suggestions are Headings, Text, Unordered Lists, Multi-Level Lists, Ordered Lists, the Start Attribute, Outlines, and Definition Lists.

**5.** Make each page name a definition term by enclosing it in **<dt> </dt>** tags.

**6.** Add a description of each page, enclosed in **<dd> </dd>** tags. For example,

```
<dt>Headings</dt>
<dd>This page displays HTML's six heading levels.</dd>
```

**7.** Close your definition list with a **</dl>** tag.

If you get stuck, review the material covered earlier in the chapter. To see a sample solution, go to this book's companion Web site at www.osborne.com.

# Find the Code Online

To find the code online for this or any of the chapters in this book, go to Osborne's Web site: www.osborne.com, and click the Free Code choice on the navigation bar. From the list of books, select the *How to Do Everything with HTML* option and you will be able to download the book files, which are linked together and organized as an offline "mini" Web site. For more on how to use the "mini" Web site, see Chapter 17.

| Use This Code For... | Look for This Filename |
| --- | --- |
| HTML template | template.htm |
| Headings | headings.htm |
| Text elements | text.htm |
| Unordered list | ulist.htm |
| Unordered list (with subpoints) | ulist2.htm |
| Ordered list | olist.htm |
| Roman numeral list | olist2.htm |
| Sample outline | olist3.htm |
| Definition list | dlist.htm |
| Sample home page | sampleindex.htm |

# Chapter 3

# Position and Modify Your Text

## How to...

- Create Line and Paragraph Breaks
- Indent Text
- Position and Align Text
- Choose Fonts
- Control Font Sizes and Colors
- Use Inline Styles for Better Control

So far, you have learned how to create a Web page and add basic text and list elements. You've also probably noticed that your results aren't too exciting. Perhaps you'd prefer using something a little fancier, with a variety of sizes and colors. In this chapter you will learn how to choose different fonts and control their size, position and colors. You also will understand one of the most important issues in HTML and Web design: the issue of structure versus presentation.

# Understand Structure and Presentation

If you've done much reading about HTML, you've probably come across the term *deprecated* more than once. The term refers to HTML elements and attributes no longer recommended for use by the World Wide Web Consortium (or W3C), the governing body that oversees the use and standardization of HTML. For example, the <font> element, which you will learn about in this chapter, is one of many elements and attributes that have been officially deprecated by the W3C. Because the word "deprecate" literally means to express disapproval for something, you might wonder why the W3C is expressing disapproval for HTML elements. To understand the answer to this question, you must learn a bit of HTML history.

## HTML Originally Defined Structure

When HTML was first developed by Tim Berners-Lee in 1989, the Internet was a very different place. It was used mostly by the government and universities and was primarily for the exchange of scientific or scholarly information. The transmitted material was documentary and looked more like a term paper than a Web page. So when HTML was created, the main concern was document structure. For example, the <h1> through <h6> elements defined heading levels

## Did you know?

## W3C Web Site

The W3C has a Web site that provides current information on HTML, XHTML, XML, style sheets, and a host of other Web-related subjects. The URL is http://www.w3.org.

one through six. Other elements—for example, paragraphs, lists, and so forth—defined how text was to appear on the page. In other words, in early HTML document structure was everything; that is, until the arrival of the World Wide Web and graphical Web browsers.

## HTML Extended to Address Presentation Issues

When the Web came on the scene, almost overnight the academic world of HTML became a world of color, pictures, and design. Prior to the Web, a document's presentation was virtually a non-issue. But advances in graphics moved presentation to the front. This created a problem: HTML was never intended to deal with design issues. Web designers found themselves struggling with the issues of how to create pleasing pages and maintain some control over how their documents appeared when viewed online. Because HTML didn't provide the tools they needed, they developed "workarounds"—they used HTML code in ways it was not intended to be used to achieve control over presentation. As time passed, HTML was extended to include new elements, such as <font>, that governed presentation rather than structure. As a result, over time HTML began to move away from its original purpose and into the design arena. The problem was that HTML's inherent limitations made it a very poor design tool.

## Use HTML for Structure; CSS for Presentation

The W3C has been working to solve the problems of HTML's limitations by separating structure from presentation. That's where *Cascading Style Sheets,* or CSS, come in. Using CSS, a designer has precise control over a Web page's presentation without having to use the old "workarounds." The W3C's wish is that you use HTML as it was intended, to define your document's structure; and use CSS to define its presentation or style. For that reason, the W3C has "deprecated" many of the elements that were developed as extensions to HTML in favor of CSS.

For the time being, you're safe using these deprecated elements, but eventually browsers will not recognize them (although that day probably is a long, long way off). However, if you plan to develop Web pages in the future, you'll need to know how to use CSS. That won't be a problem for you, because from this chapter on you'll be learning CSS along with HTML. By learning both HTML and CSS, you'll be able to work in the present and be prepared for the future. So, roll up your sleeves and get ready to learn how to control fonts on your Web page.

# Control Text Flow

If you paste a text file into your sample Web page in Chapter 2, you will notice instantly that text loses even the simplest formatting when brought into an HTML document: indents, paragraph breaks, and line spacing all are lost. But HTML provides several means for indicating breaks in your text.

## Create Line Breaks with <br /> and Paragraphs with <p>

These elements are structural in nature and help you control how your text will be divided on the page. The difference between the *line break* and the *paragraph* elements is that when you use <br /> you're telling a browser to insert a line break and go to the next line:

```
To insert a line break, use the line break element. <br />
```

The <p> element, on the other hand, will add a blank line before it starts your new paragraph:

```
<p>Use the paragraph element to identify paragraphs.</p>
```

## Insert Ruler Lines with <hr />

The *horizontal rule* element, <hr />, will draw a horizontal line wherever you place it. When it was first introduced, <hr /> didn't give you any control over how your line appeared on the page. Now you have a few options for choosing how your rules appear.

### Use the width Attribute to Specify Rule Length

For instance, you can specify the width of the rule by adding the width attribute:

```
<hr width="25%" />
```

This creates a rule that covers 25 percent of the screen and tells the browser to draw a horizontal rule and to size it at 25% of the screen size. You can specify whatever percentage you want. Another way to select the length of your rule is by the number of *pixels* (the little "dots" that make up the pictures on your monitor). To use pixels instead of percentages, simply include the number *without* the percent sign:

```
<hr width="200" />
```

This creates a rule that is 200 pixels wide.

> TIP
>
> *If you're interested in making horizontal rules flexible, use percentages rather than pixels. That way, the rule will automatically adjust itself to the monitor that displays it.*

## Specify a Rule's Thickness with the size Attribute

You can specify the thickness of the rule with the size attribute, but this time you must use pixels instead of percentages. Try modifying your rule to display 3 pixels thick (the default is 1 pixel):

```
<hr width="25%" size="3" />
```

## Use the noshade Attribute to Turn Off a Rule's Shading

Some browsers display a horizontal rule with shading that gives it a 3D look. If you prefer your rule to appear as a solid line, add the noshade attribute:

```
<hr width="25%" size="3" noshade />
```

## Use the color Attribute to Select a Rule's Color

Some browsers will display rules in color. You can choose a color by adding the color attribute:

```
<hr width="25%" size="3" noshade color="blue" />
```

Now, to experiment with some of the text control elements you have learned, open the HTML template you created in Chapter 1 and save it as text2.htm.

1. Between the <title> </title> tags, type **Text Control Elements**.

2. Just below the <body> tag, type **<p>** and then follow it with a line of text. If you can't think of what to write, you can copy the sample code from the following code listing.

3. Decide where you want the line to break and type a **<br />** tag.

4. When you've finished with your paragraph, put in a closing tag: **</p>**.

5. Begin a new paragraph with another **<p>** tag and enter some more text. Remember to use **<br />** wherever you want the browser to enter line breaks. Then close out your second paragraph with another **</p>** tag.

6. Finish your sample by putting an **<hr />** line below the last paragraph.

7. Now save your page and open it in your browser. It should look something like Figure 3-1. If your page doesn't display correctly, compare your code to the following sample code.

8. Just for fun, go back into the file and add some of the modifications to the <hr /> tag to see what results you get.

```
<html>
<head><title>Text Control Elements</title></head>
<body>
<p>In the past, you didn't need to enclose your paragraphs<br />
with the paragraph tags, but now it is advisable to do so.<br />
Actually, HTML is forgiving enough that it wouldn't be<br />
a problem if you didn't, but you can't count on that<br />
in the future, when XML rules.</p>
<p>The line break tag gives you the ability<br />
to tell HTML where to break your text<br />
instead of letting the browser do it for you.</p>
<hr /> <!-- Horizontal rule line here -->
<p>To make use of the horizontal rule, just place<br />
it wherever you want the rule to be.</p>
</body>
</html>
```

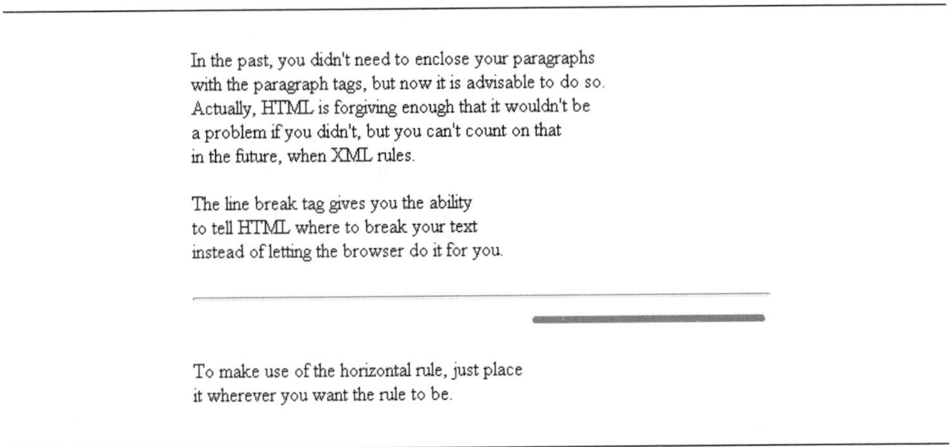

In the past, you didn't need to enclose your paragraphs
with the paragraph tags, but now it is advisable to do so.
Actually, HTML is forgiving enough that it wouldn't be
a problem if you didn't, but you can't count on that
in the future, when XML rules.

The line break tag gives you the ability
to tell HTML where to break your text
instead of letting the browser do it for you.

To make use of the horizontal rule, just place
it wherever you want the rule to be.

FIGURE 3-1    Use <p> and <br /> to properly structure your page, and <hr /> when you want to mark off divisions visually

## Indent Text

When you want to indent text in a word processor, just press the TAB key. In HTML, it's not that simple. Because Web browsers ignore normal text formatting instructions, you have to be creative to indent text.

### Use   to Add Spaces

The *nonbreaking space* entity ( ) will instruct a browser to add spaces wherever you want them. However, most commonly it is used to create an indent at the beginning of a paragraph. To use it, you type the characters ** ** where you want the spaces inserted. In case you're wondering what an *entity* is, all you need to know about them at this point is that they *always* begin with an ampersand (&) and end with a semicolon (;). The letters in between these two characters tell the browser to insert special characters (in this case, a space). If you want to have a five-space indent at the beginning of a paragraph, type five nonbreaking space entities at the beginning of the line you want to indent. (For more on entities and how to use them, see Appendix C).

### Use the Definition Description Element <dd> to Indent Text

An easier way to indent is to borrow from the list elements covered in Chapter 2. You'll remember that the dictionary list included a dictionary term <dt></dt> element and a dictionary definition element <dd></dd>. The definition description element automatically indents. So, by enclosing the top line of your text in this element, you can force an indent without typing all those entities.

## Use <blockquote> to Indent a Large Block

If you want to indent everything from the left margin, the easiest way to do it is to use the <blockquote> element. Blockquote is one of those elements that was never intended to be used for presentation purposes, but often is used that way. Its true function is to set apart long quotations. It does function well if you want to quickly indent a block of text. Keep in mind that when you enclose your text in this element, you will instruct the browser to indent the margins from both sides. By *nesting,* or enclosing, the text inside two or more sets of <blockquote> tags, you can increase the amount of the indent. Perhaps it's not an ideal way of indenting, but it will get the job done.

1.  Go back to the text file you just created and indent the first line by adding the nonbreaking space entity. Just inside the <p> tag type ** ** once for each space you want to indent. For a standard five-space indent, type   five times. Don't forget to begin each entity with an ampersand and close it with a semicolon.

2.  Now, indent your second paragraph by using the definition description element. Just inside the <p> tag type **<dd>**, and before the <br /> or </p> tag type **</dd>**. This should indent the first line. Your code will look like this:

    ```
    <p> <dd> Text </dd> </p>
    ```

3.  To experiment with <blockquote> you'll need to add another paragraph to your text. Type some text in or copy the code from below.

4.  Now insert the <blockquote> tag just inside the first <p> tag and </blockquote> at the end of the paragraph (not the line), just inside the </p> tag. Your HTML should resemble this:

    ```
    <p><blockquote>Paragraph of Text</blockquote></p>
    ```

When you view your paragraph in your browser, the entire paragraph should be indented. Just for fun, add another set of <blockquote> tags to your paragraph and see the result. Properly nested, your code will look like this:

```
<p><blockquote><blockquote>Paragraph of Text</blockquote></blockquote></p>
```

When you view your paragraph in a browser, it will be indented even more, as is the example in Figure 3-2.

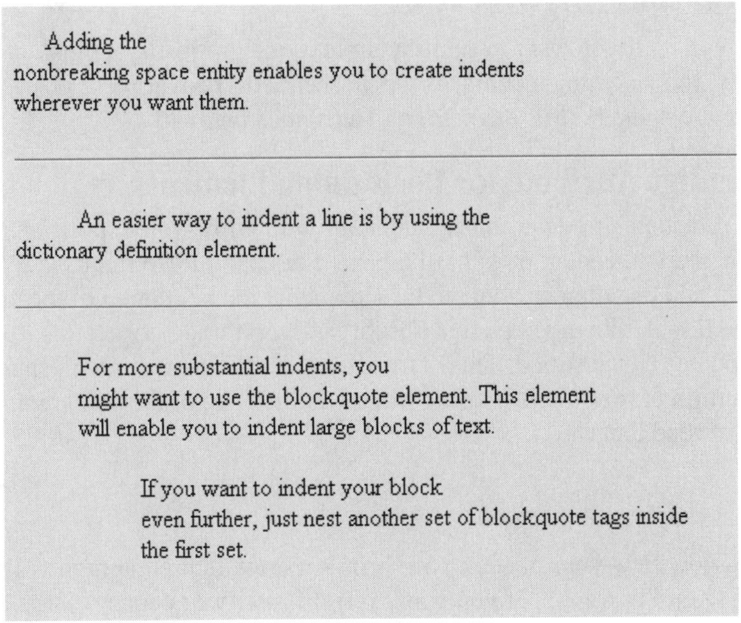

Adding the
nonbreaking space entity enables you to create indents
wherever you want them.

An easier way to indent a line is by using the
dictionary definition element.

For more substantial indents, you
might want to use the blockquote element. This element
will enable you to indent large blocks of text.

If you want to indent your block
even further, just nest another set of blockquote tags inside
the first set.

**FIGURE 3-2**   Use  , <dd>, and <blockquote> to indent

```
<html>
<head><title>Adding Indents</title></head>
<body>
<p>      Adding the <br />
nonbreaking space entity enables you to create indents<br />
wherever you want them.</p>
<hr />
<p><dd>An easier way to indent a line is by using the</dd><br />
definition description element.</p>
<hr />
<p><blockquote>For more substantial indents, you<br />
might want to use the blockquote element. This element<br />
will enable you to indent large blocks of text.</blockquote></p>
<p><blockquote><blockquote>If you want to indent your block<br />
even further, just nest another set of blockquote tags inside<br />
the first set.</blockquote></blockquote></p>
</body>
</html>
```

# Position and Align Text

What do you do if you want to center your text or right-justify a block of text? Obviously, the indenting techniques we've seen won't cover these possibilities. But, there are some HTML elements and attributes that will.

## Use the align Attribute for Positioning Elements

The align attribute, used with many elements, will allow you to position text (or images) at the left, center, or right of a page. For example, to right-justify a single paragraph, add the align attribute to the <p> tag at the beginning of the paragraph. The tag will look like this: <p align="right">. Everything between the <p></p> tags would be right-justified. This is fine if you just want to align one paragraph or a brief portion of text. To see how it works, modify one of the paragraph tags of your file to read this way:

```
<p align="center">Text</p>
```

When you view your page in your browser now, that paragraph will be centered, as in Figure 3-3. If you want to right-justify or center a large number of paragraphs, it might get a bit bothersome to include the align attribute with every one. Fortunately, there's an easier way.

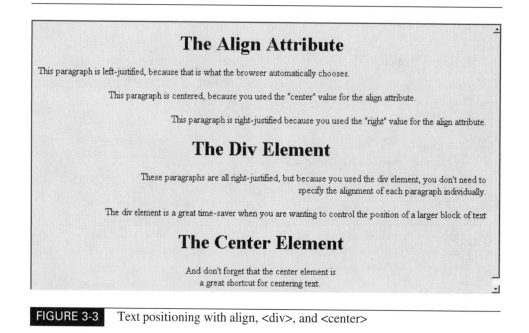

**FIGURE 3-3** Text positioning with align, <div>, and <center>

> **TIP**
>
> *When using the align attribute, it's often not necessary to specify "left" alignment, as the browser usually defaults to this arrangement anyway. There are exceptions, though, so always check to see how your pages display.*

## Use <div> </div> to Position Large Blocks

The <div> element, used with the align attribute, enables you to right-justify a large block of text. For example, to right-justify several paragraphs, you would simply enclose all the paragraphs inside the <div> element:

```
<div align="right">Several Paragraphs</div>
```

To see <div> in action, follow these steps:

1. Open your HTML template and save it as alignment.htm.

2. Now, remembering what you learned earlier, create several paragraphs of one or more lines each. Remember to use <p> and </p> at the beginning and ending of each paragraph, and <br /> where you want lines to break.

3. When you've created your paragraphs, insert the tag **<div align="right">** before the *first* <p> tag. Insert a **</div>** after the last </p> tag. Now save the page and open it in your browser.

4. When you view the page in a browser, all the paragraphs should be right-justified.

5. To change the alignment, simply change the value inside the quotes to either "center" or "left."

> **NOTE**
>
> *Aligning paragraphs is only one function of the <div> element. This element marks off a division so you can assign attributes to a large portion of a page at one time.*

## Use <center> to Center Objects and Text

If all you want to do is center your text, the <center> </center> element is the easiest way to do it. This element works the same way as the <div align="center"> tag. To see how it works, simply replace your <div> tags with <center> tags. Now check out the results in your browser. Your results should look something like Figure 3-3.

### Experiment with align, <div>, and <center>

Try reproducing Figure 3-3 by opening template.htm and saving it as align.htm. Then enter the code listed here:

```
<html>
<head><title>Text Alignment</title></head>
<body>
<h1 align="center">The Align Attribute</h1>
<p>This paragraph is left-justified, because that<br />
is what the browser automatically chooses.</p>
<p align="center">This paragraph is centered, because<br />
you used the "center" value for the align attribute.</p>
<p align="right">This paragraph is right-justified because<br />
you used the "right" value for the align attribute.</p>
<hr align="center" width="50%">
<h1 align="center">The Div Element</h1>
<div align="right"><p>These paragraphs are all right-justified,<br />
but because you used the div element, you don't need to<br />
specify the alignment of each paragraph individually.</p>
<p>The div element is a great time-saver when you are<br />
wanting to control the position of a larger block of text</p></div>
<hr align="center" width="50%">
<h1 align="center">The Center Element</h1>
<center><p>And don't forget that the center element is<br />
a great shortcut for centering text.</p></center>
</body>
</html>
```

NOTE    *The HTML for Figure 3-3 was modified to allow the text to fit on one screen. When you type in the preceding code, each paragraph will cover several lines, giving you a better illustration of paragraph alignment.*

# Choose and Modify Fonts

You now know how to move your text around and align it, but thus far you haven't exercised much control over the size, type, or color of your fonts. The text elements you learned in the previous chapter gave you a little control, but the <font> element expands your ability to control how text appears on your page.

## Control Fonts with the <font> Element

The <font> element has been officially deprecated by the W3C. That means they would rather you didn't use it in writing Web pages. But it remains a fairly easy way to manipulate a Web page's text, and until style sheets are more widely supported, you need to know how to use it. But, in all fairness to the W3C's preferences, you'll learn later in this chapter why it is to your advantage to learn how to control your fonts with CSS.

Although <font> does not give you complete control over how your fonts appear, it does enable you to specify a number of sizes, not to mention font faces and colors. To choose or modify the font for a line, a portion of a page, or even an entire page, all you need to do is enclose the text between <font> </font> tags and specify what changes you want to make with the size, face, and color attributes. Whatever text is enclosed in the tags will be changed according to your specifications.

## Adjust Font Size with the size Attribute

You can specify seven different sizes for your fonts with the size attribute. These sizes are conveniently numbered one through seven, with one being the smallest possible size and seven the largest. It works somewhat the same way as the <h1> through <h6> elements you learned about earlier, but in this case you get one extra size. The default or automatic font size is 3. To see size in action, follow these steps:

1. In the HTML page that is already open, choose any paragraph and add the following tag, just inside the <p> tag: <p><font size="7">.

2. Remember to put a closing </font> tag just inside the closing </p>.

3. Your code should look something like this:

```
<p><font size="7">Text</font></p>
```

4. Now view it in your browser. You will see that all the text within those tags is displayed in a very large font.

5. Try substituting the numbers 1–6 in place of the 7 and see what kind of results you get. Remember: 3 is the default or normal text size.

That seems easy enough. But what if you want to use a larger font size for the whole page without having to bother with <font>? For that, you use <basefont />.

## Use <basefont /> to Set Default Font Sizes

Remember that the default font setting for a Web page is 3. By the way, don't think points here, as in a 10pt or 12pt font. You'd never want to use a 3pt font on a Web page. Your visitors would need a magnifying glass just to read it. The number 3 here is relative to the seven available font sizes. So, consider 3 to be in the middle somewhere, an average font. Logically, then, the numbers 4–7 would represent fonts larger than 3, whereas 1 and 2 would be smaller. Now, if you want a little more flexibility, <basefont /> can help.

With the <basefont /> element, you can change the default font setting for the entire page either higher or lower. So, if all your text should appear in a larger font size, you would put the basefont element in your page like this:

```
<basefont size="5" />
```

That means you have changed the default font setting from 3 to 5. Now, unless you specify otherwise by using the <font> element, all your text will appear in this larger font. To try it out, just go back to your HTML document and insert the basefont tag given earlier. You can put it in either the head or body of the page—either will work. When you view your page, all the text will display in whatever font setting you have chosen.

**SHORTCUT** *If you remember that the default font size is 3, you can make it larger or smaller by adding to or subtracting from it. For instance, to use a size 7 font, you could write either <font size="7"> or <font size="+4">. Because the default size is 3, using a "+4" will result in a font size of 7. Conversely, a tag that reads <font size="-1"> will give you a font size of 2 (3-1=2).*

To get a feel for how to control font size with <font> and <basefont />, create a page and type in the following HTML code:

```
<html>
<head> <title>Font Size Experiment</title> </head>
<body>
<basefont size="5" />
<p>The default text size for this page is now<br />
basefont 5. That will result in some fairly large<br />
text</p>
<p><font size="3">By choosing a 3 value for<br />
this font, we have reset it to the default size.</p>
<p>Of course, we could have changed just
  <font size="+4">one</font>
word<br />
if we'd wanted to.</p>
</body>
</html>
```

3

Save your page as fontsz.htm and view it in your browser. It should resemble Figure 3-4.

## Control Font Styles with the face Attribute

You don't have to specify a font as long as you are happy with the default fonts that most browsers have. But as you design pages, you might decide you want to use some different fonts to jazz up your site. The way to tell the browser to use a different font is with the face attribute. Wherever you want to change fonts, simply enclose the text in the <font> element and specify the font face in the first tag.

To experiment with an Arial font instead of the default, Times New Roman, add this line to the HTML page you have been working on:

```
<font face="Arial">This text is in an Arial font.</font>
```

You can specify any font you want to. If, however, you use a lot of unusual fonts, keep in mind that some of your visitors' browsers might not have the same fonts installed. What will happen when they view your page? The browser will simply use its default fonts to display your text. It's advisable to make sure your pages look good in the default fonts as well as the ones you choose.

To further increase the chances of displaying your choice of fonts, include more than one option in the <font> tag. This way you can give the browser your first, second, and third (and more) choices. When it loads your page, the browser will look for the first font. If it isn't there, it will proceed to the next one, and so on until it either finds one of them on the user's system or has to pull out its trusty

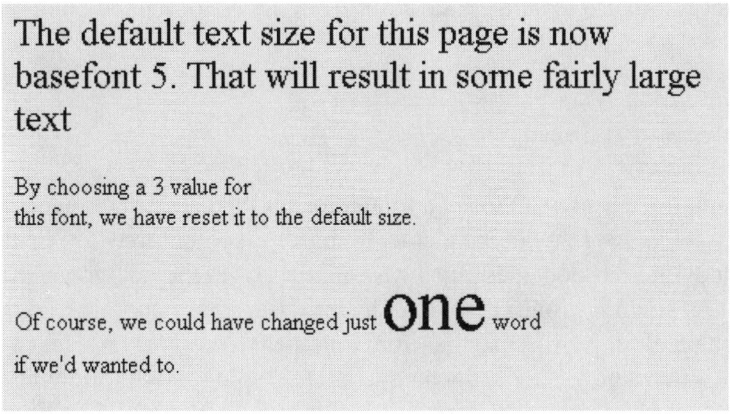

The default text size for this page is now basefont 5. That will result in some fairly large text

By choosing a 3 value for
this font, we have reset it to the default size.

Of course, we could have changed just **one** word
if we'd wanted to.

**FIGURE 3-4**    The <basefont> and <font> elements increase your control over text size

default fonts. If you want to include more than one choice in the <font> tag, write it like this:

```
<font face="Arial, Verdana">This gives
the browser two choices</font>
```

You can add as many fonts as you want as long as you separate them by commas.

## Select Font Colors with the color Attribute

If you want to dress up your page with different-colored fonts, you can do it by adding the color attribute to your font tag. Add this line to your HTML page to see a font displayed in red:

```
<font color="red">This font will be displayed in red</font>
```

If you want to specify colors by name, you have the option of using the 16 Windows colors: black, silver, gray, white, maroon, red, purple, fuchsia, green, lime, olive, yellow, navy, blue, teal, and aqua. A much larger range of colors is available, but to take advantage of them you will need to use either a Netscape-named color (see Appendix A) or the color's hex code. Because the use of color is covered in detail in Chapter 4, this chapter only focuses on how to place these color codes inside the font tag.

Try adding a line with a font tag containing the hex code for blue:

```
<font color="#0000ff">This will produce a blue font.</font>
```

If you want to use a more exotic color from the list of named colors developed by Netscape, try adding this line:

```
<font color="mediumvioletred">This is a
Netscape-Named Color.</font>
```

Incidentally, if you want to set a font color for the entire document, you can do it with <basefont />. Just put the element, <basefont color="red" />, in either the head or body of your document; this way all the text in the document will display in red unless you use <font> to instruct the browser to use another color.

To get a feel for how to use the <font> element to control how text appears on your page, open a new HTML document and try typing in the following code. Save it as fontx.htm and view it in your browser. It should look like Figure 3-5.

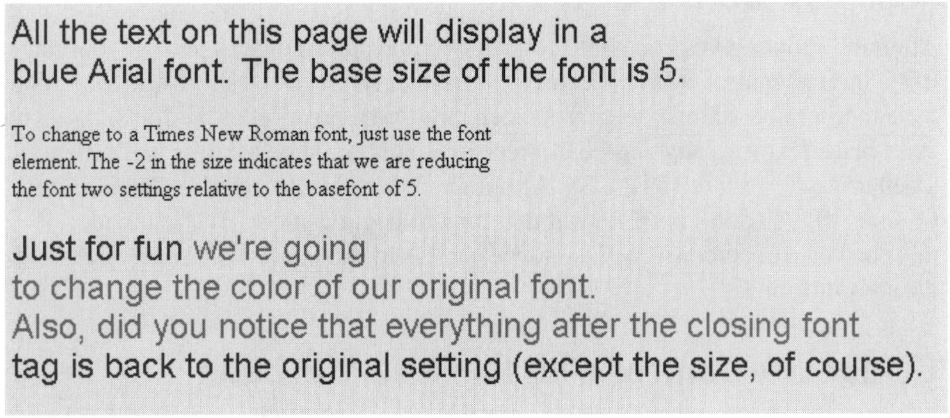

All the text on this page will display in a
blue Arial font. The base size of the font is 5.

To change to a Times New Roman font, just use the font
element. The -2 in the size indicates that we are reducing
the font two settings relative to the basefont of 5.

Just for fun we're going
to change the color of our original font.
Also, did you notice that everything after the closing font
tag is back to the original setting (except the size, of course).

**FIGURE 3-5**    The <font> and <basefont> elements allow you to control color, too

```
<html>
<head><title>Experiment with Fonts and Colors</title></head>
<body>
<basefont face="Arial" size="5" color="blue" />
<p>All the text on this page will display in a<br />
blue Arial font. The base size of the font is 5.</p>
<p><font face="Times New Roman" size="-2" color="black">
To change to a smaller, black Times New Roman font,
 use the font<br />
element. The -2 in the size indicates
that we are reducing<br />
the font two settings relative to
 the basefont of 5.</font></p>

<p>Just for fun<font color="mediumvioletred"> we're going<br />
to change the color of our original font.<br />
Also, did you notice that everything
 after the closing font</font><br />
tag is back to the original setting
 (except the size, of course).</p>
</body>
</html>
```

# Use CSS for Better Control

Although <font> gives you some control over the appearance of text on your page, it is a limited control at best because you have only seven sizes to work with. You have to use rather clumsy workarounds to adjust the position of the fonts. And you can't place text with any degree of precision. You might be asking, "Isn't there a better way?" Yes, there is: CSS. Although CSS will be covered in detail in Chapter 10, you don't need to wait that long to begin using it. The remainder of this chapter will demonstrate just how easy it is to use *inline style sheets* by using the style attribute.

## Get Precise Control with the style Attribute

Cascading Style Sheets are somewhat of a misnomer for what you are using here. The term "style sheet" implies something separate from the page, and you will see later why the term "cascading" is used. What you will work with here is called an *inline style*. It works about the same way as what you have learned already with HTML. In Chapter 1 you learned the three most important terms in HTML: elements, attributes, and values. An attribute goes inside an element and describes what you want to modify. A value is attached to the attribute and gives the details of how you are going to modify the element.

Inline style sheets are similar, but add one more term to the mix: *property*. Property is a term you will become very familiar with as you work with CSS. It functions like an attribute; that is, it tells the browser what aspect of an element you are modifying. For example, some properties you might use in adjusting a font are font-family, font-size, margin-left, margin-right, color, and so forth. You will see that you have a much larger selection of properties to work with in CSS, and you can do many more things with them.

Using inline styles is similar to using any other attribute inside an element. However, there are a few important differences in syntax:

■ Property-value combinations must be enclosed in the quotation marks that follow the style attribute:

```
<p style="All properties-values go in here">
```

■ Properties and values must be separated by a colon:

```
<p style="property: value;">
```

3

■ Property-value combinations must be separated by a semicolon:

```
<p style="property: value; property: value; property: value;">
```

For example, to choose an Arial font and display it in green, your tag would look like this:

```
<p style="font-family: Arial; color: green;">
This is a green Arial font</p>
```

To demonstrate the versatility of CSS, try telling your browser to display a paragraph in a 24pt, Verdana font, and have the font display in navy with a left margin of 1.3 inches.

1.  Once you've chosen a paragraph to modify, remove any size, face, or color attributes from the opening <p> tag.

2.  Insert the style= attribute within the tag. This tells the browser that you are using a style sheet:

    ```
    <p style= " " >
    ```

3.  To set the font, choose the font-family property:

    ```
    <p style=" font-family: ">
    ```

4.  Now specify the font style you want to display:

    ```
    <p style="font-family: verdana; ">
    ```

5.  Tell the browser to display a 17pt font. Be sure to separate each property-value combination from the next one by a semicolon:

    ```
    <p style="font-family: verdana; font-size: 17pt; ">
    ```

6.  Now choose a left margin of 1.3 inches:

    ```
    <p style="font-family: verdana;
            font-size: 17pt; margin-left: 1.3in; ">
    ```

7.  Finally, set the font color to navy:

    ```
    <p style="font-family: verdana;
            font-size: 17pt; margin-left: 1.3in;
            color: navy;">
    ```

8.  Save your page and display your newly styled paragraph in your browser. Quite a difference!

CAUTION *In CSS you have to put a hyphen (-) between related words. If you use a font that has more than one word in its name, you must hyphenate it. For example, the Cooper Black font must be written as Cooper-Black. Likewise, Times New Roman should be Times-New-Roman. If you leave out the hyphens, browsers will not recognize the term.*

This is only a sampling of what you can do with CSS. As you work your way through this book, you will learn how to use CSS to create Web pages that are attractive and of high quality.

For a comparison of a regular paragraph and one styled with an inline style sheet, type the following code and save it as styledemo.htm. View it in your browser to see the difference.

```
<html>
<head><title>CSS Inline Style Demo</title></head>
<body>
<p>This is a regular paragraph</p>
<p style="font-family: verdana; font-size:
24pt; margin-left: 1.3in; color: navy;">This
is a styled paragraph</p>
</body>
</html>
```

The following illustration compares a "regular" paragraph with a "stylized" paragraph.

This is a regular paragraph

# This is a styled paragraph

What does CSS give you that <font> does not? Control. With CSS, Web designers have precise control over how objects are displayed on their Web pages. Compared to that, <font> seems a bit klunky, doesn't it? The best part is that you can use the style attribute inside almost any element. (See Appendix C for a list of elements that do not accept the style attribute, plus a detailed listing of CSS selectors, properties, and values.)

CAUTION  *Even though CSS gives you precise control over your page's design, never forget that browsers allow their users to override your design in favor of their own preferences. Always take into account what your page will look like when viewed on a browser that gives priority to the user's font and color choices.*

# Learn Good Web Design

In this chapter you have learned how to control, position, and modify your text with <font> and inline style sheets. With style sheets particularly, your choices are virtually unlimited when deciding how your text is going to be displayed. Unfortunately, many beginning Web authors make a huge mistake at this point—they go font crazy.

## Web Design Principle: Don't Go Font Crazy

You know you've gone font crazy when your page has over 25 fonts in 15 sizes, and you have used almost all 216 browser-safe colors in one page. HTML gives you the ability to design whatever kind of pages you'd like, but it's not a license for gaudiness…well, maybe it is. At least you have the freedom to do whatever you want when designing your own Web page—but your visitors don't have to come back. And if your page overwhelms them with an endless succession of odd, varicolored, and multi-sized fonts, it's a good bet they won't.

If you want people to rave about your page rather than laugh at it, remember: Don't go font crazy.

In practical terms, that means

- Limit your fonts to two or at the most three on one page.

- Don't use a lot of different sizes; be consistent.

- Be restrained in your use of color. Harsh colors make text difficult to read.

- Avoid extremely large fonts; monitors don't display them well.

- Large fonts for logos are better done in a graphics program.

For other suggestions on good Web design, and complete reference listings for everything covered in this chapter, visit this book's companion site at www.osborne.com.

## Practice, Practice, Practice

Try improving the look of the sample home page created at the end of Chapter 2 by changing the fonts, font colors, and sizes. Experiment with the <font> element, inline style sheets, indenting, and alignment until you are comfortable working with these elements and attributes.

# Find the Code Online

To find the code online for this or any of the chapters in this book, go to Osborne's Web site: www.osborne.com, and click the Free Code choice on the navigation bar. From the list of books, select the *How to Do Everything with HTML* option and you will be able to download the book files, which are linked together and organized as an offline "mini" Web site. For more on how to use the "mini" Web site, see Chapter 17.

| Use This Code For... | Look for this Filename |
| --- | --- |
| Text elements | text2htm |
| Text alignment | align.htm |
| Font demo | fontsz.htm |
| Font size experiment | fontx.htm |
| Inline style demo | styledemo.htm |

# Chapter 4

# Introduce Color Sensibly to Your Pages

## How to...

- Specify Colors by Name
- Specify Colors by Code
- Create a Color Comparison Page
- Use Style Sheets for Color Control
- Choose Pleasing Colors

The Web is a world of color—more than 16 million colors to be more specific. All those choices can be a daunting prospect for a Web designer, making you either throw up your hands in confusion or throw caution to the wind and choose whatever colors seem good to you. This chapter covers the science and art of doing color on the Web. It is a science because you can select from those 16 million colors with mathematical precision. It is an art because a failure to use color wisely can result in a page that is difficult to read, hard on the eyes, or hopelessly gaudy. Thoughtfully chosen color combinations can say to the people who visit your site, "This is a class operation."

# Understand and Experiment with Color

You might not be an artist, but at some point in your life you've probably used paints, colored pencils, or even crayons. When you sat down before a blank sheet of paper you had 10, maybe 12 colors before you. You experimented, mixed colors, and generally had a great time creating a picture that was uniquely your own. Can you imagine what it would have been like if, maybe in school, your teacher plopped down a box of crayons that had more than 16 *million* colors? That's what you have when you work with color in HTML. With that many choices, where do you start? Try starting with the 16 basic colors.

> **NOTE** *The figure 16 million (16,777,216, to be exact) derives from the 256 possible "settings" for red, green, and blue—the three colors from which all others are created. If you multiply 256 by 256 by 256, you arrive at the figure of 16.7 million.*

# Specify Colors by Name

You won't need to read many books on Web design before you'll come across the term *palette,* which artists use to refer to the colors they have to work with at any given time. Web designers have a number of different palettes available to them; only a few need to be covered here. The easiest way to begin working with color on the Web is by using the *named* colors. These colors require no special coding for a browser to recognize them; just type in the color's name and the browser does the rest. There are two lists of named colors to choose from: the 16-color basic palette and the Netscape-named colors.

## Use the 16-Color Basic Palette

The basic palette, sometimes called the HTML or Windows palette, is a range of 16 colors, generally based on the colors that Windows makes available as default colors. The top 16 are white, black, silver, gray, red, maroon, yellow, olive, lime, green, aqua, teal, blue, navy, fuchsia, and purple. Because it's more fun to actually do something with color rather than just read about it, try setting some (or all) of these colors as background colors on a blank Web page.

To specify these colors as a background for your page, use the following:

- The color's name

- The bgcolor=" " attribute

To experiment with the basic palette, open template.htm and save it as colorcompare.htm. In the opening <body> tag, add bgcolor="blue". Your opening <body> tag should look like this:

```
<body bgcolor="blue">
```

Save the page and display it in your browser. You'll notice that the screen is a nice shade of blue. Go back into the page and change the color to any of the other color names, to see how it displays as a background color.

## Use the Netscape-Named Colors

The 16 basic colors are fun to start with, but they can be rather restricting. Who, after all, wants a bright red or drab olive background for a page? If you are yearning for a little more freedom in color choices, but still want to be able to specify the colors by name, the Netscape-named colors are worth a look. These color combinations, developed and named by Netscape, provide you with an additional 120 colors to work with (See Appendix A for the complete list). The names for the Netscape colors are reminiscent of the creative names you find on some crayons. Instead of plain old "red" and "blue," you have options like "lemonchiffon" and "orchid."

You can experiment with any of these colors by using the bgcolor attribute in the opening <body> tag, just as you did previously. However, another way to see how these colors display is to create a simple table. If you don't know how to create an HTML table yet, don't worry. Just type the following code exactly as written. You'll learn about tables and how they work in Chapter 8.

To create a one-celled color display table, open template.htm and save it as colorcompare.htm; then type in this code:

```
<html>
<head><title>Color Comparison Table</title></head>
<body>
<table border="0"  cellpadding="100">
<tr><td bgcolor="peachpuff">Sample Color</td></tr>
</table>
</body>
</html>
```

TIP    *If you are using your HTML template, the bold type indicates the new code you have to type in. Don't type in the other tags unless you are starting from scratch.*

When you have saved your page, display it in your browser. Your results should look like the example in Figure 4-1. To see any of the colors displayed, substitute the color name inside the quotation marks by the bgcolor attribute.

## Specify Colors by Code

Although the Netscape-named colors are convenient and easy to use, you might not want to use them exclusively. Whenever you design pages for the Web, you must keep in mind that many people use older browsers that do not recognize the Netscape names. When your page displays on one of these browsers, your carefully chosen "peachpuff" background probably will display as the browser's default (usually gray or white) color. Another problem you might encounter with

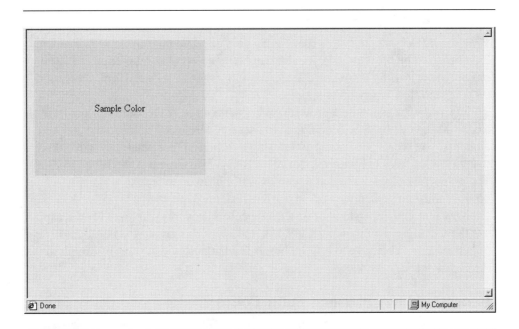

**FIGURE 4-1**    Simple Color Viewing Page

Netscape's named colors is that only a few of them are browser-safe. Not sure what browser-safe colors are? Well, it doesn't mean that the browser will crash or the computer will explode if you use unsafe colors. It does mean that your Web pages won't look very good on some monitors.

Think of the colors on a computer monitor as being made up from three master "tubes" of paint: red, green, and blue (often referred to as RGB). In this case, the "pigment" is light rather than paint. Any of the 16.7 million colors referred to earlier in this chapter can be created using a combination of those three colors of light. However, because of differences in equipment (older monitors and computer systems have limited display capabilities), the majority of those 16 million colors will be *dithered* when displayed. Dithering isn't a great problem in itself, but it does tend to make Web pages look sloppy. If you want to avoid it, you must use browser-safe colors.

TIP    *If you're not sure what dithering is, just set your computer's display to show only 16 colors; then run your Web browser. Do you see the "speckling" that shows up in most of the images? That's dithering.*

### Understand Browser-Safe Colors

Browser-safe colors are colors that have a very specific mixture of red, green, and blue light. To be browser safe, a color can be made up of combinations of RGB only in the following amounts: 0%, 20%, 40%, 60%, 80%, and 100%. Feeling a bit confused? It's really quite simple.

Say you want to create a browser-safe shade of red. You could try this formula: Red=100%, Green=20%, Blue=20%. Because you're using color in the proper amounts, you won't have any problems with dithering; but what if you decide to create a shade of red with this formula: Red=93%, Green=27%, Blue=14%? The odd percentages mean that the color is not browser safe and is likely to produce dithering when viewed on certain systems.

Now that you understand browser-safe colors, how do you tell a browser to use them? Unless you're using CCS, it's not as easy as giving the color amounts in percentages. You have to tell the browser what colors you want by supplying the colors' *hexadecimal code*.

### Understand Hexadecimal Color Codes

What is hexadecimal code? In simple terms, it is the base-16 numbering system used by computers. Trying to understand how to use hexadecimal could be very confusing, but fortunately all you need to know is how to specify the browser-safe percentages mentioned above. Check Table 4-1 for the percentages and their hexadecimal equivalents.

## How to ... Use Subtractive and Additive Color Mixing

Color does not mix the same way on a computer as it does with paint or other solid pigments. If you mix the primary colors in pigment (red, yellow, blue), you will wind up with black. This is called *subtractive* color mixing. If you mix the primary colors with light (red, green, blue), you will end up with white. This is called *additive* color mixing. If you mix green and blue pigment, your result will be mud. Mix green and blue light and you'll end up with light blue!

| Percentage | Hexadecimal Equivalent |
|---|---|
| 0% | 00 |
| 20% | 33 |
| 40% | 66 |
| 60% | 99 |
| 80% | cc |
| 100% | ff |

**TABLE 4-1**    Browser-Safe Color Percentages and Hex Equivalents

Specifying a color using hex code really is quite easy. Just remember that the individual colors you will mix are always red, green, and blue and that they are always listed in that order. To mix the shade of red mentioned in the preceding paragraph, the code would be: red-ff (100%), green-33 (20%), and blue-33 (20%). If you're not sure where the codes come from, look at the chart again. It's important that you understand this.

The code for the color is built by combining the codes for the individual RGB values and by adding the pound (or number) symbol in front. Your completed code for a browser-safe red is: #ff3333. Try it out. Open your colorcompare.htm again and in the opening <body> tag, use the bgcolor attribute to set the color to your custom browser-safe code. It will look like this:

```
<body bgcolor="#ff3333">
```

There are 216 different choices of browser-safe colors, more than enough to give your Web site that distinctive look. Try experimenting with the colors by creating browser-safe combinations from the chart listed in Table 4-1.

> **TIP**
> *This book's companion Web site, www.osborne.com, provides a chart of all the browser-safe colors. To see them side by side, go to the site and choose the colorchart.htm file.*

## Use the Basic Colors by Code

You also can specify the 16 basic colors by their hexadecimal codes. Table 4-2 lists the colors and their codes together. Notice that half of them do not fit the browser-safe

| Color | Hex Code | Color | Hex Code |
|-------|----------|-------|----------|
| Black | #000000 | White | #ffffff |
| Aqua | #00ffff | Blue | #0000ff |
| Navy | #000080 | Teal | #008080 |
| Yellow | #ffff00 | Lime | #00ff00 |
| Green | #008000 | Olive | #808000 |
| Red | #ff0000 | Maroon | #800000 |
| Fuchsia | #ff00ff | Purple | #800080 |
| Gray | #808080 | Silver | #c0c0c0 |

**TABLE 4-2**    The 16 Basic Colors with Hex Codes

description by using the specific percentages listed in the preceding (80 is equal to 50% in hexadecimal, and c0 is just less than 80%). However, because they are basic system colors, they are still considered safe to use.

Try using one of the basic colors for a background on your colorcompare.htm page. To change your background color to teal, adjust the <body> tag to read this way:

```
<body bgcolor="#008080">
```

Now, save the page and view it in your browser. Your background should be teal.

TIP    *If you want the convenience of using Netscape's named colors and the security of browser-safe colors, Appendix A gives you a formula for converting the Netscape colors to the nearest browser-safe equivalents.*

# Set Colors with bgcolor, text, <font>, and <basefont>

Now that you have learned the basics of how color works in Web browsers and experimented with color a little, it's time to see how you can make specific color choices for your Web pages. If you have been doing the exercises as you worked through the chapter, you also have created a handy tool to help you compare colors on a page. Your colorcompare.htm file should look something like the picture in Figure 4-1. As you learn to set the colors for your page, you can use this sample page to see what those colors look like side by side.

You can set colors for your page using HTML attributes and elements , or by using Cascading Style Sheets. Each has its own advantages and drawbacks. The advantage of using HTML elements and attributes (bgcolor, text, color, <font>, <basefont>) is broad compatibility. Because you are using elements recognized by all but the oldest browsers, your pages will display properly on almost all systems. The disadvantage of these attributes and elements is that most of them have been deprecated. So, although they are supported now, there is no guarantee for how long browsers will continue to recognize them. If eventually these elements and attributes are no longer widely supported, you will need to go back into your pages and change them.

## Define Page Colors Globally

By defining colors globally, you will be choosing the default colors throughout a Web page unless you specify otherwise. Generally, you set these colors inside the <body> element. Inside this element you can define your page's background color, text colors, and link colors.

### Specify Background Color with the bgcolor Attribute

To specify the background color of a page, use the bgcolor= " " attribute inside the <body> tag. The value that goes inside bgcolor can be one of the recognized color names or a color's hexadecimal code. To select a white background for a page, you could write:

```
<body bgcolor="white">
```

However, you could just as easily use the hex code for white, in which case your code would look like this:

```
<body bgcolor="#ffffff">
```

Either way, you wind up with the same result—a Web page with a white background. To do a black background, you can use either the name "black," or the hex code "#000000"; for a red background, use "red" or "#ff8080"…you get the idea.

The bgcolor attribute is useful for more than just setting a page's background color. As you already discovered, it can be used in a table to set the individual background color for cells. It also can be used to set the background color for table headings.

## Set Text Colors with the text Attribute

You can set the color for all the text in your page by using the text= " " attribute inside the opening body tag. Again, using a color's name or hex code will cause all the text in a page to display in that color. For example, if you want all the text on a page to be maroon, write your <body> tag this way:

```
<body text="maroon">
```

To have a page with a yellow background and maroon text, construct your tag like this:

```
<body bgcolor="yellow" text="maroon">
```

Modify your colorcompare file to reflect this change; then save and view it in your browser. When you view it, you will notice that the background now displays in bright yellow (hard on the eyes, isn't it?), and the text inside the table cell is maroon. The cell's background color remains unchanged.

## Set Text Colors with

As you learned in Chapter 3, you also can specify text characteristics with the element. If you include the following instruction in the body of your page:

```
<basefont color="purple" />
```

all the text will display in purple.

> **NOTE**    *If you want to try this, be sure to remove the text="maroon"attribute from the <body> tag. It will take priority over basefont.*

## Set Link Colors with link, vlink, and alink

A Web browser normally displays hypertext links as blue with an underline. When you click on the link, it turns red momentarily; this is called an *active link*. After you have visited the link, usually it will display as purple; this, as you probably have guessed, is called a *visited link*. However, you don't have to use those colors; if you use the link, vlink, and alink attributes, you can choose whatever colors you want.

For example, if you want to set the link to red, the active link to yellow, and the visited link to blue, write the body tag this way:

```
<body link="red" vlink="yellow" alink="white">
```

If you try this out, you will see that any links on the page display in the colors you have chosen rather than the default colors. Add the bold text lines to the code of colorcompare.htm to see what a link looks like with your custom colors.

```
<html>
<head><title>Color Comparison Table</title></head>
<body bgcolor="teal" link="red" vlink="yellow" alink="white">
<table border="0"  cellpadding="100">
<tr><td bgcolor="peachpuff">Sample Color</td></tr>
</table>
<a href="http://www.osborne.com"><h2>Sample Link
to Osborne's Web Site</h2></a>
</body>
</html>
```

CAUTION *Before you change the colors of your links, keep in mind that most Web surfers have gotten used to the blue/red/purple color scheme for links. Be careful that you don't make your page difficult to navigate by making your links difficult to identify.*

## Choose Local Colors

After you have set the colors for your page, you might find that there are certain places where you would like to substitute different colors. For example, although most of your text is in black, you might want to emphasize a sentence by putting it in red text. You can override the global color choices you made and select colors for certain "spots" or locations on your page. Sometimes this is called *spot* color.

### Use <font color=" "> to Change Text Color

If you want to set a particular portion of text apart by changing its color, but you want the rest of the page to retain its default color, you can do it with the <font> element and the color=" " attribute. To see how it works, add the following line to colorcompare.htm:

```
<p><h2>This line will have one  <font color="red">
red</font> word.</h2></p>
```

When you save and display your page now, you will see that the word "red" is displayed in bright red text. Remember, you also can use the hex code for red. Substitute the hex code #ff0000 for the word "red" in the <font> tag. Save and display it. You still get the same result.

## Use the color=" " Attribute with Horizontal Rules

Remember the horizontal rule <hr />? You can specify colors for it by including the color=" " attribute inside the tag. Try adding this line to your color page:

```
<hr color="yellow" width="50%" size=7 />
```

When you save and view the page, you will find a bright yellow horizontal rule has been inserted wherever you put the <hr /> element.

## Use bgcolor=" " to Set Colors for Table Cells

You have already experimented a bit with tables in this chapter. When you get to Chapter 8 you will learn that tables are used for much more than displaying columns and rows of data on a Web page. Tables are one of the most frequently used means of establishing a page's layout. The bgcolor attribute enhances this by enabling you to set different colors for individual table cells. As you will see, that enables you to create very pleasing layouts for your pages. To see how this works, try adding the following lines to the table you already created:

```
<html>
<head><title>Color Comparison Table</title></head>
<body bgcolor="teal" link="red" vlink="yellow" alink="white">
<table border="0"  cellpadding="25">
<tr><td bgcolor="peachpuff">Sample Color</td></tr>
<tr><td bgcolor="#0000ff"><font color="white"><h1>Sample
Two</h1></font></td></tr>
</table>
<a href="http://www.osborne.com"><h2>Sample Link</h2></a>
</body>
</html>
```

When you save and view this file in your browser, you'll see that another "cell" has been added just below the first one. This time the cell has a blue

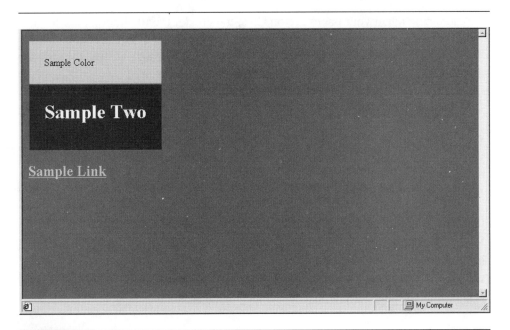

**4**

**FIGURE 4-2**    Color comparison page

background and the text displays in white. Compare it to Figure 4-2 to see how close you got.

Perhaps by now you're thinking, "There's got to be an easier way!" After all, to get some text to have a special background color, its own color, and a large size, you have to write:

```
<tr><td bgcolor="#0000ff"><fontcolor="white"><h1>Sample
Two</h1></font></td></tr>
```

What's worse is that you have to do that every time you want to produce those results! Is there a better way? You bet! You can do all this and more with Cascading Style Sheets.

# Set Colors with CSS

Cascading Style Sheets (CSS) are a mixed blessing. On one hand, they give you far greater influence over the colors on your page than does pure HTML. On the other hand, the browser support for CSS is spotty at best. What that means is that the more dependent your pages are on CSS, the greater the likelihood that they will look awful on some browsers. Does this mean you shouldn't use them at all? No. Just keep in mind that, at least for a while, you must take into account the browsers that don't support CSS. But, by all means, learn to use them.

# Set Page Colors with the Color Property

In straight HTML, your ability to set page colors is limited to the <font> element, <basefont>; and the text, color, and bgcolor attributes. CSS allows you to set page colors with a freedom you could only dream of before. You'll learn in detail what you can do with CSS in Chapter 10, but the following are some samples.

## Embed a Style Sheet with the <style> </style> Element

You learned in the previous chapter how to do an inline style sheet. But to have greater influence over the styles of text on your page, you will want to at least use an embedded style sheet. To create one, first open template.htm and save it as csscolor.htm. Then, in between the <head> </head> tags, insert the following lines:

```
<html>
<head>
<title>CSS Color Samples</title>
<style type="text/css">
</style>
</head>
<body>
</body>
</html>
```

## Set Background Colors with CSS

Setting background colors with CSS is a simple and straightforward process. Instead of using the bgcolor attribute inside the <body> element, you place a *rule* (CSS instruction) inside the <style> element.

To use CSS to set an aqua background for a page, insert the following line between the <style> tags:

```
body {background-color: aqua;}
```

Save the page and display it in your browser. The background will be aqua.

## How to ...   Define Colors with CSS

Style sheets don't just give you greater control over the appearance of your page; they give you greater flexibility in how you specify your colors. With HTML, you are limited to either named colors or using hexadecimal codes. In a style sheet you have those options, plus several others. For example, you can represent the color #ffff00 (a golden yellow) in an abbreviated form of hex code, using only one digit per color: {color: #ff0}. Another option is using color percentages: {color: rgb [100%, 100%, 0%]}. You also can describe the color with base-10 numerical color values (0 to 255): {color: RGB (255, 255, 0)}. All these produce the same color.

Recalling what you covered in the previous chapter, you used a property (background-color) and combined it with a value (aqua). But in this case, you've added another item: a *selector* (body). The selector is the HTML element you wish to be affected by your style rule. Because you want to set the background for the entire page, you chose body as your selector. You could just as easily have chosen another element and specified a particular background color for that element only. For example, try creating some level one headings with their own background colors.

### Create Headings with Colored Backgrounds

One of the most exciting things about style sheets is that you can apply your styles to any element. For example, say you want to define not one, but four, different <h1> elements, giving a different style and background color to each. With straight HTML you can do it using some of the techniques you learned in the last two chapters; but you would have to insert the control elements every single time you wanted to modify <h1>. With style sheets, you do it just one time.

Try adding the following lines in between the <style> </style> tags on your page:

```
h1 {font-family: arial;  color: navy; }
h1.red {font-family: Times-New-Roman; color: red;
            background-color: black;}
h1.white {font-family: Times-New-Roman; color: white;
        background-color: green;}
```

```
h1.lime {font-family: arial; font-style: italic;
              color: lime; background-color: olive;}
```

After you've included the style lines, add some lines in the \<body> \</body> portion of your page to see how they display:

```
<p><h1>This is my basic headline.</h1></p>
<p><h1 class="red">This is my red headline.</h1></p>
<p><h1 class="white">This is my white headline.</h1></p>
<p><h1 class="lime">This is my lime headline.</h1></p>
```

Save and display the page in your browser. Your results should resemble Figure 4-3.

Anywhere you specify one of those four classes you created, the display will look like that. You can see that using style sheets can save you a great deal of time. It also can help you develop a consistent look for your Web site that spans all of your pages.

Remember, when using embedded style sheets, always remember to enclose properties and values inside curly braces { }.

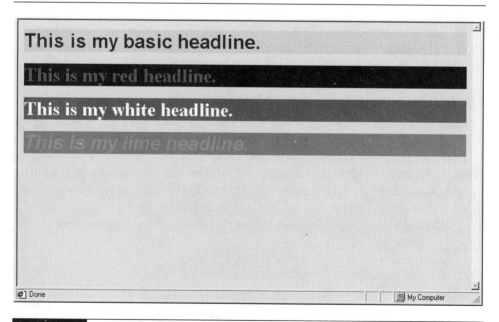

FIGURE 4-3    A sample of stylized headlines

NOTE    *For inline style sheets, the properties and values are enclosed in quotation marks (see Chapter 3).*

Properties should be separated from their values by a colon (:), and from other properties by a semicolon (;). Selectors (the elements you wish to set a style for) should be outside and to the left of the curly braces. Proper style sheet syntax is reflected in the following line:

```
selector   {property: value;  property: value;  property: value;}
```

It also can be written this way:

```
selector   {
            property: value;
            property: value;
            property: value;
            }
```

## Set Paragraph Colors with CSS

Suppose you want to include several different paragraph styles on a page, each with a distinctive look and background. You'd have a tough time creating this in HTML alone; with CSS, it's a breeze. To create three different paragraph styles for your csscolors.htm page, insert the following lines of code between the <style> </style> tags:

```
p.blackback    {font-family: arial; font-style: italic;
                font-weight: bold; color: powderblue;
                background-color: black;}
p.yellowbk     {background-color: yellow; font-size: 16pt}
p.red          {font-weight: light; color: #ff0000;
                text-align: center; font-size: 32pt;}
```

You have three paragraph styles:

■ **Blackback**    An Arial italic font, displaying in powder blue with a black background

■ **Yellowbk**    A 16-point font with a yellow background

■ **Red**    A light, 32-point font which will be centered and displayed in red

These are in addition to the undefined <p> element, which will display as it normally does. To see these new paragraph styles in action, insert the following lines of code into the <body> </body> portion of your page:

```
<p class="blackback">This is a sample of the blackback style.</p>
<p class="yellowbk">Here is how yellowbk looks.</p>
<p class="red">I enjoy this red, centered font.</p>
<p>An unmodified paragraph looks like this.</p>
```

Once you have saved the page, display it in your browser. It should look something like Figure 4-4. Are you beginning to see the possibilities?

## Set Link Colors

You can use CSS to set link colors, too, using what is called a *pseudo class*. A pseudo-class is used to define a "class" that doesn't actually exist in a page's HTML code, but exists because it fulfills certain conditions. For example, a visited link is defined by a pseudo-class because there is no specific HTML element for visited links. Instead, your visitor's browser "remembers" whether a link has been

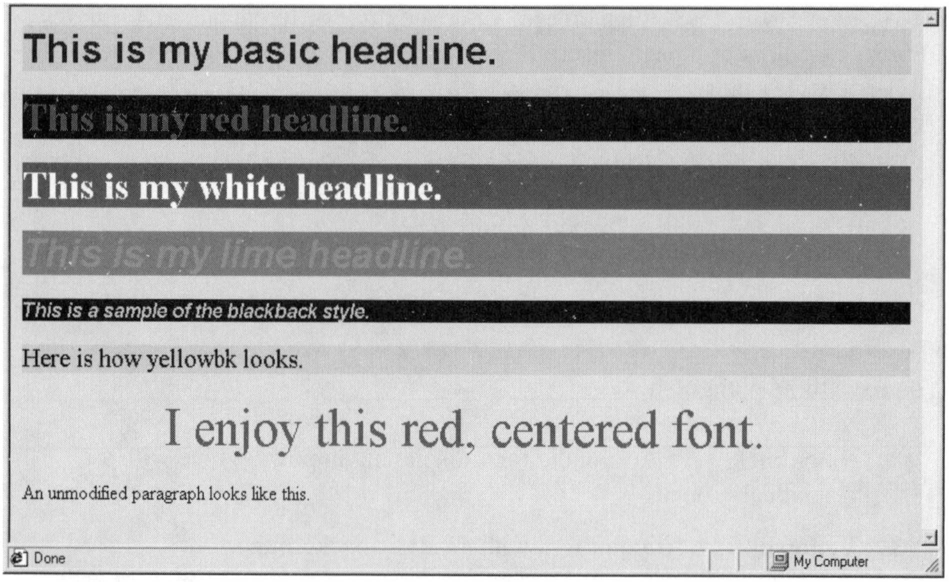

FIGURE 4-4     Headlines and fonts defined with CSS

visited. You need not worry too much about what that means right now, as it will be covered in Chapter 10. To use CSS to set link colors:

- **a:link {color: red}**    Will set link colors to red

- **a:visited {color: #0000ff;}**    Will set visited link colors to blue

- **a:active {color: rgb(0, 255, 0);}**    Will set active link colors to lime green

## Remember the Downside of CSS

Whether or not you use CSS, it's always good practice to see what your page looks like in different browsers. However, if you plan to make even minimal use of style sheets, you must do it regularly. The support for CSS is so varied you will not have to look very far to find a browser that displays your page much differently from what you'd planned. For example, Figure 4-3 shows csscolors.htm as it displays in Internet Explorer. Look at the differences when you view it with Netscape Communicator, as in Figure 4-5. The differences might not be great, but they are significant enough to negatively affect your design, if you don't take them into account. *Always* check your pages in other browsers.

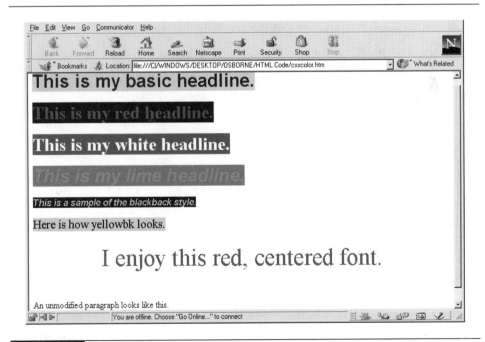

**FIGURE 4-5**    Stylized headings and paragraphs in Netscape Communicator

# Learn Good Web Design

Have you ever driven down the road and seen a house painted bright yellow with hot pink trim? Do you shudder when you think about it? Good color combinations can enhance your Web site. At best, poor use of color makes your page difficult to read and hard on the eyes. At worst, it's like the screech of fingernails on a blackboard. It will send people away from your site in droves.

## Web Design Principle: Use Gentle Colors in Pleasing Combinations

When you begin to plan your Web site, choose your colors carefully. Don't just grab them at random as if you were taking a handful of crayons out of a box. Put some thought into your colors, keeping in mind that you should

- Put at least as much thought into your color scheme as you do your site's layout.

- Compare colors side by side before you construct your page.

- Choose soft colors rather than deep, bright, or garish shades.

- Make your color scheme consistent throughout your site.

- Keep in mind the possible equipment limitations of visitors to your site.

- Never forget that visitors can set their browsers to override your designs and styles. (What will your page look like if your styles are not used?)

- Remember that some of your visitors might suffer from color blindness. Take steps to ensure your color choices do not make your pages less accessible to them.

TIP    *A great site for information on Web color in general, and color blindness in particular, is www.visibone.com. It's worth checking out.*

## Practice, Practice, Practice

Using color in Web pages is fun and tricky at the same time. If you will take the time to experiment with different color combinations, you can develop a way to reinforce some of the things you have learned about color and how to use it. Try the following exercises:

## Experiment with CSS

Cascading Style Sheets give you a great deal of flexibility in how you use and apply color to your pages. To see CSS in action, try creating some pages and using style sheets to add color. For starters, use CSS to create a page that has these color characteristics:

- A light blue background

- A paragraph style that uses navy text

- A headline style with white text on a navy background

If you get stuck, go to Appendix D and look through the CSS reference guide. You should find everything you need to help you apply colors with style sheets.

## Create a Chart of the 16 Basic Colors

For a challenging exercise, try creating a file named 16colors.htm and then type this code. It will create a chart of the basic color palette you began this chapter with. You'll be using HTML to create a table to structure the color chart. If you want to brush up on tables before you try this, you might check out Chapter 8 first. Otherwise, just be careful to type the code in *exactly* as written here:

```
<html>
<head><title>The 16 Basic Colors</title></head>
<body>
<center>
<h1>The 16 Basic Colors</h1>
<table border="1"> <!-- Table starts -->
<tr>  <!-- Row 1 -->
<td bgcolor="white">White</td> <!--TD tags define table cells-->
<td bgcolor="black" style="color: white;">Black</td>
<td bgcolor="gray">Gray</td>
<td bgcolor="silver">Silver</td>
</tr> <!-- End of row 1 -->
<tr> <!-- Row 2 -->
<td bgcolor="navy" style="color: white;">Navy</td>
<td bgcolor="blue" style="color: white;">Blue</td>
<td bgcolor="teal">Teal</td>
<td bgcolor="aqua">Aqua</td>
</tr> <!-- End of row 2 -->
```

```
<tr> <!-- Row 3 -->
<td bgcolor="lime">Lime</td>
<td bgcolor="green">Green</td>
<td bgcolor="olive">Olive</td>
<td bgcolor="yellow">Yellow</td>
</tr> <!-- End of row 3 -->
<tr> <!-- Row 4 -->
<td bgcolor="fuchsia">Fuchsia</td>
<td bgcolor="red">Red</td>
<td bgcolor="maroon" style="color: white;">Maroon</td>
<td bgcolor="purple" style="color: white;">Purple</td>
</tr>  <!-- End of row 4 -->
</table> <!-- End of table -->
</center>
</body>
</html>
```

In this chapter, you have learned only a small sample of what you can do with color in your Web pages. You are limited only by your imagination and your visitors' equipment—keep that in mind, as it is one of the unfortunate (and continual) frustrations of a Web designer. Designing Web pages will bring out the artist in you, but don't stray too far from the scientist. Test your pages to make sure they work for everyone, not just yourself.

# Find the Code Online

To find the code online for this or any of the chapters in this book, go to Osborne's Web site: www.osborne.com, and click the Free Code choice on the navigation bar. From the list of books, select the *How to Do Everything with HTML* option and you will be able to download the book files, which are linked together and organized as an offline "mini" Web site. For more on how to use the "mini" Web site, see Chapter 17.

| Use This Code For... | Look for This Filename |
|---|---|
| Easy color comparison page | colorcompare.htm |
| CSS color demonstration | csscolor.htm |
| Chart of the 16 basic colors | 16colors.htm |
| Chart of 216 browser-safe colors | colorchart.html |

# Chapter 5

# All About Links

## How to...

- Link to Another Web Site
- Link to Other Pages on Your Own Site
- Link to Different Spots on the Same Page
- Open Links in a New Window
- Create E-mail, FTP, and News Links
- Adjust the Appearance of Links
- Make Links User Friendly

The Web wouldn't be the Web without hyperlinks. No matter how much material is available on the World Wide Web, without a way to tie all that information together, it is little more than a gigantic library without a cataloging system. Prior to the development of the Web in 1990, other means of accessing information dominated the Internet. You might have heard terms like *gopher, archie, veronica,* and *jughead* and wondered what they meant. No, they're not comic book characters. They are terms that describe some of the ways to search the Internet in its early days. Although they're still around, the development of the World Wide Web and its use of *hypertext* has eclipsed gopher and company, pushing them into the background in favor of a system that radically changed the way we access information online.

# Understand Hypertext and Links

Why did the arrival of hypertext links make such a difference? You can understand it better by comparing the Internet to a vast library. What if you went into a library and discovered that the only way you could find anything was by going through multiple lists of items, each one becoming a little more specific, until you narrowed your search down to the information you were looking for? Then, when you found the book you wanted, you had to access the information in it, page by page, until you found what you needed? Thankfully, libraries don't work that way. But, if you've ever used a *gopher* server, that's about what it's like.

The development of HTML and the creation of the World Wide Web made it possible to go right to the document you want, and a lot more. Because pages are linked together, it is possible to go to the specific page you want. Even better, assuming a link is provided, it is possible to go to a precise location on the page you are looking for. And with all those pages linked together around the world…well, you see where the term "web" comes from. And it's all possible because of *hypertext*.

## Understand URLs

What is hypertext? Even if you've never been on the Web, you've probably used hypertext before. Often the "help" files of computer programs use hypertext to help you find the answer to your question quickly. Computerized encyclopedias are another place you've probably encountered hypertext. The articles in such encyclopedias and dictionaries generally have related subjects listed at the bottom. If you click on the subject, you are instantly transported to another article for more information. That's hypertext at work. To understand how to use it on the Web, you must learn a little about *uniform resource locators* (URLs). URLs are more commonly known as Web addresses, Internet addresses, and even "dot.coms." But simplistic names won't give you an idea of how a URL works.

A URL is made up of several parts, each of which helps identify a specific location where a *resource* can be found (or sent). For instance, if you want to visit Osborne's Web site, the address would be http://www.osborne.com/. The first part of the address is the *protocol,* usually *http://.* This stands for *Hypertext Transfer Protocol,* the specification for transferring documents using hypertext links or *hyperlinks.* As you'll see in the following, there are other protocols, depending on what you are trying to do on the Net; but the primary one for the Web is http://. When an Internet server sees http:// at the beginning of an address, it knows to expect an HTML document.

The next portion of a URL identifies the *host* (also called a *server*). In the case of Osborne's address, the host portion is www.osborne.com. The host is the system where the file or document you are looking for can be found, or where it is

**5**

## Did you know?    **Other Internet Protocols**

Other kinds of URLs come into play as you use the Internet, including File Transfer Protocol (ftp://) for transferring files, the Mailto Protocol (mailto:) for sending e-mails, the News Protocol (news://) for accessing newsgroups, and even Gopher (gopher://) to use menu-driven searches.

to be sent. You probably are more familiar with the term *domain name*, as in www.domainname.com. When you type in a domain name, it is translated into what is known as an IP address, which numerically describes the exact location of the server that hosts that particular Web site (see Chapter 7 for more information on IP addresses).

The last part of a URL locates the *file* on the server. You generally don't have to type in this part, as the browser supplies it for you. If it is displayed, the file location might look something like this:

```
http://www.mysite.com/index.htm
```

No directory is listed in this address because the index page usually is located in a site's main, or *root*, directory. If you are accessing a page that is in a different directory on a Web site, the address might display this way:

```
http://www.mysite.com/vacations/pictures.htm
```

In the case of this address, the file is pictures.htm; it resides in the vacations directory.

 *If you know the filename and directory of the page you are looking for, you can go straight to it without having to visit the site's home page. Just type in the complete address, including directory and filename, and you'll take a shortcut to the page.*

A complete URL points to a specific resource on the Internet by identifying the *protocol://host/directory/filename*.

NOTE *Because you normally go to the first, or "root," directory when you visit a Web site, you might not always see a directory listed in the URL.*

Table 5-1 shows how URLs change to reflect the action you are requesting.

## Link to Another Web Site with the Anchor Element, \<a\> \</a\>

Hypertext points to a precise location on the Internet by using a URL to identify where information is and what should be done with it. But how do you create the link? That's where HTML comes in. HTML stands for Hypertext Markup

| Action | URL |
|---|---|
| To access a Web site | http://www.domainName.com/index.htm |
| To use File Transfer protocol | ftp://domainName.com/directory/file.txt |
| To use the Mailto protocol | mailto:emailaddress@domainName.com |
| To access a newsgroup | news://newsserver.com/directory/filename |
| To use a Gopher server | gopher://server.address/directory/file |
| To access a local file (on your computer) | file:///c:\My_Documents\myfile.htm |

**TABLE 5-1**    URLs for the Most Common Protocols

Language. You can create hypertext links or *hyperlinks* using an element specially designed for that purpose: the anchor element, <a> </a>.

A link is simply a connection between one hypertext document and another, created by enclosing text or an image inside two anchor tags. However, the link must point somewhere, so you also must include the href=" " attribute. Href stands for *hypertext reference* and is the place where you put the URL or pointer, so your link has a destination. A link that doesn't point anywhere will look like this:

```
<a href=" ">This link doesn't go anywhere</a>.
```

If you type this link into a Web page, it will appear as the default blue underlined text that characterizes links, but it won't take you anywhere because it doesn't have an address. To give the link somewhere to take you, insert a URL between the quotation marks beside the href attribute. To make the link take a visitor to Osborne's site, change the link to read:

```
<a href="http://www.osborne.com">Go to Osborne's Web site.</a>
```

Create an HTML file from your template and try typing these lines in. You should see a pair of links that look like this:

This link doesn't go anywhere Go to Osborne's Web site.

That's all there is to creating a simple link to another Web site. Oh, but there's so much more you can do with them.

# Help People Navigate Your Site with Internal Links

One of the most common uses for hyperlinks on a Web site is for *site navigation*. Site navigation is just a fancy term for "helping people find their way around." It's good to keep that in mind as you develop your site. As you develop links to other pages on your Web site, remember that you want to make things as easy for your visitors as possible. The larger and more complex your site becomes, the more links you will find yourself using. If your links are complicated, confusing, or non-functional, visitors will becomefrustrated and probably will leave.

## Link to Pages on Your Own Site

Linking to another page on your own site is even simpler than linking to a different Web site; all you need to include is the name of the file you're linking to and the directory where it is located. If the file happens to be in the same directory, you need only the filename.

### Link to Another Page in the Same Directory

To link to another page in the same directory, simply include the filename in the href=" " attribute of the opening anchor tag. For example, to add a link to your index.htm page that will open up headings.htm, type

```
<a href="headings.htm">Headings Page</a>.
```

This will create a link that looks like this:

<u>Headings Page</u>

This kind of link will work as long as the file is stored in the same directory. However, if you have a large site, you might find it easier to organize your files in different directories, much as you do on your computer. If you do this, you will have to provide the *path* to your file.

### Link to Another Page in a Different Directory

You have two options when linking to a file in another directory: *absolute* and *relative* URLs.

**Use Absolute URLs for Simplicity** The least complicated option is to use an *absolute* URL. Although that term might sound intimidating, it simply refers to the exact "path" to the file's location, including all directories and subdirectories you have to go through to get there. It is called *absolute* because it specifies a precise address. For instance, suppose you have a site devoted to facts about famous people. One of your subdirectories might be named Biographies. In that directory, you might have several other directories; for instance, Actors, Musicians, or Presidents. If you want to link to a file named washington.htm and that file is located in the Presidents directory, you would write the URL in your link this way:

```
<a href="/biographies/presidents/washington.htm">Washington</a>
```

This tells the browser to go to the Biographies directory, then to go to the Presidents directory, and finally to load the washington.htm file.

> **TIP** *Remember that directories should be separated by a forward slash, and the filename comes last.*

If you want to create a link on the washington.htm page that will take a visitor back to the home page, you can use an absolute pathname that will go in the opposite direction:

```
<a href="presidents/biographies/index.htm">Home</a>
```

Absolute URLs work fine, provided you never move your pages to a different location. If you do, you'll have to go back into each page and rewrite the links to reflect the new paths. If you have a small site, that might not be a problem. However, if you have a large site with lots of files you can plan on spending quite a few hours just rewriting links. To avoid this problem, use *relative* URLs.

> **NOTE** *How many directories you decide to use on your site is entirely up to you. If you plan on a small and relatively uncomplicated site, or you will be your own "Webmaster," you might choose to keep your files all in a single directory, thus eliminating the need for complicated pathnames in your URLs. However, if you plan on a large, difficult-to-maintain site or if more than one person is accessing the files, you probably will want to organize similar files in directories with descriptive titles: for instance, Images, Personnel, Statistics, Reports, and so forth. This will make working on your site much easier.*

5

**Use Relative URLs for Flexibility**     If you want your site to have maximum flexibility and you definitely don't want to waste your time rewriting links, relative URLs are your solution. Whereas an absolute URL contains the exact address of the file you want the browser to load, a relative URL uses a kind of shorthand to tell the browser to go backward one or more directories. If you want to write the link from washington.htm-to-index.htm using a relative URL, it will look like this:

```
<a href="../../index.htm">Home</a>
```

The two dots followed by a slash are the code that instructs the browser to move backward (or up) one directory level. Because you must go up two levels to get to the main (or root) directory and index.htm, you must use the code twice. What makes relative URLs advantageous is that the link will work even if you move the file to another directory.

What if you want to link to a file in a parallel directory; that is, go sideways rather than backward? On our famous persons' Web site, to link to Mozart's biography, you'd send the browser to the Musicians directory. You would write a link to tell the browser to go up one directory (to Biographies), to go forward one directory (to Musicians), and to load the file mozart.htm. How would it look?

```
<a href="../Musicians/mozart.htm>Mozart Biography</a>
```

Confusing? It can be if you let your Web site structure get complicated. A good rule is to keep the structure of your Web site as simple as you can and still accomplish what you need to accomplish. In the meantime, remember that two dots followed by a slash, ../, take you backward or up one directory. To go forward, give the directory name followed by a slash, *directory/*.

TIP     *If you're struggling with the whole idea of relative URLs and how to use them, try creating several practice directories on your computer. Name your root directory home and create a subdirectory named sub-a. Make another directory inside sub-a and name it sub-b. Just for fun, create another subdirectory of home and call it sub-c. Then create an HTML page in home, naming it index.htm. Put a page in each of the other directories and practice linking them together until you are confident using relative URLs.*

# Link to Precise Spots on a Page with Named Anchors

Another practical use of links is to help visitors navigate a single, long page. Have you ever visited a site where most of the content was contained on a single page? You could scroll down through the entire page, but you might be interested in only one particular topic covered there. If the page's author included links to *named anchors,* you will find it much easier to get around.

## Create an Anchor with the name=" " Attribute

A named anchor helps visitors navigate a long page more efficiently by allowing you to create links that point, not to a different page, but to the anchor. You create an anchor with the name=" " attribute. To put a link at the bottom of a page that will take visitors back to the top without using the scroll bar.

1. Place an anchor at the top of the page by typing **<a name="top"> </a>.**

2. At the bottom of the page make a link to your anchor by typing the following:

   **<a href="#top">Top of Page</a>**

> **CAUTION** *Be sure to include the pound sign, #, at the front of the name when you use it as a URL in the link.*

3. Your code should look like this:

```
<html>
<head><title>Named Anchors</title></head>
<body>
<a name="top"> </a>
<p><h1>This is the text of your page</h1></p>
<a href="#top">Top of Page</a>.
</body>
</html>
```

> **NOTE** *It is not necessary to put your named anchor around an actual line of text or image. The browser will go to the spot where the anchor is located, whether or not it is attached to something visible on the page. However, the longer and more complicated your page is, the more desirable it is to have your anchor actually tied to something you can see.*

You can see how this can be useful for enabling people to navigate a long page; for example, a glossary of terms. You could create named anchors at each new letter of the alphabet, with links at the top of the page. Each term could include links that would take the visitor back to the alphabetical directory or just to the beginning of the particular section in which the term was found.

## Create an Anchor with the id=" " Attribute

As useful as the name=" " attribute is, it also is numbered among HTML's deprecated attributes. The HTML 4 specification recommends using the id=" " attribute instead. Don't worry, though. It works the same way as name, but with a few new wrinkles and a lot more versatility. Keep in mind the following differences:

- ID names must be unique. If you use id=" " to create your anchors, you must choose a unique name for each one you make. It can be any name you choose as long as it begins with either a letter or an underline; IDs may not begin with a number. Also, you can use the ID only one time (as an anchor) in a single document. In other words, you can't have several different elements all using the same ID.

- ID names go inside an element tag. Instead of using the anchor, <a>, tags, you can place the ID name inside the opening tag of any element you want to link to: <h1 id="heading">This is a heading with an ID.</h1>.

- The anchor element, <a>, is still used to create the link. You still must use the anchor element when creating your link and the pound sign, #, still must precede the ID: <a href="#heading">Go to Top</a>.

The code listed here has been modified to use the ID attribute:

```
<html>
<head><title>Named Anchors Using the ID Attribute</title></head>
<body>
<h1 id="header">This is a heading</h1>
<p><h1>This is the text of your page</h1></p>
<a href="#header">Top of Page</a><br />
<p>The above link will take you to the top of
```

```
the page.</p>
</body>
</html>
```

Using the name or id attribute with the *anchor* element also enables you to link to a precise spot on a page, but the usefulness of this combination does not end there. You also can use this attribute/element combo to link to a specific location on a different page or even a different Web site.

## Use Named Anchors to Link to Precise Locations on Different Pages

Suppose you are designing a site for a university and you want to create links that will direct online visitors to a brief paragraph describing a certain course, but you want to include all course descriptions in a single document. One way to do it would be to create a named anchor for each course and create a link to each course's description. It might look something like the following code:

■ Anchor (on the courses.htm page):

```
<p id="biology103">Biology 103</p>
```

■ Link (perhaps on a degree program page, listing required courses):

```
<a href="courses.htm#biology103">Click for a description
 of BI-103</a>
```

*You also can link to other pages using the name attribute. Instead of putting the name in an element, as with id, write it as* <a name="biology103"> </a>.

The preceding link will take visitors to the courses page where they will find a description of the Introduction to Biology course. The advantage of linking this way is that you can reference a single pool of information from any number of different pages.

*When using an anchor to link to a different page, the filename and anchor name or ID are not separated by any characters.*

### Use Named Anchors to Link to a Different Web Site

This same approach will work, even if you want to link to an entirely different site. All you need to know is the anchor name or the id name and the site's URL to link to a specific portion of that site.

Suppose the preceding imaginary university has several satellite campuses, each with its own site. They could access the information on the main site's servers simply by linking to the site's anchors, like this:

```
<a href="http://www.imaginaryu.edu/catalog/
courses.htm#biology103">BI-103</a>.
```

Note that you need to use the complete URL when you are trying to link to another site.

CAUTION *Although it is possible to link to any site this way, keep in mind that not everyone will be delighted by the idea of you linking to their sites; copyright issues also can come into play. Always get the permission of the Webmaster if you plan to link to another site.*

## Open Links in a New Window

If you are reluctant to include links to other Web sites because you don't want your visitors to leave your site too quickly, there are several steps you can take to encourage them to stay. One of the easiest is to set up your links so that they open a new browser window. That way, visitors can visit the site you're linked to and remain at your site. You can configure a link to open in a new window by using the target=" " attribute.

### Use target=" " to Open New Browser Windows

When a visitor clicks on a link with the target attribute, the content will open in a new browser window. To indicate a new window with the target attribute, add the value _blank between the quotation marks as in the sample here:

```
<a href="www.newSite.com" target="_blank">
This link opens a new window.</a>
```

> **NOTE** *The value "_blank" must have the underscore character before the letter "b."*

# Use Special Types of Links

Using links for site navigation and to connect with other sites only scratches the surface of what you can do with links. Remember the different protocols mentioned earlier in this chapter? The following will describe how some of them are used.

## Use mailto: to Create E-mail Links

One of the more challenging aspects of Web authoring is designing systems for your visitors to respond to your site. Many of these require venturing outside the secure world of HTML into more complex programming languages. One easy way to enable people to contact you from your site is by including an e-mail link with the mailto: protocol.

To put an e-mail link in a page you can type something like this:

```
<a href="mailto:myEmail@server.com">Email Me!</a>
```

When someone clicks on this link, it will open the browser's e-mail program with an e-mail window already addressed to you. All they have to do is write a note and click "send."

## Use ftp:// to Link to Download Sites

FTP stands for File Transfer Protocol. You will become very familiar with the ftp:// protocol when you are ready to publish your Web site to a server, because that's how you get your files from your computer to your host's. However, if you've ever downloaded a file to your computer, you've already used ftp://, even though you might not have known it. What you might not know is that there are many public FTP sites called *anonymous ftp sites*. These will allow you to log in, usually with the username "anonymous." You might want to provide a link to a site that offers information related to your site's topic. If your own host supports FTP, you might want to provide files of your own for downloading.

Suppose you're an amateur astronomer and you want to make some fantastic space pictures available to your visitors. You might create an FTP link to a NASA FTP site that offers space and astronomy pictures, such as this:

```
Find space pictures at the:<a href="ftp://
nssdc.gsfc.nasa.gov>NASA Ftp Site</a>.
```

A visitor who clicks this link will be transferred to NASA's anonymous FTP site, where they will be able to find a wealth of pictures and space information. As always, be sure you have the right to link to information on the Internet before you do. With most public sites such as this, there will be no problem.

## Link to Usenet Newsgroups with news:

The news:// protocol enables you to link your visitors to Usenet newsgroups. Newsgroups are veterans of the Internet's early days and work something like huge e-mail groups. Groups organized around common interests abound and can be a great source of information. Perhaps along with the NASA astronomy information, you might like to put visitors in touch with a link to an amateur astronomy newsgroup. You could add a link such as this:

```
<a href="news:sci.astro.amateur">
Amateur Astronomers' Newsgroup</a>
```

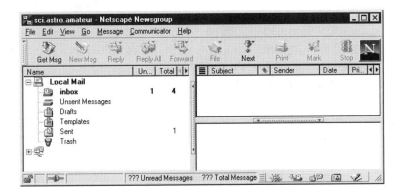

Assuming your visitors have their browsers configured for newsgroups, this link will open up their news reader and enable them to tie into the group. As you read earlier in the chapter, there are other protocols, but these are the ones you are likely to use most often.

> **TIP**   *To find newsgroups to link to, try doing a search on Usenet in any search engine.*

Until now, you have been working with plain text links—nothing fancy, and definitely not pretty. Not many years ago, that's what you would have been limited to when adding links to your page. Fortunately, things have changed. It is now possible for you to have useful links—and good-looking ones, too.

> **NOTE**   *Another way to write the newsgroup protocol is nntp://.*

# Dress Up Your Links

Links can be modified several different ways to affect their appearance and function, and even to give your visitors feedback. Unfortunately, not all of these

work with every browser, so keep in mind that these are bells and whistles; they
are nice to use, but don't make your site dependent on them.

## Give Link Details with the title=" " Attribute

The title=" " attribute is a nice little addition that unfortunately has limited browser
support. By adding the title=" " attribute to your anchor tag, you can add an
explanatory comment to your link. When a visitor's mouse passes over the link, a
small text box will appear with your comment. For example, the Webmaster of the
imaginary university referred to earlier could add the title attribute to the biology
course link, explaining what the link leads to:

```
<a href="courses.htm#biology103" title="Introductory Biology">
BI-103</a>
```

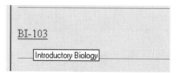

 *The title=" " attribute is a very useful "universal" attribute. You can put
it inside any element and get the same explanatory box (called a ToolTip)
in IE4 and above.*

## Modify Link Appearance with Text Elements

Virtually any of the text elements covered in Chapter 2 can be applied to a link.
You are not limited to lines of default, basic blue text for links. You can change
the size, color, and even the font. Experiment with some of the following
possibilities:

```
<h1><a href=" ">This is a link inside a heading element.</a></h1>

<a href=" "><font face="arial" color="red" size="5">This is
a size 5, Arial link.</font></a>

<small><a href=" ">Links in small text are great
for page bottom navigation bars.</a></small>

<center><a href=" ">You can center links, too.</a></center>
```

SHORTCUT *Because these links aren't leading anywhere, just leave the quotes by href empty.*

## This is a link inside a heading element.

### This is a size 5, Arial link.

<p style="font-size: small; text-align: left;">Links in small text are great for page bottom navigation bars.</p>

<p style="font-size: small; text-align: center;">You can center links, too.</p>

5

Check out the text elements in Chapter 2 and create some modified links of your own. The only limitation is that you can't put a *block level* element inside the <a></a> element. You can use most of the block level elements with links, but they must go on the outside of the <a> tags. For example, because <h1> is a block level element, it must go outside the <a> tags. See the following for more block level elements:

```
<a href=" "><h1>This won't work.</h1></a>
<h1><a href=" ">This will.</a><h1>
```

NOTE *Block level elements generally (but not always) insert a line break and space after the element. They are <address>, <blockquote>, <center>, <div>, <form>, <h#>, <hr>, <p>, <pre>, <span>, <table>, and the list elements.*

## Modify Link Appearance with CSS

If you've read Chapter 4, you've already covered much of what can be done with links through style sheets. There are a few other things you can do to modify your links, both with inline and embedded style sheets.

### Remove Underlines with Text-Decoration: None

You might decide you'd rather not have the links in your page underlined. You can turn off underlining on a link-by-link basis by using the style=" " attribute:

```
<a href=" " style="text-decoration: none;">
This link has no underlining.</a>
```

This link has no underlining.

This particular style affects only the link with which it has been included. To turn off underlining as the default setting for a page, embed a style in the <head> </head> portion of the page:

```
<style> a:link {text-decoration: none;}</style>
```

### Make Link Colors Change Dynamically with a:hover

If you've done much Web surfing, you certainly have encountered *mouseover* effects, in which an image (usually a navigation tool) changes appearance when the cursor moves over it. With style sheets you can easily create that effect in links by using the pseudo class a:hover (see Chapter 10 for more on pseudo classes). The downside of this effect is that it not recognized by Netscape. Your links will still work; they simply won't be affected by this style. The following code, inserted in the head portion of any page, will alter the links so that they have no underline and change to yellow when a cursor moves over them.

```
<style type="text/css">
    a:link {text-decoration: none;}
    a:active {text-decoration: none;}
    a:visited {text-decoration: none;}
    a:hover {color: yellow;}
</style>
```

There are many more things you can do with inline and embedded style sheets. If you want to learn more, skip ahead to Chapter 10.

# Learn Good Web Design

Nowhere does poor Web design show itself more clearly than in poorly thought-through navigation and linking. Links are the means by which visitors will find their way around your site. If your links are clear and easy to follow, you will have happy visitors. If you leave your visitors with a confusing jumble of links that seem to lead nowhere, they might visit your site one time and never come back. It doesn't have to be that way if you give some thought to planning your links.

### Web Design Principle: Make Navigation Visitor Friendly

Have you ever gotten lost because someone gave you bad directions? Frustrating, isn't it? That's how your visitors feel when they can't find their way around your site. To make things easier on them, keep the following in mind:

■ Always have a link to your home page on every page of your site. Remember, some visitors might not come to your site through the home page. If you offer them no way to get to the site's main page, they will leave.

■ Include a text-based navigation bar somewhere on each page to enable those without graphical browsers to find their way around your site.

■ Make your link names clear and self-explanatory. Nothing is more frustrating than seeing a "click here" link that gives you no idea where you'll end up if you do click it.

■ Provide a site map (a directory of the pages on your site) so people can figure out where they are and where they want to go. To learn more about site maps, see Chapters 7 and 17.

■ If you have long pages, use anchors to provide links for quicker travel to the top, bottom, and individual topics people are looking for.

■ Avoid changing the color or appearance of links too much. If people can't recognize them as links, how will they know to click on them?

■ Visit other Web sites and learn from both good and bad design. A good site to visit to learn from bad design is Vincent Flanders' site: www.webpagesthatsuck.com.

## Practice, Practice, Practice

If you've been working through the exercises chapter by chapter, you should have created as many as 15 separate Web pages. In Chapters 7 and 17 you will learn how to organize those pages into a site. You can get ready for that process by adding links to the pages you have already created.

### Create Links for Your Web Site

You can practice creating links by opening your index.htm file and developing a list of links to the other pages you have made. On each of the other pages, write a link that will take the visitor back to the index.htm page. A sample link from your index page to headings.htm might look like this:

```
<a href="headings.htm">Six Heading Levels</a>
```

The return link might be written this way:

```
<a href="index.htm">Home</a>
```

## Create a Navigation Bar

Once you've created some links, try stringing some of them together into a navigation bar. To make it more interesting, enclose it in the <small> element to reduce the size of the letters. Make it similar to the following sample:

```
<small><a href="colorcompare.htm">Color Comparison</a> -
<a href="csscolor.htm">Style Sheet Color</a> -
<a href="16colors.htm">Color Chart</a></small>
```

> **TIP**  *Remember that as long as you don't include a <br /> or <p> element, the browser will display the above links all on one line.*

<u>Color Comparison</u> - <u>Style Sheet Color</u> - <u>Color Chart</u>

Links are what have made the Web the phenomenon it has become. But to you as a Web author, they are much more. Links are the means by which you will direct your visitors to the information you want to present to them; make sure they're clear.

To find the code online for this or any of the chapters in this book, go to Osborne's Web site: www.osborne.com, and click the Free Code choice on the navigation bar. From the list of books, select the *How to Do Everything with HTML* option and you will be able to download the book files, which are linked together and organized as an offline "mini" Web site. For more on how to use the "mini" Web site, see Chapter 17.

| Use This Code For... | Look for This Filename |
| --- | --- |
| Named anchors demo | namedanchors.htm |
| ID demo | idanchors.htm |
| Links demo | links.htm |

# Chapter 6

# Add Images to Improve Your Presentation

## How to...

- Understand Graphics Formats
- Find Graphics
- Create Your Own Images
- Insert an Image on Your Page
- Control Image Placement and Appearance
- Use Image Links for Navigation
- Use CSS with Images

Web pages without pictures can be pretty dull places. The content might be great, but today's world is visually oriented. People who visit your site expect to see more than straight text. But how do you give it to them without having to invest in (and learn how to use) a lot of expensive software? The good news is that there are more resources available than you'll ever have time to check out—and many of them are free. But before you begin working with graphics, you must absorb a little background information about how graphics work on the Web.

# Understand Web Graphics

There are scores of different ways to create, save, store, and send graphics over the Internet. Fortunately, you don't need to be concerned with most of them. To put images on your Web sites you need only to have a working familiarity with two or three different formats.

## Learn the Differences in Graphics Formats

Although the sheer number of different graphics formats out there is enough to give you a headache, the three that are best suited for use on the Web are GIF, JPEG, and PNG. Each has its own unique qualities and is best used for a particular type of image. A key difference among these three formats lies in how images are *compressed;* that is, how the images are made smaller when they are saved and sent over the Web.

## Use the GIF Format for Art

If you are doing navigation buttons; using clip art; or creating banners, drawings, or anything that has large blocks of the same color, you want to use GIF (*Graphics Interchange Format,* pronounced *jiff,* like the peanut butter). GIF's particular compression format makes it ideal for these purposes.

When an image is saved, it is compressed to save space and transfer faster. Each of these formats compresses images in a different way. GIF uses something called *LZW* (named after its inventors, Lempel-Ziv and Welch) compression. When an image is saved, LZW takes rows of pixels with the same color and reduces them, in effect, by taking inventory of the number of pixels with that color. For instance, it is easy to take an image of a button that is solid red and $10 \times 72$ pixels; you would merely make a computerized notation that there are 10 rows of red pixels with 72 in each row.

## Use JPEG for Photos

If you are planning to use photos on your Web page, GIF is not your best option. The reason, again, is compression. A photograph generally has a much broader range of color varieties and shades, which makes it unsuitable for GIF's method of compression. Instead, you need to use the JPEG (pronounced *jay-peg*) format. Instead of inventorying pixels, as GIF does, JPEG uses a more complicated process that compresses an image by removing colors from parts of the photo where they are least likely to be missed.

### Did you know?

## Who Developed GIF?

GIF was developed by CompuServe, and the LZW compression algorithim is proprietary. Any software company that uses GIF compression must pay a licensing fee to Unisys, the owner of the patent. You don't have to worry about it personally, as the fee is not charged to consumers who use GIF images, only to companies that write software using LZW compression.

## Did you know?

### What JPEG Means

JPEG stands for Joint Photographic Experts Group, the group responsible for developing the JPEG format. JPEG was designed expressly with photographs in mind, so if you plan to use photos, save them as JPEGs.

### Look to the Future with PNG

PNG (pronounced *ping*), stands for Portable Network Graphics. It was developed in response to the controversy over the licensing fee being charged for the GIF compression program and looks to be a very promising format for the future. PNG combines some of the best qualities of both GIF and JPEG but doesn't have very broad browser support at the present time. For now, it's better to stick with GIF and JPEG; but don't forget about PNG—its day is coming.

> NOTE    *If you use a scanner, you can capture your images as bitmaps, or BMP. Although Internet Explorer will display bitmaps, there are two good reasons to avoid them on your Web pages. First, Netscape does not support them, so your images will not show up on Netscape browsers. An even better reason to avoid them is that bitmap files tend to be larger and will slow down your page loading time. Always convert bitmaps to GIF, JPEG, or PNG files.*

## Learn Key Terms

Whenever you are dealing with images and image-editing programs, you will encounter certain terms that come up repeatedly. Terms such as *bit depth*, *transparency*, *compression*, and so forth can be intimidating but are important to understand; they will influence which kind of format you choose for any given image on your page.

### Color Depth

The *color depth* or *bit depth* of an image refers to how much "computing power" is packed into the processing of an image. The greater the bit depth, the more colors the image can contain, and the larger the size of the file. GIF images will allow a maximum of 8 bits for every pixel. Because there are three basic colors used in video and graphics displays (red, green, and blue), each gets 8 bits. A little quick arithmetic (8×8×8) will give you 256 possible color combinations; thus GIF images can display a maximum of 256 colors. JPEG and PNG both will allow as many as 24 bits per image. With these formats you can have as many as 16.7 million colors in an image file (256×256×256). That is why JPEG and PNG images work better for photographs and images, both of which require a lot of color definition. The downside of the higher color depth is that it requires a larger file and a longer loading time.

> **TIP** *If you are creating or editing your own graphics, you can choose even smaller color depths. This is a great way to make image files load faster, as long as you don't need as high an image quality.*

6

## Transparency

When it is said that an image supports *transparency*, it means that it is possible to cause one or more of the colors in the image to act as if it were transparent, thus matching the background color of the Web page. This will make your graphics look much cleaner as you use them on different pages, allowing you to create a "cut out" effect and making the borders of the picture invisible. GIF and PNG support transparency; JPEG does not. If you are creating a logo for your page, you probably will want to use GIF or PNG.

## Lossless or Lossy Compression

Image compression is said to be *lossless* when the graphic can be compressed or saved without any loss of information. In other words, the image is exactly the same before and after the compression process. On the other hand, *lossy* compression involves a loss of data when the image is saved. GIF and PNG are lossless compression formats. JPEG is lossy, but the loss of quality generally is small.

## Interlacing

*Interlacing* is a means of saving an image so that when it loads, it gradually progresses from a low resolution to a high resolution. This gives the visitors to your Web site something to look at while the image is loading. The image itself begins "out of focus" and gradually sharpens. JPEG does not support interlacing; GIF and PNG do.

## Grayscale

Some formats support images in *grayscale*, that is, a large range of shades from white to black. If you want to put a black-and-white photograph on your site, you will want to use a format that supports grayscale. JPEG and PNG support grayscale; GIF does not.

Table 6-1 compares the main characteristics of the different kinds of graphic files that are best suited for Web use. A good rule for logos, lettering, or any image that has large blocks of color is to use GIF; for photographs or detailed images, use JPEG. Learn to use PNG, but keep it in your "to use someday" file for now, as it is not supported broadly enough to guarantee that your visitors will be able to view the images if they are in that format; hopefully that will change soon.

# Locate Graphics for Use on Your Site

There are several options before you as you search for images to use on your site. You can capture images right off the Web as you surf various sites, or you can hit one of the many free and paid clip art and image sites. If you're ambitious and want to create your own graphics, you can find a number of low-cost (and sometimes free) graphics editors to help you get the job done.

## Capture Images from the Web

The easiest way to find graphics and art is to capture it directly from the Web. You might be surprised to learn that you can save virtually any image that appears on your screen when you visit a site. It is as simple as a right-click with your mouse. To see how easy it is, follow these steps:

**1.** Go online and find a picture, logo, or graphic that you like.

|  | GIF | JPEG | PNG |
|---|---|---|---|
| **Color Depth** | 256 | 16.7 million | 16.7 million |
| **Compression** | Lossless | Lossy | Lossless |
| **Transparency** | Yes | No | Yes |
| **Interlacing** | Yes | No | Yes |
| **Grayscale** | No | Yes | Yes |

TABLE 6-1    Comparison of Web Graphics Formats

2.  Put the mouse cursor somewhere on the image and right-click.

3.  A dialog box will pop up, giving you several options.

4.  Choose Save Picture As.

5.  Either accept the image name as supplied or type in your own. You also should specify which directory you want to save the image in.

6.  Click OK.

That's all there is to it. You now will be able to insert that image into your own Web pages.

CAUTION   *Whenever you use an image or a photo someone else has created, copyright issues become involved. Even though you can easily capture any image from the Web, that does not mean you have the right to use it without its creator's permission. If you plan to use someone else's graphics, be sure to contact him or her to ask if it's okay. Generally you can find an e-mail link to the Webmaster of a site at the bottom of the main page; you also might find information about the usability of material from a given Web site.*

## Find Royalty-Free Clip Art

Fortunately, there are so many royalty-free sources for clip-art, buttons, backgrounds, and pictures on the Web, there's no need to "borrow" someone

| Site | URLs |
|------|------|
| Clip Art Directories—Online directories of Web sites offering different types of art, organized by subject | www.webplaces.com/html/clipart.htm<br>www.aplusart.com |
| Free Clip Art—Some nice sources for royalty-free art | www.clip-art.com<br>www.clipart.com<br>www.GifArt.com |
| Buttons, Banners, and Backgrounds—Sites that offer navigation buttons and background wallpaper | www.freewebtemplates.com<br>www.buttonland.com |
| Photos—Sites that provide royalty-free photographs for your use | www.stockphotowarehouse.com<br>www.freestockphotos.com |

**TABLE 6-2**     Resources for Locating Images

else's without permission. A quick search on Yahoo or any other search engine generally will bring you more sites offering free images than you have the time or desire to visit. Some helpful sites to check out are in Table 6-2.

NOTE     *Although free, www.freestockphotos.com requires that you mention the source of each of their pictures you use in your Web pages.*

## Create Your Own Graphics

If you want your site to be uniquely your own, you might want to consider creating your own images and graphics. It's not that difficult, and you might even find yourself having fun in the process. To create your own images, or modify someone else's, you will need a graphics-editing program. Playing with an image editor is sort of like using finger paints without getting messy or having to clean up. Once you try it, you might find it hard to stop.

### Choose an Image Editor

If you're working in Windows 98 or above, you already have a simple image editor available to you. It is called *Windows Imaging*, and usually you can find it by going to Start | Programs | Accessories. If you don't find it there, you might need to use your Windows CD to install it. If you're interested in an image program that packs a little bit more punch, they are available in a wide range of prices. Table 6-3 lists a few of the programs currently available.

NOTE     *Window's Imaging doesn't let you edit .GIF files. Microsoft Photo Editor does, but it doesn't have a text tool.*

| Editor | Approximate Price |
|---|---|
| Adobe Photoshop | $500–$600 |
| Corel PHOTO PAINT | $350 |
| Macromedia Fireworks | $150 |
| Microsoft Photo Draw | $100 |
| PaintShop Pro | $100 |
| ArtGem | $50 |
| IrfanView | Freeware |

**TABLE 6-3**    Image Editors Price Comparison

> TIP    *If you want to put your company logo or letterhead on your site, use a scanner. A scanner comes in handy when you have hard copies of graphics (logos and so forth) that you need to convert to digital format. If you plan to use your own photographs, you can use a scanner to convert them as well. It also is possible to scan art you find in print sources, but remember the copyright issue. Just because you can scan an image doesn't mean you have the right to use it on your site. Always get permission.*

## Create the Four Bs for Your Web Site

Although there is no limit to the kinds of images you can create for your site, you almost certainly will want to create the four "Bs," *banners, buttons, backgrounds,* and *bullets.* These four elements are great for giving your site its own look and style, not to mention they will give you some easy projects with which to learn how to use a graphics editor. The images in this chapter are not fancy, by any means. If you invest some time in learning how to use your graphics editor, you soon will be able to create some beautiful logos, banners, and icons that will give your Web pages a distinctive look.

**Create a Banner**    One way to give your site a consistent look is by incorporating a banner at the top of each page. A banner in this context is not the same as banner advertisements you have seen on many Web pages. The kind of banner in view here is more like a site "letterhead" or logo. It is something you can place on every page of your site to give it a distinctive "look."

1.  Open your image editor and select File | New. This should bring up a pop-up window, which will allow you to set some basic specifications for

your image such as *height*, *width*, *resolution*, and *background color*. There probably will be some other choices, but these are the only ones you need to be concerned with right now.

2. Set the height to 55 pixels, width to 500 pixels, resolution to 72 pixels/inch, and background color to white. Click OK.

3. Choose the text tool (usually an icon with the capital letter "A" on it).

4. Using about a 28pt font, type whatever you would like your banner to say. For this example, the text will read: How to Do Everything with HTML <Notebook>.

5. Save the file as a GIF file, named banner1.gif.

TIP    *Another good way to save .GIF files is by using names that remind you of the color, height, and width of the image. For instance, the preceding file could be named as wh55 × 500.gif. It's much easier to keep track of image sizes this way.*

**Create Navigation Buttons**    To create navigation buttons for your site, you begin by choosing File | New, this time specifing a smaller size for your image. Try setting the height at 35 pixels and the width at 100 pixels. Keep the resolution at 72 pixels/inch. This will create a rather large button, but it will give you some extra working room for your first few attempts, and you can always choose a smaller size for your button later.

1. Choose the Eyedropper icon and select a color for your button. Select the Flood-Fill tool (it looks like a bucket of paint with a drip coming out of it).

2. Click inside the image; it will change to the color you selected.

3. Next, choose Image | Effects | Buttonize. This will bring up a dialog box with some options for you to choose as you "sculpt" your button.

**4.** In the Buttonize dialog box, set the height to 9, the width to 8, and the opacity to 75.

**5.** Before you add text to your button, you might want to make some duplicates so you can have a series of identical buttons for your site. Click Edit | Copy, (or click the Copy icon). Then click Edit | Paste | As New Image. An exact duplicate of your button will appear onscreen. Repeat this process until you have enough buttons for your site.

**6.** To add some text, choose the Text tool and click one of the buttons you have created. In the Text Entry dialog window, specify a 10pt Arial font and make sure the text color contrasts well with your button's background color. The text color is displayed in the square to the right of the two smaller rectangles. To change the text color, just click in the square; the color selection window will come up. Choose a color for your letters that contrasts well and stands out from the background.

TIP

*With GIF and PNG images you can set the background color to transparent. This will make your image or banner look as if the letters were cut out and pasted individually. This is especially useful if you have a patterned background that you want to show through between the letters. If your page has a solid color background and you want to create the same effect, just set the background color in your image to the same color as your Web page. Be careful with this, though. Sometimes a user's display will not render your GIF files the same way it does a Web page, and the background will show. You're pretty safe if you stay with black or white.*

**7.** In the Enter Text Here window, type **HOME** and click OK. Your text will appear in the button in selected mode. Just move the mouse cursor over the text, hold down the left mouse button, and drag the text until it is centered on the image. Choose Selections | Select None option.

**8.** Repeat the preceding procedure for each of the buttons you have made. Some button names to use, if you are building the sample HTML site as you work through the book, are COLORS, TEXT, LISTS, LINKS, and IMAGES.

**9.** Save each of the buttons as GIF files; use a descriptive name so you won't have any trouble remembering what it is down the line: homebtn.gif, for instance.

**10.** Save a copy of the button *without* any letters on it as blankbtn.gif, so that if you decide to add new buttons in the future, you will be able to maintain a consistent look.

TIP    *By decreasing the color depth, you can reduce the file size of the image from about 10K to less than 2K. In PaintShop Pro, reduce the file size by selecting Colors | Decrease Color Depth | 16 Colors (4 bit).*

**Make a Background Wallpaper**   Now that you have a banner and some buttons, you might want to create a background wallpaper for your Web pages. There are so many different options open to you here that it would take another book just to explore a few of them. Two key things to remember in creating background wallpaper is keep them *small* and *seamless*. You don't need to create a large image for a background, as browsers know to "tile" the images by merely repeating them until they have filled the page. So, the smaller the image, the faster your background will load.

Keeping your background tiles small is the easy part; keeping the tiles seamless is what takes work. To create a reasonably seamless tile to use with a page:

**1.** Select File | New and specify the image size at 72 × 72 pixels, with a white background and a resolution of 72 pixels per inch.

**2.** Select Image | Effects | Weave; the Weave dialog box will appear.

**3.** Set the Gap size to 1, the Width to 5, and the Opacity to 13.

**4.** Select a dark gray for the Weave color and a light gray for the Gap color.

**5.** Click OK and save the image as a GIF file with the name weavetile.gif.

**6.** To view your background, create an HTML page in the same directory where you saved weavetile.gif; then add this line inside the opening <body> tag: <body *background="weavetile.gif"*>. When you view the page, you will have what appears to be a white canvas background.

There are many other ways to create background wallpaper for your Web site. The best way to discover them is to take some time to play with your image editor, trying out different effects. When you get one you like, be sure to save it, and take note of the different settings you used in making it. Just remember to keep the image small, keeping the number of colors to a minimum. The more complex the image, the longer it will take your page to load.

**Make Your Lists Stand out with Graphic Bullets**    HTML lists supply their own bullets (circle, disc, and square); but if you prefer a larger selection, why not create your own size or shape? They are among the easiest graphic images to create, and because they usually are small, they don't take a lot of time to download to the user's computer. To create a simple, circular bullet graphic:

1. Choose File | New to create a new image. The overall size isn't important, as you'll be cutting your shape out of this image and using it to create a new one. A size of $100 \times 100$ pixels will be more than enough.

2. Choose the selection tool, set to Circle with Feather set to 0.

3. Move the mouse cursor inside the image; then click and drag until you have a small circle about $20 \times 20$ pixels. (Look in the lower-left corner of the window for a measurement of the pixel size).

4. Select Cut, then Paste | As New Image.

5. You should have a nice, circular image on your screen.

6. Select a color for the bullet and use the Flood fill tool to "paint" the bullet.

7. Once you have filled the bullet with color, choose Image | Effects | Cutout.

8. Select a dark color in the same general hue as the shadow color. For instance, if your bullet is blue, choose navy for the shadow. Add the following settings: Opacity 85, Blur 10, Vertical Offset -6, Horizontal Offset 1. These settings should create a "ball-like" effect.

9. Save the image as bullet.gif.

**CAUTION**    *Be sure you have set the background color to transparent; otherwise, if you use the image on anything other than a white background, the white corners of the image will stand out like the proverbial sore thumb.*

You now have created the basic images you need to dress up your page. The next step is learning how to place them in your HTML document so they can do the job you for which you designed them.

# Insert and Modify Graphics on Your Page

HTML provides a number of ways to insert images and control their placement and appearance on the page. You have access to some basic image controls with

HTML elements. These allow you to put images on your page and use them as links, backgrounds, and navigation tools. After you have a feel for using images with HTML, you can expand your design control with Cascading Style Sheets.

## Insert a Graphic Image

Once you have your images ready, you want to place them on your page. Inserting an image is easy. You can place a graphic on your page by using the image, <img />, element and its attributes. To place an image, follow these steps:

**1.** Insert the image with the image element: **<img />**.

CAUTION   *<img /> is an empty element and has no closing tag. Don't forget to put the slash at the end of the <img /> tag.*

**2.** Identify the image's location with the *source* attribute: src=" ". The source attribute tells the browser where to find the image. If the graphic is in the same directory as the Web page, you only need to include the file name, as here:

```
<img src="graphic.gif" />
```

However, if you have placed your pictures in a different directory, you will need at least to include the directory where the graphic files is located:

```
<img src="images/graphic.gif" />
```

For more on relative and absolute file addressing, see Chapter 5.

**3.** Add a description for non-visual browsers with alt=" ". The alt (alternate text) attribute provides a place for you to include a text description of the image. Similar to the title attribute covered in Chapter 5, alt will create a pop-up text box with your description in it when the cursor moves over it. But one of alt's most important uses is to provide content for those who might have images turned off on their browsers or those few who might still be using text-only browsers. Wherever you have placed an image, visitors will see a display that tells them an image is present, and your description will be included. The same description will appear when someone passes the mouse cursor over the image.

```
<img src="picture.jpg" alt="My Favorite Picture" />
```

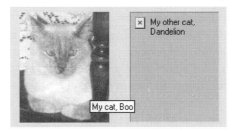

## Control Graphic Size with Height and Width

The height and width attributes enable you to specify the amount of space your image takes up on the page. With these attributes, you can scale an image up or down, depending on your needs.

*Keep in mind that height and width do not change the image file's actual size, only how it displays on a page. A 1MB image still takes up a full meg of space, even if you scale it down to a "thumbnail" size.*

- **height=" "**  The height attribute specifies the height of the image in pixels.
- **width=" "**  The width attribute specifies the image's width in pixels.

```
<img src="picture.jpg" alt="My Favorite Picture" height="100"
width="150" />
```

The smaller image is set to 100 X 150; the larger is set to 200 x 250.

6

TIP *Although using the height and width attributes is not required, it is a good idea to do it with every image. If you don't, the browser has to analyze each image as it decides how to construct the page, making the page take much longer to load and leaving visitors with a blank screen while they wait. If you supply these values in advance, the browser is capable of creating a quick page format and then displaying your text. This way, people who come to your site can still review your content while they wait for images to load.*

# Wrap Text and Align Images

To determine where your image appears on a Web page and how it relates to the text around it, you can use the align=" " attribute. Although this attribute has been deprecated in favor of style sheets, it still provides an easy and reliable way to control the positioning of your images.

## Use left and right for Text Wrapping

To control text wrapping, you use the align attribute with left or right as the value. The picture will appear on one side of the page, with the text on the other.

```
<img src="pansy1.jpg" align="left" />
<img src="pansy2.jpg" align="right" />
```

Lorem ipsum dolor sit amet, consectetuer adipiscing elit, sed diem nonummy nibh euismod tincidunt ut lacreet dolore magna aliguam erat volutpat. Ut wisis enim ad minim veniam, quis nostrud exerci tution ullamcorper suscipit lobortis nisl ut aliquip ex ea commodo consequat. Duis te feugifacilisi. Duis autem dolor in hendrerit in vulputate velit esse molestie consequat, vel illum dolore eu feugiat nulla facilisis at vero eros et accumsan et iusto odio dignissim qui blandit praesent luptatum zzril delenit au gue duis dolore te feugat nulla facilisi.

Ut wisi enim ad minim veniam, quis nostrud exerci taion ullamcorper suscipit lobortis nisl ut aliquip ex en commodo consequat. Duis te feugifacilisi per suscipit lobortis nisl ut aliquip ex en commodo consequat.Lorem ipsum dolor sit amet, consectetuer adipiscing elit, sed diem nonummy nibh euismod tincidunt ut lacreet dolore magna aliguam erat volutpat.

Lorem ipsum dolor sit amet, consectetuer adipiscing elit, sed diem nonummy nibh euismod tincidunt ut lacreet dolore magna aliguam erat volutpat. Ut wisis enim ad minim veniam, quis nostrud exerci tution ullamcorper suscipit lobortis nisl ut aliquip ex ea commodo consequat. Duis te feugifacilisi. Duis autem dolor in hendrerit in vulputate velit esse molestie consequat, vel illum dolore eu feugiat nulla facilisis at vero eros et accumsan et iusto odio dignissim qui blandit praesent luptatum zzril delenit au gue duis dolore te feugat nulla facilisi.

If you choose align="left", any text will be wrapped around the right side of your image. Align="right" will wrap the text around the left side of your graphic.

## Use top, middle, and bottom for Vertical Positioning

To control the vertical alignment of an image relative to text, another image, or anything else on the page, specify the value as top middle or bottom.

```
<img src="picture.gif" align="top" />
<img src="picture.gif" align="middle" />
<img src="picture.gif" align="bottom" />
```

- This is top alignment
- This is middle alignment
- This is bottom alignment
- This is texttop alignment
- This is absmiddle alignment
- This is absbottom alignment
- This is baseline alignment

6

## How to ... Align Graphics with Netscape Values

Another set of values, developed by Netscape, works slightly differently from top, middle, and bottom. To align an image even with the top edge of the text, use align="texttop". If you want text to align in the exact middle of the image (as if an invisible line exists through the middle if the letters), use align="absmiddle". To align an image with the absolute bottom of your text (for instance, the bottom of the "g" in align is the absolute bottom), use align="absbottom".

## Specify White Space Around Your Image

If you want to create a buffer zone of white space around your image, you can create it with the hspace and vspace attributes. *hspace* stands for horizontal space; *vspace* stands for vertical space. Adding hspace will insert space along the horizontal axis and vspace along the vertical axis.

```
<img src="pansy3.jpg" hspace="50" vspace="50">
```

The values for hspace and vspace are specified in pixels; thus in the preceding case the browser would add a space of 50 pixels around the entire image. If you want to add space on only one side or only above and below the image, simply use the attribute you need.

## Add a Border

To add a border around your image, include the border=" " attribute. You can specify the size (thickness) of the border in pixels. So, border="5" will insert a border 5 pixels in width. Adding a border to an image is a nice way to give a picture a "large image" feel with a "small image" performance.

```
<img src="boo.jpg" border="5" alt="My cat Boo"
height="100" width="50" />
```

NOTE    *If your image is a link, a border is automatically drawn around it. If you do not want a border around an image that is a link, you must specify border="0".*

# Practical Uses for Images

Images can be used purely for decoration, but they also have many practical uses on a Web page. Images can be used as links, backgrounds, buttons, watermarks, and much more.

## Create Image Links

You can use an image as a link by putting the <img> element between the anchor tags that create a link.

```
<a href="http://www.linksite.com">
<img src="picture.gif" /> </a>
```

Remember: Those who come to your site through a non-graphical, non-visual browser will need some other way to navigate. You can make things easier for them by including a text link with the image. This is done by inserting the text between the <a> tags-—just as you would for a normal link.

```
<a href="http://www.linksite.com">
<img src="picture.gif" />Text Link</a>.
```

## Insert a Background Image

You can insert a background image on your page by using the background=" " attribute inside the opening <body> tag. The browser will then "tile" the image to fill up the page. To use the background created earlier in this chapter as the wallpaper for a page, the opening body tag would look like this:

```
<body background="weavetile.gif">
```

**A page with a seamless tile background**

The image, whatever it is, will fill the page and will scroll right along with the page's content. What if you would like to have your company's logo remain stationary on the page, where your visitors can always see it? For that you need a watermark.

## Create a Watermark Effect

If you would like to create a *watermark* effect, you use an additional attribute in the <body> tag, called bgproperties. This attribute will allow the background to remain stationary while the page's content scrolls. To create this effect, make the following change to your <body> tag:

```
<body background="weavetile.gif" bgproperties="fixed">
```

Until recently, this attribute was supported only in Internet Explorer and Opera; Netscape 6 now supports the watermark effect. However, older Netscape browsers still ignore this attribute and scroll the background.

# Cut Down the Page Loading Time

The ability to add graphics is without a doubt a great asset to you as a Web author, but it comes with a downside. Images take time to load. The more images you have, the slower your page will load. If your site is purely personal, and you really don't care how long your visitors have to wait—or if they leave—no problem. But if you want to make sure that people who visit your site stay around till your page has loaded, you need to give some thoughts to speeding the process up.

Some simple solutions have already been covered. Keep your image files small—small graphics load faster; and always specify the height and width of your images. This way, at least Web surfers who visit you will have text to read while they wait on the pictures. Following are some other ways to cut down your page load time.

## Use the lowsrc Attribute with a Quick-Loading Image

One easy way to make your pages load faster is to create a lower-resolution (or smaller-sized) image and include it by using the lowsrc=" " attribute in the <img /> element. With lowsrc, the faster-loading graphic will come up first and then be replaced with the slower-loading image.

```
<img src="bigpitts.jpg" lowsrc="lowrespitts.jpg"
alt="Pittsburgh skyline" />
```

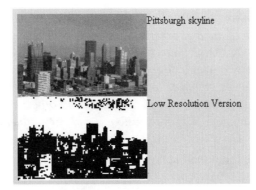

## Use Interlacing with Images

Have you ever loaded a page and noticed that the pictures start off looking fuzzy and out of focus and then gradually clear up? Those are known as *interlaced* images.

It's a way of saving an image file so that it will display an entire image in low resolution and then gradually increase the resolution until the graphic is fully loaded. If you're using a GIF or PNG image, when you create the image, be sure the Interlacing option is selected.

## Use an Inline Thumbnail Image

If you plan on using a lot of images, say for a picture gallery, consider putting *thumbnails* on your page and linking them to an *external* image. Your graphics editor will have an option for resizing the image. (If you're using PaintShop Pro, click Image | Resize, specify a new width and height in pixels and save the image with a new name.) To retain the proper proportions, be sure to check the box marked Maintain Aspect Ration of # to 1.

> **NOTE** *As its name implies, an external image is one you link to separately from the current page. You don't need to create a special HTML page to house the image; just link to the image name as you would a Web page URL.*

To use this image as a thumbnail link, make it an inline image and link it to an external version of the same image:

```
<a href="bigpitts.jpg"><img src="smallpitts.jpg" />
Click to Enlarge</a>
```

> **SHORTCUT** *If you're planning to use a lot of thumbnail images, you might want to check out one of the inexpensive thumbnail-generating programs, such as ThumbNailer, Arles Image Web Page Creator, or Au2HTML. These programs convert whole directories of images into thumbnails in one step and will even generate an HTML page, displaying the image in a "gallery" type format. You can find these and other similar programs at www.download.com, www.tucows.com, and www.zdnet.com/downloads.*

A variation on the thumbnail approach would be to crop a small portion of the picture and save it as a separate file. Then you could use it to serve as a link to the smaller image. You might create a link that looks like this:

```
<a href="bigpitts.jpg"><img src="pittscrop.jpg" />
Click to see Whole picture</a>
```

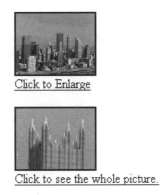

Click to Enlarge

Click to see the whole picture.

6

## Slice Larger Images into Smaller Pieces

If you have a really large image that must go on the page, you might find it simpler (and faster) to slice it up into several smaller pieces. For instance, to cut banner.gif into three smaller images in PaintShop Pro, follow these steps:

1.  Open the image.

2.  Using the selection tool, select about one-third of the banner.

3.  Click Edit | Copy and Paste As New Image to make that portion into a new graphic.

4.  Save it as banner1.gif.

5.  Make two more sections the same way, saving them as banner2.gif and banner3.gif.

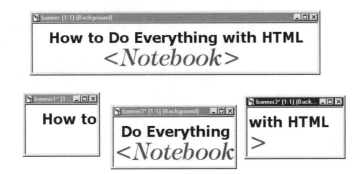

Put the images on a Web page using the <img /> element once for each small image. As long as you don't include a line break (<br />) element, the browser will position all three images side by side, making them appear as one image. Although the banner seems to load faster, it still takes about the same time; because it displays piece by piece it seems to take less time. At least it gives your visitors something to look at while they're waiting.

The following code creates a Web page using the three-part banner created earlier.

```
<html>
<head><title>Banner Sample</title></head>
<body>
<div align="center">
<img src="banner1.gif" />
<img src="banner2.gif" />
<img src="banner3.gif" />
</div>
</body>
</html>
```

How to Do Everything with HTML
*<Notebook>*

# Use Cascading Style Sheets with Graphics

If you have been working through this book chapter by chapter, you have already begun to appreciate the value and versatility of Cascading Style Sheets (CSS). If you've just jumped in here, you're about to discover how much style sheets can help you. By combining style sheets with graphics, you can create some wonderful effects for your Web pages. As always, you need to make sure that your pages are not dependent upon any of the effects you create, so that a person with a non-visual browser or one that simply does not support CSS can still enjoy your site.

## Manage Background Images with CSS

Cascading Style Sheets enable you to control background images and do all the same things covered earlier in the chapter; however, CSS throws in some extras that are not available in straight HTML. As you have already read in this chapter, HTML allows you to specify a background image, which will be tiled to fill up the page. You can use an IE extension to fix that image in place, but that's about all you can do.

The style rules for CSS background images give you a much greater range of choices:

- To specify an image for a background

```
background-image: (url)picture.jpg
```

- To tile an image to fill up the page

```
background-repeat: repeat
```

- To make an image repeat across the top of the page

```
background-repeat: repeat-x
```

- To make an image repeat straight down the page

```
background-repeat: repeat-y
```

- To cause an image to be used only once

```
background-repeat: no-repeat
```

- To allow an image to scroll with the page

```
background-attachment: scroll
```

- To fix the image in place such as a watermark

```
background-attachment: fixed
```

- To position the background image on the page

```
background-position: top (or center, bottom, left, right)
```

To use the <style> element to create an embedded style sheet that creates a background image down the left side of the page and allows it to remain fixed, you would write your HTML code as follows (if you're fuzzy on CSS style rules, check out Chapters 2 and 3):

```
<html>
<head><title>CSS Watermark Effect</title>
<style type="text/css">
body    {    background-image: url(weavetile.gif);
             background-position: left;
```

```
                     background-repeat: repeat-y;
                     background-attachment: fixed; }

</style></head>
<body>(Cut and paste some text here)</body>
</html>
```

Lorem ipsum dolor sit amet,
consectetuer adipiscing elit, sed
diem nonummy nibh euismod
tincidunt ut lacreet dolore magna
aliguam erat volutpat. Ut wisis
enim ad minim veniam, quis
nostrud exerci tution ullamcorper
suscipit lobortis nisl ut aliquip ex

**NOTE** *Are you wondering what the strange words in the preceding illustration mean? Actually, they don't mean anything. They are nonsense words (technically called greeking) used to fill up text in a layout. Greeking is a good way to experiment with layouts before you write your final copy. If you are trying to duplicate this illustration, just paste your own text into the code. If you'd like to have a copy of the text used in the illustration, go to Osborne's Web site (www.osborne.com), choose* How to Do Everything with HTML, *and download it along with the rest of this chapter's files.*

## Insert Image Bullets with CSS

Suppose you want to use some custom bullets to give your list items a little pizzazz. With CSS, it's a snap. Simply write a style rule for the <li> element that instructs the browser to use your bullet instead of HTML's default bullets. The style rule would look like this:

```
ul      {list-style-image: url(button.gif); outside;}
```

- This is list item one.
- This is list item two.
- This is list item three.
- This is list item four.
- This is list item five.

If you break the rule down, it's easy to see what each part is doing. The selector, ul, selects the unordered list, <ul>, element. The property, list-style-image, is assigned to <ul> and the value url(button.gif) instructs the browser to use an image for the bullet, instead of one of the standard HTML options. The value, outside, tells the browser to put the bullet to the left and indent the text. To apply the style in your page, simply use the <ul> element as you normally would. Only now the browser uses your image for the bullets, instead of the standard HTML choices.

```
<html>
<head><title>CSS Lists</title>
<style type="text/css">
     ul      {list-style: url(button.gif) outside;}
</style></head>
<body>
<ul>
<li>This is list item one.</li>
<li>This is list item two.</li>
<li>This is list item three.</li>
<li>This is list item four.</li>
</ul>
</body>
</html>
```

## Place a Decorative Border Around an Image

Maybe you would like to put an attractive border around your images. HTML
allows you to specify a border, its width, and sometimes its color. However, with
CSS, there are many more available options. A sample style rule that will give a
decorative red border, with something of a 3D effect, would look like this:

```
img      {border-color: red;
            border-style: inset;
            border-width: thick;}
```

To see how this looks, choose any image on your system and then copy the code
here, putting the image filename in the <img> element:

```
<html>
<head><title>CSS Image Border</title>
<style type="text/css">
body     {margin-left: .50in; margin-top: .50in}
img       {border-color: red;
            border-style: inset;
            border-width: thick;}
</style></head>
<body bgcolor="white">
<img src="filename.jpg" alt="A sample image and border"
height="200" width="300" />
</body>
</html>
```

This code creates a red "picture frame"–type border around any image that is placed on the page. It also specifies a 1/2" margin on the top and left sides of the page.

Try experimenting with some of the other CSS border properties and see what varieties you can come up with. Appendix D provides a reference guide of CSS properties and values. The best way to learn CSS (or HTML for that matter) is to play with it. Go have some fun and see what you can do.

# Learn Good Web Design

Graphics are like caramel syrup on a bowl of French vanilla ice cream. You can have a good Web site without them, but they certainly add to the total experience. But, just as too much caramel syrup can ruin a good bowl of ice cream, overdoing images can kill your Web site. In fact, it's safe to say that the number one killer of otherwise good Web sites is the poor use of graphics and images. How do you enhance your site with graphics? Very judiciously.

## Web Design Principle: Use Images Like Salt—Sparingly

There are plenty of ways to misuse images, which will keep people from coming back to your site after their first brief visit. Why? Because poorly chosen images can make a site slow to load and hard to view. Following are a few suggestions for using images to enhance a visitor's experience rather than taking away from it.

## Limit the Size and Number of Images per Page

Although graphics, pictures, and images provide necessary visual interaction for the visitors to your Web site, never forget that they slow down your page's loading time. It's simple mathematics. The more (and larger) images you have, the longer your pages will take to load. And because the majority of Web surfers still access the Internet through plain, old-fashioned telephone lines, if you have a graphics-heavy page, your visitors might have time to read the newspaper, watch TV, wash their clothes, and fix dinner all before your page loads. The solution to the problem is easy: Keep graphics small and limit their use. Imagine each of your Web pages as a small container that can hold only about 60K of material; then try to keep the sum of all your content on each page within that limit. It's not easy, but it can be done.

## Don't Use Distracting Backgrounds

Have you ever visited a site where the background image was so distracting that it hurt your eyes to look at it? Or it made the page's content so difficult to read you just gave up? A lot of really beautiful images make poor backgrounds. Remember, the most important part of your site is the content. Unless you are creating a site that depends on visual imagery (such as an art museum or a photo gallery), images are window dressing for your site. They are there to add to the experience. Don't choose garish or harsh-looking background images or patterns that make you dizzy when you look at them. You might think they look really good, but unless your content is incredibly compelling (and sometimes not even then), your visitors will not be back for a second visit.

## Remember Those with Non-Visual Browsers

Although the old text-based browsers like Lynx are slowly passing off the scene, they are being replaced by a new generation of non-visual browsers: Aural and Braille Web browsers for the blind, TTY browsers for the deaf, and other advances in technology are opening the Internet to an ever-increasing audience. If your site is heavily dependent on graphics, you might be losing a large number of people who otherwise might benefit from what you have to offer on the Web. Design with them in mind, too.

## Practice, Practice, Practice

Now that you have some images to work with, try going back to the pages created throughout the first five chapters of this book and insert the images in them. For starters, try to recreate the following page. If you get stuck, remember you can check out this book's companion Web site (www.osborne.com).

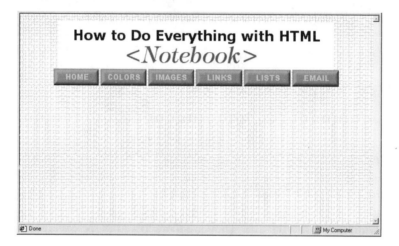

# Find the Code Online

To find the code online for this or any of the chapters in this book, go to Osborne's Web site: www.osborne.com, and click the Free Code choice on the navigation bar. From the list of books, select the *How to Do Everything with HTML* option and you will be able to download the book files, which are linked together and organized as an offline "mini" Web site. For more on how to use the "mini" Web site, see Chapter 17.

| Use This Code For... | Look for this Filename |
| --- | --- |
| Sample banner | banner.gif |
| Sample button | blankbtn.gif |
| Graphic bullet demo | bullet.htm |
| Image scaling demo | scaling.htm |

| Use This Code For... | Look for this Filename |
| --- | --- |
| Vertical alignment demo | vertalign.htm |
| Image border demo | border.htm |
| Background image demo | bgimage.htm |
| Thumbnail demo | thumbnail.htm |
| CSS fixed background | csswatermark.htm |
| CSS border | cssborder.htm |
| Background tile | weavetile.gif |
| Background tile demo | tiledisplay.htm |
| Alt attribute demo | altimage.htm |
| Text wrapping demo | textwrap.htm |
| White space demo | hvspace.htm |
| Image link demo | imagelink.htm |
| Low-res demo | lowres.htm |
| Image splicing demo | bannersplice.htm |
| CSS bulleted list | csslist.htm |
| Sample home page | samplehomepage.htm |

6

# Chapter 7

## Plan, Publish, and Promote Your Site

## How to...

- Plan Your Site for Maximum Effectiveness

- Identify Your Target Audience

- Storyboard Your Web Site

- Find a Host for Your Site

- Promote Your Site

- Make Certain Your Visitors Keep Coming Back

Once you have mastered the fundamentals of HTML that were covered in the first six chapters of this book, you are equipped to put up your own Web site. It doesn't take a lot of expensive software or programming knowledge. All it takes is your time and planning. Yet it is in the planning stage that most would-be Web authors fall short. Web authoring software has made creating a site so easy that it is commonplace for beginning authors to throw together a site in an afternoon, publish it, and sit back, confident that the world is going to rush to visit their sites.

If all you want to do is have a site online, this approach will work fine. If you actually want people to come to your site, you'd better reconsider the haphazard approach. An effective Web site not only reflects care in the design of the pages; it also reflects careful thought in its overall layout.

Just as a building contractor would never think of beginning construction on a building without a good set of blueprints, you shouldn't begin developing your site without planning it well. A good Web site "blueprint" will take into consideration your site's layout, your choice of hosts, and an idea of how you are going to promote the site.

# Plan Your Site Effectively

How do you go about planning a Web site? The best place to start is to consider why you want to put up a site in the first place. Why do you want to go to the time, trouble, and expense of constructing (not to mention maintaining) a presence on the World Wide Web?

## Identify Your Site's Purpose

The first step you take in creating your site should be to identify its purpose. Depending on whether your site is personal, informational, or for business, you will want (and need) to add different things. The more clearly you define a purpose for your site, the easier it will be to decide what needs to go into it. For example, your site could be

- A personal, family album–type site

- An informational or resource site

- An entertainment-oriented site

- A brochure site, advertising a business or organization

- An online business

By developing a concrete idea of your site's reason for existence, you will find it much easier to decide what—and what not—to put in it. For instance, if you a planning to set up an online business, you'll probably need to have a page that contains an order form and a catalog for your products. A brochure-type site isn't likely to need these, but you'll probably want to include an e-mail link so potential customers can contact you. A family album site won't need much in the way of bells and whistles, but if you're putting together an informational site about your model rocketry hobby, you might want to consider a page with a streaming video of a rocket launch.

A good rule is to put in everything you need to put in; leave out anything that won't contribute to your site's goal. The only way to know what those things are is if you have clearly defined that goal.

## Identify Your Target Audience

In addition to defining your site's purpose, you should give some thought to your target audience. Who do you want to attract to your site? How do you plan to get them there? Whether your audience is made up of friends and relatives, people with a shared interest, or potential customers, your site design, layout, and content depends on you having a clear idea of who they are.

Another question about your target audience has to do with the kind of equipment they will be using to view your site. If you're designing for a corporate intranet and you know exactly what types of browsers and monitors will be used to display your site, you'll have a great deal of freedom in design. Likewise, if you're designing for family and friends, and you don't really care whether anybody else can see your site, you are free to set up your site the way you want it. However, if you are trying to reach as broad an audience as possible, you must decide whether to design your pages with cutting-edge effects, possibly excluding those whose equipment can't display your pages properly.

As you plan your site, keep the following questions in mind:

- Who do you want to come to your site? (Family? Friends? People with a shared interest? Potential customers?)

- Is your site going to be targeted at a broad audience or a narrow one?

- Based on the age and background of your intended audience, what types of graphics and design will most appeal to them?

- Do you want to design your site so that older browsers will be able to display it, thus increasing your potential audience?

- Is your site targeted toward such a narrow group that you can use cutting-edge design without limiting your audience?

- If your site is business- or profession-related, what is its mission or goal? Is it intended for commerce, information, research, leisure, or some other purpose?

## Storyboard Your Site

Once you have identified your site's purpose and audience, you can begin drawing up a blueprint; in Web design, this is called *storyboarding*. If you've ever watched a documentary on how Walt Disney makes one of its animated movies, you're familiar with the idea of storyboarding. In the case of a movie, various parts of the story are roughly sketched out so the overall content of the film can be visualized. In a similar way, you visualize a Web site's layout and organization by storyboarding the individual pages that will make up the site.

You can storyboard a site by sketching it out on a piece of paper, using sticky notes to represent each page, or even with three-by-five cards. You can get really fancy and draw the layout with a graphics or flow chart program. Most important is that you are able to easily rearrange your layout so you can try out different approaches to structuring your site.

To create a storyboard for your site, follow these steps:

1. Decide what pages you want to start with. You will need a home or an index page, of course, but you also need to plan out your other pages. For instance, if you are constructing a family album site, you might decide on a page that focuses on each member of the family. Each of those pages could have its own series of sub-pages such as hobbies, favorite music, pictures, and favorite books.

2. Decide on your layout. Is your site going to be linear? Pyramid? This is partly determined by your site's content and purpose. If you want visitors to move progressively through your material, you might choose a linear site. If you want them to be able to take different paths, depending on their interests, a site organized like a pyramid might be more suitable.

3. Use a 3 × 5 card to represent each page, and write the page's main title on the blank side. Obviously, if you're planning to have hundreds of pages on your site, this could be cumbersome. At this point, you need to storyboard only your main pages.

4. Rearrange the cards, trying different layouts, until you find one you like.

5. Copy the layout onto a sheet of paper.

6. Revise the site design until you are satisfied.

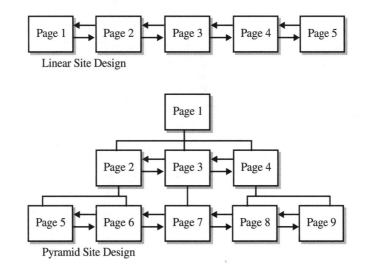

Linear Site Design

Pyramid Site Design

## How to ...    Decide What Pages You Need

If you're having trouble deciding what pages you need to include in your site, try thinking of it as if you are doing an outline. In addition to your home page, each of your outline's major points would be a page. Each sub-point could have its own page, and so on.

## Gather Your Content

In the final step of site organization you will plan and gather your content. When it comes to planning, don't skimp here. Your content will determine whether people keep coming back to your site. To find content for your site, you can

- **Write your own**    The first and most obvious place to go in looking for content is right at home. Whatever your site's subject matter, if you are going to the trouble of building a Web site, you probably have enough interest or expertise to produce a large portion of the content. If you're putting up a site dedicated to Monarch butterfly migration patterns, chances are you know enough about the subject to be your own resource for at least a portion of the site.

- **Invite others to contribute**    If you are constructing a large site or one that will provide a lot of information, you'll find it difficult to keep up with the content all by yourself. However, if you make your content needs known to others who share your interest, you might find that your only problem is finding time to put all the offerings onto your site.

- **Use a content supplier**    A great and easy way to provide fresh content for your site is by taking advantage of free Web content suppliers. These Web sites provide up-to-date news, financial, weather, and general interest content for your site and generally they are free of charge. Simply visit the site and choose what content you would like to add to your page. They will send you (generally by e-mail) some code to paste into your HTML document. That's all there is to it. To find sources, just do a search with the keywords "free Web content"; you'll find plenty of resources. The downside of these content suppliers is that a Web browser must contact their site and download the content as your page loads, thus slowing down the loading time. However, it's hard to beat them for providing fresh content on a consistent basis. You can find a list of free content providers in the following table.

| Web Content Provider | URL |
| --- | --- |
| Moreover | http://w.moreover.com/webmaster |
| Woo Doggy | http://woodoggy.com |
| IT News | http://www.it-news.com/freecontent.htm |
| Isyndicate Express | http://www.affiliate.isyndicate.com |
| Click for Content | http://www.clickforcontent.com |
| Contents Sheet | http://www.contents-sheet.com |
| Free Sticky | http://www.freesticky.com/stickyweb |

TIP *Don't forget to update your content regularly. If your site never updates or provides new information, your visitors have little reason to return. You might get new hits every week, but what you want is to get those new visitors and keep the old ones returning.*

## Develop Your Web Site

Once you've done your work in planning, it's time to begin the process of creating, testing, and previewing your pages. By this time you might be in a hurry to finish your site and get it on the Web, but take your time in this final polishing stage. You want your site to be perfectly functional when you finally put it online. This is the step in which you make sure none of your visitors sees a "404 Not Found" message when they try to access one of your pages.

## Write Your Pages

It might seem like stating the obvious, but you have to write your pages before you publish them. And with all the options available to would-be Webmasters, that might not be as simple as you think. If you've been working through the book and doing the exercises in Notepad or some other text editor, you might have wondered about the different Web authoring tools that are available and which—if any—you should use.

- **WYSIWYG programs (Microsoft FrontPage, Macromedia Dreamweaver, Net Objects Fusion, Symantec Visual Page, and so forth)**    WYSIWYG (pronounced *wizzy wig*) is an acronym for "What you see is what you get." These programs enable you to construct your pages visually, just as you might lay out a brochure or poster with a desktop publishing program. WYSIWYGs are helpful tools in that they enable you to create pages much more quickly than you can by writing the HTML code yourself. Also, many of them double as site management tools, alerting you to broken links and displaying the structure of your site. Although WYSIWYGs are helpful, they do have some disadvantages. First, they can function somewhat like a crutch and keep you from learning HTML yourself. However, you'll find that as you use these programs you'll often need to go in and play with the HTML anyway. If you don't know HTML, you're at the mercy of the program. So, even if you decide to use a WYSIWYG, take the time to learn to work with HTML first.

- **Word processors (Word, WordPerfect, and so forth)**    Most word processing programs can save pages in HTML format and many of the newest ones will even work like a WYSIWYG editor. Unfortunately, word processors are not known for writing very good code, and you might find it necessary go in and clean it up.

- **Web browsers (Netscape Composer, Microsoft FrontPage Express)**    Some Web browsers also incorporate their own Web page editing programs. These aren't bad, although their capabilities are somewhat limited compared to the WYSIWYG programs.

- **HTML editors (Amaya, HTML Kit, Coffee Cup HTML Editor, Allaire Homesite, and so forth)**    HTML editors combine the best of both worlds. They function much like a simple text editor, but also include

special features for writing HTML. In preview mode, they will give you a
WYSIWYG-like display (although you can't edit in preview mode), so you
can keep tabs on what your page actually will look like. Best of all, some
of the best HTML editors are available as freeware—just download them
and go to work! The following table lists some shareware and freeware
HTML editors you might want to check out.

| HTML Editor | URL | Approximate Cost |
| --- | --- | --- |
| Amaya | http://www.w3.org | Freeware |
| HTML Kit | http://chami.com/html-kit | Freeware |
| First Page | http://www.evrsoft.com | Freeware |
| Arachnophilia | http://www.arachnoid.com/arachnophilia | Freeware |
| Cute HTML | http://www.globalscape.com | $20 |
| CoolPage | http://www.coolpage.com | $30 |
| CoffeeCup HTML Editor | http://www.coffeecup.com | $50 |
| Hot Dog PageWiz | http://www.sausagetools.com | $70 |
| Allaire Homesite | http://www.allaire.com | $90 |
| Hot Dog Professional | http://www.sausagetools.com | $100 |
| Hot Metal Pro | http://www.hotmetalpro.com | $130 |

## Test Your Links and Site Navigation

When writing your pages, or once you have written them, the next important step
is to test your links. The larger the site you are constructing, the more tempting
it will be to let this part slide. However, there's nothing more frustrating to your
visitors than to click on a dead link; so bite the bullet and test those links. It's good
practice to begin testing as you add each new page, but whether you do it all at
once or page by page, make sure every link works.

You'll also want to make sure your site navigation is straightforward and easy
to follow. Don't leave your visitors guessing about how they should navigate your
site. At the very minimum you should provide on every page a link to the main
page and a link to a *site map*. A site map is simply a page that displays links to
all the other pages on the site.

## Preview Your Pages

If your visitors are frustrated by broken and non-functional links, you will be equally upset if you discover that the design you spent hours on looks perfectly awful on a different browser or monitor. One of the realities of designing for the Web is that your page design is affected by the user's equipment. There are many variables that can affect the look of your Web site and, as much as possible, you must take them into account:

- **Test your pages in different browsers**    You should at least check your pages out in Netscape and Internet Explorer, and it's not a bad idea to find some older versions of each browser. Another up-and-coming browser is Opera; you should display your pages in it, too.

- **See what your pages look like in browsers with the graphics turned off**    Some users with slow connections will turn off the graphics in their browsers to speed up page loading.

- **See what your pages look like when you set your monitor to different resolutions**    Depending on the capabilities of your own monitor, you can preview your pages in different resolutions by right-clicking anywhere on the Windows desktop and selecting Properties from the pop-up dialog box. When the Display Properties window comes up, click the Settings tab. This should give you the different display resolutions your monitor is capable of handling.

After you have tested your links and previewed your pages, and are satisfied with any corrections you have made, you are ready to put your site online.

# Publish Your Site

Perhaps the most intimidating part of the whole process of setting up a Web site is actually trying to put it online. When you are ready to publish your site, you must venture outside of the comfortable world of HTML and into the mysterious world of FTP, domain names, IP numbers, Web servers, and more. If you're willing to just take things step by step, you'll find it's not nearly as confusing as you imagined.

# Find a Host

The first hurdle you must cross in getting your site online is finding a host or a Web server. Actually, the only thing that makes this difficult is the sheer number of choices you now have in this area. How do you decide which server is right for you and your Web site? Your decision will be influenced primarily by your budget and your needs. Consider some of the possible choices:

- **Your own provider**   If you're putting together a Web site, you very likely already have an account with an Internet service provider (ISP). Most providers give you a few megabytes of disk space for your own home page. Three to five megabytes goes a long way; you might find it is sufficient for your needs. If so, look no further—you've found your host.

- **Free hosts**   If you plan to put together a large, complicated site and you know you'll need 50–100 megabytes of space, but you're on a budget, try one of the free servers. These advertiser-supported hosts give you lots of room to work with and generally provide quite a few resources that actually make it easier for you to set up your site. So, what's the catch? To get the free space, you will either have to consent to rotating banner ads placed conspicuously on your pages (usually at the top) or to a pop-up window that opens when someone loads your site. If you're not put off by the advertising, it's a great way to put a site online at virtually no cost to you. Some of the most popular of the free hosts are fortunecity.com, geocities.com, and tripod.com.

- **Paid hosts**   If you need space and really don't want someone else's banner ads cluttering up your page, you will need to find a paid host. A Web server works much the same way as an Internet service provider does (in fact, many of them function as both). This is one area where it pays to shop around, as you will find a wide fluctuation in prices and what you get for your money. You can find hosts for as little as six or seven dollars a month—but don't be influenced by price alone. Check them out to see if they provide

  - **Space**   At least 30–45 megs of disk space.

- **CGI bin**    You'll need this if you plan to use forms, guestbooks, or other things on your site that require a user response. See Chapter 14 for more about CGI.

- **FrontPage Extensions support**    If you plan to develop pages with Microsoft's FrontPage, your server will need to be equipped with FrontPage Extensions.

- **One or more POP3 e-mail accounts**    If you want people to contact you, it's nice to have an e-mail account that works directly through your Web site and bears your domain name.

- **Web traffic statistics**    You'll want to know how much attention your site is getting. A good server will provide a means for you to track your site's hits.

- **Good customer service**    If you have a problem, it's nice to know you have someone you can contact.

- **Support for commerce**    Will your server allow you to do business on your site, and use a transaction processor?

- **Downloads**    Will the server allow you to provide downloads?

- **Searches**    If you're going to have a large site, will visitors be able to search your site's materials?

NOTE    *A transaction processor allows you to accept payments and process transactions online. If you're planning to operate an ebusiness or just extend your current business to the Web, you should check out what's available. Some good sources are*

- *Cybercash (http://cybercash.com/webauthorize/)*
- *Signio (http://www.signio.com/products/payment.html)*
- *Visa (http://www.visa.com/nt/ecomm/merchant/main.html)*

To begin researching the market, just go to any search engine and type **Web hosting** and you'll have enough possibilities to keep you busy for quite awhile.

## Register a Domain Name

Do you really need to have a domain name? It all depends. Your domain name is your Internet identity. It is the means by which people will find—and hopefully remember—you. Although it's not mandatory that you spend the money to register your own "dot.com," it's a pretty good idea—and it's a great value.

Domain name registration used to be heavily regulated; however, when the United States Congress recently deregulated it, domain name registration opened up to competition. As a result, the price dropped to the point where it's reasonable to have not just one, but several domain names. Often, your Web server will be able to handle registering your name for you, but if they don't provide that service, it's easy enough to find someone who will. Just do a search on the words "domain name registrars" and you'll find more than enough options.

Keep in mind that when you register a name you are, in effect, leasing that name. You have the rights to it only as long as you keep the registration current. How do you find out if the name you want is available? The easiest way is to just open your browser and type in that name. If a Web site comes up, you know it's been registered. Or, you might find a "place holder" page in the case of a name that has been registered but has not yet posted a Web site. To be absolutely sure, you'll want to find a site where you can do a search on a *whois* search engine. This is an engine that specifically searches through a database of registered names. It will tell you whether or not someone has already registered the name you want. The following table lists some domain name registrars. Prices can vary, so be sure to check out several before you decide.

> **NOTE**    *You can do a* whois *search at Network Solutions' Web site. The URL is*
> *http://www.networksolutions.com.*

| Domain Name Registrar | URL |
| --- | --- |
| Network Solutions | http://www.networksolutions.com |
| Register.com | http://www.register.com |
| Domain Direct (TuCows) | http://www.domaindirect.com |
| Word Audio | http://www.wordaudio.com |
| Domain Valet | http://www.domainvalet.com |
| Signature Domains | http://www.signaturedomains.com |
| Domain Bank | http://www.domainbank.net |
| Low Cost Domains | http://www.lowcostdomains.com |
| BudgetRegister.Com | http://www.budgetregister.com |
| 123 Domain Name Registration | http://www.123-domain-name-registration.com |
| Ireg.com | http://www.ireg.com |

## How to ... Choose a Domain Name

A domain name is your Web address. As such it should be clear, easy to remember, and descriptive. Don't use acronyms or initials unless you are already known by them. Instead, try to choose a name that best describes you, your business, or the purpose for your site. Try to choose a name that will be easy for people to remember and associate with you.

NOTE
*With the boom in domain name registrations, a lot of the most popular .com, .net, and .org names have already been taken. If the name you want has been taken don't despair, as several other extensions have recently been approved and will soon be available.*

## Upload Your Site

The final hurdle in getting a site online is in actually uploading the site to your server. To upload your site, you'll need to use File Transfer Protocol, FTP; for that you'll need some special software. If you are using one of the free hosting services, generally it will provide FTP capability through its server. Otherwise, you'll need to obtain an FTP program such as CuteFTP, WS_FTP95, or one of many others.

NOTE
*WS_FTP is available free of charge at http://gavon.com/host/review/4865.html. Also, all Windows operating systems include an FTP program that is available from the DOS prompt. For Macs, a popular FTP program is called "Fetch." It is free to educational and non-profit groups and is a $25 shareware program, available at ftp://ftp.dartmouth.edu/pub/mac/Fetch_3.0.3.hqx.*

To upload your site, follow these steps:

1. Open your FTP program and make sure you are connected to the Internet. In CuteFTP, a dialog box will open, requesting some basic information about your site.

2. Label for site: This is the top window in the dialog box. Because it is for your own reference purposes, it can be any name you choose.

3. FTP Host Address: This second box is the address where the program will be uploading your files. You put your domain name in this box. For example, www.mywebsite.com.

4. FTP site User Name: You would have been given a user name by your host. Type that in the next box.

5. FTP site Password: The next input line is for your password. Again, your host would have assigned you a password; that goes here.

6. FTP site Connection Port: The next line is for the connection port. This generally is filled out automatically so you don't need to worry about it.

7. Login type: Next, you have three options from which to select under Login type: Normal, Anonymous, and Double. Check Normal.

8. After you have filled in the necessary information, click Connect. (If your computer does not dial in to your server automatically, you'll need to make sure you're online when you do this.) Once you have logged in to your host, simply transfer files as you would between two disks on your own computer. The left window generally displays the *local* files; that is, the files on your system. The window on the right will display the *remote* files. To upload your site, simply select the files on your system that you want to transfer; then make sure you have opened the proper directory on the server. If you're not sure which is the proper directory, check with your host to be certain you have the right one.

9. Click the Upload button after you have selected the files you want to transfer; the program will do the rest.

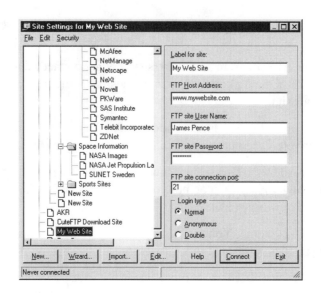

TIP    *Usually, you put your site in the root directory or a directory named* www.

# Promote Your Site

Once you have your site online, the next logical question is how to get people to come visit it. Considering that you are competing for attention with millions of other Web sites, that can be more challenging than you might think. Even if the focus of your site is narrow enough that you are competing with only hundreds of other sites, you still have a daunting task ahead of you. Because most people don't go past the first 10 or 20 sites that a search engine brings up, your job is to get your site listed in that top group. How do you do it?

## Design Your Pages with Strategic Keywords

The first thing to understand about search engines is that they look for keywords on your site. If you know where to put those keywords, you can dramatically increase your chances of being in the top 10 or 20 search engine hits.

- **Choose several keywords**   The important thing to remember here is that the people don't necessarily know that they are searching for your page. Usually they are searching on a broad topic, planning to visit whatever pages come up high on the list. You have to choose your keywords carefully so that your page is up there. For example, suppose you have a site devoted to the Monarch butterfly, and you want to attract Monarch enthusiasts. Take some time to think through what words you would use in a search engine if you were looking for a page like yours. Perhaps you would choose butterfly, Monarch butterfly, butterfly migration, insects: butterfly, and others. Notice that most of the keywords actually are more than one word; that's because search engines tend to give preference to multi-word keywords.

- **Put keywords in the <title> </title> element**    Search engines also look at the page title. Which title is more likely to attract butterfly enthusiasts: Fran's Home Page or Monarch Butterfly World?

- **Use the <meta /> element**    This element goes inside the <head> </head> portion of your page. In computer terms, the word *meta* refers to something that describes or gives information about something else; the <meta /> element provides information about the Web page. There are a number of different ways to use <meta> that are unrelated to search engines. One important use is to provide keywords that search engines access. The keywords in a butterfly page might look like this:

```
<html><head>
<title>Monarch Butterfly World</title>
<meta name="keywords" content="Monarch butterfly,
butterfly migration, Monarchs, butterflies" />
</head>
```

- **Strategically place keywords in the top part of your document**    The higher up in your document your keywords occur, the better. Search engines look toward the top of the file for keywords to categorize your site. If in constructing Monarch Butterfly World, the Web designer puts a half page of biographical information before ever getting around to his or her subject, chances are the site won't score very high in the search engine rankings.

CAUTION    *Don't think "more is better" here. If you use a <meta /> keyword too many times (usually more than seven), the search engine will ignore it. If you flood the <meta /> element with the keyword hundreds of times, as some have done, it is called spamming and it could get your site banned from the search engine.*

7

## Submit Your Site to Search Engines

Although most of the search engines are automated and will find your site sooner or later, if you want it to be sooner you'll want to submit your site to them. You can do this yourself by accessing each search engine site and manually submitting your URL, or using site submission software or a submission service to do the job for you.

To submit your site manually, follow these steps:

1. Go to a search engine site; for example, altavista.com.

2. Somewhere on the page (usually near the top or bottom) there will be a link that will read, *submit a site* or *add url*. Click that link.

3. You will go to another page that has a window where you can add the URL for your site. Just type in the URL and click the submit button. Within a few days, the engine's *spider* will crawl through your site and index it.

NOTE *A "spider" is an automated program that visits and indexes Web sites and then makes the results available to search engines.*

There are hundreds of possible search engines you could submit to. If you want to speed up the process, consider using site submission service or software. The following table lists some options you might want to explore.

| Search Engine Submission Service or Software | URL |
| --- | --- |
| Submit Express | http://www.submitexpress.com |
| Add Me | http://www.addme.com |
| Launch | http://www.nnh.co.uk/launch |
| GNet | http://gnet.dhs.org/sess |
| GetSubmitted.com | http://www.getsubmitted.com |
| Submission Pro! | http://www.submissionpro.com |
| Usubmit.Com | http://www.usubmit.com |
| The WebMasters.bc.ca | http://www.thewebmasters.bc.ca |
| Search Engine Monkeys | http://www.searchenginemonkeys.com |
| World Wide Data Link | http://www.wwpromote.com |

# There Is a Difference Between a Search Engine and a Web Directory

For example, Yahoo is a directory where sites are reviewed by people rather than spiders. If you plan to submit your site to Yahoo, be sure it will fit into one of their categories and that it is a quality site. Yahoo is very choosy; thus it is an achievement if your site gets listed with them.

7

If you prefer a faster way, try a site submission service or software to automate the process. Many of the services charge a small fee; but some offer limited submissions free of charge. With the software (which is usually shareware) you'll have to pay a registration fee, but you'll have the advantage of using the software as frequently as you want to without added fees.

■ To locate a service, do a search on the keywords *site submission services*.

■ To find software, go to an online source such as tucows.com or download.com and do a search for *site submission software.*

## Promote Your Site in Other Ways

Don't get caught in the trap of depending only on the search engines for traffic to your site. There are many other ways to get visitors, and a savvy Web author will take advantage of all of them:

■ **Promote your site through newsgroups and forums**   You have to be careful how you do this, lest you be accused of *spamming* (sending unwanted solicitations) the group. However, if you want your site to get noticed, try participating in one or two newsgroup discussions about your subject. If you add a short signature line with your URL, people might visit your site just out of curiosity. Also, as people get to know you and appreciate your expertise, they might ask you questions. You then can refer them to your site without spamming them. Check out dejanews.com and delphi.com for some possible starting places.

- **Join a Web ring**    A Web ring is a group of related sites that have interlinked. Someone who visits one site might follow the ring to your site. Yahoo! is a good place to start looking for a Web ring to join.

- **Check out banner exchanges**    Banner exchanges often are free and a great way to get some publicity for your site. You permit someone else's banner to be displayed on your site; in return you get to display your banner on their site.

- **Try paid banner advertising**    This option isn't great if you're on a budget, but if you have the funds (for example, if you have an online business) you might experiment with some paid advertising.

- **Don't forget traditional advertising**    Put your URL on your business cards, stationery, brochures, and anywhere else you think it will get noticed.

It's incredibly rewarding to see your site online for the first time. It's even better when you begin to hear from people who have visited your site. Getting your site online might seem like a daunting process, but it's really not that difficult. But don't take the trouble to publish your site without promoting it. Publishing a site without promoting it is as silly as writing a book, then not telling anyone that you've written it. Old-fashioned word of mouth is important. Tell people about your site. They'll come. And if you've got a quality site with good content, they'll come back!

# Part II

# Add Style to Your Site

# Chapter 8

# Use Tables for Layout Control

## How to...

- Understand Tables
- Create a Simple Table
- Modify Your Table's Appearance
- Create Page Layouts with Tables
- Design a Table of Links for Site Navigation

Chapters 1–7 focus on equipping you with the raw materials for creating your own Web site. With what you learned in those chapters, you could easily put together a series of Web pages that you would be proud of. However, if you have been working with some of the exercises, you also have become aware of some of HTML's limitations. The chief limitations Web designers wrestle with are presentation and layout. How do you learn how to position the various parts of your page so that your content is presented in a pleasing manner? Chapters 8–10 will cover the issues of style and how best to control it on your Web pages. In this chapter you will be introduced to perhaps the easiest (and most frequently used) method of influencing the layout and design of a page: tables.

# Understand Tables

Have you ever used a spreadsheet program? If so, you have a rough idea of what tables are and how they normally look. Tables were developed and added to the HTML standard in the early 1990s to provide a way to display structured information, such as in a spreadsheet. Before that time there was no good way to display columns of data in an HTML document; because HTML originally was devised for scientific and academic material, this presented a problem. The introduction of tables not only solved this problem, but provided a solution to an as yet undiscovered problem.

When the Internet was in its infancy, presentation and design weren't very problematic; graphical browsers changed all that. However, basic HTML did not provide the tools for control that designers were used to. In fact, a Web designer was completely at the mercy of browser, system, and HTML limitations when it came to doing Web page layouts. Placement and appearance of text and graphics were not absolute, but static. A layout that looked good on a designer's machine might be totally transformed on someone else's system.

Then Web authors discovered tables. By putting text, graphics, and other content inside table cells, designers could take advantage of a table's structure to "force" a browser to stay within a particular layout. Tables certainly did not solve all the difficulties Web developers faced, but they represented a great step forward. Even though the overall trend in the Web is toward Cascading Style Sheets (CSS)—and ultimately XSL or eXtensible Stylesheet Language—tables still are frequently used in Web design. In this chapter you'll discover why.

# Create a Simple Table

Tables are not difficult to understand or build. They can become quite complex, but the basic concept is easy. If you just keep in mind the idea of a spreadsheet, most of the structure of a table will be demystified. Tables are merely structures in which information (or parts of a Web page) is presented in rows and columns. Each individual segment of a table is called a *cell;* for example, row one, column one represents one cell; row two, column one is another; and so on. Thinking in terms of rows and columns might be confusing, though. The best way to understand how tables work is to create one.

Open template.htm and save it as tables.htm; then copy this code to construct a simple three cell by three cell table:

```
<html>
<head><title>Table Exercise</title></head>
<body>
<table>
<tr> <td>X</td> <td>X</td> <td>X</td> </tr>
<tr> <td>X</td> <td>X</td> <td>X</td> </tr>
<tr> <td>X</td> <td>X</td> <td>X</td> </tr>
</table>
</body>
</html>
```

After you've typed in the code, save your page and open it in your browser. This illustration is what you should see.

Now that you've created an uncomplicated table, take a look back through the HTML you've written to learn about each of the elements you used. You created that table with only three elements: <table>, <tr>, and <td>.

- **<table> </table>**   The *table* element creates the table. Use this element for each table you wish to create on a page.

- **<tr> </tr>**   The *table row* element establishes, as you would expect, a row. If your table is to have ten rows, you will use this element ten times.

- **<td> </td>**   TD stands for *table data*. This element creates individual cells in a row (and, by default, the table's columns). Whatever content you want to place in the table goes between the <td> tags.

As you look at the preceding code, you'll see that <tr> is used to create three rows. The <td> element occurs three times in each row; so in that particular table, you end up with three rows and three columns. These are the only elements you need to create a table. As you will see, by adding attributes and some extra elements, you can do just about anything with this little table.

> TIP    *The letter "X" has been placed between each of the sets of <td> tags because browsers will not display empty table cells. When you are designing a table, always remember to put something in each cell, even if it is not your final content.*

# Modify a Table's Appearance

Although you need only the three basic table elements, your HTML toolbox includes additional elements and attributes that can be used to modify a table's appearance. In addition, the content you choose to put in each cell will affect how your table looks on a Web page. As you work through this chapter, try modifying the simple table you created earlier by adding the lines in the following section (or sometimes modifying existing tags) and watch how your table develops.

## Add Headings and Captions

In keeping with a table's original purpose for displaying structured information, HTML provides some elements that allow you to add headings, captions, and footers to your table.

> TIP    *Sometimes existing code will be displayed to make it easier to understand where you need to add or modify code. In these cases, type in only the code that appears in boldface.*

### Use the \<th> \</th> Element to Add Headings to Your Table

To add a heading, you use \<th> \</th> instead of the \<td> element. It will create cells the same way \<td> does, but also will display the text inside the cells as centered and boldface. Try adding a heading to the table by adding this line of code above the first row:

```
<tr> <th>Col 1</th> <th>Col 2</th> <th>Col 3</th> </tr>
<tr> <td>X</td> <td>X</td> <td>X</td> </tr>
<tr> <td>X</td> <td>X</td> <td>X</td> </tr>
<tr> <td>X</td> <td>X</td> <td>X</td> </tr>
```

| Col 1 | Col 2 | Col 3 |
|---|---|---|
| X | X | X |
| X | X | X |
| X | X | X |

### Add Captions with the \<caption> \</caption> Element

A caption can be used to display a title for your table. Use the \<caption> \</caption> element just above the first row of cells. To add a caption to the sample table, add this line: **\<caption>How to Use Tables\</caption>**. The following code shows where that line should be placed in your table:

```
<table>
<caption>How to Use Tables</caption>
<tr> <th>Col 1</th> <th>Col 2</th> <th>Col 3</th> </tr>
<tr> <td>X</td> <td>X</td> <td>X</td> </tr>
```

How to Use Tables

| Col 1 | Col 2 | Col 3 |
|---|---|---|
| X | X | X |
| X | X | X |
| X | X | X |

## Display a Border

By now you probably are thinking that your table would be easier to work with if it had borders and lines defining the separate cells. To tell the browser to display a

How to Use Tables

| Col 1 | Col 2 | Col 3 |
|-------|-------|-------|
| X | X | X |
| X | X | X |
| X | X | X |

border simply add the border=" " attribute to the opening <table> tag. To add a border that is three pixels wide, go back to your code and modify the table tag to read like this: <table **border="3">**. Now look at how your table has changed.

You can change the thickness of your border by altering the number in the quotation marks. Thus, border="10" will produce a 10-pixel–wide border, and border="20" will make it 20 pixels wide. Try experimenting with some different border sizes to see what you like best.

TIP

*Although it is easier to work with tables that have borders, you might prefer to have borderless tables for your final layout. In this case specify border="0".*

## Position Your Content

As soon as the border appears, you will notice that all the "Xs" in your table are aligned to the left sides of their cells. That's because the default alignment in tables is to the left. If you want the content to be centered or right-justified, there are a couple of options for controlling its position.

### Position Content Horizontally with the align=" " Attribute

To position text (or other cell content), you must include the align attribute in each cell where you want to specify the position. For example, to center text you would modify a <td> tag to read <td align="center">. There are several options for alignment:

- **Left**  Aligns cell contents to the left. This is the default alignment.
- **Right**  Aligns cell contents to the right.
- **Center**  Aligns cell contents to the center.
- **Justify**  Also aligns the cell's contents to the left.

### Control Vertical Alignment with the valign=" " Attribute

You can determine whether your content aligns at the top, middle, or bottom of a cell by using the valign attribute. valign (vertical align) enables you to specify the vertical positioning for individual cells (<td valign="top">), entire rows

(<tr valign="middle">), or a complete table (<tbody valign="bottom">). The values you can supply with the valign attribute are as follows:

- ■ **Top**   Aligns cell contents with the top of the cell.
- ■ **Middle**   Aligns cell contents with the middle of the cell; middle is the default value.
- ■ **Bottom**   Aligns cell contents with the bottom of the cell.
- ■ **Baseline**   Aligns with a baseline shared by all the cells in a given row.

The following code and illustration demonstrate how the align and valign attributes affect cell contents:

```
<table border="3" height="200" width="200">
<tr> <td align="left">Left</td> <td align="center">Cent.</td>
    <td align="right">Right</td>
</tr>
<tr> <td valign="top">Top</td> <td valign="middle">Mid.</td>
    <td valign="bottom">Bottom</td>
</tr>
<tr> <td valign="baseline">Baseline</td>
    <td align="justify">Justify</td>
    <td>Default</td>
</tr>
</table>
```

**8**

How to Use Tables

| Col 1 | Col 2 | Col 3 |
|---|---|---|
| Left | Center | Right |
| Top | Middle | Bottom |
| Baseline | Justify | Default |

SHORTCUT   *Setting the characteristics of each element of a large table can become tedious and time consuming. Fortunately, CSS provides a way to set table properties that will control the entire table. Whenever possible, consider using CSS to develop your tables.*

### Use CSS for Alignment

Cascading Style Sheets give you more options for cell content alignment. By using an inline style sheet, you can align the contents of individual cells, much as you did with the align attribute. However, you also can use CSS to align the text in all of your table cells at once by embedding a style sheet in the head portion of your HTML page.

CSS uses the same four alignment properties: left, center, right, and justify:

- **Center alignment with an inline stylesheet: <td style="text-align: center;">**   This will control an individual cell.

- **Center alignment with an embedded stylesheet: <style type="text/css"> td {text-align: center;}</style>**   This will control all the cells in your table.

> NOTE    *The justify property works differently with CSS from the way it works with the align attribute. With CSS it causes text to be justified to both the left and right margins. The align="justify" attribute justifies only to the left.*

Try centering the contents of the sample table by adding these lines inside the <head> </head> portion of your HTML page:

```
<style type="text/css"> td  {text-align: center;} </style>
```

How to Use Tables

| Col 1 | Col 2 | Col 3 |
|-------|-------|-------|
| X | X | X |
| X | X | X |
| X | X | X |

Once you've typed in the style element, save your page and display it in your browser. Now the Xs in each cell will be centered, instead of in only the first row. As you can see, CSS can be quite a timesaver.

## Add Background Colors

Setting background colors for your table is easy. The background color attribute, bgcolor=" ", which can be used to set the color for a whole page, also works inside a table. You can set the color for individual cells, for individual rows, or for the whole table. If you would like to set the color for more than one table at once, try using CSS.

## Set Table Colors with bgcolor

The bgcolor=" " attribute will control the portion of the table in which it is placed. This attribute, used with a table, is great for creating navigation bars in your Web pages. By setting the colors for individual table cells and putting your links inside the cells, you can create an attractive—and fast loading—navigational system. To specify colors for your table, use the following:

- Place bgcolor=" " in the <table> element to control the color of the entire table.

- Place bgcolor=" " in the <tr> element to control the color of a row.

- Place bgcolor=" " in <td> or <th> element to control the color of individual cells.

8

Experiment with the colors of your table by setting the overall table color to magenta, the color of the heading row to yellow, and the color of the center cell to aqua. Your code will look like this:

```
<html>
<head><title>Table Exercise</title>
<style type="text/css">
td {text-align: center}</style></head>
<body>
<table border="3" bgcolor="magenta">
<caption>How to Use Tables</caption>
<tr bgcolor="yellow"> <th>Col 1</th> <th>Col 2</th>
    <th>Col 3</th></tr>
<tr> <td align="center">X</td> <td align="center">X</td>
    <td align="center">X</td> </tr>
<tr> <td>X</td> <td bgcolor="aqua">X</td> <td>X</td> </tr>
<tr> <td>X</td> <td>X</td> <td>X</td> </tr>
</table>
</body>
</html>
```

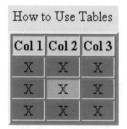

## Set Table Colors with CSS

You also can use style sheets to control table colors. The advantage here is that you can set the style for all of the tables in a page or even an entire Web site with just one set of commands. You also can control individual cells with CSS.

■ Set cell, row, or table colors with an inline style sheet:

```
<td style="background-color: blue;">
```

**NOTE**    *To set row colors, the style attribute will go in the <tr> tag. To set table colors, put it in the <table> tag.*

■ Set cell, row, or table colors with an embedded style sheet:

```
<style> td {background-color: red;} </style>
```

**NOTE**    *In the preceding examples, an individual cell was set to the color blue, whereas the overall table style was set for red cells. Which one takes precedence? In CSS, the inline style has priority over the embedded style; that's where the term cascading comes from.*

Try putting the following style sheet into the head portion of your tables.htm page. It should change your table background to blue, with white text (that's what color: white does). All captions will have a red background with yellow text. The heading cells will be gold with navy text; the center cell will be white with black text.

**TIP**    *In this style sheet, to select the colors for the center cell, a class has been created. In this case it is named td.center. To apply that style to the center cell of your table (or any other cell for that matter), modify the <td> tag for that cell to read* **<td class="center">**. *For more about classes in style sheets, read Chapter 10.*

```
<style type="text/css">
table  {background-color: blue; color: white;}
caption {background-color: red; color: yellow;}
th {background-color: gold; color: navy}
td.center {background-color: white; color: black;}
</style>
```

NOTE

*When you modify your page to add the preceding style, leave the bgcolor attributes alone. You'll see when you display your page that the style sheet overrides any colors you set with HTML attributes.*

To really see how style sheets work, try creating another table of any size in your page; will take on the characteristics of the style sheet. For a simple example, here's a once-celled table with a header and caption. Copy it into your page just after the closing <table> tag for your first table. Your results should resemble the following illustration.

```
<br /><table><caption>Caption</caption>
<tr><th>Heading</th></tr>
<tr><td>Content</td></td></table>
```

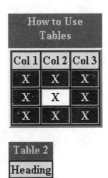

## Adjust Space In and Between Cells

So far you have learned how to construct a table and change its colors; but what about controlling the position, size, and spacing of cells? HTML provides attributes to control these aspects of a table's appearance. With cellspacing and cellpadding, you can manipulate the overall size of your tables and cells.

## Use cellspacing to Adjust the Space Between Cells

The cellspacing attribute allows you to add space between the cells in your table as measured in pixels. This attribute must go inside the <table> tag. To add a 10-pixel–wide space between the cells in your table, modify the opening <table> tag to read:

```
<table border="3" bgcolor="magenta" cellspacing="10">
```

## Use cellpadding to Add Space Inside Cells

Just as cellspacing adds space around the outside of your cells, cellpadding adds space inside them. It also adds a layer of padding (defined in pixels) around the contents of the cell. Add a 10-pixel "pad" around the content of your table cells by modifying the <table> tag to read as follows:

```
<table border="3" bgcolor="magenta" cellpadding="10"
cellspacing="10">
```

## Use CSS for More Padding Options

This is where CSS really shines. With the cellpadding attribute you are able to add padding only for the entire cell; by using CSS's cellpadding properties, you have many more options. CSS enables you to place the padding only where you want it. It also enables you to use measurements other than pixels. For example, if you want a quarter-inch padding added to the bottom of each cell, you can add a style rule in the head portion of the page that reads td {padding-bottom: .25in}.

CSS padding properties include padding, padding-right, padding-left, padding-top, and padding-bottom. CSS measurement units include inches (in), percentages (#%), pixels (#), and ems (#em).

SHORTCUT    *If you use the padding property (as opposed to padding-right and so forth), you simply put the value to the right of the property. The more values you supply, the greater the difference in how they are applied. For instance, padding: 10 would add a 10-pixel pad around the cell contents; padding: 10, 15 would put a 10-pixel pad on top and bottom and a 15-pixel pad on the sides. Three values control the top, left-right, and bottom padding. Four values control the top, right, bottom, and left sides, respectively.*

8

NOTE    *An em is a unit that is relative to the font size. For example, a padding of 1.5 ems would be one-and-one-half times the size of the font in use in the table cell.*

To apply padding to individual cells, use an inline style sheet. The HTML for the cell you want to modify might look something like this:

```
<td style="padding-right: 15">X</td>
```

To set the default cellpadding for the table with an embedded style sheet, you might write your code this way:

```
<style type="text/css"> td  {padding: 1em, 2em} </style>
```

# Make Cells Span Multiple Columns and Rows

Another way to modify the appearance of your table is to make one cell span two or more rows or columns. This is especially useful when you are using tables for layout purposes and wish to have an image in one large cell accompanied by a navigation bar made up of several cells.

To make a cell span multiple rows, insert the rowspan=" " attribute in the cell's opening <td> tag. For instance, to make the top left cell in your table span two rows, modify its <td> tag to read <td rowspan="2">. Your modified code will look like this:

```
<tr> <th>Col 1</th> <th>Col 2</th> <th>Col 3</th> </tr>
<tr> <td rowspan="2">X</td> <td>X</td> <td>X</td> </tr>
<tr> <td>X</td> <td>X</td> </tr>
<tr> <td>X</td> <td>X</td> <td>X</td> </tr>
```

**CAUTION**  *Don't forget that if you are going to make one cell take the space of two, you must remove the cell it is going to replace. Otherwise, your table will be unbalanced. When you add the rowspan attribute to the code for your table, be sure to remove one of the cells (<td>X</td>) in the second row.*

To make a cell span more than one column, use the colspan=" " attribute. If you remove one of the cells from the bottom row of your table and modify the last cell's opening <td> tag to read <td colspan="2">, it will cause the browser to display the cell across two column widths.

The code for the table rows now will resemble this:

```
<tr> <th>Col 1</th> <th>Col 2</th> <th>Col 3</th> </tr>
<tr> <td rowspan="2">X</td> <td>X</td> <td>X</td> </tr>
<tr> <td>X</td> <td>X</td> </tr>
<tr> <td>X</td> <td colspan="2">X</td> </tr>
```

## Adjust Height and Width

With HTML you can adjust both the height and the width of your tables and cells. This can be very important when you are using tables for a page's layout, as you can specify how much of a page you want the table to use. By using percentages to describe table dimensions, you can enable a browser to adjust your table to fit a monitor's display, no matter what its resolution.

### Set Height and Width with Fixed or Dynamic Design

*Fixed design* involves specifying a table's dimensions in concrete terms. For example, if you want to stretch the sample table horizontally, you could specify that the sample table you've been constructing should be 200 pixels high by 500 pixels wide by changing the opening table tag to read <table height="200" width="500">. When you display the page in a browser now, it will look quite different from the table you originally designed.

> **TIP**    *You also can use the height and width attributes to define the size of individual cells. Just include these attributes in the <td> tag of the cell you want to size.*

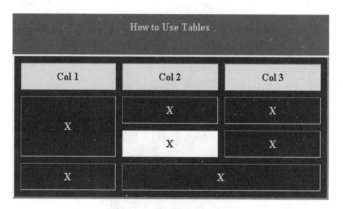

*Dynamic design* is when you describe a table's dimensions using percentages. Perhaps you want a table to take up a full screen, no matter what screen resolution your visitors' systems are set to. In this case you would describe your table's height and width with percentages: <table height="100%" width="100%">. This creates a table that will adjust dynamically to fill the browser screen. Also, by using percentages in describing the cells you can set one cell to be narrow, filling perhaps 25% of the screen, with the other taking up 75%. This is useful if you are constructing a table that will use one cell as a navigation bar and the other for page content.

> **TIP**    *Although height and width dimensions of 100% will allow your table to fill the screen, any caption you add above the table will be lost. A more practical screen-filling design is in the 85%–90% range.*

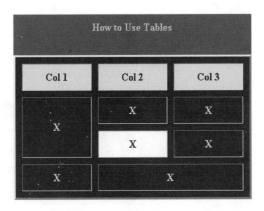

## Position Tables on a Page

Until now, the table you have been working on has been aligned to the left margin of the page; this is HTML's default alignment for tables. However, there are several ways for you to influence the positioning of tables relative to other items on a Web page. Elements such as <div>, <span>, and <center> provide a quick and easy solution for alignment. You also can position tables with the align attribute, and CSS provides an option for table placement with its float property.

### Position Tables with Elements

If you enclose your table inside the <div> or <span> elements along with the align=" " attribute, you can position the table to the left, center, or right. Any text or page content coming after the table will start immediately below it. For example, to right-align a table using <div>, you would write your code as follows:

```
<div align="right">
<table><tr><td>X</td></tr></table>
</div>
```

The <span> element will produce similar results.

8

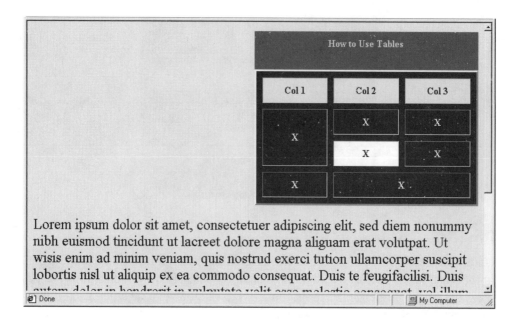

SHORTCUT

*If you want to center your table, you can bypass the need for the align attribute by using the   element instead. However, be aware that this element has been deprecated by the W3C.*

## Position Tables with Attributes

By using the align=" " attribute inside the <table> tag, you also can position a table in the center or on the right side of the page. An added advantage of using the align attribute is that, just like with images, it influences text wrapping. If you set your table to align="right", any text outside the table will wrap to the left. To right-align the sample table, modify the opening <table> tag to read <table align="right">. The following illustration shows what the page looks like with some text added.

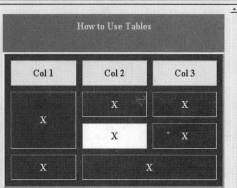

## Position Tables with CSS

Cascading Style Sheets use the float property for positioning objects on a page. To use this property you would write **float: right** (other options are left or none). There is no *center* value for the float property. If you want to center a table with CSS, you'll have to do it with margins. (For more about CSS and margins, see Chapter 10).

To left-align a single table with CSS, use an inline style sheet:

```
<table style="float: left;">
```

To right-align all the tables on a page, use an embedded style sheet:

```
<style type="text/css"> table    {float: left;} </style>
```

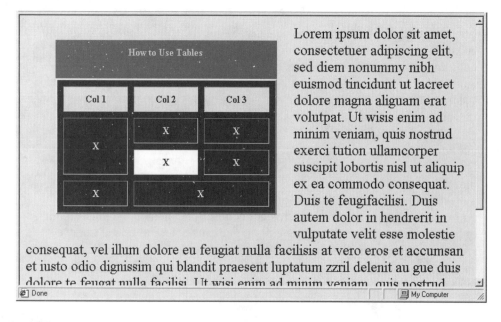

> **NOTE** *The difference between the left-right and none options for float is that text does not wrap with the none option. Any text or other content comes after the table. With left or right, the text wraps on the opposite side of the table.*

## Modify Borders and Cell Divisions

Earlier in the chapter you learned how easy it is to create a border for your table. Simply use the border attribute with a value of one or more pixels. Sometimes, though, you might want only a partial border or just rule lines drawn between the cells. How do you do that? There are ways to accomplish this using both HTML and CSS.

### Use the HTML frame Attribute to Adjust Table Borders

If you want to make changes to how the outer border of a table displays, the HTML frame=" " attribute gives you quite a few options. By inserting the following attributes, you can select portions of the table border to display, while others remain invisible:

- To display only the top: frame="above"
- To display only the bottom: frame="below"

- To display only the left side: frame="lhs"

- To display only the right side: frame="rhs"

- To display both the left and right sides: frame="vsides"

- To display both the top and bottom sides: frame="hsides"

- To display no outside border at all: frame="void"

For example, if you display a simple table with the frame="void" attribute, it might look like the following illustration:

```
<table frame="void">
<tr> <td>X</td> <td>X</td> <td>X</td> </tr>
<tr> <td>X</td> <td>X</td> <td>X</td> </tr>
<tr> <td>X</td> <td>X</td> <td>X</td> </tr>
</table>
```

8

NOTE   *The values "box" and "border" both display a border all the way around the table.*

## Use the rules Attribute to Adjust Interior Borders

Just as frame enables you to control the outer borders of a table, rules gives you control over the interior borders, or rules, between the cells. With the rules attribute you can remove all the interior borders, just the horizontal ones, or just the vertical ones:

- To display vertical rules: rules="cols"

- To display horizontal rules: rules="rows"

- To display no rules: rules="none"

- To display rules between table groups: rules="groups"

## Use CSS Border Properties for Tables

Borders are another area where HTML cannot hold a candle to CSS. In fact, the possibilities for creating attractive borders for your tables are so many and varied, it would be impractical to try to deal with them all in this chapter. Chapter 10 goes into detail about how to create borders with CSS; for a sample, use the following code to create a simple four-celled table using CSS's border properties. This code also is a good test for how well your browser supports CSS. If your display does not resemble the following example, your browser's CSS support is weak:

```
<html>
<head><title>CSS Table Border</title>
<style type="text/css">
table   { border-width: medium;
          border-color: navy;
          border-style: groove; }
td      { text-align: center;
          background-color: gold; }
</style></head>
<body>
<center>
<table><tr><td>CSS</td><td>IS</td></tr>
<tr><td>VERY</td><td>COOL</td></tr></table>
</center>
<body>
</html>
```

```
 CSS    IS
VERY COOL!
```

# Add Images and Links

Although tables originally were developed to allow scientists and researchers to display "tabular" data on HTML pages, the addition of graphics and links has made them *the* tool to use for page layouts. By using tables for layout you can add banners, photos, graphical link bars, and much more and be sure your objects will wind up where you had planned. If you've read the chapters on graphics and links, you know almost all you need to know about adding them to tables.

## Add Images with <img />

You add images to a table the same way you place them anywhere else in your page: with the <img /> element. The only difference is that <img /> must go between a set of <td> or <th> tags. To put an image into a table cell:

```
<td><image src="picture.gif" height="#" width="#" alt=" "></td>
```

Although it is not required, you will want to specify the height and width of the picture, just as you would any other time you place an image on a page. If you also have used height and width attributes for your table or cells, you might find that the combination of all the different attributes ruins your carefully planned table layout. The best thing to do is experiment by adjusting the height/width attributes on the image and the table until you come up with a combination you're happy with.

## Add Links with <a> </a>

If you want to add links to your table, use the anchor, the <a> element with a URL, the same way you create any other link. The anchor tag and its URL are cell contents; thus they go between the <td> or <th> tags on your table. You also will use the <img /> element if you want to create a graphical link.
To put a link inside a table cell:

```
<td><a href="cj.htm">Visit CJ's Page</a></td>
```

To put a graphical link inside a table cell:

```
<td><a href="cj.htm"><img src="cjhat.jpg"></a></td>
```

**NOTE** *In the preceding example, the different elements are nested inside each other. Nesting is very important when working with tables because if tags overlap, your entire table structure could become confused. If you're not sure what nesting is, see Chapter 1.*

This code creates a four-celled "Family Album" table with both text and graphical links, as shown in the following illustration. Try typing the code yourself and substituting your own pictures and filenames. As you type the code, try to think about what each element is doing and why it is there. Comment lines have been added so you can easily identify the different parts of the code. If you don't want to type it in, you can download the code from Osborne's Web site: www.osborne.com.

```html
<html>
<head><title>Family Album Table</title>
</head>
<body>
<table border="3" cellpadding="10" bgcolor="gold">
<caption><font size="+2">FAMILY ALBUM</font></caption>
<!-- This is the top picture cell -->
<tr> <td align="center"> <a href="cj.htm">
        <img src="cjhat.jpg" height="110" width="90" alt="CJ" />
        </a> <br /> <b>CJ</b> </td>
<!-- This is the top text link cell -->
        <td> <a href="cj.htm">Visit CJ's Page</a> </td> </tr>
<!-- This is the second picture cell -->
<tr> <td align="center"> <a href="cm.htm">
        <img src="cm1.jpg" height="100" width="100" alt="CM" />
        </a> <br /> <b>CM</b> </td>
<!-- This is the second text link cell -->
        <td> <a href="cm.htm">Visit CM's Page</a> </td> </tr>
</table>
</body>
</html>
```

### Use Tables for Faster Image Loading

Chapter 6 describes how to "slice" an image into multiple parts to make it load faster. That chapter used a banner for illustration purposes and used the natural left-right flow of HTML to line the image up. But what if you are slicing a large image that is made of too many pieces to line up horizontally? You use a table. Place one part of the image in each cell and put it back together, just as you would a jigsaw puzzle. To make the image appear seamless, remember that you must specify the following attributes in the opening table tag:

```
<table border="0" cellpadding="0" cellspacing="0">.
```

In this illustration, the cellpadding and cellspacing attributes are left at their default sizes of one pixel, so you can see how each cell holds part of the picture.

## Understand Weakly Supported Table Features

Several features of tables are worth noting, but at this writing do not enjoy very broad browser support. Attributes such as summary=" ", bordercolor=" ", and the <thead>, <tfoot>, and <tbody> elements can be useful. As you would with CSS, however, be cautious in using them.

### Summarize Tables with the summary=" " Attribute

The summary=" " attribute goes in the opening table tag and is supposed to contain a description of the table for non-visual browsers. This will help people who visit your site with braille or aural browsers to get an idea of what your table contains. For instance, for the preceding family album table, you could write a summary that reads as follows:

```
<table summary="This is my online family album with pictures
and links to my children's pages.  CJ's picture and link is
first and CM's picture and link is second">
```

Summary promises to be an important aspect of tables in the future, but it is not yet well supported. Still, it won't hurt to take advantage of it now. It will save you the trouble of going back and modifying your pages later.

## Set Border Colors with the bordercolor=" " Attribute

The bordercolor=" " attribute is an Internet Explorer extension to HTML that does not yet enjoy much support in other browsers. It enables you to set a color for your table borders. It's a nice addition and is safe to use as long as you remember that many of your visitors will not see the colored border. To see bordercolor in action, modify the code for the family album table by changing the opening table tag to read as follows:

```
<table border="3" cellpadding="10" bgcolor="gold"
bordercolor="red">
```

If your browser supports this attribute, you should see a red border around the table. You can give the border a 3D look by trying the bordercolorlight=" " and bordercolordark=" " attributes. See how it works by changing the preceding attributes to read as follows:

```
bordercolorlight="red" bordercolordark="maroon"
```

NOTE     *As of this writing, the bordercolorlight and bordercolordark attributes are supported only by Internet Explorer.*

## Display Long Tables

Some useful (although not well supported) elements are the <thead>, <tfoot>, and <tbody> elements. These elements enable you to display a large table with a permanent or static header and footer. If you have a lot of data on a page, the header and footer will remain stationary while the table data scrolls. You have to set up this type of table a little differently, with the <thead> and <tfoot> elements at the top, followed by the <tbody> element. A simple construction is given in the following. Notice how the browser puts the footer cell at the bottom, even though in the code it comes second:

```
<table>
<thead><tr><td>Header</td><tr></thead>
```

```
<tfoot><tr><td>Footer</td></tr></tfoot>
<tbody><tr><td>Body</td></tr></tbody>
</table>
```

**8**

# Learn Good Web Design

Although the W3C would prefer that you use Cascading Style Sheets to do your page formatting and layout, until CSS is more widely supported you probably will still do much of your page layout with tables. If you're not convinced, just log on to any major Web site and choose the View Source option on your browser; then look for the table tags you've learned in this chapter. Chances are you won't have to search long or far to find plenty of them. Tables for layout are a fact of life. So, how do you make the best use of them?

## Web Design Principle: Plan Each Table Strategically

Careful and strategic planning is essential if you are going to make the best use of tables. Just as you must take the time to storyboard a Web site, must sit down and sketch out your page layouts, particularly if you're going to use tables. As you plan your tables, keep in mind some of the following guidelines:

- **Design with Web accessibility in mind**   What will your table "look" like to those with non-visual browsers? Will it make any sense at all, or will it confuse your visitors?

- **Avoid nesting tables**   Nesting tables is putting one or more complete tables inside another table. Although it does enable you to create much more complex layouts, it slows loading time and can make your material unintelligible on a non-graphical or non-visual browser.

- **Use CSS where possible, but test your designs in a non-CSS compatible browser to make sure it's still viable**   Keep in mind that if you are planning more than one table for a page, CSS will enable you to format all the tables with one set of commands.

■ **Draw a sketch of your layout on paper before you write the code for your table**    Think through your content, images, and cell and table height and width and write them down; then write your table code based on your sketch. You'll save yourself hours of grief (and reworking) by doing it this way.

■ **Use dynamic rather than fixed design**    That is, specify size in percentages rather than pixels.

## Practice, Practice, Practice

There are many ways to use tables to lay out a page. One of the simplest is to have a banner at the top, a navigation bar down one side, and a content cell on the other. The following illustration creates a simple page layout for your HTML notebook site. Try to reproduce it by thinking through the various elements as you see them displayed. How many cells will you need? How many rows? What percentage of the screen should the different parts use? Then write the code for your own version of this page. If you get stuck, you can find the code for the page below at Osborne's Web site: www.osborne.com.

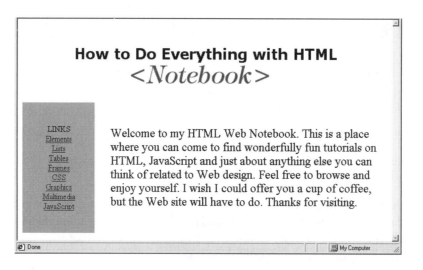

Although HTML tables can become very complex, they really are quite simple to use once you understand how they work. Cascading Style Sheets ultimately will provide a much more efficient and exact means of laying out your Web pages. However, while you're waiting for everyone to catch up, use tables to your best advantage.

# Find the Code Online

To find the code online for this or any of the chapters in this book, go to Osborne's Web site: www.osborne.com, and click the Free Code choice on the navigation bar. From the list of books, select the *How to Do Everything with HTML* option and you will be able to download the book files, which are linked together and organized as an offline "mini" Web site. For more on how to use the "mini" Web site, see Chapter 17.

| Use This Code For... | Look for this Filename |
| --- | --- |
| Basic table | basictable.htm |
| Table caption | tablecaption.htm |
| Table cell contents aligned | tablealign1.htm |
| Table background colors | tablecolor1.htm |
| Table cellspacing | cellspacing.htm |
| Table row span | rowspan.htm |
| Absolute design | absolutetable.htm |
| Right aligned (no text wrap) | tablediv.htm |
| Float left | tablefloat.htm |
| No interior rules | tablebordermodify2.htm |
| Table with graphics | tableimage.htm |
| Table with header and footer | tableheadfoot.htm |
| Table headings | tableheading.htm |
| Table border | tableborder1.htm |
| CSS cell alignment | tablealign2.htm |
| CSS background colors | tabledouble.htm |
| Table cellpadding | cellpadding.htm |
| Table column span | colspan.htm |
| Dynamic design | dynamictable.htm |
| Right aligned (text wrap) | tableright.htm |
| No outside border | tablebordermodify.htm |
| CSS border | csstableborder.htm |
| Table with reassembled graphic | slicepxtable.htm |

8

# Chapter 9

# Use Frames for Efficient Navigation

## How to...

- Understand Frames
- Create a Basic Frameset
- Modify Your Frames
- Provide Content for Non-Compatible Browsers
- Use Floating Frames
- Create a Frames-Based Navigation Layout

If you've surfed the Web at all, you have encountered frames. Chances are you also have formed a strong opinion about them; you probably either love them or hate them. Why do frames provoke such strong emotional reactions from people? Possibly because so often they are misused. When frames are used incorrectly, they can be very frustrating to those trying to sort through them. The frustration is like being given a large, gift-wrapped box to open, only to find a slightly smaller box inside it. When you open the second box, you find another, even smaller one inside, and so on. By the time you actually get to the box with the gift in it, you might not even care anymore.

Yet, frames provide an excellent tool for site navigation. They enable you to create, among other things, a navigation bar that never moves, pages that load faster, and a permanently reserved space for your site's logo or banner. Just be careful to not get carried away, because if the adage "you can't see the forest for the trees" is applicable to Web design, it is when a visitor can't see your site because of the frames.

# Understand Frames

Although frames look intimidating on the surface, they really are quite simple to construct. In fact, one of the reasons for their overuse might be that when people find out how easy they are to create, they go "frame crazy" and use them all the time. However, frames are not an all-purpose site creation tool, but a means for creating dynamic layouts and efficient navigation systems.

## Frames Allow for Multiple Page Display

What, exactly, are frames? Simply put, frames enable you to display more than one page at a time in the same window. Until now, when you have displayed your HTML pages, you've had to do it one at a time. To display more than one document at a time, you would have to open another browser window. Frames change all that. With a fairly simple set of elements, you can display two, four, eight, or even more pages in the same browser window. Why would you want to do this?

Say you are an author, and you want to put together a Web site to publicize your book. As you design the site, you decide that you want your book's cover to appear on every page, but you'd like to include a lot of different content. Perhaps you want to put some reviews on one page, an excerpt on another, and reader comments on another, but you always want to keep your book's cover in front of your potential customer.

You could design a site with tables, creating five or ten separate pages, each with the same layout but different content. Or you could construct a three-frame page that features the cover of your book and a banner with your name at the top, content on the right side, and a navigation bar on the left side. Then, when a visitor clicks a link in the navigation bar, only the content frame will change; everything else stays where it is. In this case you have made your life easier by not creating the same layout ten times. You also have made things easier for your visitor because your pages will download more quickly. Remember, only the text content has to reload; not the images in the other frames—less content equals faster load time.

## Disadvantages of Frames

Although frames provide for more efficient site design and navigation, they come with some noteworthy disadvantages attached. In fact, if you are not careful in your use of frames, you actually can make getting around your site more difficult. Consider some of the following ways in which frames can make site navigation confusing:

- Too many frames on a page presents a dizzying array of visual options and choices, often causing the focus of your site to be obscured.

- Overuse of frames can slow down loading time. Keep in mind that usually each frame is loaded a separate HTML document (although it is possible to

9

load one page into more than one frame). Each of these documents takes time to download. Thus, the more frames you use, the longer it is going to take for your site to be fully loaded on the user's machine.

■ Frames pages don't mix well with search engines. Some search engines won't even look at a frames-based site. Others will, but as you will learn later in this chapter, your *frameset* document provides no content in and of itself. If this also is the main page for your site, search engines don't have much to work with.

■ Frames pages can pose navigation problems for someone who enters your site through a "back door." If a search engine's spider has indexed the content pages on your Web site, someone might come to your site directly through one of these pages, rather than through your home page. In this case the page will display apart from the frame structure you created. If you are relying solely on frames for navigation purposes, this visitor will find no navigation bar. In other words, their visit to your site will be a dead end.

■ Although the numbers are shrinking, there are still browsers out there that don't suppport frames. Someone coming to your site with one of these browsers will find it inaccessible. Non-visual browsers for the handicapped also have trouble with frames.

You might be wondering why you should even bother with frames. After all, there are plenty of other ways to present a Web site without using them. In fact, many excellent sites use no frames at all. So why bother?

## Advantages of Frames

There are any number of reasons you would want to use frames on your site. Although frames should never become an end in themselves, they can help you accomplish certain things that would be difficult without them. For example, frames enable you to create some of the following effects:

■ Frames allow you to display multiple pages in a single window.

■ Frames allow you to keep some content static as other content changes.

■ Frames allow your visitors to access content from a different Web site without leaving yours or opening a second browser window. Thus, if you have a second site and want to include content from it, frames make it easy.

■  When you use seamless frames you can create the impression of a single page with dynamically changing content.

TIP

*If you prefer to have a link open in a separate window rather than in one of your frames, just use the target="_blank" attribute in your link tag. For example, the link <a href="www.osborne.com" target="_blank">Open Osborne's Web Site</a> will cause a new window to open. Be sure to include the underscore character ( _ ) before the word "blank."*

To keep frames in perspective keep in mind that, although frames are useful tools, no tool is right all the time. If frames will help you create a better site, by all means use them. But don't load your site with frames just because you know how to do them.

## Understand Frame Elements and Attributes

Like tables, HTML frames are very easy to build; so easy, in fact, that you will wonder why you haven't used them before now. In many ways creating a site based on frames is not as difficult as using tables. Although a frameset can become quite complicated (just as a table can), the basic concept is quite simple. You use a master document, called a *frameset* to create the frames; then you create an HTML document for each of the frames you want to be visible on the page.

Did you know?

# Who Developed the Idea of Frames?

Frames originally were developed by Netscape and first supported in Netscape 2. Later, they were made part of the HTML 4 standard. Virtually all newer browsers support frames, but there are still some that do not.

9

## Understand Basic Frame Elements

The first step in working with frames is in understanding the elements used to create them. You need only two elements to create a page with frames: <frameset> </frameset> and <frame />. Like tables, frames are a very simple construction that can quickly become complicated. The basic frame elements (and what they do) are listed here:

■ **<frameset> </frameset>**    The *frameset* element is what actually creates the multiple frames. When creating a frames-based page, you use this element *instead of* the <body> </body> element.

■ **<frame />**    The *frame* element is used to specify each of the frames that will be visible on your page. Like the <img /> element, <frame /> is an empty element and requires no closing tag.

## Understand Basic Frame Attributes

Just as with frame elements, only two attributes are essential to creating frames; the others enable you to fine-tune your frames. The essential attributes are the columns and rows attributes. These attributes enable you to control the layout, size, and number of frames that will appear on your page.

> NOTE    *Actually, you need only one of these two attributes. Unlike HTML tables, you do not need to have both rows and columns; you can create a frame page with either rows or columns.*

■ **cols= "column width"**    This attribute defines a frameset in columns. The default setting is one column, which takes up 100% of the page. If you want more than one column, specify the width of each column, separated by commas. You can specify width in pixels or percentages. By using the asterisk, *, as a wildcard, you can create a column that will dynamically adjust to whatever space is left over. In the following example, the columns attribute will create three vertical frames: one taking up 20% of the screen, the next using 30%, and the last using the remaining 50% :

```
<frameset cols="20%, 30%, *">
```

■ **rows="row height"**    The rows attribute defines a frameset in rows. The default setting is one row, taking up 100% of the page. As with columns, you can define row height with pixels (fixed design), or percentages (dynamic design), and use an asterisk as a wildcard.

> TIP  *Whenever possible, specify row and column dimensions with percentages and the asterisk. The advantage of using dynamic design is that your frames will adjust to fit browser windows, no matter how they are sized. If you give absolute dimensions in pixels and a visitor has resized his or her browser, your frames might be cropped. Also, how a page will be displayed is determined by the screen resolution your visitor is using. Visitors making a quick scan of your site might miss parts of the page that scroll off screen if they are using a low resolution (640×480).*

Although there are some other elements, and quite a few other attributes that can be applied to frames, these are more for fine-tuning the frames and how they display. These are covered later in this chapter. All you need for creating your first frames page are the elements and attributes covered earlier.

# Create a Simple Frames Page

The best way to learn HTML frames is by experimentation. By constructing a simple page with four frames, you will learn what you can do with them and how to modify them. For this example you will start by creating some display documents.

## Build Your Display Documents

Frames need something to display to work correctly. Before you begin constructing a frameset, you will want to create some simple HTML pages. For this example, these pages needn't be complicated or filled with content. A plain page with the text "This is page 1," and so on, will suffice. Just for fun, you might want to specify a different background color for each of the pages.

To create a set of display documents, follow these steps:

1. Create a directory on your hard drive, named Framesample.

2. Open template.htm and in the <body> </body> portion of the page, add this line: **<h1>This is page 1.</h1>**.

3. To add visual interest, choose a color for the page by adding a bgcolor=" " attribute to the <body> tag. If you set a page to a dark color (such as black, navy, green, maroon, or purple), you also might want to specify white as a

text color by adding the text="white" attribute to the <body> tag. (For other color possibilities, see Chapter 4.)

4.  Save the page as frame1.htm, in the Framesample directory.

5.  Create seven more pages, saving them as frame2.htm, frame3.htm, and so on.

The following code will create a black page with white text. Change the bgcolor and text values to create different combinations:

```
<html>
<head><title>Frames</title></head>
<body bgcolor="black" text="white">
<h1>This is page 1</h1>
</body>
</html>
```

After you have some documents to display, it's time to move on to the next step in making frames pages: constructing the frameset.

## Construct a Frameset

The heart of a frames page is the *frameset*. Think of it as a master document that controls the display of your frames. Although a frameset document is an HTML page in its own right, it displays no content of its own. The frameset's contents are the frames. Keep in mind that when you are doing frames you must *always* have one extra document: the frameset.

### Build a Frameset

You construct a frameset document the same way you do any other HTML page—with one important exception: A frameset page uses the <frameset> </frameset> element in place of the <body> </body> element. The reason for this is your frames make up the body of the frameset document.

NOTE *A frameset page can use the <body> </body> element, but only if it is contained within the <noframes> </noframes> element. This is to provide content for browsers that do not support frames.*

At its simplest, with no frames defined, a frameset will look like the following code listing. Using template.htm, create a frameset by replacing the <body> </body> element with the <frameset> </frameset> element. Save it as framesample.

```
<html>
<head><title>Frame Sample</title></head>
<frameset>
</frameset>
</html>
```

However, if you try to display this, you won't see much of anything because the frames have not yet been defined.

## Define Frame Structure

As mentioned earlier, you define frames using the cols=" " and rows=" " attributes. If you read Chapter 8, the idea of table columns and rows will be familiar. However, frames work a bit differently. You can have either columns or rows, or a combination of both. For example, to construct a frameset with four equal columns, you would modify the opening <frameset> tag to read:

```
<frameset cols="25%, 25%, 25%, 25%">
```

If you want instead to have a frameset with four equal rows, change to the rows attribute:

```
<frameset rows="25%, 25%, 25%, 25%">
```

To divide your frameset into four equal parts with both columns and rows, you would modify the <frameset> tag to look like this:

```
<frameset rows="50%, 50%" cols="50, 50%">
```

If you add this code to your page and try to display it, you will still get a blank page. Why? Because defining a frameset is not enough. You also must specify what pages your different frames will load. For that, you use the <frame> </frame> element.

## Specify Frame Content

Your frames provide the content for your page. If you define frame structure in the <frameset> element but don't tell the browser what to put into the frames, it will ignore the frameset altogether. Because the last example uses both rows and columns to construct four frames, you will use the <frame /> element four times.

For each <frame /> you create, you also must use the src=" " attribute to tell the browser which file to load in that frame. For instance, to use frame1.htm in one of your frames, you would include the following tag: <frame src="frame1.htm" />.

Try including the preceding line plus three others in your frameset. Your complete frameset should look like the following code and illustration:

```
<html>
<head><title>Frame Sample</title></head>
<frameset rows="50%, 50%" cols="50%, 50%">
     <frame src="frame1.htm" />
     <frame src="frame2.htm" />
     <frame src="frame3.htm" />
     <frame src="frame4.htm" />
</frameset>
</html>
```

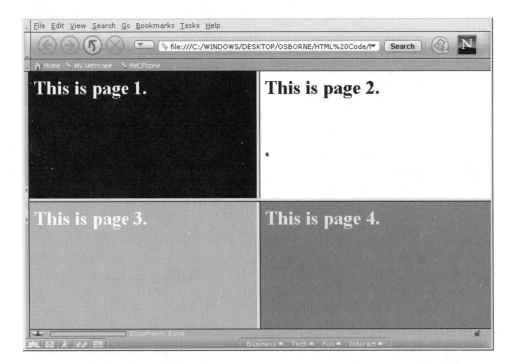

## Create Nested Frames

You can create even more complicated framesets by nesting them. Chapter 1 covers the concept of nesting, which means putting complete sets of tags inside one another.

To nest frames, you will place another set of frameset tags, *inside* your existing frameset. For instance, consider the preceding frameset, which created four equal-sized frames. What if you decide to divide the bottom-right frame into two smaller frames? One way to do it would be to add another <frameset> in place of the <frame /> tag for that frame. Your code will be changed to look like this:

```
<html>
<head><title>Frame Sample</title></head>
<frameset rows="50%, 50%" cols="50%, 50%">
     <frame src="frame1.htm" />
     <frame src="frame2.htm" />
     <frame src="frame3.htm" />
          <frameset cols="50%, 50%">
          <frame src="frame4.htm" />
          <frame src="frame5.htm" />
          </frameset>
</frameset>
</html>
```

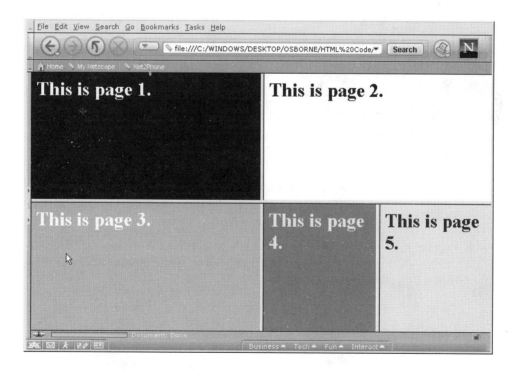

NOTE *By changing the columns and rows attributes, you can come up with many different possible frame constructions. The preceding illustration is only one possibility.*

Although it is possible to come up with many different combinations of nested framesets, you might want to think twice about doing it. Nesting frames is one way to make your pages so complicated that you destroy their effectiveness. If you have a good reason to nest frames, by all means do it. Otherwise, let nested frames remain a curiosity, but not part of your regular Web arsenal.

CAUTION *Don't forget to include closing tags and properly nest your tags. If you make any mistakes, your frames will not display properly.*

# Modify Your Frames

Both the <frameset> </frameset> and the <frame /> elements can be modified with attributes that will allow you to control how your frames are displayed and how much your visitors can modify them. For instance, you can add or remove borders, select border colors, determine whether your visitors can resize the frames on their browsers, and much more. These attributes give you the ability to fine-tune your layout.

## Use Attributes with the <frameset> Element

You used the cols=" " and rows=" " attributes to create your frame layout.. There are also a number of additional attributes you can choose from. These will allow you to control general frame appearance:

- Turn borders on and off with frameborder=" ". The values are "1" for on and "0" for off. (Netscape 3 and higher and IE 4 and higher also support "yes" for on and "no" for off.)

- Set the thickness of frame borders with border="#". With this attribute you set the thickness of the border in pixels. For example, border="5" will set a border that is five pixels thick.

■ Add space between frames with framespacing="#". This also is specified in pixels. Thus, framespacing="20" would add a 20-pixel–wide space between frames. (This attribute is limited to Internet Explorer browsers.)

■ Add color to your borders with bordercolor="color". Specify colors for your frame borders with either color names or hexadecimal code. This will affect all the frames on the page. You also can specify bordercolors for individual frames by placing this attribute in the <frame /> element.

NOTE    *The bordercolor=" " attribute only works in Internet Explorer 4 and higher and in Netscape 3 and higher.*

The following example shows how the previous illustration would look with added color, framespacing, and border thickness added. The modified <frameset> tag would look like this: <frameset bordercolor="navy" framespacing="10" border="5">.

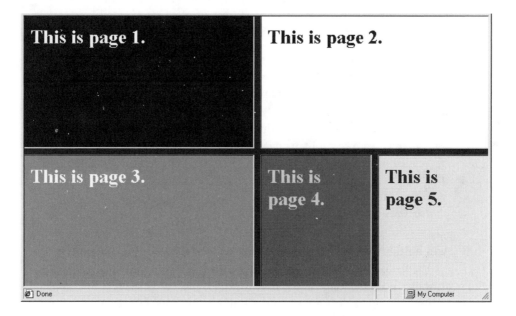

## Use Attributes with the <frame /> Element

In addition to the src=" " attribute, the frame element takes a number of other attributes. Most of these relate to how the frame functions when displayed, although a few deal with general appearance. The attributes you can use with the <frame /> element are as follows:

- **Add white space with marginheight="#" and marginwidth="#"**     As their names imply, these attributes control the margins in your frames. You can use these attribute in individual <frame /> elements to specify different margins for each. The values for these attributes can be given in pixels or percentages.

- **Prevent resizing with the noresize attribute**     This is one of the few instances in which a Web designer can override user preferences. This attribute should be written as noresize="noresize." To prevent viewers from resizing your frames according to their own tastes, use the noresize attribute. When you insert this in a <frame /> element, it acts like a toggle switch, fixing your frames at the proportions you set.

- **Add a scrolling bar with the scrolling=" " attribute**     You actually have three options where scrolling bars are concerned. If you supply a "no" value here, your frame will never display a scrolling bar, no matter how much content the page has. If you put "yes" as a value, your frame will always display a scrolling bar. By choosing "auto" for the value, the browser will determine when a scroll bar is needed and insert one automatically.

SHORTCUT     *The default setting for scrolling is auto. There's no need to use the scrolling attribute unless you want to turn scrolling off or ensure that it's always on.*

- **Add a description with longdesc=" "**     To make your Web site more accessible to those who are using non-visual browsers, consider using this attribute. With the long description attribute, you can provide a link to a URL containing a description of the frame's contents. For instance, <frame longdesc="description.htm" />

■ **Control individual frame borders with frameborder=" "**   Used in the <frame /> element, this attribute enables you to turn individual frame borders on and off. If you want to turn off the borders for some, but not all of your frames, this is a useful attribute.

■ **Control individual frame border colors with bordercolor=" "**   With this attribute you can specify a different color for a particular frame border.

■ **Turn borders on and off with frameborder=" "**   This attribute works the same way as it does in the <frameset> </frameset> element, by toggling borders on and off. Here you can control an individual frame.

■ **Assign names to your frames with the name=" " attribute**   This probably is the most important of all the attributes you can use with the <frame /> element. By assigning a name to a particular frame and using the target="attribute" in your hyperlinks, you can direct any number of different pages to display in that frame.

To see some of these attributes at work, modify your framesample.htm code to look like the following code. These changes will remove all the borders, except around the bottom-right frame. A scroll bar will be added to the bottom-left frame.

```
<html>
<head><title>Frame Sample</title></head>
<frameset rows="50%, 50%" cols="50, 50%" frameborder="0"
 framespacing="0" border="0">
    <frame src="frame1.htm" marginheight="100"
marginwidth="100" />
    <frame src="frame2.htm" noresize="noresize"/>
    <frame src="frame3.htm" scrolling="yes"/>
        <frameset cols="50%, 50%" frameborder="0">
            <frame src="frame4.htm" />
            <frame src="frame5.htm" frameborder="1"/>
        </frameset>
</frameset>
</html>
```

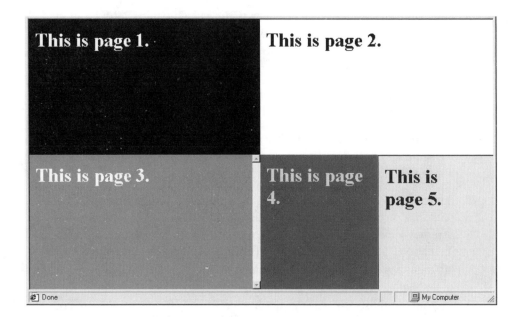

By using the different frame attributes, you can control many aspects of your frame's display. Try experimenting with the framesample.htm page by adding some of the attributes yourself and seeing what changes they make as the page is displayed.

## Address Non-Compatible Browsers with <noframes>

Although the numbers are shrinking, there still are browsers in use that do not support frames. If someone tries to access your site with one of these, they will not be able to view your pages. To assist people using these older browsers, it is wise to include special directions inside the <noframes> </noframes> element. You can either provide alternative content between these, or offer directions or even a link to a non-frames version of your site. A sample <noframes> instruction is given here:

```
<html>
<head><title>No Frames</title></head>
```

```
<frameset>
     <frame src=" "/>
     <frame src=" "/>
</frameset>
<noframes>
<body>
<div align="center">
<h3>Your browser does not support frames. Click this
link for an alternate <a href="noframes.htm">non frames
version</a> of this site.</h3>
</div>
</body>
</noframes>
</html>
```

The content in the <noframes> element will be displayed only when someone visits the site with a browser that doesn't support frames. Frame-supporting browsers will ignore it.

**9**

**Your browser does not support frames.**
**Click this link for an alternate <u>non-frames version</u> of this site.**

# Create an Inline Frame

Frames were first incorporated by Netscape. Not to be left out, the developers of Internet Explorer threw their own version of frames into the mix. However, IE's concept is quite different from Netscape's. Instead of dividing a single window into multiple frames, IE developed the concept of the *inline* or *floating* frame.

An inline frame is more like a mini-window that you can place inside a block of text or the layout of a page. Like regular frames, floating frames draw their content from a separate HTML document; unlike them, the page they are placed on can have its own content. The easiest way to picture how a floating frame works is to visualize it as you would a sidebar in a magazine article. It provides its own content, but in the context of other content.

To create an inline frame, you use the <iframe> </iframe> element. This element is a bit of an anomaly because even though it functions as an empty element (you don't put anything between the two tags), you still must have the closing tag. All the frame attributes given earlier can be applied to inline frames. You also can use the align=" " attribute to position it on the page and cause text to wrap around it (although the align attribute has been deprecated in favor of style sheets). To create a sample page that uses a floating frame, follow these steps:

1. Open template.htm and save it as iframe.htm.

2. Set the body bgcolor to "white."

3. Add the following line just below the first <body> tag:

   ```
   <iframe src="frame1.htm" align="left" width="200"
   height="300"> </iframe>
   ```

4. Add some text below this line to simulate content for the iframe.htm page.

5. Save the file in your Framesample directory and display iframe.htm on your browser.

The following illustration was created from this code:

```
<html>
<head>
<title>Inline Frames</title>
<body bgcolor="white">
<!-- Comment: notice that the iframe references lorem.htm
as its source. Any HTML file can go there. -->
<iframe src="lorem.htm" align="left" width="200" height="300">
</iframe>
<h2> <!-- Comment: Lorem.txt was pasted in here.
Supply your own text or go to this book's companion site:
www.osborne.com, and cut and paste lorem.txt in. -->
</h2>
</body>
</html>
```

9

Inline frames can be very useful, but they do have one big disadvantage. Until recently, Internet Explorer was about the only browser that supported them, even though they have been made part of the HTML 4 standard. Things are changing, though, as both Netscape 6 and Opera 5 now display inline frames. If you decide to use them, keep in mind the people who visit your site; be sure to provide alternatives for those who won't see your floating frames.

# Use Frames for Site Navigation

Perhaps the best use of frames is in providing a speedy and efficient means of site navigation. Many sites that use frames will have a column of links on one side of the page and offer content on the other. Although this can be done with tables, you also can create a snappy design with frames. The key to making this work is in using the name=" " attribute with each of your frames and the target=" " attribute with your links.

At the beginning of this chapter you were encouraged to create eight HTML pages to use as sample content. Imagine that each of those pages is a page on your Web site and that you want to create a frames-based home page that will use one frame as a navigation bar, one as a banner, and one for content. You can create your frame page by following the steps below. If you get confused, check the completed code below the numbered instructions:

1.  Open template.htm and save it as framesite.htm.

2.  Add a title such as <title> Mini Frames Site </title>.

3.  Delete the <body> </body> tags; in their place add a set of <frameset> </frameset> tags.

4.  Modify the opening <frameset> tag to read

    ```
    <frameset rows="15%, *">
    ```

5.  Create a frame and link it to frame1.htm as follows:

    ```
    <frame src="frame1.htm" /> (This will be your banner space.)
    ```

6.  Now, to construct the navigation bar and content frames, you will need to nest another frameset in the existing one. Just below the frame element you just typed, add another set of <frameset> </frameset> tags.

7.  Modify the opening <frameset> tag to read

    ```
    <frameset cols="20%, *">
    ```

8.  Define a frame for your navigation bar:

    ```
    <frame src="frame2.htm" />
    ```

9.  Now comes the part that makes the whole system work. You want to define another frame; this time for your content. However, this frame needs to have a name so you can "target" links at it. For the sake of simplicity, name this frame "content." The <frame> element will look like this:

    ```
    <frame src="frame3.htm" name="content" />
    ```

10. Make sure you have properly nested all your tags and that you have closing tags for both framesets. Save and close this document.

11. All that remains is to modify your frame2.htm page to enable it to serve as your navigation bar. To do this, open frame2.htm and add a line such as the one below between the <body> </body> tags:

```
<a href="frame4.htm" target="content">Frame 4</a><br />
```

12. Do a line like that for frame5.htm, frame6.htm, and so on (you also can use the first three documents). Be sure to include the target="content" attribute with each one, as that will tell the browser where to load it.

13. Save frame2.htm; now you're ready to try out your mini frames site. Load framesite.htm in your browser. The window should resemble the following illustration. (For the illustration, frame1.htm was modified to read, "This is your banner frame.")

```
<html>
<head><title>Mini Frames Site</title></head>
<!-- Comment: This code creates your frameset. -->
<frameset rows="15%, *">
    <frame src="frame1.htm" />
        <frameset cols="20%, *">
            <frame src="frame2.htm" />
            <frame src="frame3.htm" name="content" />
        </frameset>
</frameset>
</html>
```

# Learn Good Web Design

In this chapter, you have learned how to create a simple frameset, modify your frames, and provide content for non-frames browsers. You also have experimented with inline or floating frames. There are many more things you can do with frames; the best way to discover them is by experimenting. As you experiment, keep some design principles in mind.

## Web Design Principle: With Frames, More Is Less

Remember the adage that less is more? With frames, more is less. Carelessly used, frames can quickly overwhelm a site. The more frames you have, the less space is available, the less content you can display at a time, and the less visual interest your site has. An overuse of frames gives a Web site all the appeal of a dusty, cluttered attic. For that reason, many people shy away from using them, which is unfortunate. Used with care, frames can add to the quality of a site. Just remember some of their drawbacks as a means of staying on track. Also remember some of these guidelines:

- You have only so much screen space to divide up into frames. Don't cut your screen into so many pieces that no one wants to taste your product.

- It is your content that attracts people; not your frames. Make sure you give your visitors content.

- Be considerate to those who cannot view your frames. Provide some alternative content for them.

- Use frames because you need to; not necessarily because you want to. In other words, what will frames add to your site that other design approaches will not?

- When you plan a frames-based site, be sure to sketch it out as you would if you were using tables. Because the order in which you place elements in a frameset will affect the display, this is even more important than it is with tables.

## Practice, Practice, Practice

This chapter serves as an introduction to frames. If you want to learn to use them, you must work with them enough to become comfortable with them. Try some of these ideas to get a feel for working with frames:

- Create the same basic layout as is displayed at the end of Chapter 8, but this time do it with frames. You will need to create borderless frames to get the seamless effect. (*Hint:* Setting border, frameborder, and framespacing attributes to "0" will help.)

- Once you have a workable layout, create a links page that links to each of the HTML pages you have created thus far. Target each of the pages to display in a "content" frame as in the previous example.

- Try displaying pictures in a frame set. Experiment with different ways of doing it. (*Hint:* You can link directly to a picture or you can put the picture in an HTML page and link to the page. Which works better and why?)

# Find the Code Online

To find the code online for this or any of the chapters in this book, go to Osborne's Web site: www.osborne.com, and click the Free Code choice on the navigation bar. From the list of books, select the *How to Do Everything with HTML* option and you will be able to download the book files, which are linked together and organized as an offline "mini" Web site. For more on how to use the "mini" Web site, see Chapter 17.

| Use This Code For... | Look for This Filename |
| --- | --- |
| Basic frameset page | framesite.htm |
| Four frame frameset | framesample.htm |
| Noframes demo | noframes.htm |
| Frame documents | frame1.htm through frame8.htm |
| Modified framesets | framesample2.htm through framesample4.htm |
| Inline frame demo | iframe.htm |

# Chapter 10

## Enhance Your Site with CSS

## How to...

- Understand CSS

- Add Inline Styles

- Embed a Style Sheet

- Link to a Style Sheet

- Apply CSS Properties

HTML was developed to define the structure of a document when Web and Internet documents were entirely text based. The advent of graphical browsers and Web design stretched HTML far beyond its capacity. To accommodate the needs of Web designers, extensions were added to HTML to increase its ability to address a document's appearance and structure. Unfortunately, this was roughly similar to doing interior decorating with two-by-fours and six-penny nails. You might be able to do it, but it won't look good. Two-by-fours and big nails are useful in building the structure of a house, but for finished carpentry you want quality woods, molding, paint, wallpaper, and so on.

Likewise, HTML was not developed for controlling the appearance of a document. HTML is the equivalent of the two-by-fours and six-penny nails. For finished Web "decorating" you need better materials and tools. Enter Cascading Style Sheets. CSS offers a set of tools that will enable you to refine, finish, and polish the appearance of an element, a page, and even an entire Web site.

# Understand CSS

If you've been working through this book from the beginning, you've already used CSS and experienced the freedom it gives you in Web design. However, if you just jumped in here at Chapter 10, a brief orientation is in order. CSS often appears intimidating when you read about it in a book such as this; it seems to be completely different from HTML. After working through ten or so chapters and learning HTML, confronting something called CSS—and finding that it's written differently—can be pretty daunting. Often readers just give the CSS chapter a curious glance before moving on to the next aspect of HTML. After all, if HTML gets the job done, why bother learning CSS? Further, to get right down to the basic question, what is a style sheet, anyway?

# HTML and the Problem of Style

The introduction to this chapter summarized the problem of HTML as it relates to style. HTML simply was not intended for dealing with a document's style or presentation. Granted, the extensions added to HTML over the past decade have enabled it to address those issues, but HTML provides clumsy presentation control at best. It only makes sense to use the proper tool for the job you need to do. In the case of presentation, that tool is CSS. However, there are a few other strong reasons to learn how to use CSS. They can be summarized in three words: deprecation, accessibility, and necessity:

- **Deprecation**   If you go to the W3C's site (www.w3.org) and read the current standard for HTML, you'll discover that the term *deprecated* shows up alongside a fair number of elements and attributes. In essence, the W3C is trying to move HTML back toward its roots and is deprecating certain presentational elements in favor of CSS. Right now, elements such as <font> and attributes such as align are still supported in browsers; eventually they won't be.

- **Accessibility**   CSS2 (the second official CSS standard) addresses much more than style. It deals with accessibility issues such as how to develop pages for aural (sound) browsers. Although CSS2 is poorly supported at present, that will change. One day you will be able to create style sheets targeted toward different types of browsers and link your pages to them, opening your Web site to a much broader audience.

- **Necessity**   The heir apparent to HTML is XML (eXtensible Markup Language). Currently, a transitional form known as XHTML (eXtensible Hypertext Markup Language) is the current standard recommended by the W3C. XML requires a style sheet if you want anything other than a document's pure structure to display. In other words, when XML rules, you won't have much of a choice where style sheets are concerned.

Of course, there is one more excellent reason to learn to use style sheets: They're fun.

# Understand the Idea of Style Sheets

Style sheets take their name from the idea of style sheets in publishing. A publisher, Osborne for example, has a particular style for its publications. In addition, the publisher is not limited to a single style. It might use a general style that is reflected in all its publications, but more specific styles for certain series. For instance, if you were to examine all the books in the *How to Do Everything* series, you would notice that even though subject matter differs among books, they all reflect the same basic style in fonts, layouts, and approach. If you check out some of Osborne's other books, you will notice a similarity in style at certain points, but each series will have its own distinctive look and feel.

Cascading Style Sheets are intended to help you accomplish the same effect with your Web site. With CSS, you can plan a color scheme, set margins, create a layout, choose and modify fonts, and much more. All you have to do is save that style sheet as a separate document, link all your pages to it and, voilà, your entire Web site will take on the characteristics you specified in the style sheet.

## Understand CSS Terminology

One reason CSS confuses people who have been learning HTML is that many of the terms are different. When they read about style sheets, it's almost as if they are starting again from the ground floor. After getting used to elements, attributes, and values, it can be frustrating when the terminology shifts to selectors, properties, declarations, and rules. Actually, CSS terms need not be confusing as long as you learn to understand them in the context of HTML. Try understanding the basic CSS in the way described here:

- **Selector**   Think element here. At its simplest, a selector is an element you want to specify a style for, such as <h4> or <ol> or <table>. The only difference is that when you use an element as a selector, you don't place the "less than" and "greater than" signs around it, like you would if it were a tag. Instead, <h4> is simply written as h4. Likewise, <ol> becomes ol, and <table> becomes table. As you'll discover later in the chapter there can be more to it than this, but this is a good starting point.

- **Property**   Properties are essentially the same as attributes. Remember that with HTML, an attribute identifies a characteristic assigned to an element, such as color=" ". In CSS instead of attributes, you have *properties*. These are also written differently. In HTML the color attribute is written with an equals sign (=) and quotation marks (""), like this: color=" ". In CSS, the color property is written with a colon following it, like this: {color:}.

- **Value**   This one's easy. A value is the same in HTML and CSS. It is the specific characteristic assigned to an element or a selector. For example, purple can be a value assigned to an HTML attribute: {color="purple;"} or a CSS property: color: purple;.

- **Declaration**  A declaration is simply a complete statement of both a property and a value. In other words, {color: purple;} is a declaration. One thing to keep in mind is that after every declaration, you must have a semicolon (;). The semicolon is what tells the Web browser where one declaration ends and another begins. For instance, if you want to specify purple text with a bold font for the same selector (element), you would separate the two declarations this way: {color:purple; font-weight: bold;}.

- **Rule**  A rule is the complete "sentence" combining a selector, properties, and values. A complete declaration (properties and values) is enclosed in curly braces. For instance, the following statement would be called a rule: p {color: purple; font-size: 24pt; margin-left: .5in;}.

    If you break down the preceding rule, p is the selector (for the paragraph element); the properties are color, font-size, and margin-left; and the values are purple, 24pt, and .5in, respectively.

There are some other terms, such as *classes, pseudo-classes, pseudo-elements,* and *inheritance;* these will be covered later in this chapter.

10

NOTE  *You can put as many declarations in a rule as you want, as long as they are separated from one another by semicolons (;) and enclosed in curly braces ({}). The single exception to this is with inline style sheets, in which you use quotation marks (" ") instead of curly braces to enclose the declarations.*

## Learn Style Sheet Types

There are three ways to implement style sheets in your HTML document: inline, embedded, and linked. The primary difference between these style sheets lies in where they are placed and how much of a document they affect or influence:

- To control a single element only one time, use an *inline* style sheet. Inline style sheets, as their name implies, are placed "in line" in the individual elements of an HTML page, and control only the specific element to which they are applied. To create an inline style sheet, you use the style=" " attribute. For example, to change the text for a single paragraph to a red, italicized font you would modify the opening <p> tag to read as follows:

```
<p style="color: red;  font-style: italic;">
```

■  To control an element for a single page, use an *embedded* style sheet. Embedded style sheets are placed in the <head> </head> portion of an HTML page and make use of the <style> </style> element. An embedded style sheet will control the elements to which it is applied throughout the entire page, although an inline style rule will take precedence over it. For instance, to set the paragraph style for an entire page to navy, bold, 12-point text with a yellow background, you would create a style rule like the following one:

```
<style type="text/css">
      p       {   color: navy;
                  font-weight: bold;
                  font-size: 12pt;
                  background-color: yellow; } </style>
```

NOTE    *When using embedded and external style sheets, you also should include the type=" " attribute with the value set to "text/css", as in the preceding example. This tells the browser what type of style sheet to expect.*

■  Control elements on multiple pages with an *external style sheet.* By creating a style sheet and saving it as a separate document, you can link multiple pages to it, and the pages will take on the style specified in that sheet. For example, you could have saved the style in the preceding paragraph as a separate file, say my_style.css, and then linked your pages to it using HTML's <link> element. The <link> element should be placed in the <head> element of each page you want linked to a style sheet and would be written as follows:

```
<link rel="stylesheet" type="text/css" href="my_style.css"  />
```

NOTE    *The rel=" " attribute tells the browser the relationship between the <link> element and whatever is being linked. Since it is possible to use this element to link more than just style sheets to a Web page, it is necessary to add the value "stylesheet" to the rel=" " attribute. The href=" " attribute is added to tell the browser where to find the style sheet. The value for this attribute would be the URL where the style sheet is located. In most cases, that will simply be the name of the file, as in the preceding example.*

As you read this, perhaps you are beginning to see a potential problem with style sheets. With so many possibilities for specifying style, which one takes priority? That's where the *cascading* part comes in.

## Understand the Cascade

Why are style sheets called cascading? The term *cascading* refers to the order of priority in which styles are applied. Consider all the possible conflicting style rules that can be applied to one Web page: The browser might have its own style, the author can specify a style, and the readers (Web surfers) who visit your site might have specified their own styles for browser display. On top of that, it is possible to have different styles specified in linked, embedded, and inline style sheets. In other words, you could have six or seven different styles all competing for the right to determine what an <h1> element looks like. So, which style gets the last word? The cascade is the order of precedence or priority that different style declarations are given. The following questions give some guidelines for how a style's precedence is determined:

- **Who wrote the rule?**   The page author's styles take priority over the reader's styles; both have priority over the browser's default styles.

- **What kind of style is it?**   An inline style takes precedence over an embedded style; both take precedence over a linked or an imported style.

- **How specific is the selector?**   The selector with more detail takes priority over the selector with less detail.

- **Which style occurs last?**   Generally, the last declaration takes precedence over earlier ones in a document.

10

## How to ...   Increase a Rule's Priority

One easy way to increase a style rule's ranking in the cascade, simply include the !important property with the rule. You must be careful to include the property after the style declaration but before the semicolon that separates it from the next declaration. For example, to set a background color as important for the <h1> element but leave the text color at a normal priority, you would write the rule this way:

```
h1 {background-color: yellow !important; color: navy; }
```

# Create and Use Style Sheets

The easiest way to see CSS in action and learn how to use it is to create a sample Web page and progressively add different style rules. By doing this, you will see how the different styles affect the overall look of your page. You will also gain a feel for how certain styles take precedence over others. To create a CSS sample page, follow these steps:

1. Open template.htm and save it as css_sample.htm.

2. Cut and paste several paragraphs of plain text into the <body> of your HTML document. These can be from any text document you want. The following illustration uses lorem.txt.

3. Format your text into at least three paragraphs by using the <p> </p> element.

4. Write three headlines and insert one before each paragraph. Enclose all your headlines in the <h3> element.

   Your HTML code should resemble this:

```
<html>
<head><title>CSS Sample Page</title></head>
<body>
<h3>This is going to be a headline.</h3>
<p>Paste a paragraph of text here.</p>
<h3>This will be another headline.</h3>
<p>Paste another paragraph of text here.</p>
<h3>This will be a headline, too</h3>
<p>Paste a third paragraph here.</p>
</body>
</html>
```

When you view the page in your Web browser, you should see something similar to the following illustration. Once you have saved your basic page, you're ready to begin styling.

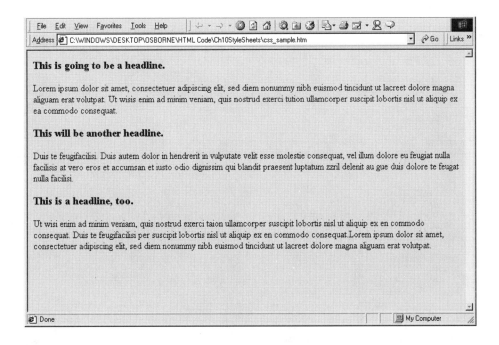

**NOTE**      *Your ability to reproduce the results you will see in this chapter depends directly on your browser's capability to support style sheets. Although most browsers have some degree of support for CSS, for best results use the most recent version of Internet Explorer. If you want to test your browser for its style sheet support, the W3C has a great testing site. Just go to http://www.w3.org/Style/CSS/Test and click the various links. It will load test pages linked to external style sheets. You'll be able to measure your own browser's support for CSS easily with this free tool.*

## Apply an Inline Style Sheet

Begin styling your sample page by adding an inline style to the second headline, changing its font to Arial, size to 18pt, color to blue, and position to center. To do this, use the style=" " attribute with the font size, color, and text align properties. The <h3> headline with an inline style sheet added should look like the following line of code:

```
<h3 style="font-family: arial; font-size: 18pt;
     color: blue; text-align: center;">This will be another
     headline.</h3>
```

With the inline style added, your page now should resemble the following illustration:

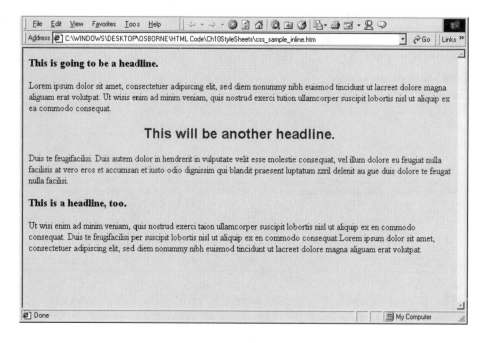

CAUTION *Be sure to enclose all the declarations in a single set of quotation marks and separate them by semicolons; otherwise, your style will not display properly.*

## Add an Embedded Style Sheet

To add an embedded style sheet to this document you will use the same syntax except that instead of enclosing declarations in quotation marks, you will use curly braces and place your style rules inside the <style> </style> element in the <head> </head> portion of your page. For your sample page, try setting a page background color of gold, a default font for the <p> element, and a default font size and color for the <h3> element. You can do this by following these steps:

1. Insert a set of <style> </style> tags in between the <head> </head> tags on your page.

2. Modify the opening <style> tag to read <style type="text/css">. Because there can be different kinds of style sheets, the type attribute tells the browser to expect text-based commands and the CSS language.

3. To set the background color to gold you will need to write the following style rule for the body selector:

```
body { background-color: gold; }
```

4. To set a style for the h3 selector that gives it a silver background, with navy-blue text, set at a size of 1.5ems, add the following line:

```
h3 { background-color: aqua; font-size: 1.5em; color: navy; }
```

5. Now, tell the browser to display the p element as bold, italicized text by adding the following rule:

```
p { font-weight: bold; font-style: italic; }
```

The completed header for your page should look like the following code:

```
<head><title>CSS Sample</title>
<style type="text/css">
body { background-color: gold; }
h3 { background-color: aqua; font-size: 1.5em; color: navy; }
p { font-weight: bold; font-style: italic; }
</style></head>
```

When you save and display your page, your style changes should look like this:

10

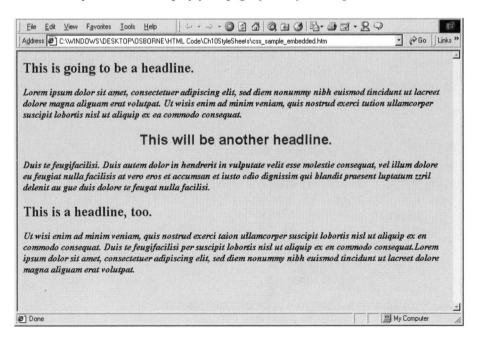

As you examine your results, you will see that your style specifications were all incorporated in the page, with one exception: The middle headline will still be blue with an 18-point Arial font. Remember: An inline style sheet overrides an embedded style sheet, so your first specification remains unchanged. You will see this even more clearly when you create and link to an external style sheet.

## Create and Link to an External Style Sheet

Fortunately, there's nothing difficult or mystical about creating an external style sheet. It is merely a text document that contains a set of style rules. As with HTML, you can create an external style sheet with a simple text editor. You only need to make sure you save the document with a .css extension so the browser knows how to identify it.

To construct a simple external style sheet, follow this procedure:

1. Create a new file in Notepad or another text editor. Save it as a plain text file named my_styles.css.

2. Copy in the following lines exactly as written:

```
body    { margin: .5in;
          background-color: silver; }

h3      { margin: .25in;
          color: white;
          font-size: 24pt; }

p.green { margin: .25in;
          color: green;
          font-family: arial;
          font-weight: bold;
          border-style: double;
          border-width: thick;
          border-color: red; }

p.large { margin-right: 1in;
          color: navy;
          font-size: 2em;
          background: gold; }
```

3. Save your style sheet and open css_sample.htm.

## How to ... Use Classes

In the preceding code, the selectors p.green and p.large are called *class* selectors. This is a way of modifying a standard selector, in this case "p," and setting it apart as a separate class with its own properties. To call a class selector's characteristics forth in a Web page, just add the class=" " attribute to the appropriate element. For instance, to apply the characteristics of p.large to a paragraph, you would write **<p class="large"> Content </p>**. Using classes gives you a virtually unlimited ability to specify style details for your page.

4.  Remove both the embedded and inline style sheets. (This is just so you can see the effects of the external style sheet without having to worry about the other styles overriding it.)

5.  Add the following line in the <head> </head> portion of the page:

    ```
    <link rel="stylesheet" type="text/css" href="my_styles.css" />
    ```

6.  Now, to apply the class in your sample page, change the first <p> to read <p class="green"> and the second <p> to read <p class="large">.

**TIP** *It's not necessary to put each declaration on a separate line, but it does make it easier to identify which styles you have assigned to the selectors and check your code for errors. As long as you have written the rules correctly and keep individual declarations together, the browser doesn't care whether they're on one line or several.*

Your revised code should resemble the following code:

```
<html>
<head><title>CSS Sample Page</title>
<link rel="stylesheet" type="text/css"
href="my_styles.css" /></head>
<body>
```

```
<h3>This is going to be a headline.</h3>
<p class="green">Paste a paragraph of text here.</p>
<h3>This will be another headline.</h3>
<p class="large">Paste another paragraph of text here.</p>
<h3>This will be a headline, too</h3>
<p>Paste a third paragraph here.</p>
</body>
</html>
```

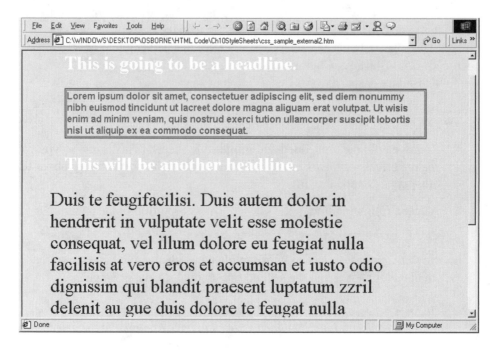

Save css_sample.htm and display it in your browser. Your page should look very different now. After you view your page, experiment by adding the embedded and inline styles back into the document to see how it affects your ultimate result.

**SHORTCUT** *When editing CSS and HTML documents at the same time, you can save time by using Wordpad for your HTML document and CSS for the style sheet. Keep both open at once, along with a browser to view the document in, and you'll have a much easier time editing your styles.*

# Understand and Use CSS Properties

By now you probably have concluded that CSS isn't nearly as difficult as you thought it was. It is merely a matter of knowing how to write a style rule and apply it to the document you want to stylize. However, although CSS is not difficult, it can become complex. The sheer volume of choices before you can become overwhelming to the point of paralysis, leading you to conclude that, although style sheets might be easy and fun, they're just not worth the trouble.

The challenge in writing a chapter on style sheets is providing you with enough detail to enable you to use them without flooding you with every single possibility. After all, the current CSS specification weighs in at a whopping 331 pages. Trying to cover even a small portion of the details is challenging enough. Attempting to cover everything in one chapter is impossible.

However, it is possible to give you enough detail to get you started; the best place to start is with properties. To keep it simple, consider properties as governing four general areas of page design: fonts, text, colors-backgrounds, and box properties (margins, padding, borders, and so on). These four groups of properties do not include everything, but they will give you plenty to start with. As you read through the list of properties, type in the code following each one; gradually you will build a sample style sheet to incorporate into the plain text Web page you created at the beginning of the chapter.

10

## Did you know?

## Where to Find Out More about CSS?

The W3C has published online the complete CSS1 and CSS2 specifications along with links to tutorials, authoring software, articles, and many other resources. To browse through them go to http://www.w3.org/css/.

## Use Font Properties for Controlling Font Display

Font properties enable you to apply styles to the fonts on your page. With these properties you can specify different fonts: their sizes, styles, weights, and so on. As each of the properties is listed, it will be added to the style rule for the <p> element. To see how it displays, import it into your original sample page. Try experimenting with CSS by substituting different values in the various declarations. Your choices for font properties are as follows:

NOTE    *Throughout these property sections you will be able to build some style rules for a sample document. It is not necessary to rewrite each line of code. The new additions are indicated in bold type.*

- **Font-family**    Allows you to specify the font you want to display. Although you can choose any font you'd like, remember that if the font is not on your visitor's system, the browser will substitute a default font. Generic values for font-family are serif, sans-serif, monospaced, cursive, and fantasy.

  ```
  p { font-family: sans-serif; }
  ```

- **Font-style**    Basically toggles between normal and italic fonts. A third possible value is *oblique*, but this generally displays as italic.

  ```
  p {font-family: sans-serif; font-style: italic; }
  ```

- **Font-variant**    Enables you to display a font as small caps. The possible values to choose from are, as you would expect, normal and small caps.

  ```
  p {font-family: sans-serif; font-style: italic;
     font-variant: small-caps; }
  ```

- **Font-weight**    Offers a greater range of choices than HTML's bold, <b>, element. You can specify values by descriptive terms such as normal, bold, lighter, and bolder, or with a numerical value of 100 through 900 (in increments of 100).

  ```
  p {font-family: sans-serif; font-style: italic;
     font-variant: small-caps; font-weight: 700;}
  ```

■ **Font-size** Sets you free from HTML's seven-step font sizes. This property enables you to specify font sizes with nine different measurements: inches (in), millimeters (mm), centimeters (cm), points (pt), picas (pc), pixels (px), ems (em), exs (ex), and percentages (#%).

```
p {font-family: sans-serif; font-style: italic;
      font-variant: small-caps; font-weight: 700;
      font-size: 14pt;}
```

■ **Color** Enables you to choose colors for your fonts by using color names, or their hexadecimal or RGB values.

```
p {font-family: sans-serif; font-style: italic;
      font-variant: small-caps; font-weight: 700;
      font-size: 14pt; color: blue;}
```

NOTE *For a chart listing CSS properties and values, see Appendix E.*

Applying this style rule to the original plain text HTML page produces these results:

10

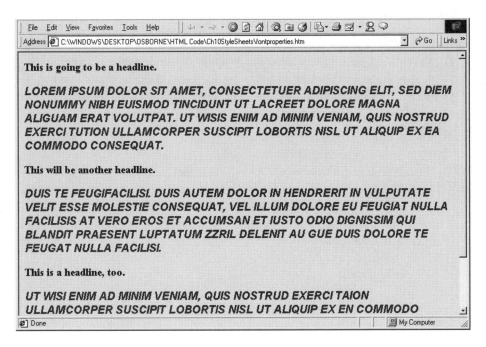

## Apply Text Properties for Spacing and Alignment

Whereas font properties deal with size, color, weight, and style of fonts, text properties handle the more mundane tasks of dealing with character and line spacing, alignment, justification, and so on. The text properties enable you to arrange your page with far greater precision than you ever could with HTML. For example, you can specify details such as the following:

- **Word-spacing**   With this property you can specify additional space between words using the same types of measurements as with font-size. The default is normal.

  ```
  h3 {word-spacing: .1em;}
  ```

- **Letter-spacing**   As its name suggests, letter-spacing allows you to add to the default spacing between letters. Again, normal is the default.

  ```
  h3 {word-spacing: .1em; letter-spacing: .2cm; }
  ```

- **Text-decoration**   With text-decoration you can add the values of underline, overline, line-through, and blink. The default value is text-decoration: none.

  ```
  h3 {word-spacing: .1em; letter-spacing: .2cm;
      text-decoration: underline; }
  ```

- **Vertical-align**   This allows you to apply the same vertical alignment properties to text elements as you did with text alignment attributes in HTML. Values include baseline, sub, super, top, text-top, middle, bottom, text-bottom, and percentage.

  ```
  h3 em { vertical-align: super;}
  ```

NOTE    *Notice that in addition to the h3 selector, this line also has em added. This is called a contextual selector. By adding an element to the selector, you can create styles for specific contexts. To create a superscript in an h3 headline, simply enclose the words you want to superscript in a set of <em> </em> tags.*

■ **Text-transform**   With the text-transform property you can automatically capitalize every word in any given element, change them all to uppercase, or make them all lowercase.

```
h3 {word-spacing: .1em; letter-spacing: .2cm;
    text-decoration: underline;
    text-transform: capitalize;}
```

■ **Text-align**   The text-align property works essentially the same way as the align attribute. You can choose from values of left, right, center, and justify.

```
h3 {word-spacing: .1em; letter-spacing: .2cm;
    text-decoration: underline;
    text-transform: capitalize;
    text-align: center; }
```

■ **Text-indent**   Using text-indent frees you from the old convention of using the non-breaking space entity,  , for indenting. Using this property you can specify exactly what kind of indent you would like. The possible values are a number, a measurement, and a percentage.

```
p {font-family: sans-serif; font-style: italic;
    font-variant: small-caps; font-weight: 700;
    font-size: 14pt; color: blue;
    text-indent: .5in;}
```

■ **Line-height**   If you want to space lines farther apart than the default setting for a browser, use the line-height property. You can specify line-height by a number, a measurement, or a percentage.

```
p {font-family: sans-serif; font-style: italic;
    font-variant: small-caps; font-weight: 700;
    font-size: 14pt; color: blue;
    text-indent: .5 in; line-height: 1em;}
```

10

Try adding these modified rules to your css_sample.htm document and compare your results to the following illustration:

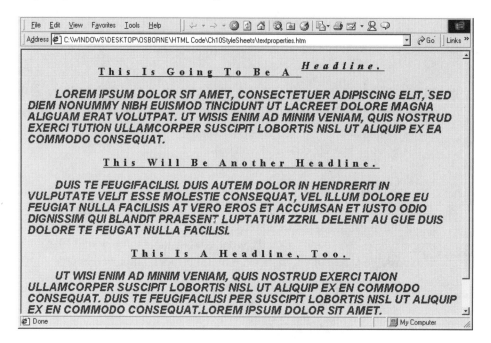

## Use Color and Background Properties

As you might imagine from the name, color and background properties enable you to control the display of background images and colors. These properties work much the same way as the bgcolor and background attributes but give you many more options to work with. The color and background properties are as follows:

- **Background-color**   With HTML you were able to set the background color only for an entire page or individual table cells. The CSS background-color property enables you to set a background color for any element.

```
body {background-color: gold; }
```

■ **Background-image**    With this property you can set a background image for any element; not just for a page.

```
body {background-color: gold;
      background-image: url(weavetile.gif); }
```

■ **Background-repeat**    This property allows you a much greater range of choices in how a background image repeats on your page. You can choose to have the image repeat (tile) through the entire page, repeat horizontally or vertically, or not at all. The values are repeat, repeat-x (horizontal), repeat-y (vertical), and no-repeat.

```
body {background-color: gold;
      background-image: url (weavetile2.gif);
      background-repeat: no-repeat; }
```

■ **Background-attachment**    To create a watermark effect with a fixed background image that allows content to scroll, you can use the background-attachment property. Your options are scroll or fixed.

```
body {background-color: gold;
      background-image: url (weavetile2.gif);
      background-repeat: no-repeat;
      background-attachment: fixed; }
```

■ **Background-position**    With the background-position property you can specify where an image occurs in an element. You can describe the position in terms of top/center/bottom and left/center/right. In other words, you can specify an image to show up in the top right, center center, bottom left, and so on.

```
body {background-color: gold;
      background-image: url (weavetile2.gif);
      background-repeat: no-repeat;
      background-attachment: fixed;
      background-position: center center;}
```

10

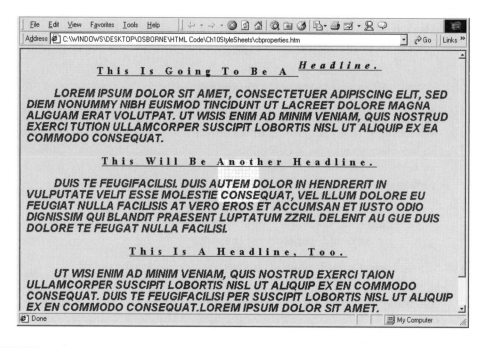

NOTE *With background-position and other position-related properties, the positioning is relative to an imaginary "box" that surrounds the element. If you would like to visualize what that box looks like with one element, open an HTML page and modify any <h1> element to read <h1 style= "background-color: blue>". The h1 element will now appear with a blue rectangle behind it. That's the invisible box. When you specify background position with any element, the background image is placed relative to the invisible box around that element; not the entire page—unless, of course, you are modifying the <body> element.*

## Control Margins, Padding, and Borders with Box Properties

Perhaps the most complicated (and useful) properties are the box properties. These allow you much greater influence over positioning, layout, borders, text flow, and so on than you ever could have with HTML. These properties can take quite a while to master, but they are great tools to have at your disposal. They are as follows:

■ **Margin-top (right, bottom, left)**   With the margin properties you can specify margins in measurements or percentages. If you don't specify margins, the browser will set them automatically (this can also be specified as "auto"). The following sets left and right margins to one inch:

```
body {background-color: gold;
      background-image: url (weavetile2.gif);
      background-repeat: no-repeat;
      background-attachment: fixed;
      background-position: center center;
      margin-left: 1in; margin-right: 1in;}
```

■ **Padding-top (right, bottom, left)**   If you think about tables and the cellpadding attribute, you will understand how padding works. Now you don't need to be limited to individual cells; you can add padding to any element.

```
p {font-family: sans-serif; font-style: italic;
   font-variant: small-caps; font-weight: 700;
   font-size: 14pt; color: blue;
   text-indent: .5 in; line-height: 1em;
   padding: .25in .50in;}
```

■ **Border-style**   If you want to add a border to any element, you can do it with this property. You can choose from eight possible options: solid, dashed, dotted, inset, outset, ridge, groove, or double.

```
p {font-family: sans-serif; font-style: italic;
   font-variant: small-caps; font-weight: 700;
   font-size: 14pt; color: blue;
   text-indent: .5 in; line-height: 1em;
   padding: .25in .50in;
   border-style: inset;}
```

■ **Border-color**   This property enables you to set the color for a border. You can specify up to four values; they are assigned the same way as margin values.

```
p {font-family: sans-serif; font-style: italic;
   font-variant: small-caps; font-weight: 700;
   font-size: 14pt; color: blue;
   text-indent: .5 in; line-height: 1em;
   padding: .25in .50in;
   border-style: inset;
   border-color: red;}
```

10

■ **Border-top-width (right-width, bottom-width, left-width)**  You can set the width of a border as thin, medium, or thick; or you can specify a unit of measurement.

```
p {font-family: sans-serif; font-style: italic;
      font-variant: small-caps; font-weight: 700;
      font-size: 14pt; color: blue;
      text-indent: .5 in; line-height: 1em;
      padding: .25in .50in;
      border-style: inset;
      border-color: red;
      border-width: thick;}
```

When you've modified your style rules to match these, save your page and compare it in your browser. It should look something like this:

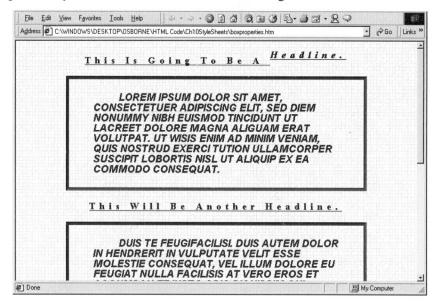

If you plan to add images, the height, width, float, and clear properties will prove quite useful. These properties correspond to the height, width, and align attributes in HTML. That is, they allow you to specify how an image will be displayed and whether text will wrap around it.

■ **Width**  This property functions much the same as the width attribute. Its best use is with graphics or to set the width of a block level element.

```
img.pansy1 {height: 200px; }
```

■ **Height**   As with width, this property sets the height of an element.

```
img.pansy1 {height: 200px; width: 320px;}
```

■ **Float**   Similar to the align attribute, this property allows you to set an element to the left or right margin, with text flowing around the opposite side.

```
img.pansy1 {height: 200px; width: 320px;
            float: left;}
```

If you have added the preceding style rule to the page (and have supplied or downloaded a picture to go with it), you will notice that the image is overlapping part of the text box as in the following illustration. If you don't want the image to float with text wrapping, use the clear property.

■ **Clear**   The clear property will prevent an image such as the preceding one from floating on top of another element, leaving one or both sides clear. The values for this property are none, left, right, and both.

```
p {font-family: sans-serif; font-style: italic;
   font-variant: small-caps; font-weight: 700;
   font-size: 14pt; color: blue;
   text-indent: .5 in; line-height: 1em;
```

10

```
padding: .25in .50in;
border-style: inset;
border-color: red;
border-width: thick;
clear: left;}
```

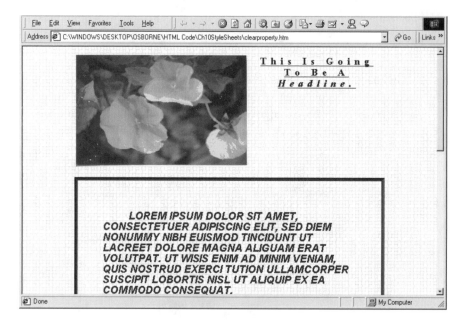

With the box properties, you now have the ability to create complex layouts for a Web page using nothing more than HTML and CSS.

# Learn Good Web Design

Cascading Style Sheets are the direction in which the Web is moving. Eventually, you will have to know how to use them; you might as well learn to use them now. However, there are good reasons to be cautious in your use of CSS for the present.

## Web Design Principle: Don't Be Afraid of CSS

Cascading Style Sheets are here to stay. Moreover, they are the wave of the future in Web design. Granted, there are still some support problems, particularly with CSS2. However, the fact remains that if you plan to do much Web design in the years to come, you will need to know CSS.

As support for style sheets grows, eventually the deprecated elements and attributes will no longer be supported. If you are building your sites on these elements, you will find yourself doing quite a bit of remodeling and redesigning. Once XML is the primary language for Web authoring, you won't have a choice. XML requires a style sheet of some sort, whether CSS, XSL (eXtensible Stylesheet Language), or some other language yet to be developed. It is to your advantage to learn to use style sheets. As you design your Web pages, try polishing your technique by applying these principles:

- Use inline style sheets in place of <font>, align=" ", and other deprecated elements and attributes. You will become accustomed to style sheet syntax by using CSS whenever possible.

- Apply embedded style sheets for your basic page layouts instead of using tables. There's no need to get into complicated design if you don't want to. Just remember that CSS was designed with page layout in mind. It might be easier to use tables, but discipline yourself to use CSS.

- Begin developing some external style sheets with plans to implement them on your site. The advantage of external style sheets is that you need to create only one; then link all of your pages to it. The result will be a unified look for your site.

10

## Practice, Practice, Practice

If you have been working through this book, you have been building a collection of HTML pages and organizing them into an HTML notebook site. Why not try creating a style for the site as an external style sheet and link the various pages to it? You will see firsthand the power of CSS for creating a unified presentation throughout a Web site.

To get you started, here is a sample style sheet based on the rules created in this chapter. Type it in and save it as a plain text file named practicestyle.css. Add a link inside the <head> portion of your pages that reads <link rel="stylesheet" type= "text/css" src="practicestyle.css" />. Remember that to use any of the selectors that are defined with classes (p.green, p.large) you must identify the class with the class=" " attribute. For example, to use the p.green selector you would write the opening tag <p class="green">.

If you don't want to write the style sheet out, download it from Osborne's Web site: www.osborne.com. Try making some modifications and additions and linking your pages to it.

```
body {background-color: gold;
      background-image: url (yourownimage.gif);
      background-repeat: no-repeat;
      background-attachment: fixed;
      background-position: center center;
      margin-left: 1in; margin-right: 1in;}

h3      {margin: .25in;
          color: white;
          font-size: 24pt;}

p {font-family: sans-serif; font-style: italic;
    font-variant: small-caps; font-weight: 700;
    font-size: 14pt; color: blue;
    text-indent: .5 in; line-height: 1em;
    padding: .25in .50in;
    border-style: inset;
    border-color: red;
    border-width: thick;
    clear: left;}

p.green {margin: .25in;
          color: green;
          font-family: arial;
          font-weight: bold;
          border-style: double;
          border-width: thick;
          border-color: red;}

p.large {margin-right: 1in;
          color: navy;
          font-size: 2em;
          background: aqua;}

h3 em {vertical-align: super;}

h3 {word-spacing: .1em; letter-spacing: .2cm;
    text-decoration: underline;
    text-transform: capitalize;
    text-align: center;}
```

# Find the Code Online

To find the code online for this or any of the chapters in this book, go to Osborne's Web site, www.osborne.com, and click the Free Code choice on the navigation bar. From the list of books, select the *How to Do Everything with HTML* option and you will be able to download the book files, which are linked together and organized as an offline "mini" Web site. For more on how to use the "mini" Web site, see Chapter 17.

| Use This Code For... | Look for This Filename |
| --- | --- |
| Web Page without CSS | css_sample.htm |
| Web page with embedded style | css_sample_embedded.htm |
| External style sheet | my_styles.css |
| Text properties demo | textproperties.htm |
| Box properties demo | boxproperties.htm |
| Clear property demo | clearproperty.htm |
| Background tile sample | Weavetile2.gif |
| Web page with inline style added | css_sample_inline.htm |
| Web page linked to external style sheet | css_sample_external.htm |
| Font properties demo | fontproperties.htm |
| Color/Background properties demo | cbproperties.htm |
| Float property demo | boxproperties2.htm |
| Pansy photo | pansy1.jpg |
| Practice style sheet | practicestyle.css |

**10**

# Part III

## Bells and Whistles to Adorn Your Site

# Chapter 11

## Enhance Your Pages with Audio and Video

## How to...

- Understand Formats and Delivery Methods

- Find Audio and Video Files

- Link to a Sound or Video File

- Add a Background Sound

- Embed Sound and Video

- Use Streaming Audio and Video

Nowhere are the sweeping advances in the technology of the Web more evident than in the area of multimedia. When the Web started it was little more than typewritten text on a screen. Next came graphics and the capability to add pictures and fonts of different sizes and colors. Now you can include animation, audio, and video to bring life to your designs. You might be tempted to avoid multimedia on the grounds that it's too difficult for you to learn and use; however, nothing could be further from the truth. In fact, if you know how to add a link to a Web page, you already know enough to link to an audio or a video file.

# Understand Formats and Delivery Methods

As you explore multimedia, it's best to start with the different formats that are available. Just as with graphics, certain formats work best for certain purposes. For example, when deciding on sound files you might be influenced by the desire for a quick download time as opposed to good sound quality. On the other hand, sound quality might be important to you and you really don't care how long it takes a file to download. Perhaps both are important to you. All these factors will influence the choice you make.

## Compare Audio Formats

You will encounter several different audio formats as you enter the world of multimedia. Some you will definitely use; others you just need to know about. The formats listed in the following do not represent all possible choices, only those most commonly used and best supported.

- **μ-Law**   Pronounced *moo-law*, this format is sort of the granddaddy of them all. If you're familiar at all with audio files, you might recognize its file extension, .au. This is the file type used on UNIX systems. Although this type of file is supported on most PCs, it doesn't offer great sound quality.

- **MIDI**   Musical Instrument Digital Interface is a very different way of producing music and other sounds. Whereas most sound files actually record and reproduce sound and music, MIDI does not. Instead, a MIDI file is somewhat similar to storing the information from a printed page of music in digital format. Although that might be an oversimplification, that's the basic concept. MIDI doesn't store music; it stores instructions for creating music. The advantages of MIDI files are that they are very small and download quickly. The disadvantage is that you are limited in the sound you can reproduce because sound is not actually recorded. For example, MIDI files cannot be used for voice recordings.

- **Waveform Audio**   If you use a Windows system, you already use Waveform (or Wave) Audio. The sounds your PC produces when you load and unload Windows, not to mention other Windows sounds, are produced by .wav files. These files allow for good sound quality but can be very large and take a long time to download.

- **MPEG**   This is the format that has been in the news lately. MPEG (Motion Picture Experts Group) files are compressed, enabling music to be easily downloaded. The amount of compression is striking. For example, a single song saved as a .wav file can use 40 megabytes of space or more. The same song saved as an .mp3 file might be 1 or 2 megabytes. In light of this, you can understand the Napster controversy. Who would want to take the time to download an album of 12 songs at 40 megabytes each? On the other hand, what if each song is only 1.5 megabytes?

- **AIFF**   Originally developed for Macintosh systems, Audio Interchange File Format (.aif, .aiff) files provide high quality, although the file size tends to be large. Even though it was a Mac development, .aif files are supported in the Windows environment and can easily be converted to other formats.

- **RM**   RealMedia files are a special file format designed by RealNetworks for streaming media. RealProducer, the program that creates these files, is available as freeware.

11

So, which file type should you use when you are putting together sounds for your Web site? It all depends. If you want to have background music that begins when the page loads, you want a small file that downloads quickly. Your best bet is a MIDI file. If you don't like the computerized sound that tends to go along with MIDI files, try a very short WAV file. Also, if you want to emphasize sound quality, you'll lean toward WAV. If your sound clips are long, you probably are going to want to take advantage of MPEG's compression capabilities. MPEG files do lose some quality in the compression process, but generally it is not significant.

## Compare Video Formats

A slightly less daunting array of choices awaits you when you consider the different video formats that are available. Again, although there are more formats than those discussed here, those listed in the following are the most common and enjoy the greatest support:

- **Audio/Video Interleaved**   This format was developed for Microsoft's Video for Windows. Audio/Video Interleaved (.avi) is the standard for the Windows platform and is used for many applications requiring video. For instance, if you have an encyclopedia on CD-ROM, you'll find that most (if not all) of the video clips contained on it are in the .avi format.

- **QuickTime**   QuickTime (.mov) is used widely and works well on all platforms. Developed for the Macintosh, it is nevertheless supported in both Internet Explorer and Netscape. Its ease of use and the availablility of inexpensive encoding software make the .mov a good choice for newcomers to the world of multimedia.

- **MPEG**   Developed by the Moving Picture Experts Group, MPEG (.mpg) files, like their JPEG counterparts, can be compressed significantly yet lose little quality. If you are loooking for high-quality video reproduction for your site, this is the format of choice. However, MPEG can be complicated, and you will need special software for encoding the videos. This makes MPEG an unlikely choice for a casual user.

Which format should you choose? The main consideration here probably is file size, as video files tend to be very large. For simply attaching a video link or embedding a file, you probably will want to use either QuickTime or AVI. The advantage of using QuickTime is that it is already supported on both Windows and Mac systems. However, if you use AVI clips on your site, Mac users will need to download a plug-in to enable them to view the files.

## Understand Delivery Methods

There are two different ways to deliver audio or video to your visitors: *download* and *streaming*. Your choice of one or the other probably will be governed by the size of the file you are planning to use.

If you plan to use only very short clips of a few hundred kilobytes or less, use download as your delivery method. When you link to an audio or a video file, or when you embed multimedia into your pages, the normal method of delivery is by download. In other words, the entire file is downloaded into your visitor's computer before it is played. With short clips and small file sizes, most people won't mind waiting. However, if you're planning to include a long clip—perhaps a lecture, complete songs, or 15 minutes of your Hawaiian vacation video—your visitors probably will move on before the file has time to download. In cases such as this you might want to consider *streaming* audio and video.

The difference between streaming and downloadable media is very simple: Downloadable audio and video is like filling a glass of water before you take a drink. You wait until the glass is full; then you enjoy the water. On the other hand, using streaming media is like going to a water fountain. You drink the water as it streams up from the fountain's nozzle. No need to wait for a glass to fill up. With streaming media, the visitor gets to watch the video or listen to the music while the file is downloading.

SHORTCUT  *Even with downloadable files, it is to your advantage to use streaming media. Because streaming audio and video use the UDP protocol (no error checking; hence faster downloads) rather than TCP, the same size file will take less time to download to your visitor's browser. A longer clip could be used without hindering performance.*

11

# Find Multimedia Files

Obviously, if you're going to do the exercises in this chapter, you're going to need some audio and video files to work with. How do you go about finding them? It might not be as hard as you think. Consider some of these possible sources:

- **Your Own PC**   If your computer is of fairly recent vintage, you might be astonished to learn how many audio files are already stored away on your hard drive. On Windows 95 or 98, just click Start, Find, Files or Folders. On the line that reads Named:, type an asterisk followed by an audio or a video file extension (for example, **\*.mov**). Click Find Now and watch as your computer searches for the files.

■ **CD-ROMs**    These can be a great source of potential files. Just pop one in your drive and use the same process as outlined earlier (remembering to specify the CD-ROM drive as the one to search); you could find plenty of files to experiment with.

■ **Online**    There are a number of ways you can obtain audio and video files online. Web sites such as www.freeaudioclips.com and www.multimedialibrary.com are sources worth checking out. Also, although it won't always work, try right-clicking any links to videos on Web sites. Your browser usually will give you an option to download and save the video file.

■ **Osborne's Web Site**    Some of the audio files used in the examples for this chapter are available on Osborne's site: www.osborne.com. Check the chart at the end of this chapter for a list of which files you will find there.

■ **Create Your Own**    There are quite a few shareware and even freeware programs available that will enable you to create your own audio and video files. Try visiting some sites such as www.download.com, www.tucows.com, or www.zdnet.com/downloads, and search for audio and video editors or multimedia authoring tools. You'll find a large range of selections to choose from. Table 11-1 lists a few you might start with.

| Program Name | What It Does | Publisher URL | Approximate Price |
|---|---|---|---|
| Cooledit 2000 | Audio editor | www.syntrillium.com | $69 |
| GoldWave | Audio editor | www.goldwave.com | $40 |
| Total Recorder | Audio editor | www.highcriteria.com | $12 |
| Ulead Video Studio | Video editor | www.ulead.com | $100 |
| QuickTime Pro | Makes QuickTime movies | www.apple.com | $30 |
| Windows Media Encoder | Produces audio and video for Windows Media | www.microsoft.com | Freeware |
| RealProducer | Creates streaming audio and video | www.real.com | Freeware |

**TABLE 11-1**    Audio and Video Editors

> TIP
>
> *If you want to create your own audio or video files, you will need both the hardware and software to get the job done. For audio, your computer must be equipped with a sound card (standard equipment nowadays), and you'll need audio editing software. For video, you must install a video capture card on your computer. This will enable you to plug a VCR, video camera, digital camera, and so on into your system.*

Once you have some multimedia files to work with, you're ready to see how they function on a Web page.

> CAUTION
>
> *When dealing with audio and video, copyright issues quickly become relevant. It might seem harmless for you to include your favorite song as background music for your site, but if you do not have permission to use it, you are violating the law. The same holds true for video, still photos, art, software, or just about anything that has been created by someone else. ASCAP (American Society of Composers, Authors, and Publishers) is a good place to start if you want to use copyrighted music on your site. Check out their Web site: www.ascap.com/weblicense/.*

# Add External Audio or Video

Just as you can link to an external image, you can add audio and video to your page simply by linking to a file. This is without a doubt the easiest way to add multimedia to your site. For example, in Chapter 8 a family album page was created to demonstrate the use of tables for layout. What if you decided you would like to have a recorded message available as a link? The message wouldn't play automatically, nor would it be embedded as part of the page. Rather, it would be kept as a separate file; if anyone wanted to listen to it, they would just have to click the link.

Assuming you had already created the audio and video files you want to link to, all you need to do is use the anchor element <a> </a> with the href=" " attribute. The value for href=" " will be the filename of the audio/video clip. For an audio clip, your link might look like this one:

```
<a href="greeting.wav">Listen to a greeting.</a>
```

11

For a video clip, everything's the same except for the filename:

```
<a href="homemovie.mov">Watch my home movies.</a>
```

Your link will appear as any other link would; but instead of linking to another page, a browser will load a plug-in (a special "helper" program) that will play the sound.

```
Listen to a greeting.
Watch my home movies.
Listen to music
```

Adding audio and video to a page can be that simple. Of course, although using an external link might be the easiest way to add multimedia to your site, it might not be the best way. In fact, one of the more important aspects of adding multimedia is learning to sort out the different ways of including it on your site and choosing the right one for your purposes.

# Embed Sound in Your Page

Have you ever visited a Web site and found yourself listening to background music that started playing automatically? Or perhaps you heard a recorded greeting, welcoming you to the site? This is an easy way to begin using audio. As long as you keep the clips short, the resulting file size will be small and manageable. You won't need to worry about long download times delaying your sounds.

## Embed a Background Sound with

The good news about the element is that it is very simple to use. The bad news is that it works only on Internet Explorer. However, it's a nice, easy way to practice with audio files.

To insert a background sound with the element, just use the src=" " attribute to identify the sound file you want to attach. In the case of the following example, the name of the file is bgsound.wav, but you could put the name of any audio file in there as a value. One additional attribute is loop=" ". The loop attribute will allow you to specify how long the sound should play. If you want an endlessly repeating loop, add the value "infinite." If you want the greeting to play only once when the page is loaded, insert a numerical value of **1**. By increasing the numerical value, you increase the number of times the sound plays. Thus, a value of 10 will cause the sound to play ten times.

Try typing in the following code to create a simple page with a background sound. Save it as bgsound.htm. Experiment with different sound files and different values for the loop attribute.

```
<html>
<head>
<title>Bgsound Sample</title>
</head>
<body>
<h1>This is a sample of a page with a background sound</h1>
<bgsound src="bgsound.wav" loop="3" />
</body>
</html>
```

It's a shame that the <bgsound /> element was never incorporated into the HTML standard, as it's undoubtedly the simplest way to embed a sound on a page. However, Netscape provides a different model for creating a page with inline sound.

# Embed Inline Sounds

What is an *inline* sound? It's simply a sound that has been placed in a page inline, like any other element. Sometimes inline sounds are referred to as *embedded* sounds. The idea is the same as with external and inline images. If you merely write a hypertext link to an image file as you would with any other page, you are using an external image. When someone clicks on the link, the browser displays the image as a separate entity, rather than as part of the page that linked to it. On the other hand, if you use the <img /> element to actually place the image on your page, you are using an inline or embedded image. Sound files work the same way; however, instead of the <img /> element, you embed sound files with either the <embed> or <object> element.

## Add Inline Sound with <embed> </embed>

Netscape's <embed> </embed> extension is more versatile than IE's <bgsound />. With <bgsound /> you are limited (as its name implies) to embedding a background sound. The <embed> element, on the other hand, enables you to place different objects in your page, including audio and video files. Although <embed> is supported by both Netscape and IE, it has been deprecated in favor of the <object>

element. Unfortunately, some older browsers will not recognize <object>. So, for
the present it's not a bad idea to be familiar with <embed>. To experiment with
the <embed> element, try the following steps:

1.  Open bgsound.htm and save it as embed.htm.

2.  Delete the line that reads:

    ```
    <bgsound src="bgsound.wav" loop="3" />
    ```

3.  In its place type

    ```
    <embed src="embed.wav">
    ```

 *If you don't want to download the embed.wav file, substitute any sound
file you choose.*

4.  Add the autostart=" " attribute to tell the browser not to start the audio
    clip automatically:

    ```
    <embed src="embed.wav" autostart="false">
    ```

5.  Specify the size of the "player" the browser will display by using the
    height=" " and width=" " attributes:

    ```
    <embed src="embed.wav" autostart="false"
      height="20" width="125">
    ```

6.  Add a closing tag:

    ```
    <embed src="embed.wav" autostart="false"
      height="20" width="125"> </embed>
    ```

NOTE    *Even though embed works like an empty element (nothing in between
the two tags), a closing tag is required.*

Your HTML for a page with an embedded sound file should resemble this code:

```
<html>
<head>
<title>Using the Embed Element</title>
</head>
<body>
```

```
<embed src="embed.wav" autostart="false"
  height="20" width="125"> </embed>.
<h1>This is a sample of a page<br />
with an embedded sound</h1>
</body>
</html>
```

When you save your page and display it in a browser, you should see a set of controls in the upper-left corner of the browser window. These controls function like the controls on a tape recorder and allow the visitor to play and replay a sound.

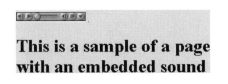

## Use &lt;embed&gt; for Background Sound

What if you want to create a background sound using the &lt;embed&gt; element? You merely have to add one attribute and modify another. You must add the loop=" " attribute as you did with &lt;bgsound&gt;. With &lt;embed&gt;, however, loop=" " uses a different set of values. Instead of numerical values or "infinite," here loop can be given a value of only *true* or *false*. False turns the loop off; true makes the sound loop endlessly. In addition to adding the loop attribute, you must change the value in the autostart=" " attribute to "true." You also can delete the height and width attributes, as they are not needed for a background sound. This will cause the sound to begin automatically. Your modified code would look like this:

```
<embed src="embed.wav" autostart="true"
 loop="true"> </embed>.
```

## Use &lt;embed&gt; and &lt;bgsound /&gt; Together for Maximum Compatibility

Because both &lt;embed&gt; and &lt;bgsound /&gt; are extensions that are not part of the official HTML specification, you might encounter compatibility problems with some browsers if you use only one of them. If you plan to use these elements to add background sound to your pages, it would be wise to use both of them. For instance, if you were to modify the original page created in this chapter, bgsound.htm, to include both &lt;bgsound /&gt; and &lt;embed&gt;, your code might look like the following.

11

```
<html>
<head>
<title>Bgsound Sample</title>
</head>
<body>
<h1>This is a sample of a page
with a background sound</h1>
<bgsound src="bgsound.wav" loop="3" />
<embed src="embed.wav" autostart="true"
 loop="true"> </embed>.
</body>
</html>
```

## Use <noembed> </noembed> for Non-compatible Browsers

If you're concerned about visitors to your site who might be using browsers that
do not support the <embed> element, you can provide substitute content for them
with the <noembed> element. Similar to the <noframes> element, <noembed>
will display alternative content in browsers that do not recognize the <embed>
element. You could include a textual description or a title for your video, thus
providing your visitors with some idea of what they are missing.

## Embed Sound Files with <object> </object>

Although you can embed sound with the <embed> element, according to the W3C
the method of choice should be the <object> </object> element. The W3C isn't
trying to be picky here. As you'll see, the <object> element is in a class by itself.
Object is sort of a generic element, used for putting objects in Web pages, an object
being defined as just about anything you want to put in a Web page. Its use is
not restricted to audio or video files. It also can be used for embedding graphics,
Active-X controls, Java applets, text, and even other Web pages. Object truly is
an all-purpose element. Eventually, the <object> element will be the normal way
of embedding anything in a Web page.

 *You can position objects with the align=" " attribute, insert them in table
cells, and so on. Be creative in your design.*

The procedure for embedding a sound file with <object> is very similar to that
used with <embed>, but there are a few different attributes you must use. This is
because <object> can embed many different types of objects. Obviously, you must

inform the browser just what kind of object you are putting in. To embed a sound file in a Web page with the object element, follow these steps:

1. Open template.htm and save it as object.htm.

2. Add the opening object tag:

```
<object>
```

3. Use the data=" " attribute to tell the browser where to find the file you want to embed. The value for this will be the URL of the file you want to embed:

```
<object data="object.wav">
```

4. Now that you've told the browser where to find the file, you must tell it what kind of file it will be embedding. For this, you use the type=" " attribute with the *MIME type* of the file. In this case, it will be audio/wav:

```
<object data="object.wav" type="audio/wav">
```

5. You should add the height and width attributes to specify the amount of space allotted to the plug-in:

```
<object data="object.wav" type="audio/wav"
    height="125" width="125">
```

6. Add the autostart="true" attribute to allow the sound to play as soon as it loads:

```
<object data="object.wav" type="audio/wav"
    height="125" width="125" autostart="true">
```

7. Add the closing tag. As with <embed>, the <object> element functions as an empty element, but still requires a closing tag:

```
<object data="object.wav" type="audio/wav"
    height="125" width="125" autostart="true">
</object>
```

Just to give the page some substance, try adding a line that reads, <h1>This page shows the &lt;object&gt; element in action</h1>. Your finished code should look like the HTML code that follows:

```
<html>
<head>
<title>Embed Sounds with the
```

11

```
        Object Element</title>
</head>
<body>
<object data="object.wav" type="audio/wav"
height="125" width="150" autostart="true">
</object>
<h1>This page shows the &lt;object&gt;<br />
element in action.</h1>
</body>
</html>
```

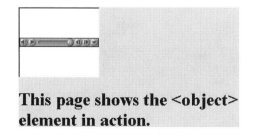

**This page shows the &lt;object&gt;
element in action.**

<blockquote>
TIP    *Any time you want to display an HTML tag as part of a Web page, you must
enclose the text with the character entities for the "less than," &lt; , and
"greater than," &gt; , signs. If you typed in only the tag, the browser would
interpret it as an element and not as part of the text of your document.*
</blockquote>

## Understand MIME Types

In the preceding example you had to identify what kind of file the browser should
expect by using the type=" " attribute. The value you supplied was called the *MIME
type.* MIME stands for Multipurpose Internet Mail Extensions. It was developed as
a means for enabling non-text files to be transferred by e-mail. When you use the
<object> element to embed a sound or video file, you must identify the file by its
MIME type. This includes a basic file type such as audio, image, video, and so on,
followed by a slash and a more specific type (often the file's normal extension).
For example, the preceding entry was for a .wav file. In that case you entered
type="audio/wav".

<blockquote>
NOTE    *You can find a comprehensive list of MIME types at ftp://ftp.isi.edu/in-notes/
iana/assignments/media-types/media-types.*
</blockquote>

The MIME types you generally will encounter with audio and video files are
listed in Table 11-2.

| Media Type | File Extension | MIME Type |
| --- | --- | --- |
| μ-Law | .au | audio/basic |
| Wave | .wav | audio/wav |
| MPEG | mp3 | audio/mpeg |
| QuickTime | .mov | video/quicktime |
| MPEG | .mpg | video/mpeg |
| Microsoft Video | .avi | video/msvideo |

**TABLE 11-2**    MIME Types

So, how do you sort out the <bgsound /> , <embed>, and <object> elements; particularly because all three can accomplish the same goal? <bgsound /> is a great element but because it's supported only by IE, you probably won't want to use it unless you're sure only IE users will be accessing your page (or if you don't care whether or not they hear the sound). With <embed> and <object>, it's a little tougher call. Even though the <embed> element is proprietary and not part of the official HTML specification, it is supported by all but the oldest browsers. That makes it pretty safe to use. On the other hand, the <object> element is gaining support but still is less supported than <embed>. If you're concerned about getting the largest possible audience, go with <embed>, but be forewarned that you will need to become familiar with <object> sooner or later.

## Embed Video in Your Page

Once you have embedded some audio files in an HTML document, adding video is easy. You simply use the <embed> or <object> element to embed the video into the page and write the code essentially the same way as you would for an audio file. If you want to start off with an easy option, however, Internet Explorer has provided an uncomplicated way to include video on a page without using either of these elements. You can add video files using the <img /> element with the *dynamic source*, dynsrc=" ", attribute. Unfortunately, dynsrc is not supported beyond Internet Explorer so you might not want to use it extensively. However, it's an easy way to begin experimenting with video files. Besides, if you happen to be designing pages for a corporate intranet and you know everyone will be viewing your pages with IE, this is a simple technique.

NOTE    *Even with Internet Explorer, you might experience difficulty with <img dynsrc=" " />, as the most recent version apparently no longer supports this attribute.*

11

## Add Video with the dynsrc=" " Attribute

Using the dynsrc=" " attribute to add video to a page is as easy as adding an image. If you have read Chapter 6 on adding graphics, you will remember that a graphical image can be embedded in a page with the <img /> (image) element. For a JPEG or GIF image, the element is written <img src="filename.jpg" />. To add a video, you use the dynamic source attribute instead of using the source attribute. For example, to use dynsrc to add a video to a page, you would write the image element like this: <img dynsrc="myvideo.avi">. The following HTML code will create a page with the sample.mov file displaying as soon as the page is loaded.

> TIP
>
> *If you're having trouble finding a video to practice with, go to Apple's site and download the free version of QuickTime (www.apple.com/ quicktime.download/). A file named sample.mov will be included as part of the package.*

```
<html>
<head>
<title>Use Dynsrc for Video</title>
</head>
<body>
<img dynsrc="myvideo.avi" />
<h1>This video is added with the<br />
dynsrc attribute.</h1>
</body>
</html>
```

When you display this page, you should see something like this:

**This video is added with the dynsrc attribute.**

Some other attributes you can add to work along with dynsrc=" " are

■ **loop=" "**    As with you can specify infinite to create an endless loop or a numerical value for the number of times you want the video to play.

■ **start=" "**    This allows you to specify when the video should start playing. Your choices are fileopen or mouseover. With fileopen (the default), the video begins playing as soon as the file loads. With mouseover, the image will not play until the mouse moves over it. Try modifying the preceding file to read <img dynsrc="sample.mov" start="mouseover" />. Save the file and load it. Once the page has loaded, move your cursor over it and see what happens.

## Add Video with <embed> and <object>

Because adding video with the <embed> or <object> element is essentially the same as adding audio, this is a good chance to practice some of the HTML you have learned. Add a little variety to your multimedia page by embedding two videos on a single page and structuring them inside a table. Use the <embed> element for one and the <object> element for the other.

NOTE    *This exercise provides a side-by-side comparison of the <embed> and <object> elements. Because of long download times for video, you probably wouldn't do this on the Internet. It would work okay for an intranet, though.*

11

To create your page, follow these steps:

**1.** Open template.htm and save it as twinvideos.htm.

**2.** Inside the <body> </body> element, add the   element. This will center the table.

```
<html><head><title>Twin Videos</title></head>
<body>
</body>
</html>
```

**3.** Create a table with a set of <table> tags. To assist you in laying out your table, set the border=" " attribute to 1.

```
<html><head><title>Twin Videos</title></head>
<body>
<table border="1"> </table>
```

```
</body>
</html>
```

4. Add a row with two headings: Video 1 and Video 2.

```
<html><head><title>Twin Videos</title></head>
<body>
<table border="1">
<tr> <th>Video 1</th> <th>Video 2</th>
</table>
</body>
</html>
```

5. Add another row with two data cells.

```
<html><head><title>Twin Videos</title></head>
<body>
<table border="1">
<tr> <th>Video 1: Embed</th>
<th>Video 2: Object</th> </tr>
<tr> <td> </td> <td> </td> </tr>
</table>
</body>
</html>
```

6. Inside the first cell use the <embed> element to add a video file. For this illustration, sample.mov will be used.

```
<tr><td><embed src="myvideo.avi"
    height="200" width="200"
    autostart="true" loop="false"> </embed></td>
```

7. Inside the second cell use the <object> element to add another video file. This can be the same one or a different one—your choice.

```
<td><object data="myvideo2.avi" type="video/quicktime"
    height="200" width="200" autostart="true"
    loop="false"> </object></td></tr>
```

8. Add a line below the table to finish your creation.

```
<h1>These are my twin videos</h1>
```

Check your finished code against the code that follows:

```
<html><head><title>Twin Videos</title></head>
<body>
<table border="1">
```

```
<tr> <th>Video 1: Embed</th>
<th>Video 2: Object</th> </tr>
<tr><td><embed src="myvideo1.avi"
    autostart="true" loop="false"
    height="200" width="200"> </embed></td>
<td><object data="myvideo2.avi" type="video/quicktime"
    autostart="true" loop="false"
    height="200" width="200"> </object></td></tr>
</table>
<h1>These are my twin videos</h1>
</body></html>
```

Now, save the file and display it in a browser. Your display should look something like this:

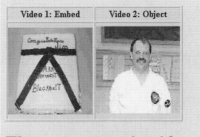

# Add Streaming Audio and Video

Putting audio and video on your site presents a number of problems, but the most serious is download time. Even short clips can result in fairly large file sizes. For example, the four-second clip used early in this chapter still came out to almost 100K. That's twice the recommended size for your entire page.

You can see how audio and video can slow your site down significantly. What is the solution? Streaming media. With streaming media your visitors can watch or listen to your files as they download. Are streaming files difficult to create? Not at all. Expensive? Definitely not. (Some of the best software for creating streaming media is freeware.)

What is the downside, then? Primarily that your Web host must be able to support streaming media, and not all currently do. If you spend a little money and invest in Apple's QuickTime Pro, you don't even have to worry about that. In any case, you shouldn't have to search long to find a server that will support streaming audio and video. With its increase in popularity, more and more Web hosts are upgrading their services to support streaming media.

If you want to provide streaming content on your site, a program such as RealProducer will enable you to create the files you need. You can record your own sound with a microphone, plugged directly into your sound card. You can also input an audio through the sound card's line input jack with a CD, cassette, or even record player. If you have a video capture card, you can do the same with video input. Once you have recorded your file, RealProducer converts it into a special format that is suitable for streaming. It will even create a special Web page to serve as the link to your streaming file. The "wizards" built into the program will enable you to easily and quickly create RealAudio or RealVideo files. When you save the file, the program will use the .rm extension, marking them out as RealMedia files.

## Did you know?

## How Streaming Media Works

You know what streaming media is, but do you know how it works? Streaming media, such as that used by RealAudio and RealVideo uses a different protocol than you normally encounter when you surf the Internet. The protocol is called *User Datagram Protocol* (UDP). The standard Internet protocol is *Transfer Control Protocol/Internet Protocol* (TCP/IP). So what's the difference? Perhaps a simple comparison could be found in mail delivery. You can't carry the analogy too far, but TCP/IP might loosely correspond to registered mail, special delivery. The data that your Web browser has requested will be delivered because TCP/IP keeps checking for errors and delivering until everything that has been requested has also been received. On the other hand, UDP could correspond to bulk mail. There are less guarantees involved and less error checking. So, while there is greater chance of data loss, the information is delivered more quickly. That's also where the analogy breaks down. Bulk mail is definitely not quicker. However, the comparison is with the security of the data and guarantee of delivery. Simply speaking, streaming media is faster because there's less error checking in the download.

Once you have created your files and uploaded them to your Web server, you need to put a special link into your page to help it find the file. This is similar to linking to an external audio or video file, with one exception: You must create a special document and link to it. The document (also known as a *metafile*) serves as a pointer, directing the browser to your streaming file. Just create a blank file in Notepad or another text editor and type in the full URL for the file you are going to link to.

For instance, say you converted video of your Hawaii vacation to RealVideo and saved it as hawaii_trip.rm. Once it's uploaded to your server the URL might be something such as http://www.cheapinternethost.com/hawaii_trip.rm. You simply type that line—and nothing else—into your text file and save it with a .ram extension; for instance, the filename could be hawaii.ram. Then simply link to the .ram file. When visitors click it, their browsers will launch a special "plug-in" that will play a streaming video of you enjoying Hawaii's sun and surf. The code for such demonstrates how such a link might look, as does the illustration that follows:

```
<html><head><title>Streaming Video</title></head>
<body>
<a href="hawaii.ram">Check out
    my Hawaiian vacation</a>
</body>
</html>
```

# My Hawaiian Vacation

*Click the link above for some video of my vacation in Hawaii. And eat your heart out!*

Streaming media is the way to go if you plan to use a lot of audio and video files on your site. However, be sure that you have a lot of storage space on your Web server—those files are large.

# Learn Good Web Design

As you've read this chapter, you probably have already figured out one of the main problems with video and audio on the Web: file size. If you plan to use a lot of audio and video as part of your Web site, ask yourself this question: "What do audio, video, and molasses have in common?"

## Web Design Principle: Sweet, but Slow

Yes, it's really fun to watch a video you created displayed in all its glory on your own Web page. But if your visitors have to wait 10 minutes for it to download, what's the point? By the time it's downloaded, they'll be long gone. People don't like to wait when they're surfing the Web. That's why high-speed Internet service is all the rage. But until everyone has a high-speed connection, you must keep in mind that most people have to wait for even small files to download. Have mercy on them by following these principles:

- If you have a number of different audio or video clips, don't embed them in your pages. Link to them externally. That way, your visitors don't need to wait for them to download unless they have chosen to view, or listen to, them.

- For background music or recorded greetings, keep it short and sweet. Even a 10- or 15-second clip can take a while to download.

- Don't use endlessly looping background music. Like elevator music, it will drive your visitors crazy. If they can't turn the sound off, they won't stay long and they probably won't be back.

- If you must embed a longer audio or video clip, be sure that it really will enhance your site and your visitor's experience. Don't just put it in for the fun of it.

- If possible, deliver long video and audio portions via streaming media. Your visitors will bless you for it.

## Practice, Practice, Practice

Try experimenting with different ways to use audio without slowing down your site. For example, create a page with a gallery of audio links attached to images—perhaps a photo album with thumbnail photos that will give a recorded greeting when you click on the link. Add some video links. If you already have a Web host, upload your pages and see how long it takes for them to download.

# Find the Code Online

To find the code online for this or any of the chapters in this book, go to Osborne's Web site: www.osborne.com, and click the Free Code choice on the navigation bar. From the list of books, select the *How to Do Everything with HTML* option and you will be able to download the book files, which are linked together and organized as an offline "mini" Web site. For more on how to use the "mini" Web site, see Chapter 17.

| Use This Code For... | Look for This Filename |
|---|---|
| Bgsound sample | bgsound.htm |
| Embed sample | embed.htm |
| Object sample | object.htm |
| Twin video demo | twinvideos.htm |
| RealAudioLink page | realaudio.htm |
| Sample audio file (before processing) | realaudio1.wav |
| Sample audio file (after processing) | realaudio1.ra |
| Sample audio file | object.wav |
| Dynsrc demo | dynsrc.htm |
| Sample video file | videosample.avi |
| RealAudio ram file | realaudio.ram |
| Sample audio file | bgsound.wav |

11

# Chapter 12

## Make Your Pages Come Alive with GIF Animations

## How to...

- Animate Text with HTML
- Understand GIF Animation
- Create and Use GIF Animations
- Create a Streaming Slide Show
- Understand Vector Graphics and Flash
- Understand How to Use Animation

In about a decade, the World Wide Web has been swept by a whirlwind of change. Beginning with simple, hyperlinked text documents, it has seen the addition of graphics, sound, video, and more. The Web experience of the new millennium promises to be one of dynamic interactivity. Some of the most dramatic additions have been in the area of animation.

Animation can bring a vitality to your site that is impossible to achieve with static images. Better yet, adding animation to your site is easy—much easier than you might expect. Be careful, though, because with Web animation it is very easy to cross the line from interesting to annoying.

# Create Animation with HTML

As you'll discover in this chapter, most Web animation techniques involve special software for creating, and sometimes for viewing, the animation. However, there are a few ways you can create some simple animation with HTML alone. Keep in mind, though, that the term "animation" is applied very loosely here. Basically, it involves moving text around, making it blink, and causing it to change color. Another problem with these HTML techniques is that, as you'll see, cross-browser support for them is weak. But they are fun to play with and provide a nice introduction to Web animation. Just don't become too dependent on them.

## Create a Scrolling Marquee

A very simple way to add animation to a Web page is with the <marquee> </marquee> element. Any text enclosed inside this element will scroll across the page, much the same way as a bar of text will move across your TV screen when the station wants to pass on some news without breaking into a program. The <marquee> element's greatest disadvantage is that it is proprietary (not part of the HTML specification) developed by Internet Explorer. Only IE browsers support this element.

## Use <marquee> to Make Text Scroll

Create a blank HTML page by opening template.htm and saving it as marquee.htm; then add the following line in the <body> </body> portion of the page:

```
<p><marquee>Welcome to my Web Site!</marquee></p>.
```

Save the page and view it with Internet Explorer. Your welcome line should be scrolling across the top of the page in an endless loop. Now, if you have Netscape or Opera on your computer, try viewing the page in either one or both. Those browsers will ignore the <marquee> element entirely and display the text as if it were a simple paragraph.

NOTE    *While you probably are familiar with Netscape, you may not have heard of Opera. Opera is a nicely designed Web browser that is known for its speed in downloading pages. Although it used to cost around $40, it is now advertiser-supported freeware. If you're looking for an alternative to Internet Explorer and Netscape, you might want to download Opera and try it on your system. Their Web address is www.opera.com.*

12

## Modify the Marquee with Attributes

If you watch the marquee.htm page on IE very long, you probably will notice some eyestrain as you try to focus on the small moving letters. You'll probably also notice that your marquee's movements seem jerky. Most important, an endlessly looping string of text can become distracting to the point of being irritating. However, there are some attributes that will alter a marquee's appearance and behavior:

- **behavior=" "**   This attribute enables you to tell the browser how to scroll your text. "Scroll" (the default value) allows the text to scroll endlessly. "Slide" will bring the text in from either the left or right side of the screen and slide it to the opposite margin. "Alternate" will keep the text moving between the left and right margins (as if it were bouncing off both sides).

- **loop=" "**   You can use this attribute to determine how many times you want the text to scroll, slide, or alternate. "Infinite" (the default value) keeps the text moving indefinitely. A numerical value will cause the action to be performed for that number of times. For instance, loop="10" will scroll the message ten times.

- **direction=" "**   With this attribute you can choose the direction in which your text will move. The values are "left" and "right."

- **scrollamount=" "**   If the motion of the scrolling text seems too jerky, you can use scrollamount to smooth it out. Add a numerical value to represent the number of pixels you want the text to move each time. For example, scrollamount="2" will move the text a distance of two pixels each time it moves.

- **scrolldelay=" "**   The scrolldelay attribute also can be used to control the movement of the text, this time by delaying each separate movement for a specified period of time. The values for this attribute must be in milliseconds; thus, a delay of 100 milliseconds would be equivalent to one tenth of a second.

Some other attributes that can be used to modify the size and positioning of the marquee are height=" " (height of the marquee in pixels), width=" " (width of the marquee in pixels), hspace=" " (adds space on the sides of the marquee), vspace=" " (adds space above and below the marquee), and bgcolor=" " (enables you to specify a background color for the marquee).

To modify the appearance and behavior of the simple marquee created in the previous example, try the following steps:

1. Set the marquee's background color to red:

   ```
   <marquee bgcolor="#ff0000">
   ```

NOTE   *#ff0000 is the hexadecimal code for the color red. For more on color and hex codes, see Chapter 4.*

2. Change the direction so the text scrolls from left to right:

   ```
   <marquee bgcolor="#ff0000" direction="right">
   ```

3. Let's slow down the motion of the text so it's not so hard on your visitors' eyes:

```
<marquee bgcolor="#ff0000" direction="right"
scrolldelay="100" scrollamount="2">
```

4. To reduce the annoyance factor, set the text to scroll across the window and stop at the opposite side:

```
<marquee bgcolor="#ff0000" direction="right"
scrolldelay="100" scrollamount="2"
behavior="slide">
```

5. Just for fun, let's throw in a little style with CSS:

```
<marquee bgcolor="#ff0000" direction="right"
scrolldelay="100" scrollamount="2"
behavior="slide" style="color: white;
font-family: arial; font-size: 24pt;">
```

6. Save the page as marquee2.htm and view it in Internet Explorer. Your finished marquee should resemble this:

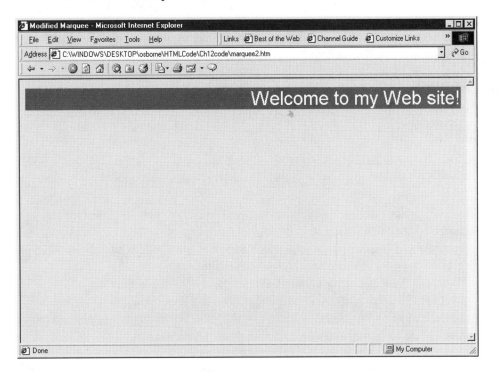

For a good example of why you must be careful with using <marquee>, try displaying the page in Netscape or Opera. Because neither browser supports the <marquee> element, all you will see is a line of plain text.

Why bother learning about <marquee> if the browser support is so weak? First, if it's tastefully used, you can use it to create a nice animation effect that a fair portion of visitors to your Web site will see. Second, it's a good way to learn about how irritating animation can be if it is just carelessly thrown in. To see for yourself, go back into your code for marquee2.htm and change the value in the behavior attribute to either scroll or alternate. You also might want to remove the scrollamount and scrolldelay attributes, allowing the text to scroll at its default speed; then load the page in IE and watch it for a while. It shouldn't take very long before you are ready to leave the page behind.

If you think that an endlessly scrolling line of text is irritating, you haven't seen anything until you've seen what results from Netscape's infamous <blink> element.

## Create Blinking Text

Internet Explorer has not cornered the market on potentially obnoxious animation effects. In fact, Netscape's <blink> element has a worse reputation than <marquee> could ever have hoped for. Pick up any number of books on Web design and you'll find authors virtually pleading with you to never use the <blink> element for the rest of your natural life. Do you wonder why?

### Add Blinking Text with Netscape's <blink> </blink> Element

Try adding the following line to the marquee2.htm page just below the line for your scrolling marquee:

```
<p style="font-size: 24pt;">This is a sample of
<blink style="color: red;">red, blinking text.</blink>
```

Save the page as blink.htm and view it in your browser. You will need to use Netscape to see the blinking text, as neither IE or Opera support the blink element. As with the previous example, just watch the page for a little while if you want to get a feel for how annoying constantly blinking text can be.

Whereas the <marquee> element at least can be modified to make it less objectionable, <blink> takes no attributes. The only thing you can do with it is make the text blink on and off—endlessly. Are you beginning to understand why so many Web authoring and design books preach against using it?

### Add Blinking Text with CSS

Despite the <blink> element's capability to irritate most Web surfers, for some reason the capability to create blinking text was included in the CSS specification. So, instead of using <blink> to create the effect, you can write a style rule that will do it. To see it work, add the following line to blink.htm:

```
<p style="text-decoration: blink; color:blue;
font-size: 24pt;">
This is a sample of blue blinking text,
done with CSS</p>
```

However, even using CSS you will not find much more browser support. Internet Explorer does not support blinking text in either CSS or with the <blink> element, although Opera does.

# Create and Use GIF Animation

The techniques outlined in the previous section show how to create some simple blinking and scrolling effects with HTML. However, the animation workhorse of the Web is, at least at present, GIF animation. If you read Chapter 6, you already know that GIF stands for Graphics Interchange Format, a graphics format developed by CompuServe. As you might expect, GIF animations are simply a collection of GIF images organized in successive frames and combined into what appears to be a single, animated image.

## Understand GIF Animation Tools

GIF animations are easy to create and, if properly optimized, can be fairly small files. However, to create GIF animations you do need graphics software capable of creating GIF images and animation software to assemble the animation. For suggestions on graphics software, see Chapter 6. Table 12-1 provides a list of a few of the possible software choices for creating animations. As you can see, most of these programs are in the $30–$40 range and can be downloaded as free demos.

| Program | Publisher's Web Site | Approximate Cost |
|---|---|---|
| CoffeeCup GIF Animator | www.coffeecup.com | $30 |
| Ulead GIF Animator | www.ulead.com | $40 |
| Animagic GIF Animator | www.rtlsoft.com | $30 |

TABLE 12-1     Animation Software Choices

| Program | Publisher's Web Site | Approximate Cost |
|---|---|---|
| GIF Movie Gear | www.gamani.com | $40 |
| Jasc Animation Shop (Also comes bundled with PaintShop Pro) | www.jasc.com | $50 |

**TABLE 12-1**    Animation Software Choices *(continued)*

There are three basic steps to making your own GIF animations. First, you must use a graphics editor to create the individual pictures' frames that will make up your animation. Second, use animation software to assemble the animation. Finally, you must optimize the animation. By optimizing, you reduce the file size as much as possible so it doesn't take too long for the animation to load onto your visitor's computer. Once the animation has been created, you insert it in your Web page just as you would any other image.

## Create Frames for an Animated Banner

The types of animations you could create are limited only by your imagination. However, on the Web GIF animations most frequently are used for banners, buttons, icons, animated links, and so on. Although it is beyond the scope of this book to explore the details of how each of these might be created, it will be helpful for you to work through the steps of creating at least one animation. For this exercise, you will create an animated banner. You will need to use a graphics editor capable of saving in the .GIF format. If you want to create the banner as you work through the chapter, you should download a .GIF program (see Table 12-1). CoffeeCup GIF Animator is the program used later in this chapter.

To create an animated banner, follow these steps:

1. Start with a banner-sized blank frame. Open your graphics program and create a blank document that is 468 pixels long by 60 pixels high. Save the blank banner as banneranim.gif. It should look like the following example:

TIP *The standard banner size for use on the Web is 468×60 pixels. If you plan to create banners for exchanges and advertising, always use these dimensions unless instructed otherwise.*

**2.** Select File | New, and create another image with properties and dimensions identical to the first. (or choose Edit | Copy, and then paste a new picture). A second blank frame identical to the first should appear on the screen.

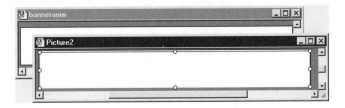

**3.** Use a text tool (generally represented as a capital letter on the image editor's toolbar) to add some text to your second frame. Click the Text tool for a Text Entry window to come up. Choose a font and color, set it at 26 points, and type **Come**. Your text should appear inside the banner (with some programs you might have to position the text). Save the image as banneranim1.gif. The following illustration shows what your second frame might look like:

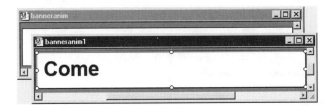

TIP *To change text color in PaintShop Pro, click inside the large square to the right of the two smaller rectangles. In Microsoft Photo Draw, select the Fill option from the Text dialog box.*

**4.** Repeat the preceding process, this time copying your second banner and pasting it as a new image. You now should have three banner frames in your window.

SHORTCUT *Using PaintShop Pro you can copy and paste as a new image simply by clicking on the toolbar's copy button and then on the paste button.*

12

5. Using the text tool add the word "visit" to your third banner frame. Position it and save this frame as banneranim2.gif. You've created three frames so far.

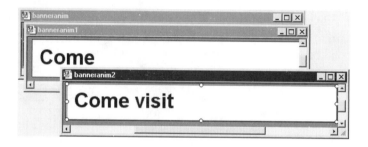

6. Create another frame by copying and pasting banneranim2.gif as a new image. Use the Text tool to add these words: **Mywebsite.com**. Once you have positioned the text, save the image as banneranim3.gif. You now should have four frames, each adding to the previous one.

7. Now, to add a little color, copy and paste banneranim2.gif (the next to the last) as a new image. Select the text tool and click inside the banner. When the text entry box appears, change the color of Mywebsite.com. Depending on your graphics program, you might not have to retype the text. Be careful to position the text in exactly the same place as in banneranim3.gif. Remember to use the Zoom and Grid features of your image editor to help you position the letters accurately. If you don't, the letters will appear to

move when the animation runs. While you may want that for some animations, for this one you simply want the text to appear to be changing color.

You have created the frames that will become your animation. Although this is a fairly simple animation, you could make it more complex by adding more frames. For instance, you could have it spell the message out letter by letter, or you could use a series of pictures, and so on. Keep in mind, though, that the more frames you add, the larger your final file size will be. That will make your animation take longer to load and slow the overall process of page loading. As you'll see later, there are steps you can take to optimize your file; but first you must create the animation.

## Create a GIF Animation

You have created the raw materials for your animation, but now you need a way to combine and play them. A low-cost GIF animator will do the job nicely and requires very little expertise on your part. The animation in the following illustrations was created with CoffeeCup Software's GIF Animator, but you can just as easily use a program listed in Table 12-1.

NOTE    *Most of the software mentioned in this chapter can be downloaded as shareware or as trial versions.*

12

CoffeeCup's GIF Animator gets you up and running quickly with an Animation Wizard. Select File | New to bring up the wizard; then follow these steps:

1. Use the size of the first animation. This will automatically set the frame size of all the images to match the first one.

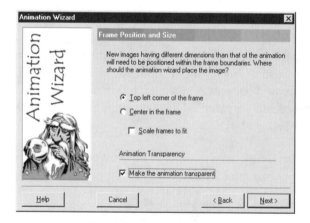

2. The second box will offer a choice of either a Transparent or Opaque background. Select, Make the Animation Transparent.

3. This box also deals with options that are necessary if you are using frames of different sizes and dimensions. Because all the frames in this animation have the same dimensions and are identical in size, you don't need to make any adjustments. Accept the default options by clicking Next.

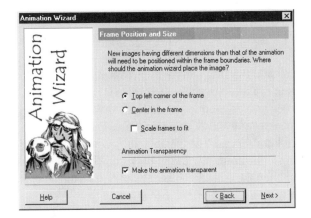

4.  The next dialog box contains two very important options. First, you can either allow the animation to loop indefinitely or set it to run for a certain number of loops. As with the <blink> element, an endlessly looping animation can become very distracting, particularly if the person who is visiting your site plans to stay there a while. Set the animation to loop about five times and stop. Its purpose is to draw attention to the banner; several cycles should do it. Of course, there might be times when a continuous animation is warranted—but be sure it's necessary before you do it. The second option is for determining the amount of time between frames. The number you choose here should depend largely on the kind of animation you are trying to achieve. If you are doing a cartoon-type animation and you want to create the illusion of movement, you must use more frames and rotate them fairly quickly. For the kind of animation you are doing here, slower is better. Set the animation for 25 (one fourth of a second). Click Next to move to the next dialog box.

**12**

TIP    *A motion picture runs at 24 frames per second (fps). Video moves at about 30 frames per second. For the Web, 15 fps is plenty fast.*

5. Now you can add the files for your animation. Click Add Image in the dialog box and open the directory where you saved the frames you created earlier. Click the files you created in the order you want them to appear. You can insert the files as many times as you want. For example, banneranim3 and banneranim4 are repeated at the end, followed by the original blank frame. This will cause the color to change back and forth on the "Mywebsite" letters a few times; then the frame will blank out before the animation begins again. Click Next to move to the next dialog box.

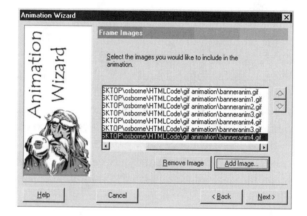

6. Once the files are added, click Finish; the program will assemble the animation for you. It will display in a small window in which you can view your animation frame by frame. There also is a button on the toolbar that will enable you to play the animation.

When you push the Play Animation button on the toolbar, the program will play back your animation. You can make adjustments, add new frames, and so on, working with the animation until it is exactly what you want. If you prefer an even more automated approach, a program such as Microsoft's PhotoDraw enables you to create an animation by merely creating a single image. Then, when you choose the GIF Animation option, you are given a number of options to choose from. As the following illustration shows, you can create some pretty sophisticated effects with these programs.

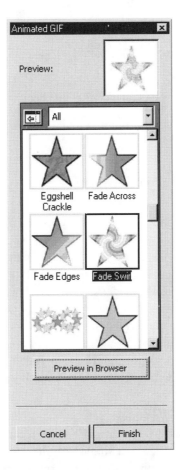

12

NOTE    *Remember that when you add special effects you are adding more frames to the animation, thus increasing the file size and download time.*

After you select your special effect, PhotoDraw gives you the option of previewing it in your browser. Select the Preview in Browser option in the GIF Animation dialog box, and you will see a sample of your animation displayed. For the animation created with CoffeeCup's GIF Animator, you can preview it in the software itself. The following illustration shows the animated banner "running" in CoffeeCup's GIF Animator:

After you have viewed your animation and are satisfied with it, you are ready to optimize and save it.

## Optimize Your GIF Animation

Animations can quickly become very large. Consider the sample animation you just built. Although you created only five frames, you added some of them more than once. What if you wanted to create a really sophisticated animation that displayed 15 different frames per second? For a 5-second animation, your final count would then be a whopping 75 frames. That might not sound like much until you remember that that means there are 75 GIF images making up that single animation. Can you imagine adding almost seventy separate pictures on one Web page? That's basically what you are doing. Those pictures take time to download before they ever display. If you plan to use detailed animations, and you want your visitors to hang around long enough to watch them, they'd better be pretty breathtaking. However, you can speed things up by taking the time to optimize your animation.

### Understand Optimization

Many of the techniques used to optimize GIF animations are the same as what you would use to reduce the size of a single GIF image. Of course, there are some others that are unique to GIF animations. When optimizing your animation you might consider some of the following adjustments:

■ **Reduce the number of frames.** This perhaps is the simplest solution for reducing file size.

■ **Reduce the size of the animation frames**    For something with a specified size, such as a banner, this isn't always an option. However, if you can make the actual frames smaller, they will load faster.

■ **Reduce the number of different colors**    The greater the color depth in your images, the bigger the file. Use as few colors as possible without degrading the quality of your image.

■ **Turn off antialiasing when you create the images**    Antialiasing is the way graphics programs smooth out the choppy look that occurs when pixels are used to display letters and other curved lines. It results in a better look but takes up more space. If you can get away with it and still have a good-looking image, turn this option off.

## Use an Optimization Wizard

In addition to the previous steps, you can further optimize your animations by taking advantage of your animation software's optimization wizard. The software can further reduce your file sizes by using some advanced compression options. For example, to optimize the animation created earlier with CoffeeCup's GIF Animator, follow these steps:

1.  With the animation file still open, select Tools, Optimize Animation. In the opening dialog box, select the Replace Current Animation with Optimized Version check box. These check boxes allow you to choose whether to create an entirely new animation or merely optimize the one you just created. Unless you have a particular reason for saving your original animation, go ahead and replace it, and then click Next.

**12**

2.  You will see another dialog box that asks you what you want to do with the color palettes for the animation. Choose the first two options: Sort Palettes and Remove Unused Entries and Optimize All Palettes (Global and Local) This will optimize your colors. (See Chapter 6 for more about color depth in images.) Click Next to continue.

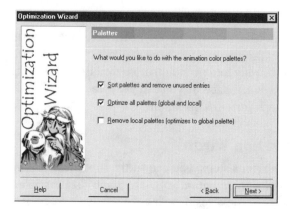

3.  This box prompts you to optimize the frames by removing any unnecessary parts. Select at least the first two options, and then click Next.

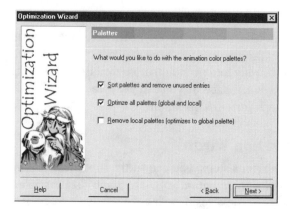

The final box will show you how much your file has "shrunk" since you began optimizing, plus an estimate of how long it will take to download. If you think the download time is too long, you can run the Optimization Wizard again and try to further reduce the size of the file. Otherwise, click Finish and save the file as animation1.gif.

Once your animated banner is complete, you are ready to try it out on a Web page to see how it works.

SHORTCUT *If you want to save time creating banners, Jasc's Animation Shop has a banner wizard that enables you to create simple banners with nice effects much more quickly.*

## Display Your Animation on a Web Page

Although creating an animation can be a time-consuming process, adding one to your Web page is simple. You treat it just as you would any other image. In fact, it is even saved with the same .GIF extension as a static image. To display your animation on a Web page follow these steps:

**1.** Open template.htm and save it as animation.htm.

**2.** In the <body> </body> portion of the page, add these lines:

```
<center>
<img src="animation1.gif"  />
</center>
```

**3.** Modify the opening <body> tag to change the background color to white:

```
<body bgcolor="white">
```

NOTE *You could also have specified the color as bgcolor="#ffffff".*

Your finished code should resemble the following:

```
<html>
<head>
      <title>Gif Animation</title>
</head>
<body bgcolor="white">
<center>
<img src="animation1.gif" />
</center>
</body>
</html>
```

Save the page and open it in your browser. It should look like the following Web page illustration:

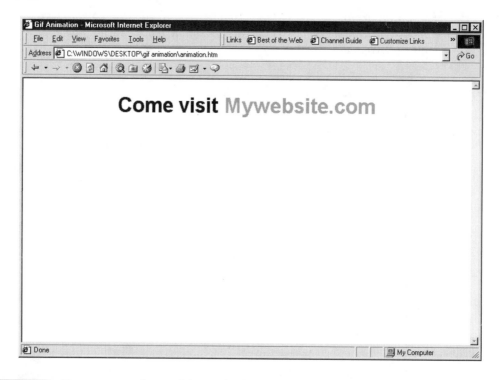

TIP     *Because you chose white as the background color for both the page and the banner, the banner disappears and the text appears to be part of the Web page. This is a nice trick for giving text a dynamic feel.*

# Additional Animation Options

Although GIF animations certainly are the most frequently used on the Web, there are other ways to liven up your page that go far beyond GIF's capabilities. For instance, say you want to create a slide show that uses JPEG images of your family photo album. Or perhaps you're a realtor and would like a page that displays pictures of some of the houses you're selling. Although creating GIF animations can be fun (sort of like making flip books when you were a kid), there are other ways to liven up your page. Maybe you don't want to go to the trouble of creating your own animations. Can you download animations to use on your Web site. For instance, you might be wondering if you can create an animation using JPEG images. One of the most exciting programs, Real Networks' Real Slide Show, makes use of streaming media to enable you to create beautiful slide shows.

## Consider a Streaming Slide Show

Have you ever seen a slide show where multiple projectors were used, and the images "dissolved" from one to the next? You can create that kind of effect with Real Networks' Real Slideshow. This program uses the same streaming media technology that was covered in Chapter 11. However, instead of using an audio or video file, you simply drag images into a slide show "storyboard" and the software automatically imports them. You can add background music and narration, change the transition time between slides, control how long each slide displays, and more. How is this useful? If you are constructing a "family album" site, you could create a slide show that enables your visitors to see all your slides presented as if you were sitting right there with them You can even add your own narration. What if you are a real-estate agent and want to display some choice homes for sale on your Web site? This program is perfectly suited for creating that kind of display.

**12**

TIP *You can download RealSlideshow at www.real.com/slideshow. RealSlideshow is a freeware program. However, if you want to add titles and captions, you'll have to purchase the full version: RealSlideshow Plus.*

The advantages to this kind of approach are that you are placing the "animation" at the discretion of your visitors. They can choose whether they want to watch your slide show or not. One of the biggest problems with GIF animations is that they are usually set to loop endlessly, and can become quite annoying. A slide show is a much more tasteful approach to adding some life to your page. Another advantage of using streaming media for animation effects is that you can use JPEG images. Obviously, GIF animations have that name for a reason: you can only animate GIF images. JPEG doesn't support animation. A slide show program enables you to at least create an animated effect with JPEGs, if not a true animation. However, if you really want to animate photographs, there is a way to do it.

After you download and install a copy of Real Slideshow, follow these simple steps to creating your first streaming slide show:

1. Click on File | New Project. Real Slideshow will open as a storyboard with a line for images, a timeline, voice, and music tracks.

2. Add imges to the slide show by clicking on File | Add images. A dialog box will open, displaying a directory for your computer along with a preview window. Select the image you want to add, and click Open. Add as many images as you want by repeating this process.

SHORTCUT    *You also can drag and drop image files directly onto the storyboard where it says, Drag Images Here to Start.*

3. Once you have added your images, you should see a thumbnail version of each one displayed on the storyboard. To increase or decrease the time each slide displays, place your cursor on the left side of the thumbnail you want to modify and drag it horizontally to either shorten or lengthen it. To modify the overall time for the show, click the plus and minus buttons on the timeline.

4. You can add a soundtrack either by recording your own audio files (see Chapter 11), using a prerecorded file, ore even a CD. Click File, add Background Music for a dialog box that will enable you to add sound to your slide show.

5. The final step is clicking the Generate button. This will instruct the software to create your slide show. When it has finished, Real Slideshow will display a box with a list of the files it created. The program even provides a wizard that will upload your finished slide show to your Web server. If you are in need of a server that supports streaming media, the wizard suggests some servers that offer free hosting and streaming media support.

## Understand JPEG Animation

Even though the JPEG format does not support animation, it is possible to work around that problem by using a *Java applet*. A Java applet is a "mini" program that can be embedded into your Web page, enabling your page to perform tasks impossible with just HTML. Adding a Java applet to your page is easy, and you don't need to be a programmer to do it. You just need to know the proper HTML code for setting up the applet you need, and even that is supplied for you. All you have to do is supply the file names for the images you want to "animate," along with the amount of time you want each to display. The applet takes it from there. (For more on how to use Java applets, see Chapter 15 and Appendix B).

You can download the from the Boutell.com web site. The JpegAnim applet was developed by Boutell and is free for use on any Web site. Boutell requests (but does not require) that you put a link back to their site if you use the applet. You can find full instructions for downloading and configuring the applet for your page at Boutell.com's Web site: http://www.boutell.com/JpegAnim.

## Use Downloadable GIF Animations

Suppose you want to use some GIF animations on your site, but you have neither the time nor the inclination to do your own? What then? Are you left out in the cold with a static, "immobile" Web site? Not in the least. As with almost any other Web resource out there, you can find a host of animated GIFs (many of them free-of charge) just waiting for you to download them and insert them on your page. Table 12-2 provides a list of just some of the sites where you can find ready-to-use animations.

12

| Resource | URL |
|---|---|
| Ulead Systems Web Utilities | http://www.webutilities.com/gif_ani |
| Espresso Graphics | http://www.espressographics.com/gif |
| Club Unlimited Animated GIFs | http://www.clubunlimited.com |
| GifsNow.com | http://www.gifsnow.com |
| Global Presence Animation Creations | http://www.animationcreation.com |
| Animation City | http://www.animationcity.com |
| GIF Animation on the WWW | http://members.aol.com/royalef/gifanim.htm |

**TABLE 12-2**    Sources for GIF Animations

NOTE

*If you visit some of the sites mentioned in the preceding tables you'll notice that GIF animations are sometimes referred to as GIF89a animations. This refers to the "version" of the GIF format that supports animation. An earlier version, GIF87a, did not support animation.*

As good as GIF animations can be, at their best they still leave something to be desired. They are necessarily small and limited in scope. If you find that GIF and JPEG animations seem to choppy or simplistic for your tastes, and you desire something "flashier," scalable vector graphics (SVG) is what you want to explore.

## Understand SVG Animation

Although you might never have heard of vector graphics animation, if you've spent any time on the Internet recently, you've undoubtedly seen it. When you load a Web page and a smooth, professional-looking graphical animation greets you—and you feel as if you're watching a movie or TV program—you've probably just come face to face with a vector graphics animation. The best known of these are Macromedia® Shockwave and Flash™ animations.

Macromedia® Shockwave and its somewhat less complex sibling Flash are too complex to deal with in detail here. Also, the software is a bit pricey for the casual user (more than $300 for Flash). Macromedia® Director, which produces Shockwave files, is considerably more expensive. What makes Flash appealing is its ability to create very sophisticated animation yet maintain a reasonably small file size. The disadvantage to Flash is that a visitor to your site would need to have the Flash plug-in installed to see the graphics.

If you are interested in experimenting with Flash animation, you can download a fully functional demonstration copy from Macromedia's site: www.macromedia.com.

### Did you know?

## Vector Graphics

Vector graphics are to other graphic files what MIDI is to other audio files. MIDI files are not recordings of music but mathematical descriptions of music. Likewise, vector graphics do not draw a picture by means of mapping out pixels, as other types of graphic files do. Instead, a program such as Macromedia Flash™ creates the graphics by describing them mathematically.

The software comes with a built-in tutorial that will get you up and running quickly. Soon you'll not only be able to create dramatic graphics such as those in the following illustration; you'll be able to animate them.

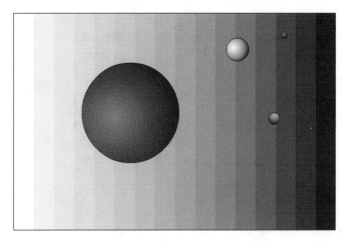

# Learn Good Web Design

In this chapter you have learned how to create several different types of animations and add them to your Web pages. The question remains: Should you? When you decide to use animation in a Web page, you stroll the very thin line between making your site attractive and making it gaudy.

## Web Design Principle: Keep the Irritation Factor in Mind

There are certain givens about human beings. One of them is that people tend to be irritated by things that repeat endlessly. Think of that dripping faucet in the kitchen or the too-loud ticking of the clock on your wall. How about a neon light right outside your bedroom window, blinking on and off all night? What about your neighbor's dog, which has been barking incessantly since two in the morning? Do you get the idea?

There is nothing more irritating than visiting a Web site that is loaded down with images that are constantly blinking, flashing, changing colors, or scooting about the page. It's like trying to read a book with 20 people shouting in your face. Eventually you say, "Enough already. I'm outta here."

That's generally what visitors will say to a Web site whose designer is in love with animation. There's nothing wrong with animation—just keep the irritation

12

factor in mind when you use it. You can do that by remembering some of these principles:

- Limit your animations drastically. The purpose of animation is to attract the visitor's attention. If you have 10 or 15 different animated GIFs on each page, all you'll succeed in doing is driving your visitor crazy.

- Don't allow animations to loop endlessly. When you create them set them to run about four, maybe five, times. That should be enough to draw a Web surfer's attention.

- If you want to use <marquee>, use it with the slide value. That will allow your text to slide onto the page, making a nice entrance without making people feel as if they're staring at a theater marquee.

- Please don't use the <blink> element for the duration of your natural life.

## Practice, Practice, Practice

Keeping the preceding principles in mind, try creating a few tasteful and creative animations on your own. Use one of the GIF animation programs and experiment with the different special effects you can add. For example, try making a splash page for your site that builds letter by letter; then have the letters change to a different color and fade out, replaced by a logo or a picture. Add the following line inside the <head> </head> portion to redirect the browser to your main page after ten seconds:

```
<meta http-equiv="refresh"
content="10; url=nextpage.htm" />
```

When you load your splash page, your animation will run and you will be automatically redirected to the nextpage.htm that you list in the meta refresh attribute.

NOTE *A splash page is an introductory page that functions something like a book cover. It tends to be more artistic in nature and then gives way to the site's main or index page, which is really the site's home page. Many splash pages use sophisticated animation to act as a welcome mat to the Web site.*

# Find the Code Online

To find the code online for this or any of the chapters in this book, go to Osborne's Web site, www.osborne.com, and click the Free Code choice on the navigation bar. From the list of books, select the *How to Do Everything with HTML* option and you will be able to download the book files, which are linked together and organized as an offline "mini" Web site. For more on how to use the "mini" Web site, see Chapter 17.

| Use This Code For... | Look for This Filename |
| --- | --- |
| Marquee sample | marquee.htm |
| Blinking sample | blink.htm |
| Animation frame 2 | banneranim1.gif |
| Animation frame 4 | banneranim3.gif |
| Slideshow Web page | sampleslideshow.htm |
| Slideshow Realpix clip | sampleslideshow.rp |
| Slideshow file | sampleslideshow.smi |
| Pittsburgh photo | sampleslideshow-bigpitts.jpg |
| Baby picture | sampleslideshow-charlene1.jpg |
| Little boy with pickle | sampleslideshow-cjpickle.jpg |
| Modified marquee | marquee2.htm |
| Animation frame 1 | banneranim.gif |
| Animation frame 3 | banneranim2.gif |
| Animate banner | animation1.gif |
| Slideshow ram file | sampleslideshow.ram |
| Slideshow RealText clip | sampleslideshow.rt |
| Slideshow project file | slideshowsample.rpj |
| Cat photo | sampleslideshow-boo.jpg |
| Little boy with chalk | sampleslideshow-cjchalk.jpg |

12

# Chapter 13

# All About Image Maps

## How to...

■ Understand Image Maps

■ Map Different Shapes

■ Create a Client-Side Image Map

■ Create an Image Map with Mapping Software

Have you ever visited a Web page and found—rather than a series of link buttons—a picture or some other type of graphic that served as a navigation tool? Maybe it was a map of the United States or perhaps it looked like a bookshelf. Whenever you clicked on a different part of the image it took you to a different page. You were navigating by means of an *image map*. Image mapping is another Web design technique that looks difficult but is really easy—once you know how to do it.

# Understand Image Maps

What exactly is an *image map?* It is a single image or graphic that has had portions mapped out and identified in your HTML code. The mapped portions, sometimes known as *hot spots,* are linked to other Web pages. When visitors to your site click on different parts of the graphic, they will be taken to different places depending on where they clicked. With careful planning, an image map can add a professional look to your Web site.

## Understand Image Mapping Terms

Creating an image map is not difficult, although it can become complex depending on how you are designing it. However, you will find it helpful to understand some of the basic terminology behind image maps. Key terms to keep in mind as you work with an image map are as follows:

■ **Server-side image maps**   A server-side image map resides and operates on your Web host. You create the map, but it actually is processed by the Web server. This kind of image map is somewhat complicated to create. Also, because the work is done on the server, it can be slower to respond.

■ **Client-side image maps**   A client-side image map resides and operates on your visitor's computer. You write the code for the map and include it in the HTML for your page. Client-side image maps are faster, reduce the load on the server, and are easier to create. This chapter will focus on creating client-side image maps.

■ **Hot spots**   A hot spot is a portion of an image that has been mapped and linked to another page. When visitors click on a hot spot they will be taken to the new page.

■ **Coordinates**   You use coordinates to map out the portions of your image that you want to turn into hot spots. The coordinates are simply numbers that are associated with the pixels used to create the image. Coordinates always begin at 0,0 at the upper-left corner of an image and increase in number toward the lower-right corner. (The horizontal coordinate comes first; vertical comes second.)

■ **Shapes**   You can map coordinates in three basic shapes: circles, rectangles, and polygons. Circles and rectangles are self-explanatory. Polygons include complex shapes that won't fit into the preceding definitions.

## Did you know?

# What Is the Difference Between a Client and Server?

Anytime you hear the term *client* in Web design it means the computer of the person who is visiting your site. The term *server* refers to the Web server that hosts your site. When an application (such as an image map or a script) is referred to as *server-side*, it is operating on your Web host's computer. A *client-side* application is downloaded with your Web page and uses the resources of your visitor's computer. Client-side applications tend to operate faster because information does not have to pass between your visitor's computer to the server and back again. Thus, they are generally the better choice for Web authors.

13

TIP

*If you're having trouble with the concept of coordinates, think of the game Battleship. There is a grid mapped out into squares with numbers along the vertical axis and letters along the horizontal axis. To fire at an opponent, you name a coordinate. For instance, A-5 would be the first line, five squares from the left. Image coordinates work the same way, except you use numbers for both horizontal and vertical. Coordinates of 47, 22 would represent a position on an image that is 47 pixels across from the upper-left corner and 22 pixels down from the top.*

## Understand Image Map Elements

As you might expect, there are special HTML elements for both server-side and client-side image maps. By becoming familiar with each of these elements you can demystify the process of creating your own image map. The image map elements are as follows:

- **\<map> \</map>**   Defines a client-side image map on your Web page.

- **\<area />**   Used for specifying the coordinates of hot spots in client-side image maps. You will use one \<area /> element for each hot spot on the image. Note that \<area /> is an empty element.

- **\<img />**   You will use the image element to specify the image you want to use for your image map.

## Understand Image Map Attributes

A number of different attributes come into play when you construct an image map. These will do everything from assigning a special name for your map to laying out the coordinates for your hot spots. The image map attributes are as follows:

- **ismap**   This attribute actually is used with server-side image maps. Even though this chapter does not discuss how to create server-side maps, as you will see later, the ismap attribute can prove useful in helping you identify the coordinates for your hotspots.

- **shape=" "**   The shape attribute is used with \<area /> and can take values of circle, rect (rectangle), and poly (polygon, the default). You use it to define the shape of your hot spots.

- **coords=" "**   The coordinates attribute is used within the \<area /> element to plot the coordinates for your hot spots. The values are the pixel numbers of the coordinates, separated by commas. Circles, rectangles, and polygons all are plotted differently, as will be demonstrated later in the chapter.

■ **name=" "** The name attribute works in the <map> element to assign a name by which browsers will recognize your map. You can choose whatever name you wish for your map. An easy-to-remember, descriptive term usually is the best choice. For example, for this chapter you will be working with a map named practicemap.

■ **usemap=" "** The usemap attribute is placed within the <img /> element and tells the browser which map to look for when applying the coordinates. The proper way to identify the map is with the name you created for it, preceded by a pound sign (#). For instance, if you were telling a browser to use the practicemap mentioned earlier, you would write **usemap="#practicemap"**.

# Create an Image Map

If you want to use an image map on your page, you have a number of options for creating it. There are quite a few different programs available that will create image maps for you and take care of writing all the necessary HTML code. These generally are inexpensive ($30–$50) and will speed up the process considerably. If you plan to do a lot of Web design and will be creating image maps frequently, undoubtedly these are the way to go. However, if you are doing only a few image maps and time isn't a problem, you might enjoy the process of creating it on your own.

## Choose an Image

Because image maps are used for navigation, it's important to choose or create your image with that in mind. For some reason, image maps seem to bring out the artistic side of Web authors. Although that is not a problem in itself, it can become a big problem if you are so artsy with your image map that visitors can't figure out your navigation scheme.

Yet it's not uncommon to find many sites whose authors have decided to use image-based navigation alone, allowing the visitors to figure out the system on their own. You can avoid this by choosing or creating an image that will provide a self-explanatory means of navigation. For instance, say you took a wonderful summer trip through four southern states—Texas, Oklahoma, Arkansas, and Louisiana—and you want to put together a Web site that displays stories and pictures from each state you visited. You could create a simple map of the four

states and make each state a separate hot spot on your image map, as in the
following illustration:

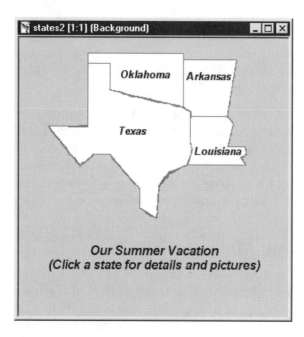

You can just as easily use a photograph for your image map. However, Because
a photo is not self-explanatory, you might want to use an image editor to add some
directions for your visitors as in the following illustration:

TIP    *You can use any image format that will work on a Web page.*
*Your primary choices are GIF, JPEG, and PNG images.*

## Find the Coordinates

The most time-consuming process of doing image maps is determining coordinates.
It's not hard; however, depending on how refined you want the hot spot to be, you
can find yourself sorting through a lot of numbers. The trick is keeping them
straight. The other challenge is figuring out the coordinates in the first place.

### Determine Coordinates with ISMAP

If you know the size of your image and don't care too much about accuracy, you
can always determine the coordinates for your hot spots by estimating them. As
a rule, though, you probably are going to want to be a little more precise when
creating an image map. Therefore, you need to have some way to determine the
exact coordinates of different spots on your image. The most common way of
doing this is with an image-editing program (see Chapter 6 for a list of available
software) or with image mapping software. However, if you don't want to invest
in either of these, there is a way to determine pixel coordinates by using your Web
browser by using the ismap attribute.

Ismap is used with server-side image maps, but it also can be used to tell your
browser to display an image's coordinates on the status bar at the bottom of the
screen. To do this you merely need to create an HTML page using the image you
want to plot as a link. It's not necessary for the link to actually point to a real Web
page. Include the ismap attribute to fool the browser into thinking the image is
linked to a server-side image map. The browser will display the image's coordinates
on the status bar.

Ismap should be included in the <img /> element, enclosed in a practice "link"
as follows:

```
<a href="nolink.htm"><img alt="Coordinate Shortcut"
src="practicemap.gif" ismap /></a>
```

NOTE    *The practice link does not need to really link to anything. It just needs*
*to be there.*

To see this work, try typing in the following code and saving it as
coordinatemap.htm. You can include any image file in the src=" " attribute.
The image file used for the following illustration is practicemap.gif, which can

13

be downloaded from Osborne's Web site. (See the table at the end of the chapter for instructions on how to find the file.)

When you have saved your page and displayed it in your browser, move your mouse cursor over the image. You should see a set of numbers in the status bar at the bottom of the page. Those numbers should change whenever you move the mouse over the image. They should disappear entirely if you move the cursor off the image. Notice in the following illustration that the status bar lists the coordinates where the cursor is pointing as 304, 313. That means the cursor is placed at a point that is 304 pixels from the left and 313 pixels down from the top.

NOTE     *ISMAP does not require a value. Its presence in the link is all that is needed.*

```
<html>
<head>
<title>Determining Coordinates with ISMAP</title>
</head>
<body>
<p style="font-size: 14pt; text-align: left;">This is a
trick for determining coordinates.</p><br />
<a href="nolink.htm"><img alt="Coordinate Shortcut"
src="practicemap.gif" ismap /></a>
</body>
</html>
```

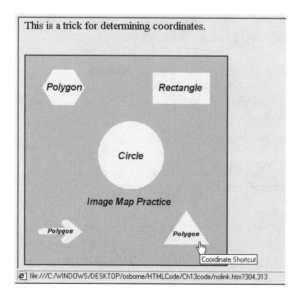

## Determine Coordinates with Image Editing Software

The most common way to determine pixel coordinates is with an image editor such as PaintShop Pro. All you have to do is open the image in the program, move the mouse over the image, and you will see the pixel coordinates displayed at the bottom of the screen. As with the preceding illustration, whenever you move the cursor the coordinate numbers will change. The following illustration shows what you should see when using an image editor:

# Plot Coordinates

Once you have a way of finding coordinates, the next step is to plot them. Plotting coordinates is simply the process of finding the key portions of your image that you want to turn into hot spots, determining their coordinates, and writing them down in a way that a Web browser can understand them. You will plot coordinates differently, depending on the kind of shape you are trying to map. With a rectangle you always go from upper left to lower right. For a circle you begin at the center. If you are mapping a complex shape, such as a polygon, you proceed in a clockwise direction, beginning from the upper left.

## Plot a Rectangle

The simplest shape to plot is a rectangle. You need to find only two sets of coordinates: the upper-left corner and the lower-right corner. Find these by putting the mouse cursor over the upper-left corner and noting the two numbers. For example, in Figure 13-1 (practicemap.gif) the coordinates for the upper-left corner of the rectangle are 221, 27. The coordinates for the lower-right corner are 320, 79.

13

> TIP
>
> *If you are using an image editor, you will find it much easier to be exact if you enlarge the image several times. The pixel count won't change and you'll greatly increase your accuracy with complex images.*

To plot this rectangle and turn it into a hot spot, you would write a line of code using the <area /> element along with the shape, coords, and href attributes, like this:

```
<area shape="rect" coords="221, 27, 320, 79"
href="rectangle.htm" />
```

The shape attribute tells the browser what kind of shape to look for. The coords attribute gives the location of the shape. Finally, the href attribute provides the link that makes the shape a hot spot. Be sure to separate your coordinates by commas.

> TIP
>
> *It is not necessary to use parentheses or brackets to combine the pairs of coordinates. The browser automatically takes them in pairs. However, you might find it easier to follow your own code if you add an extra space between pairs of coordinates. The browser will ignore the white space and you'll find it easier if you ever have to go back in and edit your code.*

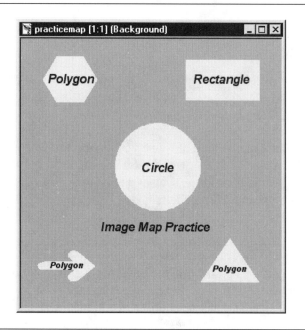

FIGURE 13-1　Practice image map

## Plot a Circle

Plotting a circle is a little different from plotting a rectangle. Instead of going to the upper-left corner of the circle (a difficult proposition, as there is no corner), you start by estimating the circle's center. You don't need to be perfectly precise here. Just get as close as you can. Again, you might find it easier to enlarge the image to help you make a better estimate. Once you've eyeballed the center of the circle, note the coordinates. The next number you give will not be a pair of coordinates, but rather the *radius* of the circle.

> **TIP**  *To find the radius of the circle, place the cursor on the left side of the circle, as near the middle as possible and note the horizontal (first) coordinate. Move the cursor to the right side. Watch the coordinates to make sure the vertical (second) coordinate does not change. Note the second horizontal coordinate. Subtract the smaller number from the larger, divide the result in half, and you will have the radius.*

Once you have determined the center coordinates and the radius, plot your circle like this (the first two numbers are the center; the third is the radius):

```
<area shape="circle" coords="184, 164,  57"
href="circle.htm" />
```

The coordinates in the preceding line are taken from the circle in the practicemap.htm image displayed in Figure 13-1. If you download this file from Osborne's Web site (www.osborne.com), you will be able to practice along with the text in this chapter.

## Plot Polygons

A polygon is any shape that requires multiple corners, angles, and points of reference. For example, a polygon could be something as obvious as the triangle or hexagon in Figure 13-1. It also would be the arrow in the same figure, the shapes of the four states in the vacation image, and even the outlines of the two children in the photo image map. These various shapes would be plotted as polygons (which is why it is the default value for the <area /> element).

To plot a polygon, use the upper-left corner as your starting point. If the image doesn't have a corner as such, choose the uppermost left point. Note the coordinates for that point and move clockwise to the next angle or corner. Also note those coordinates and proceed to the next angle until you have moved around the outside of the image and back to your starting point.

13

**Plot a Triangle** For example, to plot the triangle in Figure 13-1, begin at the top corner and note the coordinates: 281, 259. The coordinates for the bottom right corner are 320, 316, and those on the bottom left are 242, 316. Now, apply those coordinates into the <area /> element like this:

```
<area shape="poly" coords="281,259, 320,316, 242,316,"
href="triangle.htm" />
```

**Plot a Hexagon** The hexagon in the upper-left portion of Figure 13-1 presents a slightly more complex shape to plot. If you simply remember to start at the uppermost left corner and move clockwise from angle to angle, you'll find that it's not really any more difficult.

For the hexagon, beginning at the upper-left corner, the coordinates are displayed in this illustration:

To turn the hexagon into a hot spot, take the preceding coordinates and list them in order, moving clockwise, as in the following line of code:

```
<area shape="poly" coords="48,23, 85,23, 104,53,
85,83, 47,83, 29,53," href="hexagon.htm />
```

**Plot an Arrow Shape** The only shape yet to be plotted on practicemap.gif is the arrow in the bottom left of the picture. Even though this is the most complicated shape you've had to deal with in this chapter, by now you should find it very easy. You begin at the upper-left corner of the arrow and plot each angle in a clockwise direction. Just as you did with the other shapes, include them in the <area /> element. The coordinates in this code come reasonably close to defining the rounded edges of the arrow:

```
<area shape="poly" coords="70,275, 101,295, 74,315,
67,314, 72,300, 26,300, 22,294, 32,288, 70,288, 65,283"
href="arrow.htm" />
```

## How to ...  Keep Track of Coordinates

As you can see, the more complex the shape you are mapping, the larger the number of coordinates you have to deal with. How do you keep track of them if you are not using image-mapping software? The simplest means is to draw a simple sketch of the shape on a piece of paper and write the coordinates down as you plot them. Your sketch does not need to be a precision drawing, just a close approximation of the shape. Draw a short line to each corner or angle and write the coordinates down there. You will find it an easy reference if you lose your place when writing your HTML code.

CAUTION    *Be careful to not omit a comma—you can throw your whole scheme off.*

NOTE    *It is not necessary for your coordinates to be precise unless you want the clickable area to coincide exactly with the shape on the screen. The general principle is this: The more precisely you want the shape defined, the more coordinates you need. Generally, though, you'll do fine with fewer measurements.*

## Complete the Image Map

Now that the coordinates for practicemap.gif have been plotted, all you need to do to finish your image map is write the rest of the code for your page. Open template.htm, save it as imagemap.htm, and follow these steps to turn practicemap.gif into a functioning image map:

**1.** In the \<body\> section of the page, insert the \<map\> element.

```
<html>
<head><title>Practice Image Map</title></head>
<body>
<map> </map>
</body>
</html>
```

13

2. Modify the opening <map> tag by adding the name=" " attribute, with practicemap as the value.

```
<html>
<head><title>Practice Image Map</title></head>
<body>
<map name="practicemap"> </map>
</body>
</html>
```

3. Add the area elements you have already written. There should be one <area /> element for each shape you have defined, and they all should be nested inside the <map> </map> element.

```
<html>
<head><title>Practice Image Map</title></head>
<body>
<map name="practicemap">
<area shape="rect" coords="221, 27, 320, 79"
href="rectangle.htm" />
<area shape="circle" coords="184, 164,  57"
href="circle.htm" />
<area shape="poly" coords="281,259, 320,316, 242,316,"
href="triangle.htm" />
<area shape="poly" coords="48,23, 85,23, 104,53,
85,83, 47,83, 29,53," href="hexagon.htm />
<area shape="poly" coords="70,275, 101,295, 74,315,
67,314, 72,300, 26,300, 22,294, 32,288, 70,288, 65,283"
href="arrow.htm" />
</map>
</body>
</html>
```

4. Add the <img /> element to insert your map on the page. You also will insert the usemap=" " attribute with the name #practicemap so the browser will know the image is an image map.

```
<html>
<head><title>Practice Image Map</title></head>
<body>
<map name="practicemap">
```

```
<area shape="rect" coords="221, 27, 320, 79"
href="rectangle.htm" />
<area shape="circle" coords="184, 164,  57"
href="circle.htm" />
<area shape="poly" coords="281,259, 320,316, 242,316,"
href="triangle.htm" />
<area shape="poly" coords="48,23, 85,23, 104,53,
85,83, 47,83, 29,53," href="hexagon.htm />
<area shape="poly" coords="70,275, 101,295, 74,315,
67,314, 72,300, 26,300, 22,294, 32,288, 70,288, 65,283"
href="arrow.htm" />
</map>
<img src="practicemap.gif" alt="Practice Image Map"
usemap="#practicemap" />
</body>
</html>
```

**5.** To really see how the image map works, create five HTML pages and name
them rectangle.htm, circle.htm, triangle.htm, hexagon.htm, and arrow.htm.
Save them in the same directory as your imagemap.htm file.

Now load imagemap.htm into your Web browser and move your mouse over
each of the images. You'll notice that the status bar at the bottom of the browser
window changes as the cursor goes over each different shape. If you click on each
shape, it should take you to the page you created for that part of the image map.

# Understand Image-Mapping Software

13

Although it is possible to create an image map with nothing more than a Web
browser for plotting coordinates, it can be a time-consuming process, particularly
if you are mapping complex shapes. Just as HTML editors and WYSIWYG programs
can make creating Web pages easier, image mapping software can speed up the
process of creating image maps.

There are a number of different programs available; most are in the $20–$60
range. Although you might not feel like investing in an image-mapping program
for just a few images, if you plan to do a lot of Web design and work on multiple
sites, these can be great timesavers. Several of the most popular programs are

listed in Table 13-1, with the URL for the publisher and an approximate price. These programs are available as trial downloads.

Image-mapping software makes your job easier by allowing you to click on various portions of an image while the software plots the coordinates and writes the code for you. Some of the programs, such as MapEdit, are quite simple. Others are more complex and include the capability to add advanced features such as mouse rollovers and so on. To get a feel for working with image-mapping software, try downloading one of the sample programs in the preceding table and creating some complex image maps.

# Use Image-Mapping Software for Complex Tasks

Earlier in this chapter you saw how a simple line drawing of four states could be used as an image map. Because of the complex shapes involved, turning that image into an image map would be a tedious process. However, with a program such as MapEdit the job is greatly simplified.

You begin the process by creating your Web page and placing your images just as you normally would. Once your page design is complete, you open MapEdit and begin the process of converting the image into an image map. The software will bring up a dialog box asking you to open the page you want to work on; then

| Image-Mapping Program | Publisher Web Site | Approximate Price |
|---|---|---|
| Ulead Smart Saver Pro | www.ulead.com | $60 |
| CoffeeCup Image Mapper | www.coffeecup.com | $20 |
| MapEdit | www.boutell.com | $25 |
| CuteMap | www.globalscape.com | $20 |
| LiveImage | www.mediatec.com | $30 |

TABLE 13-1    Inexpensive Image-Mapping Software Choices

it will give you another box with a list of images on that page. You can choose whichever image you wish to map. After the image is selected, MapEdit will bring it up in a window, as in the following illustration:

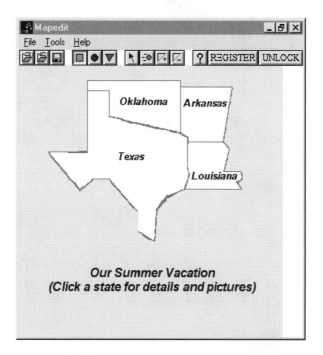

In the toolbar at the top you can choose from a rectangle, circle, or triangle (polygon) button. Once you have chosen the polygon, simply left-click around the borders of one state (in this case, Oklahoma). Click at each point where you want a set of coordinates fixed. Once you're finished, click the right mouse button and another dialog box will appear. This one gives you options for the URL you want to link to, for ALT text, advanced options for mouseovers, and so on.

13

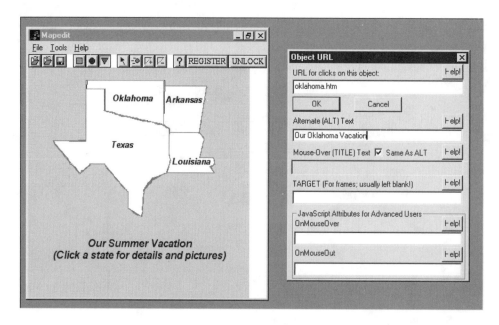

Once you have clicked around the borders of all four states, MapEdit allows you to test your hot spots by selecting the arrow tool. With this button selected, when you click a hot spot it will highlight it and bring up the dialog box you filled out for that spot. This gives you the opportunity to make any edits you need before you save the image map.

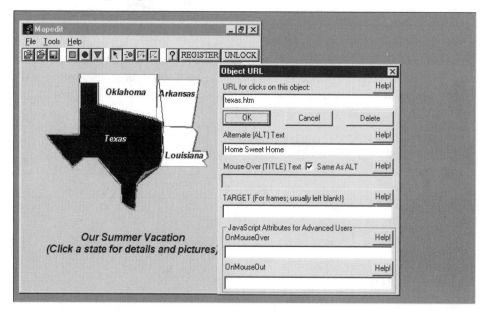

When you are satisfied with the map, links, and any other features you have added, simply click the Save button and MapEdit will write the HTML code that creates your image map. With complex shapes such as the ones in this illustration, you could easily spend a half-hour or more mapping out and plotting coordinates. The software reduces the time spent to about five minutes. The following Web page is the result of a very brief session with MapEdit.

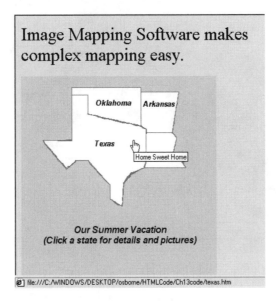

You might wonder why you should bother learning how to do image maps at all if it is so much easier with software. It's the same reason you should learn HTML even though you can create a Web page with a WYSIWYG program. You might just find it necessary to go in and fine-tune your Web pages. If you don't know how an image map works, you won't be able to "get under the hood" and work with it if you need to.

That's why some programs, such as CuteMap, display the code as the software creates it. You can see exactly what the software is doing and make adjustments on the fly if necessary. This makes it ideal for difficult images such as the two children. You can refine your image map and make it very precise with tools such as the following illustration.

**13**

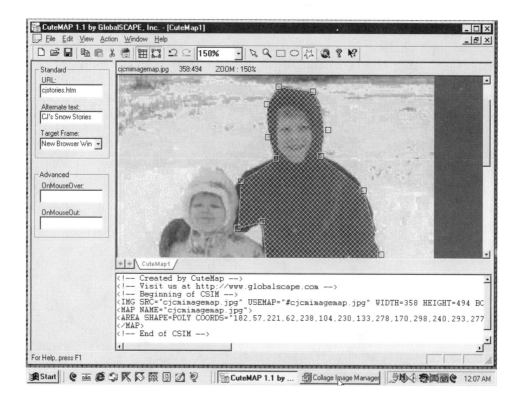

# Understand the Sliced Image Alternative

Although image maps can be fun to create and can give your site a professional look, you might not want to bother with them. If you are interested in having the same kind of look without the hassle of plotting coordinates, you might consider using a program that will slice a single image into several pieces and reassemble it into a seamless table. You then can make each part of the image into a link, just as you would any other kind of image link. For more on how to slice an image and reassemble it, see Chapter 6.

NOTE    *You can use an image editor to slice an image into pieces, but it's more difficult to achieve precise results when the image is reassembled. It actually can take you more time to do this yourself than if you had done an image map the conventional way. If you are inclined to slice your images, you would be well advised to use a program such as CoffeeCup Image Slicer (www.coffeecup.com). A sample can be downloaded along with the CoffeeCup HTML Editor as a 30-day free trial. This software will do the work and produce much better results in less time.*

# Learn Good Web Design

Image maps are fun to create and can give you a real feeling of accomplishment the first time you see them working on your Web site. However, that feeling of accomplishment should not be allowed to cloud some of the problems that come along with image maps.

## Web Design Principle: Navigation Aids Must Aid Navigation

If you plan to use image maps, please make them clear and understandable. Your visitors should not have to waste their time figuring out where your links will take them—or if they are even there. The Web designer and author Vincent Flanders calls this obscure kind of navigation "mystery meat navigation." His point is well taken. Don't be guilty of mystifying your visitors and making them feel like they must figure your navigation system out before they can find their way around. Keep some of the following principles in mind:

- Always provide some alternative form of navigation at the top, bottom, or sides of your page. This isn't only to accommodate those who might be using non-visual browsers (for example, braille and aural browsers). It's also a courtesy to those who don't want to take the time deciphering what an unclear image map might mean.

- Choose your images carefully. Don't select a beautiful landscape for your image map just because you think it's attractive. If you are going to depend on images for navigation, they should be reasonably self-explanatory.

- If your images are not obvious, use an image editor to add some captions that will help visitors decipher the links and where they will lead.

- Make use of the ALT attribute by adding a brief description of where each link will lead. This will pop up when your visitor moves a mouse over the different parts of your image.

- Don't let art subvert practicality. Navigation aids are to help people navigate. If they don't accomplish this, they're not doing their job.

## Practice, Practice, Practice

If you want to practice creating an image map for some of the pages you have created throughout this book, try using the following image to make an image

**13**

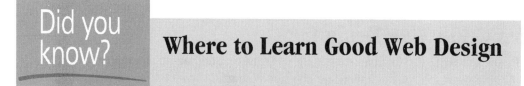

## Where to Learn Good Web Design

Vincent Flanders's Web site, www.webpagesthatsuck.com, probably is the best site on Web design out there, bar none. It operates on the principle that the best way to learn good design is by looking at bad design. He offers one or two new sites every day as examples to learn from. His site also has a number of different pages that display classic examples of poor design. If you want to get a handle on Web design, visit his site often.

map. Instead of linking to a different page with the e-mail image, try using a mailto: link to bring up a browser's e-mail program. To download this image as a completed image map, visit Osborne's Web site. Click the Free Code option at the top of the browser window; then click the link for *How to Do Everything with HTML.*

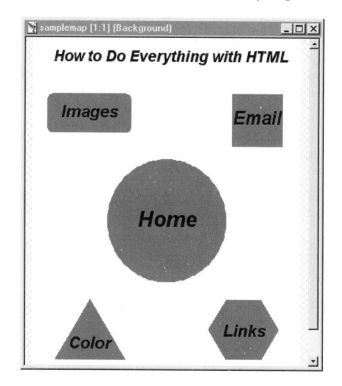

# Find the Code Online

To find the code online for this or any of the chapters in this book, go to Osborne's Web site, www.osborne.com, and click the Free Code choice on the navigation bar. From the list of books, select the *How to Do Everything with HTML* option and you will be able to download the book files, which are linked together and organized as an offline "mini" Web site. For more on how to use the "mini" Web site, see Chapter 17.

| Use This Code For... | Look for this Filename |
|---|---|
| Ismap demo | coordinatemap.htm |
| Sample image | samplemap.gif |
| Image map photo | cjcmimagemap.jpg |
| Practice image | practicemap.gif |
| States map | states2.gif |
| Hexagon image with coordinates | hexagoncoord.gif |

13

# Chapter 14

# Add Interactivity with Forms

## How to…

- Understand Form Elements

- Create a Simple Guestbook

- Create a Survey Form

- Use Tables for Form Structure

- Understand CGI

- Locate and Use CGI Resources

If you are content with creating a static Web site, such as an online brochure or a family album, and you don't really care whether your visitors have the opportunity to respond to you, you can skip this chapter without missing much. On the other hand, if you want to enable your visitors to interact with you and respond to your site, you might want to stick around and read about HTML forms. With HTML form elements you can add a guestbook, put a menu on your site, add password protection, create a survey, construct a catalog, develop an order form, and much more. Best of all, forms are easy to create—once you've sorted out the various elements involved. The process of getting a form to actually work (deliver information to you) is a bit trickier, but once you learn to take advantage of the available resources you'll soon be creating and using forms like a pro.

# Understand Form Elements

When creating a form with HTML, whether it's a guestbook, a catalog, an order form, or an e-mail form, you will use the <form> </form> element along with a combination of *controls*. As you would expect, the <form> element creates the form, whereas the controls determine what kind of information your visitors can send you. The kind of form you want to create will determine the types of controls you choose to include in it.

## Create a Simple Guestbook Form

Before you experiment with different form controls, try creating a simple guestbook for your Web site. This form will provide a text box where your visitors can write you a note that will be e-mailed to you when they press submit. Open template.htm and save it as formsample1.htm; then create a form by adding the <form> element to your code, like this:

```
<html>
     <head><title>Forms Sampler</title></head>
          <body>
               <form>
               </form>
          </body>
</html>
```

If you save and view this page in your browser, you'll only get a blank page. You must add the form controls before you will see anything. However, before you begin adding the controls to your form, you must include some attributes in the <form> element that will tell the browser (and the server) what to do with the data your visitors type in. To do this you use the *action* and *method* attributes.

## Understand the action=" " Attribute

The action=" " attribute tells the browser where to send information in the form. Most of the time it will tell the browser to use a *Common Gateway Interface* (CGI) program to process the data. (The CGI program then will send the information to you.) CGI is covered later in this chapter in the section "Make Your Form Work with CGI," so you needn't be too concerned with it at this point. For now, just keep in mind that a CGI program is stored on your Web server and serves as an information handler.

> NOTE
>
> *Why do you even need CGI? Because HTML is not a programming language. Remember, HTML is a markup language that was created to structure documents and enable them to be shared easily. To process data, you need a little more programming power than HTML has. CGI programs usually are written in Perl or some other programming language and pack a little more punch than HTML. If you know how to program, you can write your own CGI programs (usually called scripts). If the idea of programming causes you to break out in hives, don't despair. There are plenty of CGI scripts available online and many are free of charge. Later in the chapter you'll learn how to incorporate a pre-written CGI script into a form. Check out the table later in this chapter for sources for ready-to-use CGI scripts.*

14

For this illustration, you will use the mailto: protocol as your action. This will tell the browser to e-mail the contents of the form directly to you. This isn't really the best way to handle form data, although it is unquestionably the easiest. Because not all browsers allow you to use the mailto: protocol for form processing, if you plan to use a lot of forms you will want to learn how to use CGI scripts. However, mailto: is a great tool for learning how to work with forms. To add the action=" " attribute and mailto: protocol to your form, modify the opening <form> tag to read as follows:

```
<html>
    <head><title>Forms Sampler</title></head>
        <body>
            <form action="mailto:my_e-mail@my_server.com">
            </form>
        </body>
</html>
```

Once you've specified the action, you're almost ready to begin designing your form. However, before you begin adding buttons, menus, and text boxes you must tell the browser how to handle the data it receives. To do this, add the method=" " attribute to the opening <form> element.

## Understand the method=" " Attribute

Whereas the action=" " attribute tells the browser where to send the information collected from a form, the method=" " attribute tells it how to send it. You have two possible choices (values) with this attribute: get or post. The "get" value simply tacks the information on to the end of the URL where the information is to be sent. Post sends the information separately to the specified location. Each method has its pros and cons; for the most part you will want to stick with "post."

To add the method=" " attribute to your sample form, modify the opening <form> tag as in the following listing:

```
<html>
    <head><title>Forms Sampler</title></head>
        <body>
            <form action="mailto:my_e-mail@my_server.com"
                method="post">
            </form>
        </body>
</html>
```

## Add Structure to Your Form with \<table> \</table>

Before you begin adding controls, you will want to define some type of structure for your form. Use the table element to structure your form. Using tables will enable you to create a balanced layout for your form. By using CSS to set your fonts and colors, you can customize your table to give your form a sharp, professional look. If you skip this step, your form's appearance will be at the mercy of every browser that displays it—and often it will turn out looking pretty ragged.

> TIP
>
> *If you are going to use a table to structure your form, you might find it helpful to sketch your table layout on a piece of paper before you write your code. You also might find it helpful to put an "x" inside each of the table cells to get them to display before you add your form elements.*

To insert a table inside your form, simply nest a set of \<table> tags in between the \<form> tags; then create whatever cells you need to give the form the design you want it to have. The following code will create a simple, four-row, no-column table to contain your guestbook form.

> NOTE
>
> *Some other presentation adjustments have been made by using the \<style> and \<div> elements. These are in bold type, along with the table elements you will be adding.*

```
<html>
<head><title>Forms Sampler</title>
    <style type="text/css">
        body        {background-color: white;}
        table       {background-color: aqua;}
    </style></head>
    <body>
    <div align="center">
<p style="font-size: 2em">Sample Guestbook Form</p>
    <form action="mailto:my_e-mail@my_server.com"
      method="post">
     <table>
        <tr><td> </td></tr>
        <tr><td> </td></tr>
        <tr><td> </td></tr>
        <tr><td> </td></tr>
     </table>
    </form>
```

14

```
    </div>
   </body>
</html>
```

# Add Controls to Your Guestbook Form

For a simple guestbook form, you need only a few controls: an input line for your visitor's name, a text box for a brief note, and submit and reset buttons. As you add these controls, you will be learning the basics of using the <input> element and its numerous attributes. The <input> element enables you to create a form specifically suited to your needs. Along with input, you will use the type=" " attribute to tell the browser what kind of controls to display.

## Add Lines of Text with <input type="text" />

To add lines for text input (for names, addresses, and so on) use the <input /> element with the type="text" attribute. Input is an empty element so you don't need to include a closing tag. (Don't forget to put the slash at the end of the tag.) The type=" " attribute specifies the type of control you want to place in the form. By choosing "text" as a value for the type=" " attribute, you are telling the browser to create a small, one-line text box.

You can tell the browser how many characters to accept by adding the size=" " attribute and supplying a number. For example, a value of 40 will allow a visitor to input 40 characters. The name=" " attribute is used to assign an identifying name to the information that the user inputs. This is the name by which the information will be identified when it is relayed to you. When you create your form, choose the values you put in the name=" " attribute carefully so you won't have difficulty understanding or sorting your data.

To add a text input line for a visitor to insert their name, modify the table in your guestbook form to look like the following code listing:

NOTE    *The first line, which reads "Please sign my guestbook," is not a necessary part of the form. You could leave it out without affecting the form's operation at all. However, it is a good idea to add instructions such as this to make your forms clear and understandable for your visitors.*

```
<tr><td>Please sign my guestbook.</td></tr>
<tr><td>Name: <input type="text" name="name"
           size="15" maxlength="30"/></td></tr>
```

> **TIP** *If you want a text window to accept more characters than it actually displays, use the maxlength=" " attribute. For example, if you set a text box to read size="15" maxlength="30" only 15 characters will display. However, your visitor will be able to enter up to 30 characters.*

## Add a Text Box with <textarea>

The next item your form will need is a larger text box for your visitors to use when writing comments about your site. Although you could do this with a text line as in the preceding example, it would not allow your visitors to view more than one line at a time while they wrote their messages to you. Therefore, instead of using the <input /> element with a type="text" attribute, you will use the <textarea> </textarea> element.

The <textarea> element allows you to create a larger working space for your form data. You tell the browser how large to make the text box by using the rows=" " and cols=" " attributes. For example, if you want to display a text box with 10 rows and 45 columns, you would add the attributes as in the following listing:

```
<textarea name="message" rows="10" cols="45"> </textarea>
```

Notice also that the <textarea> element functions as an empty element. Even though it has a closing tag, nothing goes in between the two tags. All the information necessary to create the text area goes inside the opening tag.

After you have added your text box, you must create a way for your visitors to send you the information they have typed in. Or, if they don't like what they have written, you must provide them with a way to clear the form and start over. You can do that by adding submit and reset buttons.

## Add Submit and Reset Buttons with <input />

Creating buttons for your forms is easy. As you'll see later in the chapter, you have quite a bit of room for creativity when you put buttons into your forms. However, if you just want to add submit and reset buttons, you can do it by simply using the <input /> element with the type=" " attribute set either to "submit" or "reset." You can add these buttons to your guestbook by modifying the bottom data cell in your form/table to read like the following listing:

```
<input type="submit" /> <input type="reset" />
```

TIP *You can add "white space" between your buttons by merely adding space between the <input /> elements.*

Once you have added the various lines described in the preceding paragraphs, you will have a simple guestbook form that will work with many browsers. If you post it on your site and someone clicks the submit button, it should send you the data by using your visitor's e-mail server. If you haven't done it already, try adding the form elements just described to formsample.htm. Then save it and display it on your Web browser. It should look something like the illustration that follows the code listing:

```
<form action="mailto:my_e-mail@my_server.com"
      method="post">
   <table>
      <tr><td>Please sign my guestbook.</td></tr>
      <tr><td>Name: <input type="text" name="name"
            size="15" maxlength="30"/></td></tr>
      <tr><td><textarea name="message" rows="10" cols="45">
            </textarea></td></tr>
      <tr><td><input type="submit" /> <input type="reset" />
            </td></tr>
   </table>
</form>
```

Sample Guestbook Form

# Create a Visitor Survey

Now that you have created a simple form and have a feel for how forms work, you will want to discover the other form tools available in the HTML toolbox. There are so many to choose from; the best way to learn how to use them is to build a form that would be useful (so all this work won't be wasted) but that will allow you to use all the various form elements. The form that will best accomplish these goals is a visitor survey.

## Plan Your Survey

A visitor survey is self-explanatory: It is nothing more than a form on your site that asks your visitors' opinions on whatever you want to ask them about. For example, if you have a site devoted to cooking, you could survey your visitors about their favorite cookbooks, cooking shows, spices, recipes, and so on. You could even create a guestbook that would allow them to add recipes to your site for other visitors to use. In other words, a visitor survey can be whatever you want it to be.

NOTE *For the purposes of learning HTML forms, a visitor survey is useful in that it will allow you to experiment with most of the different form elements and use them in a practical way. The survey you will create in this chapter is geared toward readers and book lovers. If you want to modify the form so that it will better fit your own needs, simply change the information in the form elements to ask for different information. By modifying this form rather than merely copying the code, you'll find that you will learn how to use forms even more quickly.*

The first step in creating your survey is to decide what information you wish to collect from your visitors. If you are developing a survey for book lovers, you will want to obtain basic information such as names, ages, where your visitors live, and so on. You also will want to collect specific information about their reading and purchasing preferences. As you develop a list of the information you want to collect, you might come up with some of the following possibilities for a book-lovers survey:

- Your visitors' names
- Where they live

14

- Their ages

- Male or female, married or single

- Reading preferences (fiction or non-fiction)

- Fiction genres (mystery, romance, thriller, historical, and so on)

- Non-fiction topics (computer, cooking, parenting, history, and so forth)

- How/where they buy books (online, bookstores, used books)

- Favorite authors

- Comments on their favorite book this year

You could come up with other possible options, but these will give you enough to create a form using most of the possible form elements. To begin building your form, open template.htm and save it as formsample2.htm. Add a set of <form> </form> tags to create the form. When your code looks like the following listing, you are ready to begin building your survey.

```
<html><head><title>Visitor Survey</title></head>
<body>
    <form action="mailto:my_e-mail@my_address.com"
          method="post">
    </form>
</body>
</html>
```

## Build Your Survey

There are many different ways you can structure a visitor survey; however, the simpler it is, the better. Arrange the elements logically so your visitors will not have to spend time trying to understand your form and what you are asking for. Also remember to use tables to help develop a pleasing layout for the survey.

### Add Text Input Lines with <input type="text" />

Because you have already practiced adding a text line to your form, this part will be easy. Because you are surveying only your visitors' opinions, it won't be necessary to collect complete address information. However, you will want to at least know the part of the country (or world) where your visitors live; thus, the first part of your form will be primarily text input lines. Remember that to add these lines you will use the <input /> element with the type="text" attribute. Add the following lines to formsample2.htm:

```
First Name: <input type="text" name="fname"
                    size="15" maxlength="20" />
Last Name: <input type="text" name="lname"
                    size="15" maxlength="20" />
City: <input type="text" name="city"
                    size="15" maxlength="20" />
State: <input type="text" name="state"
                    size="2" />
Country: <input type="text" name="country"
                    size="15" maxlength="20" />
```

> **TIP**  *As you write the code for the form, be sure to observe how each attribute functions in the <input /> element. You might even want to experiment by adjusting some of the values. The more you play with the code, the faster you'll learn how it works.*

When you save this code and display it in your browser, you will understand why most forms are laid out with tables. Simply using form elements without some way to give them structure will leave you with a form that works but is not visually appealing. For example, the preceding code will produce a form that looks like this:

First Name: ____   Last Name: ____   City: ____   State: __  Country: ____

When you enclose the code in a table, you can add structure and a pleasing appearance to your form. Notice how different the same data fields look when they are put into a table, as in the code listing and illustration that follow:

```
<table>
<tr><td>First Name:</td><td><input type="text" name="fname"
                    size="15" maxlength="20" /></td></tr>
<tr><td>Last Name: </td><td><input type="text" name="lname"
                    size="15" maxlength="20" /></td></tr>
<tr><td>City: </td><td><input type="text" name="city"
                    size="15" maxlength="20" /></td></tr>
<tr><td>State: </td><td><input type="text" name="state"
```

**14**

```
                              size="2" /></td></tr>
<tr><td>Country: </td><td><input type="text" name="country"
                              size="15" maxlength="20" /></td></tr>
</table>
```

First Name:
Last Name:
City:
State:
Country:

## Offer a Single Choice with Radio Buttons

When you want your visitors to select a single item from a list of possible choices, you might want to use "radio buttons." If you are familiar with older cars, you won't have much trouble figuring out why these controls are called "radio buttons." Old car radios usually had a series of five or six buttons for preselected stations. When you wanted to go to a favorite station, you simply pushed the appropriate button. One thing you obviously could not do with the radio buttons was to select more than one station at a time. Likewise, the radio buttons you use in a form will allow your visitors to choose only one option. The following list demonstrates how a single radio button element can be constructed:

1. To add radio buttons to your form, use the <input /> element with the type=" " attribute set to "radio".

   ```
   <input type="radio" />
   ```

2. Be sure to give all your radio buttons the same "name" attribute. That's how the browser knows to associate all of the choices. Because these radio buttons are used to ask your visitors' ages, the most logical value for name=" " is "age".

   ```
   <input type="radio" name="age" />
   ```

3. You also will need to assign a value with the "value" element. You didn't have to do this with text boxes because your visitors add their own values

when they input text. With radio buttons and other controls where *you* supply the choices, you also must add the values.

```
<input type="radio" name="age" value="31-40" />
```

**4.** To preselect an option, add the "checked" attribute to one of the <input /> elements. This attribute does not require a value (at least for now—see the following Did You Know box). Simply adding the word "checked" is sufficient.

```
<input type="radio" name="age" value="31-40"
    checked="checked" />
```

For example, if you want your visitors to specify their ages by choosing from a series of age ranges, and want the 31–40 age range preselected, you could write something that resembles the following listing and illustration (on the next page):

```
<p style="font-size: 1.1em;">Your age (choose one):</p>
    10-18 <input type="radio" name="age" value="10-18" /><br />
    19-30 <input type="radio" name="age" value="19-30" /><br />
    31-40 <input type="radio" name="age" value="31-40"
            checked /><br />
    41-50 <input type="radio" name="age" value="41-50" /><br />
    51-60 <input type="radio" name="age" value="51-60" /><br />
    61-99 <input type="radio" name="age" value="61-99" />
```

## Did you know?

# Values Will Be Required for All Attributes

As the Web moves from HTML to XHTML (already the current recommendation), and ultimately to XML, the standards will be much more strict. All attributes will require values. Eventually, adding the word "checked" as a standalone attribute will no longer work. Therefore, it's a good practice to get into the habit of always using values with attributes. In this case it would be checked="checked".

Your age (choose one):

```
        10-18  ○
        19-30  ○
        31-40  ◉
        41-50  ○
        51-60  ○
        61-99  ○
```

TIP *The line break element, <br />, is placed at the end of each of the input elements to move the next one to a new line on your page. If you want the options to display side by side, simply omit the line breaks.*

## Use Check Boxes for Multiple Choices

If you want to provide a visitor with multiple choices, you want to use check boxes rather than radio buttons. In the book-lovers' survey you are building, you will want to ask your visitors about their reading preferences. Obviously this is a situation in which you want to provide more than one option. With check boxes, your visitors can choose as many items as they like.

To create a check box, you will again use the <input /> element. However, this time you must add the type=" " attribute with the value set to "checkbox". As with radio buttons, if you want to preselect an item you simply add the word "checked" to the <input /> element. As in the preceding example, you also will need to assign the same "name" to all your options. You also will need to specify the value of each option. The code for a series of check boxes might look something like the following code and illustration:

```
Fiction Preferences:<br />
(Choose as many as you want.)<br />
<input type="checkbox" name="fictionpreferences"
   value="historical" />Historical<br />
<input type="checkbox" name="fictionpreferences"
   value="literary" />Literary<br />
<input type="checkbox" name="fictionpreferences"
   value="mystery" />Mystery<br />
<input type="checkbox" name="fictionpreferences"
   value="romance" />Romance<br />
<input type="checkbox" name="fictionpreferences"
   value="thriller" />Suspense/Thriller<br />
<input type="checkbox" name="fictionpreferences"
   value="western" />Western<br />
<input type="checkbox" name="fictionpreferences"
   value="horror" />Horror<br />
```

## Create Pull-Down Menus with <select> </select>

If space is a consideration or if you want to add a bit of variety to your form, you can create a pull-down menu for your visitors to choose from. These menus are easy to create, and they can function either as single choice lists (like radio buttons) or as multiple option lists (like check boxes). Although constructing pull-down menus is not difficult, the elements you use are somewhat different from those you've worked with so far.

To build a pull-down menu, use the <select> </select> element instead of <input />. You can add choices with the <option /> element and use the name=" " and value=" " attributes. To see how easy it is, add a pull-down menu to the survey that allows your visitor to select from either "male" or "female". You would write your HTML code like this:

```
<p>Your sex:</p>
<select name="    ">
    <option value="male" >Male</option>
    <option value="female" >Female</option>
</select>
```

To create a list with several options, or a list that will display more than one choice at a time (sometimes called a scrolling list), you must add the following attributes to the opening <select> tag:

- **Size=" "** The size=" " attribute, with a numerical value added, will tell the browser to display more than one option in the pull-down list. For instance, size="4" will display four choices simultaneously.

- **Multiple=" "** The multiple=" " attribute allows for more than one selection to be made from the list (similar to check boxes). As with the "checked" attribute, you can get away with inserting only the word

14

"multiple" in the <select> tag, but it's better practice to include a value. In this case it would be multiple="multiple". Keep in mind that for your visitors to actually be able to select more than one option with a menu list, they probably will have to hold down the CTRL key while clicking. It's good to add an instruction to your form, in case they don't know how to do this.

In the sample form you are building, perhaps you want to find out where your visitors buy their books. Although you could do this with a series of check boxes, a scrolling menu also works well. By typing in the following code, you will create a menu that will display five bookstores and allow the visitor to scroll down to display more. They also will be able to select more than one option because the "multiple" attribute has been added.

```
<p>Bookstore Preferences</p>
<select name="bookpurchasepref" multiple="multiple" size="5">
<option value="Amazon">Amazon.com</option>
<option value="B&Ncom">B&N.com</option>
<option value="B&N">Barnes and Noble</option>
<option value="Borders">Borders</option>
<option value="Bdalton">B. Dalton Booksellers</option>
<option value="Hastings">Hastings</option>
<option value="Walden">Waldenbooks</option>
<option value="HPBooks">Half Price Books</option>
<option value="Joes">Joe's Used Bookstore</option>
</select>
```

CAUTION    *The <option> element often is used without its closing tag. Although your form will work properly if you write it this way, it's not good practice. Remember that to guarantee future compatibility, you must always use either closing tags or (in the case of an empty element) a slash at the end of the opening tag, like this: <empty_element />.*

The controls you have covered thus far in this chapter are those you will use most often. They will enable you to create virtually any kind of form you need. However, there are some other controls that enable you to add more specialized functions to your form.

## Use Special Form Controls

The following form controls will enable you to add password boxes to a form, create customized buttons, and much more. You might not use these all the time, and some of them (such as the password box) might require a "script" to make them work, but it's good to have them in your form designing arsenal:

- **\<input type="password" />**   By using the "password" value with the \<input /> element, you can create a password input field. If you've spent more than five minutes on a computer or the Web, more than likely you have encountered a password field. What makes it distinctive is that the characters typed in are masked to keep your password secret. An asterisk (*) displays for each character entered.

  ```
  <input type="password" size="10" />
  ```

CAUTION *Just using the password field does not mean you will have a password-protected or encrypted page; you will need to have a CGI script to accomplish that task. The password field merely works with the script to help get the job done.*

- **tabindex=" "**   If you've filled out many forms on Web pages, you've probably discovered that you can move from field to field by using the TAB key. What you might not know is that as a form designer, you can tell the browser in which order you want your visitors to be able to tab through your forms. By inserting the tabindex=" " attribute in each field and adding a numerical value, you can set the priority for your form fields. To see how this works, put the following code inside a set of form tags, save the page as tabindex.htm, and then tab through the fields.

  ```
  First name: <input type="text" name="fname"
              tabindex="1" size="10" /><br />
  ```

14

```
Last name: <input type="text" name="lname"
            tabindex="3" size="10" /><br />
Mother's name: <input type="text" name="momname"
            tabindex="5" size="10" /><br />
Father's name: <input type="text" name="dadname"
            tabindex="4" size="10" /><br />
Cat's name: <input type="text" name="catname"
            tabindex="2" size="10" /><br />
```

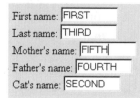

- **type="hidden"**    There will be times when you need to add hidden fields to your forms. These cannot be seen or altered by your visitors, and generally they are used to provide necessary information to your server. You do this by using the <input /> element with the type=" " attribute set to "hidden".

```
<input type="hidden" />
```

- **type="image"**    If you want to be creative with your forms and use images as buttons, one way you can do it is with the type="image" attribute. Used with the <input /> element, this attribute will allow you to convert any image into a clickable button.

```
<input type="image" src="mybutton.gif" name="surprise" />
```

- **type="button"**    You can create a more conventional-looking custom button with the type=" " attribute set to the "button" value. This creates a generic button that has no function in and of itself. However, as you'll see in Chapter 15, you can assign functions to the button with JavaScript or other scripting languages.

```
<input type="button" value="Custom Button"
name="surprise2" />
```

TIP *The text that displays on the face of the button is created with the value=" " attribute.*

■ **<button> </button>**    The newest (and preferred) way to create buttons is with the <button> element. With this element, you can convert images and even text to buttons. By using the type=" " attribute, you can assign a value to your buttons that will allow them to function as submit or reset buttons, or (as with the preceding example) to respond to script-related functions.

```
<p><button value="button"><img src="mybutton2.gif" />
    </button></p>
<p>(This is a generic button created with the
    button element<br />and with mybutton2.gif.)</p>
<p><button value="submit">This is a submit button<br />
  created with the button element.</button></p>
<p><button value="reset">This is a reset button<br />
  created with the button element.</button></p>
```

(This is a generic button created with the button element and with mybutton2.gif.)

> This is a submit button
> created with the button element.

> This is a reset button
> created with the button element.

14

Thus far you have learned how to create a form, how to tell the browser what to do with it, and how to add form controls. Then you saw some special form elements in action. All along, you've been working to build a survey form that will collect information from your readers. However, at this point your form is about as useful as a car without an engine. It might look nice, but it won't actually do anything. If you want your form to work, you have to venture from the safe and comfortable harbor of HTML into the uncharted waters of CGI.

# Make Your Form Work with CGI

What is CGI and why do you need it? CGI stands for the Common Gateway Interface. It's sort of a fancy name that describes another protocol. If you remember from Chapter 5, a protocol refers to how information is exchanged on the Internet. CGI is a protocol that deals with the exchange of information from your visitor's Web browser (the client) to your Web host (the server) and, ultimately, to you (the Webmaster). The best way to understand why you need CGI is to learn what CGI does.

## Understand CGI

As was mentioned earlier in this chapter, HTML is wonderful—but limited in its scope. Even though HTML can collect information through forms, it was never designed to process that information. For that, you need a program (generally called a script) that resides on the Web server in a special location (usually what's known as a cgi-bin). When a visitor (client) fills out your form and clicks the "submit" button, the information on the form is sent by the client browser to your cgi-bin, where the script processes the data and sends it on to you, usually by e-mail. The script can be written in one of several different programming languages; usually it's done in a language called Perl. Is this beginning to sound complicated? It can be. That's why some beginning Webmasters might want to consider some alternatives to using CGI.

## Consider Alternative Form Processing

If you want to collect information from your visitors but don't want to deal with the headaches of using the Common Gateway Interface, there are some alternatives. Unfortunately, they all tend to have their problems, too. Some possible ways to avoid CGI include the following:

- **Avoid forms altogether**   If your site does not really depend on collecting information from your visitors, don't worry about CGI. Remember, just because you can do something with HTML doesn't mean you have to do it. Forms are like any other element of Web design: If you don't need them, don't bother with them.

- **Use the mailto: protocol**   At the beginning of this chapter you learned how to have form data e-mailed to you with the mailto: protocol. The main drawback to this approach is that not all browsers support it; thus, you might exclude some of the visitors who want to use your forms. Another issue is security related. When someone sends you information this way, they reveal their e-mail address to you. In these security-conscious days, people are increasingly hesitant to allow personal information to be revealed to someone they do not know.

- ■ **Locate a form-processing service**    There are services that will (for a fee or by displaying advertisements) handle your forms for you. In this case all you have to do is link to them and all the form processing is handled from their end. If forms are a must for you, you might consider this an option. You can find them by doing a simple search on Yahoo or another search engine, using the keywords "form hosting". The following table lists some free and fee-based form-processing services you might want to explore.

| Form-Processing Service | URL |
| --- | --- |
| Freedback.com | http://freedback.com/?matt |
| Response-o-Matic Free Form Processor | http://response-o-matic.com |
| CN Form Builder | http://www.commercialnewtorks.com |
| TipJar Generic Form Handler | http://www.tipjar.com/generic.html |
| FormSite.com HTML Form Builder | http://www.formsite.com |
| BYOApp (Build Your Own Application) | http://server.com/siteapps/byoapp/index.html |
| i-Depth | http://www.i-depth.com |
| MouseCGI Millennium (MouseMail) | http://www.mousehk.net/mousemail |
| World Wide Mart | http://www.worldwidemart/fullcgi.html |
| DataTrend Software CGI Scripts | http://www.datatrendsoftware.com/cgi.html |

14

If these options don't sound appealing to you or if you just like a challenge, put on your waders and step into the sometimes-intimidating waters of the Common Gateway Interface.

## Understand CGI Form Processing

If the thought of CGI and programming in Perl makes you break out in a cold sweat, relax. If you already know how to program and can understand how to work in Perl or a similar language, you're way ahead of the game. However, knowing how to program isn't absolutely necessary as long as you know what kind of script you need, where to look for it, and how to implement it.

### Find a Script

To figure out what kind of script you need to make your form work, you must ask yourself what you want the form to do. Is it a guestbook form? If so, you need to look for a guestbook script. Is it an online catalog or order form? Look for a shopping cart script. Is it a survey or general information form? If so, you will want a simple form script.

There are many sources for free CGI scripts on the Web. Although usually these scripts are copyrighted, generally the only requirement is that you leave the header portion of the script (which contains information about the author) untouched. Others might not want you to make any modifications to the script (other than those necessary to make it functional for your pages). A handful of the sources for CGI scripts are listed in the following table:

| Script Source | URL |
| --- | --- |
| Matt's Script Archive | www.scriptarchive.com |
| FreeScripts.com | www.freescripts.com |
| BigNoseBird.com | www.bignosebird.com |
| TuCows | www.tucows.com (Search for "cgi scripts") |
| Free Dynamic CGI Scripts | www.websitestop.com/dynamic |

NOTE  *There are many different kinds of CGI scripts. As you explore some of these sites, you might be tempted to try out more than just form processing with CGI.*

Once you have found the script that will meet your needs, download it and unzip it (if necessary). Depending on the kind of script you are going to use, you might find that you have been given a CGI script, written in Perl (filename.pl), perhaps one or two HTML files, and usually a ReadMe file. This file will have the instructions you need to get your script up and running. Once you have sorted out your files, you are ready to begin phase two of your CGI experience: configuring the script.

## Configure Your Script

Obviously, a generic script is not likely to fit your form perfectly. Once you have downloaded your script, you will need to tailor it to meet the needs of your form. In some cases (as with a form script) you might also need to tweak an HTML file, or copy the code from the file you downloaded into your own page. It all depends on what your script needs to work properly. Most scripts you download will include a ReadMe file that gives you the instructions for modifying and configuring the script for your own use.

Because every script is different, and your forms and Web accounts will be unique to you, it's difficult to give precise instructions for configuring a script. That is why the ReadMe file included with your script is essential to properly setting it up. You also might need to contact your Web host to find out about how to use CGI on its server.

## Did you know?

## Not All Web Hosts Support CGI

14

It's important to check with a prospective Web host to learn whether you will even be allowed to use CGI. For example, Yahoo Geocities free server does not allow you to use CGI scripts. Because CGI raises some security issues (as you will see in the next few paragraphs), some servers do not support it. If forms and other server-side applications will be important to the functioning of your site, be sure to find out whether you can use CGI before you commit your funds to setting up a site on a particular server.

Another part of the configuration process that might or might not be necessary is that of adjusting the form, guestbook, and so on to meet your needs. Often, the scripts you download are "zipped" files that include the basic Web pages you need to execute them. However, you probably will prefer to custom tailor the Web page to fit the look of your site. Most of the time that can be done by either modifying the page directly, cutting and pasting the relevant code into one of your own pages, or by linking the page to a style sheet you have created. Once you have done that, you can turn a plain form page into a customized page that will fit the look of your site, as in the illustration that follows:

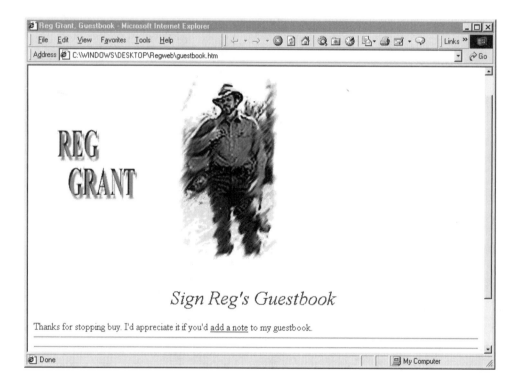

## Upload Your Files

Once you have configured your script (and your form, if necessary), the next step is to upload the files to your server. This is the easiest part of the whole process. You use your FTP program just as you would for any of your other Web pages. The only things you need to remember are that your CGI script needs to go into the cgi-bin directory, and you should put the other files in the location you specified when you configured the script.

## Change Permissions

Perhaps the most confusing—and scary—part of using some CGI scripts is that you might have to change some of the security settings for the files on your server. For example, with a guestbook program, it is necessary to configure the server to allow your visitors to leave messages that will be added to an HTML file. That means that people who visit your site actually are given permission to write information onto your server's hard drive. "Are you beginning to grasp the security implications?" What if someone with a little know-how decided it would be fun to make some modifications you (or your server) had not planned on? That is why not all servers allow you to use CGI. If you need to change permissions (and, remember, not all CGI scripts require it) you can contact your server's technical support to find out exactly how to go about it.

## Test Your Form

After you have configured your files, uploaded them, and made any changes to the file permissions, you are ready to test your form. Log on to your site, fill out your form (or guestbook), and press Submit. Hopefully, you won't receive an error message; instead you'll be celebrating the first successful addition to your Web site's guestbook.

# Learn Good Web Design

Probably the most challenging aspect of putting forms together is learning how to construct them in a manner that is both pleasing to the eye and easy to understand. As you have seen in some of the preceding illustrations, form controls left to themselves follow a linear pattern, just like text on a page. Unfortunately, this is neither pleasant nor easy to follow. On the other hand, you might organize your form so that it looks good but follows no logical pattern. Both looks and logic are important; so, when designing forms, keep some of these design principles in mind.

## Web Design Principle: Balance Sense with Sensibility

As with any other part of Web design, forms done on-the-fly are not likely to be very good. A good form requires thoughtful planning as you create its layout. Some principles to remember as you design your form are

■ Plan your form on paper before you do it on a computer.

14

- Use tables to give your form a stable structure.

- When you are building your form, turn the table borders on so that you can have a visual reference point for your structure.

- In a large form, try to group questions and input controls by related topics.

- Add instructions within your form whenever something is not self-explanatory.

- When you have finished constructing the form, turn the tables off.

## Practice, Practice, Practice

Throughout this chapter you have been working with different elements of a book-lovers' survey form. A complete version of the form (including additional controls) is displayed in the following illustration. Try either duplicating the form or modifying it to your own needs. The table borders have been left on and a border color has been added to make them stand out. This will help you see the form's structure more clearly. The form (and the code used to create it) can be found at Osborne's Web site.

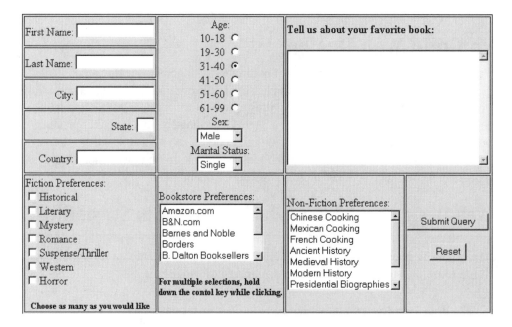

# Find the Code Online

To find the code online for this or any of the chapters in this book, go to Osborne's Web site: www.osborne.com, and click the Free Code choice on the navigation bar. From the list of books, select the *How to Do Everything with HTML* option and you will be able to download the book files, which are linked together and organized as an offline "mini" Web site. For more on how to use the "mini" Web site, see Chapter 17.

| Use This Code For... | Look for This Filename |
|---|---|
| Simple guestbook | formsample1.htm |
| Complete survey | formsample3.htm |
| Tabindex demo | tabindex.htm |
| Custom button | custombutton.htm |
| Button image #1 | mybutton.gif |
| Button image #2 | mybutton2.gif |
| Sloppy controls | formsample2.htm |
| Password demo | passwordsample.htm |
| Image Button demo | homemadebutton.htm |
| Button element | buttonelement.htm |

# Chapter 15

# Improve Interactivity with JavaScript

## How to...

- Understand Scripting Languages
- Write a Script that Identifies Your Browser
- Write a Script that Displays the Date and Time
- Add a "Last Modified" Line to Your Page
- Understand Events and Event Handlers
- Understand Java Applets

Have you ever gone onto a Web site and noticed that part of the site changed when your mouse cursor moved over it? No doubt, you have. Have you ever filled out a form incorrectly and had it "kicked back" to you with a request for additional information? Maybe you've hit a site where the Web page told you what kind of browser you were using and suggested a different one. Did you ever wonder how it knew? Chances are, it was all done with JavaScript.

# Understand Web Page Scripting

Although you can accomplish much in the area of Web design with HTML, many of the exciting things that make Web sites come alive are far beyond HTML's scope. Even with the added power of Cascading Style Sheets, you are still bound by HTML's limitations as a markup language. Because it is not a programming language, HTML cannot enable you to do much more than create static Web pages. If you want to create pages that your visitors can interact with, or pages that change dynamically, or even pages that are generated on-the-fly, you'll need to give HTML a shot in the arm. Although there are many ways you can do this, one of the best—and most popular—places to start is with JavaScript.

Before you begin working with JavaScript, you'll find it helpful to understand a little about Web page scripting. Chapter 14 introduced the term *script* when dealing with the Common Gateway Interface (CGI). If you read that chapter, you might have noticed that sometimes the text referred to a CGI program, whereas other times it was called a CGI script. Although sometimes the two terms are used interchangeably, there is a distinct difference between a program and a script.

# Understand Scripts and How They Work

A script is a program; yet it differs from other types of programs in that it cannot stand on its own. For instance, you can't download a script and run it on your computer like you can a spreadsheet, word processor, or computer game. For a script to function, it must work hand in hand with another application (such as a browser).

The CGI script mentioned in Chapter 14 is a *server-side* script. That means it remains on and works through your Internet server's computer. JavaScript usually is used for *client-side* scripting. This type of script works on your visitor's (the client) Web browser and uses their computer to process information. How does it get to their computer? It is either downloaded as part of the Web page (like an inline or embedded style sheet) or can exist on your server as a plain text file that the browser reads whenever necessary (like an external style sheet).

## Scripts Speed Information Processing

Why are scripts useful? For one thing, because they operate on your visitor's computer they can speed up the processing of information. For instance, say you have a catalog and an order form on your site, and you want your visitors to see a tally of their orders before they submit them. You could do this using a CGI script, but then the browser would have to send the information to the server. Once it had the data, the server would have to process it and then send it back to your visitor's computer. All that takes time.

With a client-side script, all that processing can be done on your visitor's computer without the need to send anything to the server. That saves your visitor time and might result in a happier customer. Additionally, not only can scripts speed things up; they can make your pages more interesting.

## Scripts Add Interactivity

Buttons that change when a mouse moves over them, pictures that display when your cursor hovers over a link, Web pages that seem to "talk" to your visitor—all this and more is possible when you use a script. How is this interactivity accomplished? It is done largely with *events*. What, exactly, is an event? Basically, an event is something that happens; however, in Web page scripting the term means a lot more than that. An event is something that happens on your visitor's browser. For example, when they move their mouse cursor over a button, that's called a *mouseover* event. When the cursor is removed from the button, that's called a *mouseout* event. When an event occurs, it can be used to activate an *event handler*. An event handler is what you use to program your page's response to certain events.

15

Web page scripts enable you to anticipate different events and use event handlers to plan a response. The event acts like a trigger, causing the event handler to spring into action and do whatever you told it to. For instance, for a mouseover event, you would use the *onMouseover* event handler. Likewise, for the mouseout event, you would use the *onMouseout* event handler. Sound pretty complicated? Perhaps the best way to see how these work is by a little experimentation.

> **NOTE** *There are many more event handlers than onMouseover and onMouseout. Later in this chapter you will find a chart of some of the more commonly used event handlers.*

To see an event handler in action, try writing a simple script using the *onClick* event handler. Open template.htm and save it as clickevent.htm; then add the following line of code to your blank HTML page:

1. Create a button with the <input /> element and type="button" attribute.

   ```
   <input type="button" />
   ```

2. Put some text on the button itself. You do this with the value=" " attribute. With a button, you now have a possible "event" on the page.

   ```
   <input type="button" value="Trigger an Event" />
   ```

3. Add an event handler. In this case it will be onClick. By using this event handler, you are telling the browser that something is to be done whenever the button is clicked.

   ```
   <input type="button" value="Trigger an Event"
       onClick=" " />
   ```

4. Tell the browser what to do when the event occurs. For this illustration you will tell it to bring up an "alert" box with a message.

   ```
   <input type="button" value="Trigger an Event"
       onClick="alert('Good Job!');" />
   ```

> **CAUTION** *Whereas HTML is very forgiving, scripting languages are not. If even a quotation mark is out of place, you will receive an error message. Some things you need to watch for will be covered later in the chapter. For now, make sure you copy the code exactly as written.*

Once you have put the preceding line of code on your page (from step 4), save it and display it in your browser. You should see a button in the upper-left corner of your screen that reads "Trigger an Event." When you click the button, an alert window should pop up with the message "Good Job!" as in the following illustration:

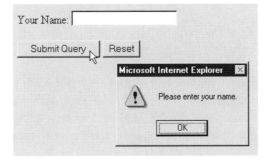

The creative use of events and event handlers will enable you as a Web author to add a dimension to your pages that simply is not possible with HTML alone. However, speed and added interactivity are not the only benefits of using a scripting language. A Web page script also can extend HTML's capabilities.

## Scripts Can Give HTML a Boost

As a markup language, HTML is essentially limited to creating a document and defining its structure. For example, as is demonstrated in Chapter 14, you can collect data with an HTML form, but for the form to actually do anything with the data it receives, you need a CGI script. However, Web page scripting can give HTML a boost by extending some of its capabilities. For instance, you can use a script to validate a form (make sure it has been correctly filled out) before it is sent off. If your visitors fail to fill out one of your required fields, they'll receive a prompt that encourages them to try again, as in the illustration that follows:

15

## Scripts Have Their Disadvantages

There are certain disadvantages inherent in Web page scripting. First, scripting languages are considerably more complex than HTML or even CSS. Remember, even though they are limited in their application, scripting languages are programming languages. That implies that if you plan to write your own scripts, you will have to think (and write) like a programmer. In other words, you will need to logically think through the task you want the script to accomplish; then choose the appropriate commands to bring about the desired results. You can avoid this problem by using prewritten scripts; however, even with these you'll need to understand the script well enough to debug it if you have a problem.

Another disadvantage of scripting is that a script can interfere with a search engine's capability to *index* your site. Many search engines use automated programs that browse your site and index it according to the words they find near the top of the document. A large script, placed in the <head> </head> portion of your page, can skew the results because it will have a lot of text that is unrelated to the purpose or subject of your site.

> TIP *If you decide to use scripts and want to avoid problems with search engines, save them as text documents (myscript.txt) and link to them. You'll learn how to do this later in this chapter, in the section "Link to an External Script."*

Also, some older browsers do not support Web page scripts. Thus, your page can suffer doubly when such a browser loads it. The script will not run and (if the script is in the <body> of the page) the browser will ignore the <script> tags and treat the script as text to be included in the Web page. The results are not very attractive, as is shown in the following illustration:

```
function CheckForName() { if (document.Name.fname.value < 1){alert("Please enter your name.");}}
```

Your Name: [                    ]

[ Submit Query ]  [ Reset ]

Another disadvantage with scripts is that your visitor is not required to make use of them. This is just another reminder to you as a Web author that you do not have ultimate control over how your page is displayed when it arrives on your visitor's browser. Visitors can turn off images, specify their own fonts and colors, use their own style sheets, and even disable JavaScript if they want to. Thus, if you have a page that is heavily dependent on scripts and someone visits you with their browser's script option set to "off," your page might suffer.

> NOTE
>
> *Realistically, probably very few Web surfers turn off the JavaScript option on their browsers, so it's not really a major threat to the integrity of your page. Likewise, the problem of older browsers not supporting JavaScript probably encompasses only a small minority of browsers. Don't allow the support issue to discourage you from trying scripts.*

All things considered, you still are likely to find Web page scripting to be a useful addition to your Web authoring toolbox. It will enable you to accomplish many things on your site that you couldn't do otherwise. With that in mind, by now you might be wondering which scripting language you should use.

## Understand JavaScript

Although JavaScript is not the only language to choose from, it is without a doubt the best supported. The other alternatives are VBScript, which is based on Microsoft's Visual Basic programming language, and JScript (Microsoft's counterpart to JavaScript). However, because JavaScript is supported on all the major browsers (Internet Explorer, Netscape, and Opera), it probably should be your language of choice.

## Did you know?   JavaScript Is Not Related to Java

JavaScript was developed by Netscape and originally was named LiveScript. As the result of an agreement with Sun Microsystems, the name was changed to JavaScript to take advantage of the growing popularity of the Java programming language. However, JavaScript is in no way related to or descended from Java. Neither is it a scaled down form of Java. There might be similarities in syntax (how it is written); these are because many programming languages have certain elements in common. JavaScript, however, is a distinct language in its own right.

Although it is beyond the scope of this book to teach you to program in JavaScript, it is possible to give you a chance to experiment with it. Hopefully, by doing so you will at least develop a feel for how Web page scripts work and what you can do with them. To begin with, you need to know how to properly include JavaScript in your Web page.

## Add a Script to a Web Page

As with Cascading Style Sheets, there are multiple ways to put a script into a page. Sometimes a script can be included as part of an HTML tag and other times as part of the <body> of the page. A script also can be placed in the page's <head> portion or saved as a separate text file and linked to the page. If your script is going to be inline or embedded, you will need to use the <script> </script> element to identify it and to let the browser know not to display it as part of the page. Try adding a script with the script element by opening template.htm, saving it as js1.htm, and following these steps:

1. Type the opening <script> tag.

   ```
   <script>
   ```

2. Add an opening HTML comment tag just below the <script> tag.

   ```
   <script>
   <!--
   ```

3. Add the language=" " attribute to identify what scripting language you are using. In this case it will be language="JavaScript".

   ```
   <script language="JavaScript">
   <!--
   ```

4. Add the type=" " attribute to give the MIME type for the script. For JavaScript, you will write type="text/javascript".

   ```
   <script language="JavaScript" type="text/javascript">
   <!--
   ```

5. Add a closing HTML comment tag.

   ```
   <script language="JavaScript" type="text/javascript">
   <!--
   -->
   ```

**6.** Type the closing </script> tag.

```
<script language="JavaScript" type="text/javascript">
<!--
-->
</script>
```

**7.** Insert a line of script on the line between the comment tags.

```
<script language="JavaScript" type="text/javascript">
<!--
document.write("My first JavaScript script");
 -->
</script>
```

Save the file and display it in your browser. As in the following screen shot, you should see a page with the line "My first JavaScript script." Not very exciting, perhaps, but it's a start.

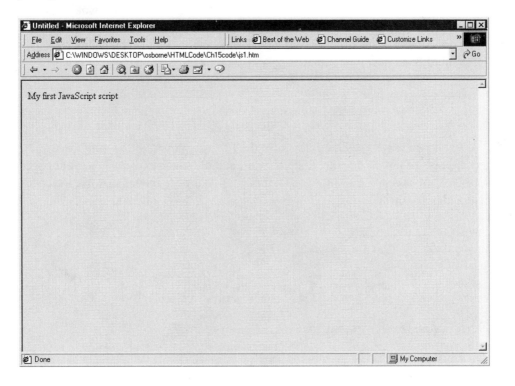

> **TIP**
>
> *Use comment tags (<!-- -->) to hide your script from older browsers. Browsers that do not support JavaScript will ignore the script lines, whereas browsers that do support scripts will execute the lines (ignoring the comment tags).*

Although most scripts will be enclosed in the <script> </script> element, sometimes you will insert JavaScript commands inside a tag. For example, with the "Trigger an Event" button created earlier in the chapter, the event handler was placed inside the <input /> element. With long scripts or scripts you might want to use on more than one Web page, you probably will want to use an external script.

## Link to an External Script

This exercise will modify your first JavaScript page (js1.htm) to include an external script that sets the background color to gold and adds a line of text with the <h1> </h1> element. The first steps in linking to an external script are creating the script itself and saving it as a text file. You don't need to use <script> tags when writing this script, only the commands that you want the browser to execute. Open Notepad, Wordpad, or another text editor and type the following lines on the blank page. Remember, you must type the lines exactly as they are here:

```
document.bgColor = "gold";
document.write("<h1>This is an external script.</h1>");
```

When you have typed the lines, save the file as a plain text file with the name extscript.js. To link to this file, first you must add the <script> element to your page. Open js1.htm and save it as js2.htm. The code for your page should look like the code listing that follows:

```
<html>
<head><title>First JavaScript</title>
</head>
<body>
<script language="JavaScript" type="text/javascript">
<!--
document.write("My first JavaScript script");
-->
</script>
</body>
</html>
```

To modify this code to link to the external script, add a second set of script tags. They can be placed either in the <head> or <body> portion of the page, as long as they are not inside or overlapping the other script tags. In the following listing, the additional script tags have been placed in the <head> of the page:

```
<html>
  <head><title>First JavaScript</title>
    <script language="JavaScript" type="text/javascript"
     src="extscript.js">
    </script>
  </head>
<body>
  <script language="JavaScript" type="text/javascript">
<!--
document.write("My first JavaScript script");
-->
</script>
</body>
</html>
```

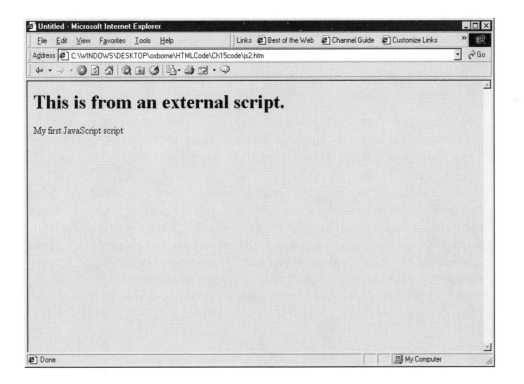

15

## Understand Key JavaScript Concepts

Once you know how to put a script on a page, you are almost ready to begin having some serious fun with JavaScript. However, before you start it's good to nail down some of the key concepts that make this language work. With HTML you learn to work with elements, attributes, and values. In CSS you use selectors, properties, and values. With JavaScript, your primary tools are *objects, properties,* and *methods.* Understanding these concepts will take you a long way toward being able to use JavaScript. Consider the following explanations of the key JavaScript concepts:

- **Objects**    JavaScript is an *object-oriented* language. That means when you work with JavaScript you must think in concrete rather than abstract terms. For example, the browser is an object. The HTML page you are creating is the *document object.* If you want a new window to open, you are going to work with a *window object.* If you create a form, you will have made a *form object.* Although the hierarchy of objects is very complex, it's important to be object oriented in your thinking so you know how to construct the commands that make your script work.

- **Properties**    A property is a characteristic of an object. For instance, in the preceding example, you set the background color of a page to gold with the following line: document.bgcolor = "gold";. What you did, in JavaScript terms, was modify the background color *property* of the document *object.*

- **Methods**    A method is an action that is taken with respect to an object. In previous examples, the line document.write("text"); used the method "write" to cause text to be written to the document object.

Now, if all this seems a bit fuzzy, perhaps a practical illustration would help. You might tell your son or daughter to wash the car. In this case the car is the object, and wash is the method. What if you have three cars: one red, one white, and one teal, but you only want the red car washed? You throw in a property to clarify things. You tell your child to wash the red car. If you wrote the command in JavaScript, it might look like this: car.red.wash("Now!");. This might be an oversimplification, but it should help you better grasp the idea of objects, properties, and methods.

## Avoid Common Errors in Coding

Writing any kind of computer code is tricky because programming languages are not at all forgiving. Be prepared to have to "debug" your JavaScript, as no matter how careful you are errors will slip in. However, if you keep in mind some of the more common errors, you should be able to catch most of them:

- JavaScript is case-sensitive. That means that onClick and onclick are not the same thing in the eyes of the browser that is interpreting the program. Always make sure you are consistent in how you write and capitalize.

- Every JavaScript line should end with a semicolon (;).

- You shouldn't break up a single line of code into multiple lines. You can do this with HTML; JavaScript will treat it as an error.

- Many parts of your code will have to be contained in quotation marks. You can use either single or double quotation marks, but if you put one set inside another, you must alternate them.

  ```
  "This 'is an' acceptable construction."
  "This construction "is not" acceptable."
  ```

If you plan to use JavaScript in your Web design, you will be well advised to test your pages on a Netscape browser. Although both Internet Explorer and Netscape will let you know when you've got an error in your code, IE will merely give you an error message in an alert box, as in the following illustration.

NOTE *It is a good practice to install each of these four browsers in a separate directory (IE 4.x, IE 5.x, Netscape 4.x and 6.0), being careful to choose the default options during installation. (This is how your visitors probably have installed their Web browsers.) Check your scripts using each browser.*

15

On the other hand, Netscape actually will help you debug the code. If you run a page that has a JavaScript error, a message on the status bar at the bottom of the browser will instruct you to type **"javascript:"** in the location bar (where you normally type Web addresses). This will bring up a JavaScript console that actually will show you where the error(s) occurred.

```
Communicator Console - Netscape                                          _ □ ×

JavaScript Error:
file:/C|/WINDOWS/DESKTOP/osborne/HTMLCode/Ch15code/js2.htm,
line 11:

unterminated string literal.

document.write("My first JavaScript script."');
...............................................^



javascript typein


[                                                                    ]
  Clear Console    Close
```

Of course, you will still need to know enough about JavaScript to know how to correct the errors in your code, but at least you won't need to waste a lot of time trying to find them.

# Experiment with JavaScript

A good way to start experimenting with JavaScript is with some easy but practical applications. These will not only get you used to working with JavaScript, they will give you some useful tools you can use on your page. Also, you might gain a better understanding of objects, methods, and properties as you apply them in the following exercises.

## Write a "Last Modified" Script

You have undoubtedly seen a line at the bottom of many Web pages that reads, "This page was last modified on," and then the page included the date on which the Webmaster made changes to it. You might have wondered if the Webmaster had to go in and adjust that line every time the page was changed. Actually, there is a way to have the date line correct itself automatically, and it only takes a few lines of JavaScript to do it. Open template.htm and save it as lasmod.htm; then add the <script> element and comment tags (<!-- -->) to the <body> portion of the page. When your code looks like the following listing, you'll be ready to add your script:

```
<html>
<head><title>Untitled</title></head>
<body>
<script type="text/javascript" language="JavaScript">
</script>
</body>
</html>
```

To write a one-line JavaScript that will add a "last modified" line to your page, follow these steps:

1.  Because you are going to be writing to your HTML document, you will be using the "document" object and the "write" method to instruct the browser to write a line of text. Insert it in your code like this:

    ```
    <script type="text/javascript" language="JavaScript">
    document.write( );
    </script>
    ```

2.  Inside the parentheses you will put a property that will cause the browser to display the date and time the document was last modified. In this case use the document object with the "lastModified" property. If you save the page and view it in your browser, you will see a line at the top left of the screen that displays the date and time (of the last modification).

    ```
    <script type="text/javascript" language="JavaScript">
    document.write(document.lastModified);
    </script>
    ```

**15**

CAUTION *Don't forget to write lastModified exactly as you see it. In JavaScript, when two words are put together, a capital letter often is used to distinguish where one ends and the other begins. Because JavaScript is case sensitive, your browser will not understand what you are asking for if you write lastmodified, LastModified, or Lastmodified.*

3. Because your visitors will not necessarily understand what that date and time refer to, you will want to add an explanatory note, such as "Date last changed: ". To add your text, enclose it in quotation marks and put it inside the parentheses, along with your document.lastModified.

```
<script type="text/javascript" language="JavaScript">
document.write("Date last changed:" + document.lastModified);
</script>
```

Save the page and display it in your browser. As in the following illustration, you should see a line displaying the time you saved the document (down to the very second). It might not be very attractive, but you can change that by adding a little HTML.

Date last changed: 03/27/2010 14:48:36

By putting your script inside a table cell and adding a little HTML to the command, you can "dress up" the display. The HTML for creating such a design is in the following listing. Modify your page to include the changes; then save it as lastmod2.htm. As in the illustration that follows the code, your "last modified" display will look a little more pleasing.

NOTE *The line of JavaScript in the following listing has been broken into two lines because of this book's layout. However, it's important to remember that it should be written on a single line. Otherwise, the browser will think it is two separate statements and will return an error.*

```
<html>
<head><title>Untitled</title></head>
<body style="background-color: white;">
<center>
<table border="1">
<tr><td>
<script type="text/javascript" language="JavaScript">
```

```
<!-- Comment tags to hide script from older browsers
document.write("<h5>Date last changed: " +
   document.lastModified + "</h5>");
-->
</script>
</td></tr>
</table>
</center>
</body>
</html>
```

> **Date last changed: 03/27/2010 14:50:48**

# Write a Script that Identifies Browsers

In JavaScript the browser is considered an object. Identified as a *navigator* (remember, JavaScript was developed by Netscape), the browser object allows you to design a page that will gather information about the browser that is viewing it. Once you get comfortable with JavaScript, you can even design your code to load different pages depending on which browser your visitor is using. To see the capabilities of the *navigator* object, open template.htm and save it as navigator.htm. Once you've added a set of script and comment tags, add the following lines of JavaScript:

1. Add a line that will identify the browser that is displaying the page.

   ```
   document.write("Your browser is: " + document.appName +
   "<br />");
   ```

2. Add a line that will display the browser's version number.

   ```
   document.write("The version is: "document.appVersion   +
   "<br />");
   ```

3. Write an instruction that displays the type of platform (computer) on which the browser is running.

   ```
   document.write("Your platform is: " + document.platform   +
   "<br />");
   ```

   Your finished code should look like the following code listing:

   ```
   <script language="Javascript" type="text/javascript">
   <!--
   ```

15

```
document.write("Your browser is: " + navigator.appName +
"<br />");
document.write("The version is: " + navigator.appVersion +
"<br />");
document.write("Your platform is: " + navigator.platform +
"<br />");
-->
</script>
```

To see this script in action, you should try it on different browsers. Your results will be different for each different browser, version, or system on which the page is displayed. For instance, if you view this page with Netscape, your results will look like the illustration that follows:

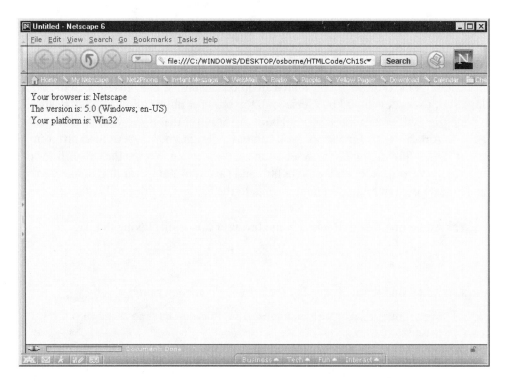

However, if you use Internet Explorer to display the page, your results will be different. As in the following illustration, the application name and version number will change to reflect the browser with which the page is being displayed.

```
Untitled - Microsoft Internet Explorer                                    _ □ ×
 File   Edit   View   Favorites   Tools   Help    Links  Best of the Web  Channel Guide  Customize Links  »
 Address  C:\WINDOWS\DESKTOP\osborne\HTMLCode\Ch15code\navigator.htm          ▼   Go

 Your browser is: Microsoft Internet Explorer
 The version is: 4.0 (compatible; MSIE 5.0; Windows 95; Creative; DigExt)
 Your platform is: Win32




 Done                                                      My Computer
```

Because most people already know what browser they are using to surf the Net, you might be wondering what possible use that little bit of JavaScript can be. Granted, just as an informational tool it's not all that exciting. However, you also can use the navigator object to analyze the kind of browser a visitor is using; then display an appropriate page.

For instance, say you want to use some aspects of HTML that were supported in Netscape but not in Internet Explorer. You don't want to exclude your faithful visitors who might not be using Netscape. So to alert your viewers that they will gain the most benefit from the page if they use Netscape, you can write a code that will test the browser and return a special prompt if it is not Netscape. Open template.htm and save it as navtest.htm; then add the following script to the page:

```
<script language="Javascript" type="text/javascript">
<!-- Comments hide script from older browsers
document.write("<h3>You are using ")
     if(navigator.appName == "Netscape")
          {document.write("Netscape. Proceed</h3>")}
```

```
        else{(document.write( "a non-Netscape browser. This page is
best viewed with Netscape.</h3>"))};
// You can stop hiding the script, now. -->
</script>
```

Don't get too confused by some of the unfamiliar parts of the script; the best way to understand the script is to examine it line by line:

- The first line should look somewhat familiar. In it you use the "write" method and the "document" object to have the browser write the phrase "You are using." Note the addition of the <h3> element inside the quotes:

  ```
  document.write("<h3>You are using ")
  ```

- Next you set up a condition that the browser should look for with an "if, else" statement. The idea is that the browser should look for a certain condition. "If" it is true, the browser is instructed to take one action. If the condition is not true ("else"), it is to take a different action. This line sets up the condition the browser is to look for. Notice the use of a double equal sign. In JavaScript, a single equal sign is used to assign a value to something. To convey the idea of one thing being equal to another, you must use two equal signs, as shown here:

  ```
  if(navigator.appName == "Netscape")
  ```

- The next line tells the browser what to do if it is a Netscape browser. In this case it uses the "document.write" command to write a line that says "Netscape. Proceed." Note that the entire statement is contained in curly braces:

  ```
  {document.write("Netscape. Proceed</h3>")}
  ```

- The final line of the script gives the "else" condition. This statement tells the browser what to display if it is not a Netscape browser. Notice again that after the "else" command, the entire statement is enclosed in curly braces:

  ```
  else{document.write("a non-Netscape browser.<br />This page is
  best viewed with Netscape.</h3>")}
  ```

Once you have typed the script, save it and display it in a Netscape browser. Your results should look something like the following illustration:

## You are using: Netscape. Proceed

If you try viewing the page in Internet Explorer, you should see a different display, as is reflected in the screen shot that follows:

**You are using a non-Netscape browser.**
**This page is best viewed with Netscape.**

## Write a Script that Displays the Current Date

Have you ever visited a site that displayed the current date and time? This is easy to do with JavaScript. It also gives you the opportunity to work with the "date" object. To see how easy it is to use JavaScript to display a date, open template.htm and save it as datetime.htm; then follow these steps:

1. Add your script and comment tags.

```
<script language="javascript" type="text/javascript">
<!-- Hide your code from older browsers
// Stop hiding -->
</script>
```

2. Create a date with the date object. You will assign the name "Today" to the date. You can name it whatever you want to, but "Today" seems appropriate.

```
Today = new Date( );
```

3. Tell the browser to display the date by using the document.write command. Notice that you use the name (Today) that you assigned to the date object. The phrase "Today's date is: " is enclosed in quotation marks because it is a text string. The two are connected with a plus sign (known as a *concatenating operator*).

```
document.write("Today's date is: " + Today);
```

4. Your completed script should look like this:

```
<script language="javascript" type="text/javascript">
<!-- Hide your code from older browsers
Today = new Date( );
document.write("Today's date is: " + Today);
// Stop hiding your code -->
</script>
```

15

If you save this page and display it in your browser, you will see the current date and time displayed in the upper-left corner of the page. The following illustration shows what you should see:

Today's date is: Sat Mar 27 19:58:30 CST 2010

Realistically, you probably would want to display the date in a slightly more conventional manner. It's not much more difficult to do that; you just need to instruct the browser to display only certain parts of the date. Using the getMonth, getDay, and getYear methods, you can make your display more specific. Each method is connected with a period to the date (Today) you already defined. Your line of JavaScript would be modified to read like the following listing:

```
Today = newDate();
document.write("Today's date is: " + Today.getMonth() + "/"
+ Today.getDay() + "/" + Today.getYear());
```

The three methods mentioned in the preceding paragraph are connected with the plus sign (+), and a slash is added between the parts of the date by enclosing it in a set of quotation marks ("/").

Also, using style sheets you can enhance the appearance of the JavaScript display. Consider the difference it makes when you add some CSS style rules to improve the look of your page. Modify your code to match the following listing. As the following illustration shows, your date display can be made to look quite attractive:

```
<html>
<head><title>JavaScript Date Display</title>
<style type="text/css">
body    {background-color: tan;}
table   {background-color: peach;
        border-style:outset;
        border-color: yellow;}
td      {font-family: Arial;
        font-size: 12pt;
        font-weight: bold;
        color: brown;}
</style></head>
<body>
<table>
<tr><td>
```

```
<script language="javascript" type="text/javascript">
<!-- Hide your code from older browsers
Today = new Date( );
document.write("Today's date is: " + Today.getMonth() + "/"
+ Today.getDate() + "/" + Today.getYear());
// Stop hiding your code -->
</script></td></tr>
</table>
</body>
</html>
```

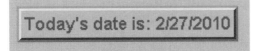

Today's date is: 2/27/2010

Unless you are familiar with programming, you have encountered a number of unfamiliar ideas and constructions as you've worked with JavaScript. Although this chapter cannot go into every possible detail, some of the aspects of JavaScript "grammar" you have used thus far are reviewed in Table 15-1.

| To Do This... | Write It This Way... |
| --- | --- |
| Add a single-line comment to JavaScript. | // Your comment goes here |
| Add a multiple-line comment to JavaScript. | /* Your comment goes here */ |
| Hide JavaScript from HTML. | <script> <!-- Script goes here --> </script> |
| End a complete JavaScript statement. | Use a semicolon (;) |
| Use a method or function. The method or function's *arguments* go inside parentheses. (Arguments are the specific actions a method or function performs.) | method( )  function( ) document.write("Hello") |
| Connect multiple JavaScript statements. | Enclose in curly braces {  } |
| Connect (concatenate) groups of literal characters (strings). | Use the "plus sign" (concatenate operator) "string" + "string" + "string" |
| Say that something is "equal to" something else (as in 2 + 3 = 5). | Use double equal signs ( = = ) if {date = = Today} |
| Assign a value to a variable (something that can change). | Use a single equal sign ( = ) var = Variable |

**TABLE 15-1**     Some Basic JavaScript Grammar

15

NOTE    *A more detailed summary of JavaScript syntax can be found on the inside back cover of this book.*

# Work with Events and Event Handlers

By now you're probably either very excited about JavaScript or thoroughly intimidated by it. Realistically, not everyone finds programming an easy thing to do. Fortunately, a number of the more impressive things JavaScript can do also are some of the easier things to accomplish.

Earlier in this chapter you read about events and event handlers. To refresh your memory, an event is something that happens on your visitor's browser, generally in response to an action they have taken (for example, loading a page, unloading it, clicking on something, and so on). An *event handler* is a JavaScript statement that is triggered by a particular event. Table 15-2 lists some of the most commonly used event handlers and the events that trigger them.

| Event | Event Handler |
|---|---|
| Your visitor stops a page that is loading. | onAbort |
| Your visitor tabs out of a form field. | onBlur |
| Your visitor tabs into a form field. | onFocus |
| A page loads into the browser. | onLoad |
| Mouse cursor moves over a part of the page. | onMouseOver |
| Mouse cursor moves away from a button or other part of the page. | onMouseOut |
| Visitor clicks the "submit" button. | onSubmit |
| Visitor clicks the "reset" button. | onReset |
| Visitor holds the mouse button down. | onMouseDown |
| Visitor releases the mouse button. | onMouseUp |
| Visitor clicks on part of your page. | onClick |

TABLE 15-2    Some Events and Event Handlers

# Experiment with Event Handlers

Event handlers allow you to create a page that responds to the actions of your visitor. Whether it is through mouseovers, keypresses, or simple clicks, you can use event handlers to create a responsive environment on your Web site. The best part about event handlers, though, is that they are easy to use.

## Create a "Ticklish" Button

To see how easy it is to use event handlers (and to have some fun doing it), try creating a "ticklish" button. This little JavaScript effect demonstrates how you can make a page change dynamically in response to a visitor's actions. The effect begins by displaying a button that says "Click for a surprise." When you move a mouse over the button, it triggers the onMouseOver event handler and the button changes to read, "That Tickles!" If you move the mouse off the button, the onMouseOut event handler changes the button to read, "Come Back." Then, if you hold the button down, it triggers the onMouseDown event handler, which alters the button to read, "Ready for the surprise?" Finally, when you release the button, it disappears and the word "Surprise!" appears in its place.

The code for the ticklish button is reproduced in the following listing. As you type it in, note that you do not use the <script> element. Often, event handlers are placed right inside an HTML element, as in the code here. For the ticklish button, all the event handlers are in the same <input /> element.

```
<html><head><title>The Ticklish Button</title>
<style> body {background-color: white; color:navy}
</style></head>
<body>
<div align="center">
<h1>The Ticklish Button</h1>
<form>
<table border="1"><tr><td>
<input type="button" value="Click for a surprise."
```

15

```
onMouseOver = "value='That tickles!'";
onMouseOut = "value='Come back!!!'";
onMouseDown = "value='Ready for the suprise?'";
onMouseUp = "document.write('<h1>SURPRISE</h1>')"; />
</td></tr></table>
</form></div></body></html>
```

When you have typed the code, save it as ticklish.htm and open it in your browser. The opening screen will resemble the following illustration. However, when you move your mouse over the button and back out, the button should respond to your movements.

# The Ticklish Button

Come back!!!

## Create a Rollover

A more practical use of event handlers is with mouse rollovers for navigation buttons. To create a simple rollover effect, you must create two buttons that are nearly identical. For this illustration two buttons, hibuttonoff.gif and hibutton.gif, differ only in the color of the text, as is shown in the following screen shot:

These two buttons will be used to create your rollover. To try this for yourself, open template.htm and save it as hibutton.htm. Then, follow these steps to use the onMouseOver and onMouseOut event handlers:

1.  Create a simple image link using the hibuttonoff.gif image.

    ```
    <a href="falselink.htm"><img src="hibuttonoff.gif" /></a>
    ```

2.  Add the name=" " attribute to the image element to assign a name to the image. For this exercise, the name will be "hiThere".

```
<a href="falselink.htm"
<img src="hibuttonoff.gif" name="hiThere" /></a>
```

**3.** Modify the anchor <a> </a> element to add the onMouseOut event
handler. The event handler will refer to the name that you assigned
to the image (hiThere).

```
<a href="falselink.htm"
onMouseOut="hiThere.src='hibuttonoff.gif'">
<img src="hibuttonoff.gif" name="hiThere" /></a>
```

**4.** Add the onMouseOver event handler to the <a> element.

```
<a href="falselink.htm"
onMouseOut="hiThere.src='hibuttonoff.gif'"
onMouseOver="hiThere.src='hibuttonon.gif'">
<img src="hibuttonoff.gif" name="hiThere" /></a>
```

Save the code and display it in your browser. Your complete page should look like
the following code listing and the illustration that follows:

```
<html><head><title>Rollover Demo</title>
</head>
<body>
<a href="falselink.htm"
   onMouseOut="hiThere.src='hibuttonoff.gif'"
   onMouseOver="hiThere.src='hibuttonon.gif'">
<img src="hibuttonoff.gif" name="hiThere"/></a>
</body>
</html>
```

# Learn Good Web Design

If your first taste of JavaScript has left you with an appetite for more, you might be
wondering where to go to learn more about it. On the other hand, if writing JavaScript
gives you a headache, but you'd still like to take advantage of some of its benefits,

## How to ... Include a Java Applet on Your Page

As mentioned earlier in this chapter, JavaScript is not the same as Java. You might be wondering what Java is and whether you can use it in your Web pages. Java is a powerful object-oriented programming language with capabilities and possible applications that extend far beyond the Internet. However, one way you can use Java is by inserting *applets* on your Web pages. Java applets are actually miniprograms that enable you to add animations; scrolling text; special visual effects; and even things like arcade games, clocks, and calculators. You don't need to know how to program in Java to be able to use an applet. By visiting one of the many sites that offer free downloads (for instance, www.javaboutique.com), you can choose from many different applets.

You can use the <applet> </applet> element to include an applet on a page. However, because <applet> has been deprecated, you should learn to use the <object> </object> element if you plan on including Java applets. (See Chapter 11 for more about how to use the <object> element.) At its most basic, a line of code including an applet on a page might look like this:

```
<applet code="www.myaddress.com/applet.class" height="100" width="100">
Whatever is between the tags functions like "alt" text. Browsers that
don't support Java or have Java disabled will display this text.
</applet>.
```

you might be wondering who you can pay to write your scripts for you. The good news is that whether you want to learn JavaScript or merely find prewritten scripts to incorporate on your pages, some of the best JavaScript resources are freely available to you online.

## Web Design Principle: Work Smarter, Not Harder

Did you ever hear the adage about "working smarter, not harder?" That saying applies very directly where JavaScript is concerned. Unless you just simply love programming and get an adrenaline rush from writing JavaScript, there's really no need to go to the trouble of writing your own scripts. Sure, there's a feeling of accomplishment to be derived from writing a successful script, but after several hours of debugging, that feeling diminishes considerably. On top of that, scripting takes valuable time that you might not have to spare. So how do you benefit from JavaScript?

Learn enough JavaScript to plug it into a page without having to write your own scripts. There is a wealth of information on the Internet about JavaScript. There are almost certainly prewritten scripts available to accomplish whatever you need. You might need to tweak them a bit, but in the long run they probably will be better than anything you could write yourself. So, to take advantage of JavaScript while keeping headaches to a minimum, find some good online tutorials that will give you enough of a background that you can perform minor adjustments to scripts. Then, find the scripts online and plug them into your page.

If you are serious about learning JavaScript, you can find tutorials targeted at all levels of experience. If you would rather just download some prewritten scripts to include on your page, you will be pleased to know that there are more free scripts out there than you'll ever be able to take advantage of. Table 15-3 lists a few of the Web sites that you can check out for JavaScript tutorials and resources.

## Practice, Practice, Practice

From a beginner's standpoint, the fastest way to get up and running with JavaScript is by downloading a prewritten script and including it in your browser. If you really want to use JavaScript on your site, visit some of the Web sites referenced in Table 15-3, download some scripts you find interesting, and design a page including one of those scripts. As you work with the script, try breaking it down and thinking through what each part of the script is doing. The more you work with JavaScript, the quicker you will learn to write your own scripts.

15

| Site Name | URL |
|---|---|
| **1001 Tutorials**   A clearing house for tutorials that links to multiple sites. A great resource for beginners as well as advanced Webmasters. | www.1001tutorials.com/javascript |
| **Page Resource.Com**   This site offers both tutorials and free prewritten scripts. | www.pageresource.com/jscript |
| **JavaScript.Com**   For the more experienced Web author, this site offers cut-and-paste scripts and provides a wealth of resources and articles. | www.javascript.com |
| **HTML Goodies**   Joe Burns's site provides easy-to-follow primers and a lot of practical resources. | htmlgoodies.com |
| **JavaScript City**   This site is a good source for downloadable scripts and even hosts a "How do I?" forum where you can ask questions about JavaScript. | javascriptcity.com |
| **A Beginner's Guide to Javascript** This site provides a JavaScript tutorial for the "absolute beginner." It's a good starting place if you want to learn more. | www.javascriptguide.com |

**TABLE 15-3**    Sites for JavaScript Downloads and Tutorials

# Find the Code Online

To find the code online for this or any of the chapters in this book, go to Osborne's Web site, www.osborne.com, and click the Free Code choice on the navigation bar. From the list of books, select the *How to Do Everything with HTML* option and you will be able to download the book files, which are linked together and organized as an offline "mini" Web site. For more on how to use the "mini" Web site, see Chapter 17.

| Use This Code For... | Look for This Filename |
|---|---|
| onClick demo | clickevent.htm |
| My first script | js1.htm |
| External script | extscript.js |

| Use This Code For... | Look for This Filename |
| --- | --- |
| Improved "Last Modified" page | lastmod2.htm |
| Browser test page | navtest.htm |
| Enhanced date display | datetime2.htm |
| Rollover demo | hibutton.htm |
| Button "on" image | hibuttonon.gif |
| Form validation script | formvalid.htm |
| Page linked to external script | js2.htm |
| Last modified page | lastmod.htm |
| Browser ID page | navigator.htm |
| Current date display | datetime.htm |
| Ticklish button | ticklish.htm |
| Button "off" image | hibuttonoff.gif |

# Chapter 16

## Liven Up Your Site with DHTML

## How to...

- Understand DHTML
- Create a Layered Page
- Control Object Positioning
- Use DHTML to Create Animations

Have you ever been visiting a Web site, clicking from page to page, when suddenly a page dissolved before your eyes as it changed to the next? Perhaps the next page disappeared with a sideways "window blind" effect. If you've ever seen such an effect, very possibly it was done with Dynamic HTML. JavaScript alone will enable you to create interactive pages—but Dynamic HTML takes a quantum leap beyond JavaScript.

# Understand Dynamic HTML (DHTML)

Dynamic HTML, or DHTML, is a hybrid of sorts. Instead of being a distinct language, DHTML represents a composite of several different Web development technologies. In fact, one of the more problematic aspects of DHTML is that there are two different (and largely incompatible) versions of it in existence: Microsoft's and Netscape's. Both are working with the W3C to create a definitive standard, but that does not yet exist. However, before considering the differences in the various versions of DHTML, you might want to learn what it is.

## Understand DHTML Essentials

Dynamic HTML enables you to control, position, and animate the various elements of your Web page by making use of four essential components or "ingredients." Even though Microsoft, Netscape, and the W3C might add their own distinct flavors to it, at the most basic level Dynamic HTML is a combination of the following:

- **HTML**   Obviously, HTML must be a part of DHTML. HTML provides the foundation for Dynamic HTML. Pages created with DHTML are standard Web pages in the sense that any browser capable of displaying a page written in HTML 4 (almost all browsers) should have no trouble with a DHTML page.

- ■ **CSS**   Cascading Style Sheets are the next major component of DHTML. Style sheets enable a Web author to position elements on a page with a great degree of precision. It is this ability to position elements that is very important to the functioning of DHTML.

- ■ **JavaScript**   JavaScript (or another scripting language) adds the "dynamic" element to DHTML. By using sophisticated scripting techniques in conjunction with style sheets, a Web author can create some very dramatic effects.

- ■ **DOM (Document Object Model)**   The Document Object Model is a way of understanding a Web "document" that allows the page's designer to apply Web page scripting to virtually any part of the page. If HTML, CSS, and JavaScript provide the structure for Dynamic HTML, the DOM is the blueprint.

Although all of these "ingredients" are a part of any version of DHTML, there are some significant differences in how they are implemented.

## Understand Netscape's and Microsoft's Versions

Dynamic HTML has developed directly along the lines of the "browser wars." Although both Netscape's and Microsoft's versions have been built from the same four components mentioned in the preceding section, unfortunately the two companies originally implemented DHTML in very incompatible ways.

### Netscape's DHTML

Netscape's vision for DHTML was based on *layers* (see the following Note). To understand the idea of layers, think of your Web page as if it is on a table in front of you. However, instead of a single page, you have a collection of elements: text, pictures, and so on. You could stack your pictures one on top of another, or perhaps lay them so they overlap each other. You might take your headline text and have it overlapping a picture. That's the basic idea of layers.

Through the use of Netscape's proprietary <layer> and <ilayer> elements, you can take portions of your page and position them wherever you'd like to. The precise positioning is accomplished with CSS's absolute and relative positioning capabilities. To make the page dynamic you use JavaScript to adjust the positioning of the various elements on your page. Of course, there's quite a bit more to it, but that's a simple explanation.

16

## Microsoft's DHTML

Microsoft's approach to DHTML is rooted in *styles*. In other words, with Netscape you use the <layer> element; with the Microsoft approach you use Cascading Style Sheets and the <span> or <div> element. Instead of using HTML attributes to position the layers, you use CSS syntax, either as a style attribute inside the element or as an embedded or external style sheet. However, you get the same basic control over the positioning of your elements. The only difference is how you write the code. Unfortunately, that's the big problem. Because there are so many differences in how Microsoft and Netscape have implemented DHTML, their two approaches simply won't work together. Thus, the challenge for any Web author who wants to make use of Dynamic HTML is to create pages that are compatible with both browsers.

NOTE     *Netscape's latest browser release (version 6) no longer supports the <layer> and <ilayer> elements. This represents a hopeful move in the direction of resolving the problems of incompatibility in DHTML. Nevertheless, because <layer> is easy to use and self-explanatory, it's still a good place to start when learning about DHTML.*

# Experiment with DHTML

Dynamic HTML is such a complex subject; this chapter cannot do much more than give you a taste of it. To develop serious applications for your Web site that are cross-browser compatible can be quite a daunting task, particularly if you are a beginner. However, by experimenting with DHTML's capabilities you can get familiar with how it works and what you can do with it. As with JavaScript, if you find that you want to learn more about Dynamic HTML, there are many resources available, some of which will be covered later in this chapter.

## Create a Page with Netscape's Layers

The concept of layers is fundamental to the Netscape version of DHTML. By using Netscape's <layer> element, you can position items on top of one another, overlap them, and place them precisely on the page. You also can enclose text and images, and even nest other elements within the layer element.

### Create a Stack of Colored Squares

An easy way to get a feel for how the <layer> element works is to use it to create a stack of different-colored squares. As you will see, once you have created your layers you will be able to manipulate them in a way you never could with HTML alone. Begin by opening template.htm and saving it as dynlayer1.htm, and then follow these steps:

1.  Add the <layer> </layer> element to your code.

    ```
    <layer> </layer>
    ```

2.  Define the dimensions of your layer by first positioning it. With Netscape's version of positioning, you consider the upper-left corner of the browser window as (0,0). Position the layer by setting the number of pixels from the top of the window and from the left side. Thus, values of top="25" and left="25" will set your layer 25 pixels from the top and left sides of the browser window.

    ```
    <layer top="25" left="25"> </layer>
    ```

3.  Give your layer some dimensions of its own. You set these like you would for an image, with the height and width attributes. For this layer, create a box that is 250×250 pixels.

    ```
    <layer top="25" left="25" width="250" height=250">
        </layer>
    ```

4.  So that you can see your layer, use the bgcolor attribute to set its background color to blue.

    ```
    <layer top="25" left="25" width="250" height=250"
      bgcolor="blue"></layer>
    ```

5.  Save the page and display it in your browser. You should see a blue square in the upper-left portion of the screen that resembles the following illustration:

**16**

NOTE    *You will need to use nothing lower than Netscape 4 or higher than Netscape 4.7 to view the <layer> exercises properly.*

6.  To add more layers, simply copy the preceding line and change the values for the top and left attributes. You also will want to change the bgcolor attribute to several different colors so you can differentiate the layers. The following code listing will create a stack of six different-colored, overlapping boxes:

```
<layer top="25" left="25" width="250"
    height="250" bgcolor="blue"></layer>
<layer top="35" left="35" width="250" height="250"
    bgcolor="red"></layer>
<layer top="45" left="45" width="250" height="250"
    bgcolor="yellow"></layer>
<layer top="55" left="55" width="250" height="250"
    bgcolor="navy"></layer>
<layer top="65" left="65" width="250" height="250"
    bgcolor="aqua"></layer>
<layer top="75" left="75" width="250" height="250"
    bgcolor="green"></layer>
```

7.  When you save your page and display it in Netscape, you should see a stack that looks like the following illustration:

Now, think of this stack of layered squares as a pile of cards. By changing the top and left attributes for each layer, you can move them around the page independently of one another just as you would several squares of colored cardboard. As you can see in the following illustration, you can position them anywhere on the page:

The code used to create the preceding illustration can be found in the following listing. Of course, you also could modify the size of the layers by adjusting the height and width attributes.

```
<layer top="25" left="145" width="250" height="250"
bgcolor="blue"></layer>
<layer top="35" left="350" width="250" height="250"
bgcolor="aqua"></layer>
<layer top="45" left="45" width="250" height="250"
bgcolor="yellow"></layer>
<layer top="95" left="250" width="250" height="250"
bgcolor="magenta"></layer>
<layer top="135" left="65" width="250" height="250"
bgcolor="red"></layer>
<layer top="125" left="375" width="250" height="250"
bgcolor="green"></layer>
```

NOTE    *In addition to the <layer> element, Netscape has added an element named <ilayer>. Ilayer stands for inline layer. The difference between the two is simple: The <layer> tag is used to designate an "absolute" position for your layer (that is, the layer's position relative to the entire page). On the other hand, the <ilayer> element is used to designate a "relative" position for the layer (that is, the layer's position relative to the element in which it is enclosed). You will see how this works in the following section.*

## Add Images and Text to Your Layers

Although moving around colored squares might be interesting and fun, you might be wondering what value it has. The way to begin to discover the power of layers is by adding some images and text to them. Find some GIF or JPEG images on your computer's hard drive (or download the ones in this chapter from Osborne's Web site, www.osborne.com) and then follow these steps. Figure 16-1 displays the finished product, and you can refer to it as you write your code.

1.  Because the layers overlap in the order that they were added to the page, start by adding an image to the sixth layer. That way, your image will not be obscured by other layers. You add an image to a layer the same way you

16

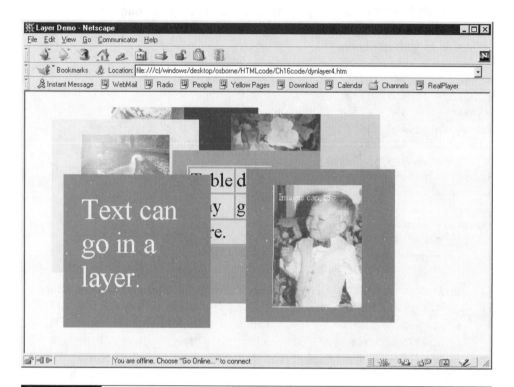

FIGURE 16-1    Layers can contain text, images, tables, and even other layers

would put any other image in a page. The only difference is that you put it
in between <ilayer> tags and nest it inside the first set. By using this nested
layer you can position the image within the layer.

```
<layer top="125" left="375" width="250"
   height="250" bgcolor="green">
   <ilayer top="25" left="50">
      <img src="cjpickle.jpg" width="150" height="200" />
   </ilayer>
</layer>
```

2. To see how you can use multiple layers nested within one another, add a
   layer of text to the preceding listing. This layer should be nested inside the
   second set of layer tags.

```
<layer top="125" left="375" width="250" height="250"
    bgcolor="green">
  <ilayer top="26" left="45">
      <img src="cjpickle.jpg" width="150" height="200" />
```

```
    <layer top="10" left="10" style="color:white">
Images can, too.</layer>
  </ilayer>
</layer>
```

3.  To add some variety, put some text in the next layer. Notice that in the outer layer (the parent), the style attribute has been added to set the font to 36 points and the color to white. Because of CSS's concept of *inheritance*, the style information will pass to the inner layer (the child) and affect the display of your text.

```
<layer top="135" left="65" width="250" height="250"
    bgcolor="red" style="font-size:36pt; color:white";>
    <layer top="30" left="30">Text can go in a layer.</layer>
</layer>
```

4.  Try adding a table to the third layer. To make the table stand out, give it a border and set the background color of the individual table cells to gold. To do this, you'll need to add a style line in the head portion of the page or in the <tr> or <td> cells. The easiest way is to embed a style in the <head> portion of the page as in the following:

```
<head><style>
td  {font-size:24pt; background-color:gold;}
</style></head>
```

5.  Your table should be nested inside the <layer> tags for the third layer from the bottom (the magenta layer), like this:

```
 <layer top="95" left="250" width="250" height="250"
    bgcolor="magenta">
  <layer top="25" left="25">
    <table border="2">
      <tr><td>Table</td><td>data</td></tr>
      <tr><td>might</td><td>go</td></tr>
      <tr><td colspan="2">here.</td></tr>
    </table></layer>
</layer>
```

6.  Select some images or add some text to the remaining three layers; then save them and display them in Netscape. Your results should resemble Figure 16-1. The complete code for the layered page is given in the following listing, and comments have been added to make it easier to identify the various parts.

```
<html>
<head><title>Layer Demo</title>
```

16

```
<style>
td  {font-size:24pt; background-color:gold;}
</style></head><body>

<!-- This is the blue layer -->
<layer top="25" left="145" width="250" height="250"
bgcolor="blue">
<img src="boo.jpg" width="125" height="150" />
</layer>

<!-- This is the aqua layer -->
<layer top="35" left="350" width="250" height="250"
bgcolor="aqua">
<img src="pansy1.jpg" width="150" height="125" /></layer>

<!-- This is the yellow layer -->
<layer top="45" left="45" width="250" height="250"
bgcolor="yellow">
<layer top="25" left="50"><img src="goose.jpg" width="150"
height="125" /></layer>
</layer>

<!-- This is the magenta layer -->
<layer top="95" left="250" width="250" height="250"
     bgcolor="magenta">
<layer top="25" left="25"><table border="2"
style="font-size:24pt; background-color:gold;">
<tr><td>Table</td><td>data</td></tr>
<tr><td>might</td><td>go</td></tr>
<tr><td colspan="2">here.</td></tr></table></layer>
</layer>

<!-- This is the red layer -->
<layer top="135" left="65" width="250" height="250"
bgcolor="red" style="font-size:36pt; color:white";>
<layer top="30" left="30">Text can go in a layer.</layer>
</layer>

<!-- This is the green layer -->
<layer top="125" left="375" width="250" height="250"
bgcolor="green">
<layer top="26" left="45">
<layer top="10" left="10" style="color:white">
```

```
Images can, too.</layer>
<img src="cjpickle.jpg" width="150" height="200" />
</layer></layer></body></html>
```

Once you finish typing in the code, save the page as dynlayer4.htm and view it in Netscape; then try viewing this page with Internet Explorer 4 or higher. As the following illustration demonstrates, IE doesn't support Netscape's layer element, and your page doesn't look anything like what you designed. If you want to create a layered effect in Internet Explorer, you must take an entirely different approach.

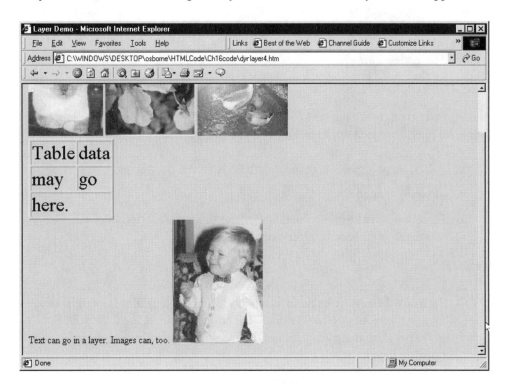

## Create Layers for Internet Explorer

Microsoft's approach to creating a layered Web page is by using the <span> and <div> elements, along with the Cascading Style Sheet "position" property. Although written somewhat differently, the concept is basically the same as Netscape's. The <span> and <div> elements act as the containers for your text or images. CSS positioning allows you to move, stack, and overlap whatever is contained in the <span> and <div> elements.

Although you could create precisely the same effect for IE as you did for Netscape, for the sake of variety try creating a page with several layers of text. To demonstrate

## Did you know?

## The Difference Between \<span\> and \<div\>

Although, the \<span\> and \<div\> elements perform very similar functions, they are different in at least one important way: The \<div\> element functions as a "block" level element. Block level elements (\<p\>, \<h#\>, and \<hr /\> for instance) all mark off divisions in a page's structure. As such, generally they add blank lines before and after their content. On the other hand, \<span\> is not a block level element. It functions as an inline generic container that you can use to insert almost anything into a page.

the layered effect, make the text in different colors and sizes. Open template.htm and save it as dynstyle.htm; then follow these steps to create your first layer:

1. Add a set of \<span\> tags inside the body of the document.

```
<span> </span>
```

2. Place some text between the tags. Make the text descriptive of what it ultimately will become: Very Big Green Text.

```
<span>Very Big Green Text</span>
```

3. If you display the page right now, you will only see a simple line of text. To make the text fit its description, add some style information. For this text, set the font size to 96 points, the color to "green," and the font family to "serif." Use the style attribute to place the style information in the opening \<span\> tag.

```
<span style="font-size:96pt; color:green;
font-family:serif;">Very Big Green Text</span>
```

**4.** Add the layering effect by inserting some position information into the style attribute. For this layer, set the position property to absolute, the top property to 20 pixels from the top, and the left property to 25 (25 pixels from the left).

```
<span style="position:absolute: top:20; left:25; font-size:96pt;
color:green; font-family:serif;">Very Big Green Text</span>
```

**5.** Copy the rest of the code from the following code listing. Notice the different position numbers for the various layers of text.

```html
<html>
<head>
        <title>Internet Explorer DHTML</title>
</head>
<body style="background-color: white;">

<!-- A layer of very large green text -->
<span style="position:absolute; top:20; left:25;
font-family:serif; font-size:96pt; color:green;">
Very Big Green Text</span>

<!-- A layer of large blue text -->
<span style="position:absolute; top:40; left:100;
font-family:arial; font-size:42pt; color:blue;">
Large Blue Text</span>

<!-- A layer of medium red text -->
<span style="position:absolute; top:35; left:150;
font-size:36pt; color:red;">RED TEXT</span>

<!-- A layer of very small text with yellow background -->
<span style="position:absolute; top:30; left:125;
background-color:yellow;">Small Text</span>
</body>
</html>
```

16

As the following illustration demonstrates, your text will be overlapped (layered) the same as it was with the Netscape <layer> element:

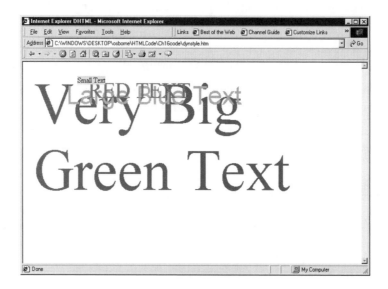

## Control Stacking Order in Layers

Although layering is an interesting effect, what's the use if you can't control how the layered parts of your page are stacked? If you refer to Figure 16-1, you'll notice that all but the top two layers are partially obscured. If there was no way to move things around, you would be wasting your time. That's what makes DHTML so much fun: You can move things around. Although it's handled somewhat differently in Netscape and Internet Explorer, the idea of stacking order is called the *z-index*.

### Adjust Layers for Netscape

To change the order in which the layers are stacked on your Netscape page, add the z-index=" " attribute to each of the six major layers (the colored squares). Because this attribute is inherited, any layers that are nested in the major ones also will be moved. The principal is simple: The higher the z-index number, the closer to the top the layer will be stacked. For instance, if you want to take the square in Figure 16-1 that has the table and move it to the top of the pile, give it a z-index of 6. You would add it like this:

```
<!-- This is the magenta layer -->
<layer top="95" left="250" width="250" height="250"
    bgcolor="magenta" z-index="6">
```

```
<layer top="25" left="25"><table border="2"
style="font-size:24pt; background-color:gold;">
<tr><td>Table</td><td>data</td></tr>
<tr><td>might</td><td>go</td></tr>
<tr><td colspan="2">here.</td></tr></table></layer>
</layer>
```

To see how it works, give the following z-index values to the layers on your Netscape (dynlayer4.htm) page:

■ **Blue layer**   z-index="3"

■ **Aqua layer**   z-index="4"

■ **Yellow layer**   z-index="5"

■ **Magenta layer**   z-index="6"

■ **Red layer**   z-index="2"

■ **Green layer**   z-index="1"

When you are finished, save the file as dynlayer5.htm and open it in Netscape. Your results should resemble the illustration that follows:

You can see that the ability to rearrange your stack of layers is as simple as changing one attribute of the <layer> element. However, remember that more than one way of rearranging layers exists. Although Internet Explorer also uses the concept of z-index, it applies it a little differently, as you will see.

## Modify Stacking Order for Internet Explorer

If you are writing a page that you want to be compatible with Internet Explorer, you will still use z-index, but you will place it in the style attribute and use CSS

16

syntax. For instance, to reverse the stacking order of your Internet Explorer page, add z-index to each of the <span> elements as in the following listing:

```
<!-- A layer of very large green text -->
<span style="position:absolute; top:20; left:25; z-index:4;
font-family:serif; font-size:96pt; color:green;">
Very Big Green Text</span>

<!-- A layer of large blue text -->
<span style="position:absolute; top:40; left:100; z-index:3;
font-family:arial; font-size:42pt; color:aqua;">
Large Blue Text</span>

<!-- A layer of medium red text -->
<span style="position:absolute; top:35; left:150; z-index:2;
font-size:36pt; color:magenta;">RED TEXT</span>

<!-- A layer of very small text with yellow background -->
<span style="position:absolute; top:30; left:125; z-index:1;
background-color:yellow;">Small Text</span>
```

When you've typed in the code, save your page as dynstyle1.htm and then open it in Internet Explorer. As the following illustration shows, now the green text will be stacked on top with the order of the other colors reversed.

NOTE    *Netscape versions 4.7 and 6.0 also display this version with no problems.*

Now that you've learned how to shuffle the deck, so to speak, there still is another key way of manipulating layers. DHTML also enables you to control a layer's *visibility*.

## Control a Layer's Visibility

Controlling visibility means you are able to determine whether a layer displays or does not display. In effect, you can turn layers on or off. By controlling visibility you could create a page which has images or text that displays in response to some event on the page, say a mouse click or mouseover. Are you beginning to see where the dynamic part of DHTML comes from?

### Visibility Control with Layers

As with z-index, the basic concept of visibility control is the same with both IE and Netscape; however, the application is different. To control the visibility of layers on a page for a Netscape browser, add the visibility attribute to the layer. If you want to turn the layer off and make it invisible, set the value to "hidden." To turn the layer on (the default setting), set the value to "visible." For example, to set two of the layers from Figure 16-1 as "hidden," modify the lines to read like the following listing:

```
<layer top="35" left="350" width="250" height="250"
z-index="4" bgcolor="aqua" visibility="hidden">
<img src="pansy1.jpg" width="150" height="125" /></layer>

<layer top="45" left="45" width="250" height="250"
z-index="5" bgcolor="yellow" visibility="hidden">
<layer top="25" left="50"><img src="goose.jpg"
   width="150" height="125" />
</layer>
</layer>
```

If you save the page, check your results in Netscape; you should see that two of the layers have disappeared. Actually, they are still there; they're just not being displayed. The following illustration shows how the page looks with the invisible layers:

To create the same effect for an Internet Explorer browser, you will use the CSS visibility property and include it in the style attribute for the layer you are modifying. Thus, to set the visibility to "hidden" for the layer of "Very Big Green Text" created earlier, you would change the line to look like the one that follows:

```
<!-- A layer of very large green text -->
<span style="position:absolute; top:20; left:25; z-index:4;
visibility:hidden; font-family:serif; font-size:96pt;
color:green;">
Very Big Green Text</span>
```

If you make that change and save the page and view it in Internet Explorer, you will see that the line of green text is no longer visible, as in the following:

Although there are more details involved in positioning, z-index, and visibility, the ones covered thus far are enough to give you an idea of the basic elements of DHTML. However, even though you have created, positioned, and moved layers, you still haven't created interactivity. That's what you will experiment with next.

## Use JavaScript to Bring DHTML to Life

The chapter on JavaScript introduced events and event handlers. These are the "switches" that will bring your page to life. Thus far, you have seen how parts of your page could be positioned, stacked, and made invisible, but all the pages have still been static. The way to bring them to life is with events, event handlers, and JavaScript.

A simple but fun way to see DHTML in action is by creating a little game that will move an image around the page. This Dynamic HTML page will make use of HTML to create the actual Web page, styles to control positioning, and JavaScript to create the action. Begin by opening template.htm and saving it as dynsample.htm. The following steps don't necessarily need to be done in this particular order, but it might help you keep track of the overall process if you do:

1.   Add an embedded style sheet to the <head> to set the overall style of the page and to position the image:

```
<style>
body {background-color: white;}
p    {font-weight: bold; font-size: 1.1em;}
<!-- Use an ID selector to set the picture's position. -->
  #pansy {position: absolute; top:255; left:50;}
</style>
```

TIP

*An ID selector enables you to create a unique selector for an HTML page. To create an ID selector, you use the pound sign (#) and whatever identification name you want. As in the preceding listing, it can be a name, or it can be a number or a combination of letters and numbers. The only requirement for ID is that it must be unique; that is, it cannot be applied to more than one part of the page. To apply the ID, you must insert the id=" " attribute into the element that you want associated with it.*

2. You will need to add some JavaScript functions to move the picture around. A function basically is a set of instructions to which you have assigned a name, which can be called by the browser in response to an event. JavaScript comes with some built-in functions, but for this page you will write your own. The four functions in the following listing contain instructions for repositioning the image:

CAUTION

*Be sure to type the script exactly as it is written.*

```
<!-- Use JavaScript functions to move the picture. -->
<script language="javascript" type="text/javascript">
    function movePansy() {pansy.style.posLeft +=100;}
    function movePansyBack() {pansy.style.posLeft -=100;}
    function movePansyUp() {pansy.style.posTop -=100;}
    function movePansyDown() {pansy.style.posTop +=100;}
</script>
```

3. Add the instructions for the game to the <body> of the page.

```
  <!-- Add instructions for the game. -->
<center>
<h1>Catch the Pansy</h1>
<p>
This picture can be very cantankerous!<br />
It doesn't like to be touched and will run away<br />
when you put your cursor over it.<br />
```

16

```
If you are patient, though, you can use your<br />
left mouse button to move it where you want it to go.<br />
Hold the button down to move the pansy toward the top of
the screen.<br />
Release the button to move the pansy toward the left side
of the screen.<br />
(But first you have to figure out how to catch it!)<br />
</p></center>
```

4. Following the instructions, add the image by inserting the <span> element with the <img /> element in between the <span> tags.

```
<span><img /></span>
```

5. As you normally would, modify the <img /> element by adding the source, height, and width attributes.

```
<span><img src="pansy1.jpg" height="125" width="150" /></span>
```

*You don't need to download the "pansy1.jpg" image to do this exercise. Any image you have can be placed in the <img /> element.*

6. Associate this image with the #pansy ID by adding the id=" " attribute to the opening <span> tag.

```
<span id="pansy">
```

7. Add event handlers to the opening span tag.

```
<span id="pansy"
onMouseOver="movePansy()"
onMouseOut="movePansyDown()"
onMouseUp="movePansyBack()"
onMouseDown="movePansyUp()">
```

*Each event handler calls a particular function. Thus, when someone's mouse cursor moves over the image (onMouseOver), it will move to the right 100 pixels. The reason is that in the function named movePansy, the style of the "pansy" selector is modified by adding 100 pixels to its left position (pansy.style.posLeft). Likewise, the other functions modify the top and left styles for the image by either adding or subtracting pixels from its position.*

The complete code for dynsample.htm is given in the following listing. Try experimenting by adding another image, or even two, and making them move dynamically around the page.

```
<html>
<head><title>Dynamic Sample</title>
<style>
body {background-color: white;}
p    {font-weight: bold; font-size: 1.1em;}
<!-- Use an ID selector to set the picture's position. -->
  #pansy {position: absolute; top:255; left:50;}
</style>
<!-- Use JavaScript functions to move the picture. -->
<script language="javascript" type="text/javascript">
   function movePansy() {pansy.style.posLeft +=100;}
   function movePansyBack() {pansy.style.posLeft -=100;}
   function movePansyUp() {pansy.style.posTop -=100;}
   function movePansyDown() {pansy.style.posTop +=100;}
</script>
</head>
<body>
<!-- Add instructions for the game. -->
<center>
<h1>Catch the Pansy</h1>
<p>
This picture can be very cantankerous!<br />
It doesn't like to be touched and will run away<br />
when you put your cursor over it.<br />
If you are patient, though, you can use your<br />
left mouse button to move it where you want it to go.<br />
Hold the button down to move the pansy toward the top of
the screen.<br />
Release the button to move the pansy toward the left side
of the screen.<br />
(But first you have to figure out how to catch it!)<br />
</p></center>
<!-- Add the picture and the event handlers. -->
<span id="pansy"
    onMouseOver="movePansy()"
    onMouseOut="movePansyDown()"
```

```
        onMouseUp="movePansyBack()"
        onMouseDown="movePansyUp()">
<img src="pansy1.jpg" height="125" width="150" /></span>
</body>
</html>
```

Once you have copied the code and saved your page, try it out in Internet Explorer. As you move your mouse over the picture, it should scoot away toward the right side of the screen. If your cursor moves off of the picture, the picture will go toward the bottom of the screen. By holding down the left mouse button, you can make the image move toward the top of the screen; when you release the button the image should go toward the left. As the following illustration shows, you will see the layering effect when the image moves over the page's text:

**TIP**    *The trick to catching the image is in approaching it from the right-hand side of the screen. That way, when the mouseover makes the image move to the right, your cursor will still be on it. To adjust the degree of difficulty, simply make the image larger or smaller with the height and width attributes. The larger the image, the easier it will be to control; the smaller it is, the harder it will be to catch.*

# Learn Good Web Design

Now that you have had a limited introduction to the world of DHTML, the obvious question is how big a part, if any, it should play on your Web site. The temptation to use DHTML is great, considering what you can do with it. As a Web author, you now are free to create pages that respond to your visitors in a way unheard of in the early days of the Web. However, does that necessarily mean you should use it?

## Web Design Principle: Too Many Cooks...

Perhaps the development of DHTML is one of the best illustrations of the adage "Too many cooks spoil the soup" that you will ever find. Because of the different approaches taken by Netscape and Microsoft, to make use of DHTML you must create pages containing instructions that both browsers can understand. Although it's not impossible to do this, when you consider the complexity of the scripts you'll have to write and weigh them against DHTML's overall benefits, and it's probably not worth the trouble. Netscape's move toward supporting the W3C's Document Object Model is a positive sign for the future of DHTML. However, in the final analysis, although DHTML can produce some cool effects, in the long run it probably won't give your site an edge over anybody else's—at least not now.

## Practice, Practice, Practice

Absolute and relative positioning, z-index, visibility, and event handlers enable you to add some life to your pages. You don't need to make your pages heavily dependent on DHTML or write a lot of complex scripts to do it. By experimenting with some of the pages created for this chapter, you can develop a feel for how to manipulate these characteristics of your Web pages.

For instance, try modifying the stack of images created for the first part of this chapter to create a "clickable" stack. You'll need to write a function that will

16

change the z-index of an image when you click on it. That way, you can create a photo album–type page that will display a stack of pictures and bring the "clicked" picture to the front. If you want to see a sample of the page, plus the code that created it, you can find it online along with all of the other code from this chapter.

# Find the Code Online

To find the code online for this or any of the chapters in this book, go to Osborne's Web site, www.osborne.com, and click the Free Code choice on the navigation bar. From the list of books, select the *How to Do Everything with HTML* option and you will be able to download the book files, which are linked together and organized as an offline "mini" Web site. For more on how to use the "mini" Web site, see Chapter 17.

| Use This Code For... | Look for This Filename |
|---|---|
| A single blue box | dynlayer1.htm |
| A stack of six colored boxes | dynlayer2.htm |
| Colored boxes rearranged | dynlayer3.htm |
| Colored boxes with added elements | dynlayer4.htm |
| Layered text | dynstyle.htm |
| Dynlayer5 rearranged with z-index | dynlayer5.htm |
| Catch the Pansy | dynsample.htm |

# Chapter 17

## Finishing Touches

## How to...

- Set Up a Web Site in 10 Steps
- Validate Your HTML Code
- Check Your Style Sheets
- Use Web Developer Resources

You've read this book and feel competent to write your own HTML code, but perhaps you also feel like you've been handed the pieces of a jigsaw puzzle that you don't quite know how to assemble. Admittedly, creating Web pages and putting a Web site together are two different things. Now that your HTML toolbox is filled, this chapter will cover some of the steps to putting a Web site together and some finishing touches you might want to consider. Also, if you've been working through the book and creating your own Web pages with the exercises, this is where you will pull all those pages together into your reference Web site.

# Assemble a Simple Web Site

There are many ways to go about setting up a Web site; you can plan precisely or haphazardly add pages as inspiration strikes you. Although you might not need to go to the same extremes of planning that a Web developer does, your site undoubtedly will benefit if you develop it systematically. The steps that follow are not the only way to organize a Web site, but they will give you a basic framework from which to plan and construct your own site.

## Step 1: Define Your Site

Your first step should always be to define your site. Defining your site can include everything from writing down your site's goals to the number and types of images you want to include. The more time you spend defining your site, the less time you'll have to spend constructing it. Think of it as if you were building a house. When you build your own home, you have hundreds, if not thousands, of decisions to make. You have to choose doors, windows, hardware, paint, wallpaper, and carpet. However, even before that you've got to buy land, select blueprints, find a contractor, and so on. Once the decisions are made and the materials assembled, construction begins. Why not try approaching your Web site that way?

As you plan your site and work toward a clear understanding of what you want it to be and do, consider some of the following possibilities:

■ Describe your site in one brief sentence: "My site is . . ." For instance, "My site is a personal family album site," or "My site is an online used book store." Whatever you want your site to be, try to describe it as clearly as possible.

■ After you describe your site's purpose, focus on its goals. Make up a list of things you want your visitors to be able to find and/or do when they come to your site. For example, "I want my visitors to learn about model rocketry by seeing pictures of model rockets, having access to plans for rockets, watching a video of a rocket launch, reading about rockets and safety," and so on.

■ Describe your visitors in one sentence: "My visitors are . . ." You might write something like, "My visitors are people who are interested in gardening," or "My visitors are old movie buffs." The clearer the picture you have of who your visitors are, the better you will be able to focus your site.

■ Make a blueprint for your site by storyboarding it. Storyboarding a site involves making a drawing of how you want your site to be organized. Whether you lay your Web site out with 3×5 cards or sketch it out on a piece of paper, storyboarding enables you to develop a visual perspective of how your pages should be linked together. It also helps you avoid a haphazard approach to site design that can leave your visitors wandering through your site and wondering where to go. (For more on storyboarding, see Chapter 7.)

Based on your storyboard and purpose statements, decide what you will need to include on your site in the way of content, images, forms, and other bells and whistles. Will you need to have audio and video? Before you answer "Yes" to that question, ask yourself how audio and video will enhance your site. Do you want to add it because you need it or because it's cool? Do you need a *splash* page done with Flash? Will it bring more visitors or drive away those who don't want to wait for it to download? The basic principle is, "Think before you add."

17

TIP     *As you storyboard your site, list a filename for each page you want to create. If you name your files at this point, you will be able to build your navigational links before you actually create all the individual pages.*

Once you have taken time to focus on your site's purpose and the raw materials you will need to assemble it, you are ready to create a template page and plan your layout.

## Step 2: Create a Template Page and Layout

Chapter 1 covers how to make a simple HTML template. If you have worked through any of the succeeding chapters, you opened your template.htm file many times as you created different practice pages. As you design your Web site, you will find it helpful to create a template page specifically for your site. This page serves as a canvas to plan and test your layout, experiment with colors, and so on. It also enables you to give your site the same (or similar) look on every page.

### Create a Template

You can create your template page by opening template.htm and saving it as sitetemplate.htm. Keep your browser open as you begin to plan your layout, and view your page as you make adjustments to it. You also might want to add some sample text for this preliminary stage, using some of the page elements you think you'll need for your site. Later, as you work on your style sheet, you'll be able to see how your styles affect the overall appearance of the page.

SHORTCUT    *If you're planning to build more than 10 pages that will share the same basic formatting, you might want to consider an external style sheet rather than a template.*

### Plan Your Layout

Planning a layout for your Web site is what enables you to give your site its own distinctive look. The best place to start your planning is by visiting other sites and observing their designs. Set up a special Favorites folder on your browser so you can easily revisit sites that you find appealing. You also can save the pages on your hard drive for online access. However, resist the temptation to "borrow" from someone else's site by merely copying the pages and changing the content to fit your own needs. Your site will mean more to you if it has your distinctive stamp on it. Besides, it can be embarrassing if one of your visitors also has visited the site from which you borrowed. Learn and get ideas from other sites, but make your site your own.

What should your layout planning include? A good layout includes a color scheme for the site, general page design, background colors and images, font choices, image placement, and navigation material. By planning these out ahead of time, you can give your site a consistency of appearance that you'll never achieve with a haphazard, design-as-you-go approach.

## How to ...   Download and Save a Web Page

If you want to save some Web pages for offline viewing, you do it in much the same way you would if you were merely saving a file. In Netscape, click File, Save Page As; then choose the directory where you want to save the file. For Internet Explorer, click File, Save As, and when the dialog box opens, make sure that the Save As Type option has "Web Page, complete" displaying in the selection box, as in this:

If you find the idea of choosing and developing a layout for your site a daunting task, why not start with something simple and work up from there? A basic, three-celled table layout can be the foundation of a very nice-looking site, and it's easy to do. The following code features an uncomplicated design with a top logo panel, a left-side navigation bar, and a right-side content panel. As you can see in the illustration that follows, it is a simple design that easily can be modified into more complex layouts.

```html
<html>
<head>
<title>Sample Layout Template</title>
</head>
<body style="background-color:white;">
<table border="2" width="100%" height="100%"
cellpadding="0" cellspacing="0">
```

17

```
<tr>
<!-- Row 1, Cell 1: Logo -->
<td colspan="2" height="15%">
Top bar is for your logo or heading</td>
</tr>
<tr>
<!-- Row 2, Cell 1: Nav bar -->
<td class="nav" width="20%" height="85%">
<p>Left side bar is for navigational links</p>
<a href="nolink.htm">Sample Link</a></td>
<!-- Row 2, Cell 2: Content cell -->
<td width="80%" height="85%">
Right panel is for your content
<h1>First level heading</h1>
<h2>Second level heading</h2>
<h3>Third level heading</h3></td>
</tr>
</table>
</body>
</html>
```

With a little shuffling around, you can take the preceding code and rearrange it to produce a layout with the navigation bar on the right, or even with top and bottom navigation bars and a center panel for content.

TIP

*The borders for the table have been set to 3 to make the layout easier to visualize. However, once you're finished designing your layout, you'll probably want to turn them off. You can easily remove them by setting the table border attribute to 0.*

Once you've settled on a design for your site, you can develop a style sheet. You can use style sheets to control virtually any aspect of your pages' appearance. However, controlling appearance is only one of the strengths of CSS. CSS can also be a real timesaver.

## Step 3: Develop a Style Sheet

Although style sheets are not required for you to construct a site, you will find that they save you time in the long run. For instance, say you build a fairly large site containing 50 or more pages but decide not to use style sheets. Down the line, if you decide you'd like to change the overall look of your site, you'll have to go in to every single page to make your changes. On the other hand, if you had used a style sheet to begin with, you'd simply make the changes on the style sheet and they would be instantly reflected in every page that is linked to it.

As you develop a style sheet for this practice site, be sure to save it as you go and link the template page to it as in the following: **<head><link rel="stylesheet" type="text/css" href="practicesite.css" /></head>**. Although you can write very complex and detailed style sheets, for a simple site it's really not necessary. In fact, too many different styles, fonts, and colors can make your page look "busy" and distract from your content. It's best to start simple and add to your style sheet as you need to.

The following style sheet code gives the page a tan, left-side navigation bar with links that light up and change color when a mouse passes over them. It sets the basic background color to white and the font color to navy.

```
body       {background-color:white; color:navy;}
h1         {color:navy; font-size:2em; text-align:center;}
p            {color:navy; font-size:1.2em; margin-left:4em;}
table      {background-color:white;}
td.nav     {background-color:tan;
            text-align:center;
            font-family:sans-serif, arial;
            font-weight:bold;}
a:link       {text-decoration: none;}
a:active     {color:gold;}
a:visited    {color:navy;}
a:hover      {color:red; background-color:yellow;}
```

17

```
img.logo    {height:100; width:600;}
img.smlogo  {height:75; width:450; float:right;}
```

When you link this style sheet to your sitetemplate.htm file and display it in your browser, you'll see that the page has changed to conform to your style sheet.

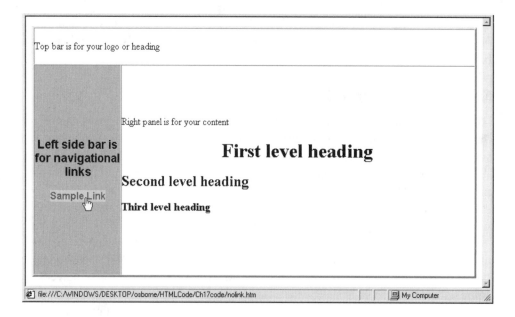

## Step 4: Add Navigational Links

As you consult your storyboard, you will at least have an idea of what your major navigational links should be. In the navigation panel of your template page, add links to each of your primary pages. Be sure to create a link back to your home page so that your visitors don't have to depend on the Back button on their browsers to go back to your main page. You also will want to create a link to a *site map,* which is a directory page linked to all the other pages on your site.

To add a set of navigational links to your practice site, modify row 2, cell 1 by replacing the cell and its contents with the following code:

```
<td class="nav" width="20%" height="85%">
Links to Code by Chapter
<hr width="25%" />
<a href="chapter1.htm">Chapter 1</a><br />
```

```
<a href="chapter2.htm">Chapter 2</a><br />
<a href="chapter3.htm">Chapter 3</a><br />
<a href="chapter4.htm">Chapter 4</a><br />
<a href="chapter5.htm">Chapter 5</a><br />
<a href="sitemap.htm">Site Map</a><br />
<a href="index.htm">Home</a><br /></td>
```

If you are developing a reference site for the pages you have created in working through this book, you will need to add an additional link for each chapter. Of course, if you are following these steps to create your own Web site, you will want to substitute your own links. The following illustration shows what the page looks like with basic links added.

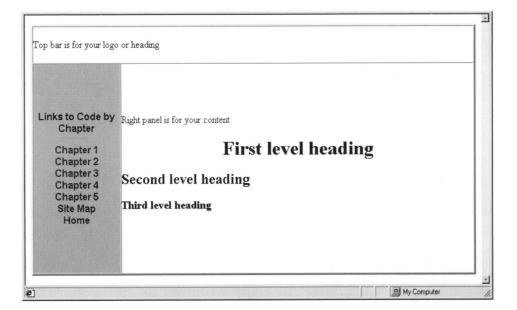

## Step 5: Duplicate Your Template Page

When you have tinkered with your style sheet and it looks the way you want it to, you can build your site. There's no need to write the HTML for each page separately; particularly if all of the pages on your site are going to have the same general look. Simply design and save a template page. Remove any sample text you've put in; then copy it as many times as you need to. Save each of your template pages with one of the names you've already specified in your links. After you've created a page for each of the major parts of your site, you're ready to add content.

17

## Step 6: Add Your Text

Once you have established the basic structure or "skeleton" of your site, you can go in page by page and add your text. You can write your text in the Web page itself or in Notepad, Wordpad, or your favorite word processor; then cut and paste the text into your page. If you use a word processor that has a Web page creator built in, avoid using that feature. Word processors tend to add unnecessary elements, use the <font> element, and generate code that you'll probably have to go in and clean up eventually, anyway. Save yourself the trouble and put only pure text into your pages. As the following illustration shows, once you add content, your pages begin to take shape. However, even though the page is looking better, it still looks a bit bare. You'll correct that with the next step: adding images.

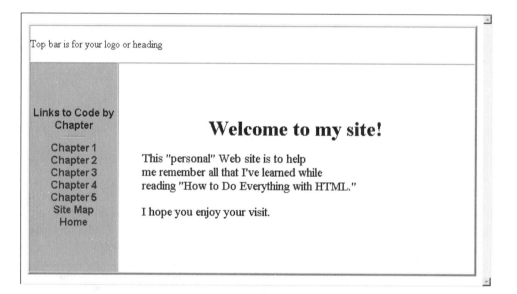

## Step 7: Add Your Images

Why should you add your images after you have put in your primary content? Well, there's no official rule that says you have to do it that way. However, unless your images *are* your primary content, they are there to decorate and enhance your site—to give it eye appeal. Back to the house building analogy: Get the structure built before you start hanging wallpaper. By including images after you put in your textual content, you can see how the images will affect the overall look of your site. Also, you can experiment with different image sizes and positions while watching how they affect your text.

For the practice site's start page, banner.gif (created in Chapter 6) has been added to the top cell as a logo. Another image, htmlimg.gif, has been placed in the content cell to offset the text and take up some of the white space. As the following code and illustration show, even simple images can enhance a site's appearance:

```html
<html>
<head>
<title>Sample Layout Template</title>
<!-- Style sheet link -->
<link rel="stylesheet" type="text/css"
href="practicesite.css" />
</head>
<body style="background-color:white;">
<table border="0" width="100%" height="100%"
cellpadding="0" cellspacing="0">
<tr>
<!-- Row 1, Cell 1, Logo panel -->
<td colspan="2" height="15%"><center>
<img src="banner.gif" alt="Logo" class="logo" />
</center></td>
</tr>
<tr> <!-- Row 2, Cell 1, Nav bar -->
<td class="nav" width="20%" height="85%">
Links to Code by Chapter
<hr width="25%" />
<a href="chapter1.htm">Chapter 1</a><br />
<a href="chapter2.htm">Chapter 2</a><br />
<a href="chapter3.htm">Chapter 3</a><br />
<a href="chapter4.htm">Chapter 4</a><br />
<a href="chapter5.htm">Chapter 5</a><br />
<a href="sitemap.htm">Site Map</a><br />
<a href="index.htm">Home</a><br /></td>
<!-- Row 2, Cell 2, Content panel -->
<td width="80%" height="85%">
<h1>Welcome to my site!</h1>
<img src="htmlimg.gif" alt="HTMLimage" class="htmlimg" />
<p>This "personal" Web site is to help<br />
me remember all that I've learned while<br />
reading "How to Do Everything with HTML."</p>
```

17

```
<p>I hope you enjoy your visit.<br /></p></td>
</tr>
</table>
</body>
</html>
```

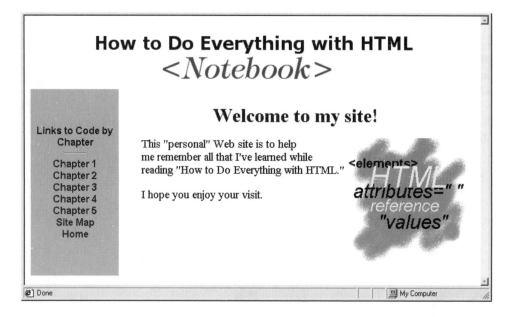

SHORTCUT   *An easy way to keep track of your images is to keep them in a separate folder as you create or select them. When you upload your site, upload the entire folder. That way, you won't have to search through all your HTML documents if you are looking for a particular image.*

## Step 8: Add the Fancy Stuff

After you have added text and images to your site, you can incorporate any of the bells and whistles that you plan on adding to your site. Some of these might include forms, streaming audio and video, animations, JavaScripts, Java applets, and any other fancy things you want to add to your site. This is also a good time to play with your style sheet if you want to experiment with different looks. Make adjustments to your style rules, and then check to see how they affect your pages. Once you have added all your bells and whistles, you're almost ready to launch your site.

## Step 9: Create a Site Map

Don't forget to create a site map. As its name implies, a site map is a page that will function as a directory of all your pages. If your visitors want to get a bird's-eye view of your site rather than following your navigational links, they can go to this page. A site map can be very simple, such as a plain text page of links, or it can be done with graphics and images and made as attractive as the rest of your site. How much time you invest in creating your site map is up to you. However, by all means include one so that your visitors can quickly find their way to a particular page. The following illustration and code listing demonstrate how you can create a bare bones site map for your reference site using HTML list elements:

```
"My Reference Site" Site Map

Chapter 1 Main Page

Chapter 2 Main Page
        Basic Template (template.htm)
        Headings (headings.htm)
        Text Elements (text.htm)
        Unordered Lists (ulist.htm)
        Unordered List with Subpoints (ulist2.htm)
        Ordered List (olist.htm)
        Roman Numeral List (olist2.htm)
        Sample Outline (olist3.htm)
        Definition List (dlist.htm)
        Sample Home Page (template.htm)

Chapter 3 Main Page
        Text Elements (text2.htm)
        Text Alignment (align.htm)
        Font Demo (fontsz.htm)
        Font Size Experiment (fontx.htm)
        Inline Style Demo (styledemo.htm)
```

```html
<html><head><title>Site Map</title></head>
<body>
<h2>"My Reference Site" Site Map</h2>
<dl>
<p><dt><a href="chapter1.htm" />Chapter 1 Main Page</dt></p>
<p><dt><a href="chapter2.htm" />Chapter 2 Main Page</dt>
<dd><a href="template.htm" />Basic
     Template (template.htm)</a></dd>
<dd><a href="headings.htm" />Headings (headings.htm)</a></dd>
```

**17**

```
<dd><a href="text.htm" />Text Elements (text.htm)</a></dd>
<dd><a href="ulist.htm" />Unordered Lists (ulist.htm)</a></dd>
<dd><a href="ulist2.htm" />Unordered List with Subpoints
(ulist2.htm)</a></dd>
<dd><a href="olist.htm" />Ordered List (olist.htm)</a></dd>
<dd><a href="olist2.htm" />Roman
      Numeral List (olist2.htm)</a></dd>
<dd><a href="olist3.htm" />Sample Outline (olist3.htm)</a></dd>
<dd><a href="dlist.htm" />Definition List (dlist.htm)</a></dd>
<dd><a href="sampleindex.htm" />
      Sample Home Page (template.htm)</a></dd></p>
<dt><a href="chapter3.htm" />Chapter 3 Main Page</dt>
<dd><a href="text2.htm" />Text Elements (text2.htm)</a></dd>
<dd><a href="align.htm" />Text Alignment (align.htm)</a></dd>
<dd><a href="fontsz.htm" />Font Demo (fontsz.htm)</a></dd>
<dd><a href="fontx.htm" />Font Size
      Experiment (fontx.htm)</a></dd>
<dd><a href="styledemo.htm" />Inline
      Style Demo (styledemo.htm)</a></dd></dl>
</body></html>
```

# Step 10: Test Your Site

Before you upload your pages to your server, you must test your entire site. You want to be certain all your links work and that you don't have bugs in any of your scripts. However, these are not the only tests you need to make. Following is a list of some other tests you might want to run on your site:

- **Browser compatibility**    Test your pages at least on Internet Explorer 4 and higher and Netscape 4 and higher. It's good practice to have these browsers installed on your system and to routinely check your pages with them. By doing this you can anticipate and correct any problems that might arise as you develop your pages

- **Screen resolution**    Check your pages in different screen resolutions to see how your pages display when viewed on a higher or lower resolution than you used when creating the page. If your monitor is capable of displaying multiple resolutions (and most are nowadays), simply adjust the monitor resolution by right-clicking anywhere on your desktop and choosing the Properties option. In the Display Properties dialog box, choose the Settings tab and move the slide bar in the Desktop area to a higher or lower setting.

NOTE    *If your monitor is not capable of handling a higher resolution, just wait. If you don't confirm the new setting, Windows will go back to your previous setting after 15 seconds.*

■   **Colors**   Another monitor-related issue you might want to check is how your colors display on other systems. Save some of your pages to floppy disk and visit your friends. When you display your pages on their systems, you might be surprised at what you see. You also might decide you need to adjust some of your colors to the browser-safe variety. (Remember that the Netscape named colors in Appendix A are *not* browser safe. You must convert them to the nearest browser-safe equivalent if you want to avoid dithering.)

After you have tested your site, fixed any broken links or images, and corrected any problems you might have discovered with displays or style sheets, you are ready to upload your site. (For details on uploading your site, see Chapter 7.) However, there are a few last checks you should perform sooner or later. These aren't essential in the sense that your pages won't function without them; however, they will become, increasingly important in the coming years.

# Validate Your HTML Code

Valid HTML (as opposed to not valid) is something you probably wouldn't have heard much about several years ago. However, with the move toward XML, the Web authoring language of the future, the concept of validating your code has moved to the forefront. What does it mean if your code is valid? It means that your HTML conforms to the standard. Two terms to understand in this whole concept are *valid* and *well formed.* Your HTML documents should be valid; they need to be well formed.

## Understand Valid and Well-Formed Documents

A well-formed HTML document is properly constructed. In other words, it is good HTML. You've used closing tags where they are required. All your elements are properly nested, with no overlapping tags. This is why your pages need to be well formed. If you are writing sloppy HTML and committing some of the previously mentioned errors, there's a good chance your pages won't work properly. However, it is possible for your document to be well formed yet still not valid.

A valid document is not only properly written; it conforms to a certain standard. The standard is known as a *document type definition* (DTD). That's something that

17

comes from HTML's parent language (SGML). A document type definition is what defines the various elements, attributes, and so on that make up HTML. Often, Web pages identify what DTD they claim to conform to.

If you use an HTML editor or a WYSIWYG program to create your Web pages, you might see something like the following line at the top of the page: <!DOCTYPE HTML PUBLIC "-//W3C//DTD HTML 4.0 Transitional//EN">. This statement is what is known as a *document type declaration*. It's simply a statement that identifies precisely which standard the page conforms to. In this case it's HTML 4.0 transitional.

Are you thoroughly confused yet? You needn't be. The reason this has become such an issue is because the Web is in the midst of a transition from HTML to XML as the language of choice. Because an overnight change from one to the other would leave many Web surfers out in the cold, with browsers that wouldn't recognize the new language and because people will take a while to adjust to using XML, the W3C has set up a transitional language known as XHTML. This is sort of a *bridge* (transitional) language that possesses the characteristics of both HTML and XML. Older browsers will still understand this bridge language; yet it also represents a huge step toward XML as the primary language for Web authoring.

## Understand Document Validation

So what's all this got to do with validation, and why do you need to even be concerned about it? Right now, you probably don't need to be concerned—at least about whether your pages will work. However, if you want to avoid problems with your pages down the line, not only must you make sure they are well formed, you must ensure that they conform to at least the XHTML transitional standard. The strict standard means you use no tags related to layout at all; you handle style entirely with style sheets. The transitional standard still allows for using some presentational attributes.

How do you validate your pages? Many HTML editors have built-in validation programs that will point out where your pages need to be changed if you want them to be validated. Some programs, such as HTML Tidy, actually will make the changes for you. The W3C even has a validation service (see the following illustration) that will check out your pages free of charge. You simply go to their site, enter the URL of the page you want validated into the form, and in a few seconds you will have a generated report showing where your page stands up against the standard you've chosen.

> NOTE
>
> *The HTML Tidy program is freeware and can be downloaded from the W3C's site at www.w3.org.*

## Validate Your Style Sheets

After you have validated your HTML code, you also might want to think about validating your style sheets. Although CSS is not particularly difficult to learn, it is complicated enough that you will benefit from some help in writing your style sheets so that they are as effective and error free as possible. This help can be found in a CSS validation program or service. The Web Design Group provides a free CSS validation service at www.htmlhelp.com. You simply give the service the address of the style sheet you are using, and it will look it over and generate a report that tells you where your code needs to be corrected. Often, you can also cut and paste your style sheet into the submission form and have it checked out before you've put it online. As you can see in the following, the reports can be very instructive and are a great way to learn how to write better style sheets:

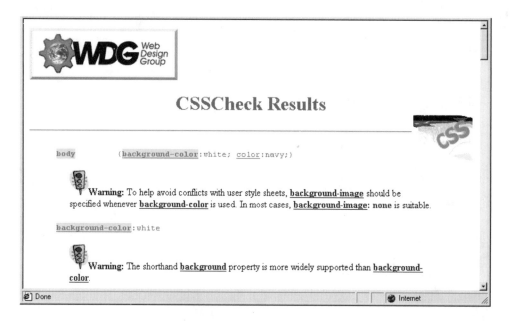

## Learn Good Web Design

Once you have a site online, hopefully you will be adding to it and changing it, and you might even be starting new sites. Who knows? You might even go into Web design as a second career or write a book on Web authoring. It's important to remember that learning Web authoring is an ongoing process. You always want to keep learning.

## Web Design Principle: Keep on Learning

Whether you are considering Web design as a career or only as a hobby, it offers a fascinating array of possibilities. New technologies and methods of creating Web pages are constantly being developed. Computers are becoming faster, and browsers are capable of handling more and more bells and whistles. The only way for you to keep your site on the cutting edge is to keep learning. Don't just put your site online, sit back, and never touch it again. Keep learning and working to make it better. If you surf the Web a lot, you see that sites often are redesigned, updated, and improved. Make that the case with your sites, too. Some developer resource Web sites you might want to check out as you continue to learn how to be a Web author can be found in Table 17-1.

## Practice, Practice, Practice

In this chapter you developed a framework for creating your own Web site. Perhaps you are already well along the way to having your site online, or maybe you are working on collecting the different pages and files you created in this book and assembling them into a reference notebook.

If you're having trouble with that idea, one resource you may want to take advantage of is an offline "mini" Web site, constructed from the Web pages

| Web Site | URL |
| --- | --- |
| Web Developer's Virtual Library | www.stars.com |
| Webmonkey | www.webmonkey.com |
| Projectcool Developer Zone | www.projectcool.com/developer |
| HTML Goodies | www.htmlgoodies.com |
| Web Design Group / HTML Help | www.htmlhelp.com |
| Tucows | www.tucows.com |

**TABLE 17-1**    Web Site Developer Resources

17

created for this book. This site uses the layout developed in this chapter, and all the pages are organized according to the chapters they come from. This site also includes a style sheet that governs the basic appearance of all the pages and a ReadMe file with instructions on how to use it. You may download the entire site as a Zip file from Osborne's Web site: www.osborne.com. After you have unzipped it and installed it on your computer, you can access all the pages and view the source code for each. Once you are comfortable with the idea of how to lay out a Web site, continue working through the steps in this chapter and don't stop until you have developed a complete site. It doesn't have to be huge and impressive. It just needs to be your own. You'll be surprised at the feeling of satisfaction you get when you see your own site online.

# Find the Code Online

To find the code online for this or any of the chapters in this book, go to Osborne's Web site, www.osborne.com, and click the Free Code choice on the navigation bar. From the list of books, select the *How to Do Everything with HTML* option and you will be able to download the book files, which are linked together and organized as an offline "mini" Web site.

| Use This Code For... | Look for This Filename |
| --- | --- |
| Sample style sheet | practicesite.css |
| Banner logo | banner.gif |
| HTML image | htmlimg.gif |
| Basic layout | samplelayout1.htm |
| Modified layout | samplelayout1a.htm |
| Modified layout with links added | samplelayout1b.htm |
| Final layout with images added | samplelayout1c.htm |
| Site map | sitemap.htm |

# Chapter 18

# Experience the Future with XML

## How to...

- Understand XML
- Create a Page with XML
- Create a Style Sheet for Your XML Page
- Understand XHTML
- Make Sure Your HTML Is XML Ready

If you have worked through this book chapter by chapter, perhaps occasionally you have become frustrated by HTML's limitations. You may have said to yourself, "I think I'd have done this differently if *I'd* been the one developing HTML." Maybe you have even wished that you could create your own markup language that better suited your specific needs. If so, you'll be pleased to know that all of these issues have been addressed in a new language called *Extensible Markup Language* (XML).

# Understand XML

The explosive growth and development of the World Wide Web has stretched HTML far beyond its capacity. After all, HTML was not created with the intent of enabling designers to craft attractive Web pages; it was developed to enable scientists and researchers to more effectively exchange information. Thus, presentation issues were not part of the original HTML picture. Cascading Style Sheets were introduced to address the problem of HTML's presentational limitations. However, an even better language is available today: XML. What makes XML better than HTML? XML enables you as a Web author to create your own markup language.

## XML Is a "Meta" Language

You read it correctly: XML is not just another markup language; it's a *meta language*. In programming terminology, the word "meta" refers to description. Remember the <meta> element that goes in the <head> of your HTML page? That element is used to provide descriptive information about your document. Well, a meta language is a language that can describe other languages. For example, SGML (Standard Generalized Markup Language) is the meta language that was used to create HTML. If you go to the W3C's site and read the current specification for HTML, you can actually read the SGML code that is used to define and describe HTML.

Extensible Markup Language is also a "child" of SGML, but it has one important distinction from its sibling, HTML. XML is *extensible.*

## XML Is Extensible

HTML is a "fixed" language. That is, you can't modify it to suit your own purposes or needs. HTML has a set structure that you must follow if you want your pages to work. With HTML you have a certain collection of elements and attributes with which to work, and you cannot customize it by adding your own elements. XML, on the other hand, is a meta language in its own right. You don't use XML to create Web pages; you use XML to create your own "tags." Then you use your own tags to create the Web pages. That's where the term "extensible" comes in. You *extend* XML by creating other markup languages with it.

# Create a Page with XML

Although XML is too detailed to cover completely in a single chapter, it is possible for you to work with it enough to get a "taste" of its capabilities. As you do this, you will quickly see what makes XML the prime candidate to succeed HTML as the "next" language of the World Wide Web. However, before you try working with this language, you need to familiarize yourself with a few of its building blocks.

## Familiar Territory: Elements, Attributes, and Values

Assuming you know some HTML, as you start to explore XML you'll find that you are on familiar ground from the very beginning. An XML document is built with elements, attributes, and values, just as the HTML document's you are

## Did you know?

### XML Can Be Used for More than Web Pages

XML is much more than a fancy new way of creating Web pages. Because it is a meta language, XML can be used to write markup languages for many different kinds of applications, such as ATM machines, databases, and much more. It is a powerful tool for creating other languages and works much like its parent language, SGML. XML's advantage over SGML is that while SGML is extremely complicated, XML is relatively easy to learn and use.

18

familiar with. The primary difference is that the elements, attributes, and values tend to be unique with each version of XML you encounter because authors can create their own tags. For example, the following code listing provides an example of how the markup in an XML document might look:

```
<webpage>
  <heading>Welcome to my XML page</heading>
  <paragraph1>This is my page of the future.</paragraph1>
  <logo> <!-- This will display a logo --> </logo>
  <paragraph2>It is written in XML.</paragraph2>
  <closing>Good bye!</closing>
</webpage>
```

Another example demonstrates the possibilities for using XML to create a database markup language. Suppose an XML-savvy librarian decided to create a "Library Markup Language" (LML); it might look something like this:

```
<book>
<title>Friendly Revenge</title>
<author>James H. Pence</author>
<publisher>Hard Shell Word Factory</publisher>
<genre>Young Adult Suspense</genre>
<catalog>F-YA PE</catalog>
<format>Ebook</format>
<isbn>ISBN: 1-58200-518-4</isbn>
</book>
```

With XML's elements, attributes, and values, the sky's the limit. You can create whatever you need. There are certain rules you must follow, of course, but for the most part you make those up, too. To see how an XML page comes together, open a text editor and type in the "webpage" markup. Save the page as a text file with the name webpage.xml. Before you do, try adding a few more important (but not essential) components.

NOTE   *If you want to view your XML page you will need to have at least Internet Explorer 4 or higher, Netscape 6, or Opera.*

## How to ... Write XML by the "Rules"

Keep in mind as you work with XML that it is case-sensitive. You can use both upper- and lowercase letters, but you must be consistent. For instance: <TAG> is not the same as <tag> or <Tag>. A good practice is to write all your elements, attributes, and values as lowercase. Also, XML *always* requires closing tags. If you are using an empty element, the closing slash must be added, like this: <empty_element />. There are other rules for writing XML, but these are covered later in this chapter.

## Create a Document Type Description (DTD)

Although a *document type description* (DTD) is not absolutely necessary, it's a good idea to write one—especially if your markup is going to be complicated. Essentially, a DTD is where you write down the rules for your new markup language and define your elements. You also decide what attributes and values you want each element to accept. Then, when a *validating parser* loads your document, it will check your DTD—read the rules—and interpret the page accordingly.

NOTE    *When discussing how XML documents are dealt with, you normally will hear the term "parser" used, rather than browser. This is because XML deals with more than just Web pages. There are two basic kinds of parsers: validating and non-validating. A non-validating parser merely checks to make sure your XML document is "well-formed;" then it will display the page. A document is well-formed if it does not have any syntax errors (overlapping tags, missing closing tags, and so on). A validating parser also checks your document against a DTD to see if it conforms to the DTD's specifications. Your document is considered "valid" if it follows the standard laid down in the DTD. What DTD is used for this check? Whichever one you choose—or write.*

18

What does a DTD look like? If you added one to the "webpage" markup language in the preceding example, it might look something like this:

```
<!ELEMENT webpage (heading, para1, para2, closing)>
<!ELEMENT heading (#PCDATA)>
<!ELEMENT para1 (ANY)>
<!ELEMENT logo (ANY)>
<!ELEMENT para2 (ANY)>
<!ELEMENT closing (#PCDATA)>
<webpage>
  <heading>Welcome to my XML page</heading>
  <para1>This is my page of the future.</para1>
  <logo> <!-- This will display a logo --> </logo>
  <para2>It is written in XML.</para2>
  <closing>Good bye!</closing>
</webpage>
```

In this simple DTD, you have laid down the rules for your own markup language. For the sake of simplicity, this particular example is keeping to the very basics: elements. No attributes, values, or entities were defined, although they could have been. If you look at the DTD line by line, it's not difficult to figure out what each line is doing:

■ **<!ELEMENT webpage (heading, para1, logo, para2, closing)>**   The first statement is made up of three parts, the ELEMENT declaration, the element name (webpage), and the element's "children" (other elements that must be nested inside it).

> NOTE   *The first element declaration is arguably the most important part of your DTD, because in it you define your root element. You can have only one root element in an XML document, and all the others must be nested within it. For instance, in an HTML page the root element is <html> </html>; all other elements must go inside it. For the page described in the preceding example, the root element is <webpage> </webpage>.*

■ **<!ELEMENT heading (#PCDATA)>**   This line defines the <heading> element. Again it has three parts: the ELEMENT declaration (this tells the parser that you are defining an element), the element's name (heading), and the type of data it can receive (#PCDATA). The #PCDATA statement stands for *parsed character data*, which simply means that text can be contained in that element.

- **<!ELEMENT para1 (ANY)>**   By now, you should be getting a feel for what these lines are doing. This line declares and defines the <para1> element. The main difference in this line is that instead of #PCDATA, this element can accept any data. For example, this element can also contain other elements, whereas the preceding <heading> element cannot. Although all the lines in this DTD are virtually identical, except for the element names and data types, in a more complex DTD you will have various types of elements (other than the #PCDATA type), attributes, values, and even entities.

> **NOTE**   *There is no particular reason the keywords in the sample.xml page were chosen, except to demonstrate the variety of keywords available. If you were actually developing a markup language that you hoped to use, you would want to give careful thought to each of your elements and to what kind of data they would be capable of accepting.*

With a clearly written document type description, your XML page is nearly complete. However, two more components must be added before it is ready to display: an XML declaration and a document type declaration.

## Add an XML Declaration

The XML declaration is simply a line at the beginning of the file that identifies your document as an XML document. Strictly speaking, you don't have to add this line, but again it's a good idea to include it. To add an XML declaration to the beginning of our "webpage" document, you will add a line that looks like this:

```
<?xml version="1.0"?>
```

This resembles an HTML tag with attributes, except for the question marks at the beginning and end of the tag. What this declaration does is identify for the parser what version of XML you are using, and you can also add additional information such as character encoding, whether the document is a "standalone" (not using a

DTD), and so on. For the following code, only the simple version declaration will be added. The "webpage" document now looks like the following:

```
<?xml version="1.0"?>
<!ELEMENT webpage (heading, para1, para2, closing)>
<!ELEMENT heading (#PCDATA)>
<!ELEMENT para1 (ANY)>
<!ELEMENT logo (ANY)>
<!ELEMENT para2 (ANY)>
<!ELEMENT closing (#PCDATA)>
<webpage>
  <heading>Welcome to my XML page</heading>
  <para1>This is my page of the future.</para1>
  <logo> <!-- This will display a logo --> </logo>
  <para2>It is written in XML.</para2>
  <closing>Good bye!</closing>
</webpage>
```

With the addition of an XML declaration, the "webpage" document is almost ready to display. However, another optional but helpful addition is a *document type declaration.*

## Add a Document Type Declaration

If you have ever looked at HTML code that was generated by an HTML editor or WYSIWYG program, you have most likely seen a document type declaration before. This line, which is included after the XML declaration, but before the first line of your code, "declares" which DTD your page conforms to. This declaration is optional, provided you do not intend to link to or embed a DTD in your page. However, if you plan on using a DTD, you will need to include a declaration as well, at least if you want the parser or browser to "validate" your document against it.

NOTE *The acronym initials of a document type declaration are also DTD, but generally it is not referred to this way in the interest of avoiding confusion with the document type description.*

There are two ways to include a document type declaration. The first is used to link to an external DTD. This is basically the same idea as linking an HTML page to an external style sheet or JavaScript. The statement is made up of three parts: the !DOCTYPE statement, the name of the DTD that you want the parser to use (the name of the root element), and the location of the DTD (so the parser can find it). For instance, if you plan on saving your DTD as a separate file and linking the page to it, the document type declaration for the "webpage" document might look like this:

```
<!DOCTYPE webpage SYSTEM "webpage.dtd">.
```

The SYSTEM keyword identifies the URL of the document type definition. Notice that the "webpage.dtd" is identified in quotation marks following the system keyword.

> TIP
>
> *As is the case with style sheets, it's a good idea to save your DTD as a separate file and link to it. This way, you can use it with more than one document. If you embed it in the document itself, you "tie it down" to that one page.*

If, as in the "webpage" sample, your DTD is relatively simple and you want to embed it in the document, you actually include it as part of the document type declaration. You do this by enclosing the entire DTD in square brackets *inside* the document type declaration tag. Because you are not linking to an outside document, you can leave out the SYSTEM keyword. With the document type declaration included in the "webpage" sample, the completed code will look like the following listing:

```
<?xml version="1.0"?>
<!DOCTYPE webpage [
<!ELEMENT webpage (heading, para1, para2, closing)>
<!ELEMENT heading (#PCDATA)>
<!ELEMENT para1 (ANY)>
<!ELEMENT logo (ANY)>
<!ELEMENT para2 (ANY)>
<!ELEMENT closing (#PCDATA)> ]>
```

18

```
<webpage>
  <heading>Welcome to my XML page</heading>
  <para1>This is my page of the future.</para1>
  <logo> <!-- This will display a logo --> </logo>
  <para2>It is written in XML.</para2>
  <closing>Good bye!</closing>
</webpage>
```

Try saving this page as a text document with the name, sample.xml, and then open it in Internet Explorer 4 or higher and you will see your first XML page displayed. You might also be surprised at how it looks. As you see in the following illustration, it appears to be displaying your XML code:

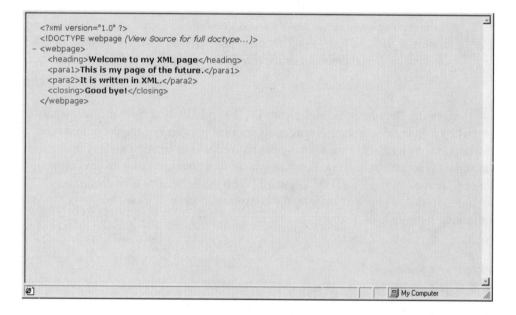

If you were writing HTML and your page displayed like this, you would know instantly that you had made an error somewhere. However, in this case, the page is displaying exactly as it is supposed to. In fact, if you made even the slightest error, the page simply would not have displayed at all, as the following illustration demonstrates:

```
The XML page cannot be displayed

Cannot view XML input using style sheet. Please correct the error
and then click the Refresh button, or try again later.
_____

Expecting whitespace or '?'. Line 1, Position 20

<?xml version="1.0">
```

You see, whereas HTML is "forgiving," XML is not. Your code must be written correctly, down to the last quotation mark. If it isn't, an XML browser or parser will not display it. There's no room for sloppy coding with XML. However, that doesn't answer the question of why your XML code displayed, instead of the Web page you may have been expecting. The reason is that there is one more "component" an XML page must have: a style sheet.

# Create a Style Sheet for Your XML Page

XML accomplishes what HTML can't—a complete separation between structure and presentation. When you write your XML code and display it, only the structure of your data will display. If you want your page to look like a Web page, you have no

18

choice but to write a style sheet for it. Fortunately, you are again on familiar ground because you can use CSS to create the styles for your XML page. There are other style sheet languages you can use, such as *eXtensible Stylesheet Language* (XSL), but because you are familiar with CSS already (if you've been working through this book), CSS will be fine for this example.

## Design Your Style Sheet

You design the style sheet for your page essentially the same way you would for an HTML page, but with a few differences. The primary difference is that you will be specifying styles for your own selectors (elements) rather than for HTML elements. Another important difference in using style sheets with XML is that you can't take anything for granted. You must specify how you want each element to display, where it should be positioned, how large the margins are, and so on. If you leave the browser to itself, it will display everything in a linear fashion, as in the following illustration:

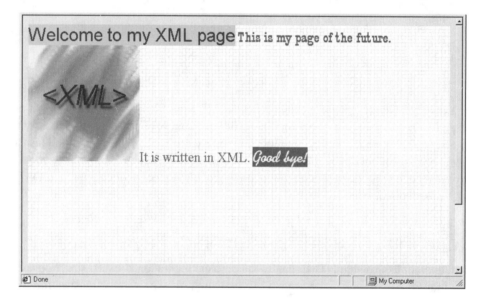

Therefore, leave nothing to chance: Use the CSS positioning properties and lay out your page carefully.

TIP *If you're working with a text editor, have your browser open and the XML page loaded. Then, open your style sheet in your text editor and make adjustments, toggling back and forth between the browser and style sheet to see how your changes affect the overall look and positioning of the elements.*

As you go through the following steps, you will need a background image to include on the page, as well as an image for the logo. (As with each chapter, you can find the files you need at Osborne's Web site: www.osborne.com. See the end of this chapter for details.) The following style rules are in the order the elements occur on the page, but you can write them in whatever order you want:

- For your "root" element, "webpage," specify a background color of white (#ffffff) and include a background image for the page. Set the background image to repeat, so that it will function as "wallpaper," and set the background-attachment to "fixed." A width and height set to 100% will fill the browser screen. Set the display property to "block." Add a little space to the bottom margin by setting it to 20px (pixels):

```
webpage   {display: block;
                   background-color: #ffffff;
                   background-image: url(weavetile2.gif);
                   background-repeat: repeat;
                   width=100%;
                   height=100%;
                   margin-bottom: 20px; }
```

- For the <heading> element, set the display to "block," and set a font family, size, and color for the <heading> element. Align the text to the center of the page. For fun, give it a border and its own background color. As a final touch, add a margin of 10 pixels all the way around:

```
heading   {display: block;
                 font-family: arial;
                 font-size: 2em;
```

18

```
color: maroon;
text-align: center;
border-style: inset;
border-color: brown;
background-color:#ffcc99;
margin: 10px;}
```

■ For the <para1> element, set the display property to "block." Positioning
properties should be set to "absolute" with a z-index of 3. (For more on
positioning and z-index, see Chapter 16.) A bold "fantasy" font will give
this element a little different look. Don't use a background color for this
element, but set the text color to "brown." Also, make some adjustments
to the top, left, and bottom margins to better size and position the element:

```
para1    {display: block;
          position: absolute;
          z-index: 3;
          font-family: fantasy;
          font-weight: bold;
          font-variant: italic;
          font-size: 1.5em;
          color: brown;
          margin-top: 15px;
          margin-bottom: 10px;
          margin-left: 50px;}
```

■ For the <logo> element, the only settings that are unique are the "top" and
"left" properties, which refer to the position of the logo image, and the "height"
and "width" properties, which specify its size. A z-index of "1" will ensure
that the logo does not overlap any of the text in either the <para1> or
<para2> element:

```
logo     {display: block;
          position: relative;
          z-index: 1;
          top: 55px;
          left: 280px;
          height:200px;
```

```
width:200px;
background-image: url(xmllogo.gif);
background-position: center;
background-color: white;}
```

■ For the <para2> element, set the font size to 1.5 ems and the text to dark green. Align this text with the right margin, but add 50 pixels to the right margin to move the text toward the left:

```
para2     {display: block;
                position: relative;
                z-index: 2;
                font-family: Times-New-Roman;
                color: #336600;
                font-size: 1.5em;
                text-align: right;
                margin-top: 15px;
                margin-bottom: 15px;
                margin-right: 50px;}
```

■ For the <closing> element, set the font to cursive, the font size to 1.75 ems, the text to yellow, and the background color to brown. Align this text in the center of the page. A little padding on the top and bottom will give the text some breathing room:

```
closing   {display: block;
                font-family: cursive;
                color: #ffff66;
                font-size: 1.75em;
                background-color: brown;
                text-align: center;
                margin-top:30px;
                margin-bottom: 10px;
                margin-left: 100px;
                margin-right: 100px;
                border-style: inset;
                border-color:#ffff66;
                padding-top: 10px;
                padding-bottom: 10px;}
```

18

Your completed style sheet should look like the one in the following listing:

```
webpage    {display: block;
            background-color: #ffffff;
            background-image: url(weavetile2.gif);
            background-repeat: repeat;
            background-attachment: fixed;
            width=100%;
            height=100%;
            margin-bottom: 20%;}

heading    {display: block;
            font-family: arial;
            font-size: 2em;
            color: maroon;
            text-align: center;
            border-style: inset;
            border-color: brown;
            background-color:#ffcc99;
            margin: 10px;}

para1      {display: block;
            position: absolute;
            z-index: 3;
            font-family: fantasy;
            font-weight: bold;
            font-variant: italic;
            font-size: 1.5em;
            color: brown;
            margin-top: 15px;
            margin-bottom: 10px;
            margin-left: 50px;}

logo       {display: block;
            position: relative;
            z-index: 1;
            top: 55px;
            left: 280px;
            height:200px;
            width:200px;
```

```
          background-image: url(xmllogo.gif);
          background-position: center;
          background-color: white;}

para2     {display: block;
          position: relative;
          z-index: 2;
          font-family: Times-New-Roman;
          color: #336600;
          font-size: 1.5em;
          text-align: right;
          margin-top: 15px;
          margin-bottom: 15px;
          margin-right: 50px;}

closing   {display: block;
          font-family: cursive;
          color: #ffff66;
          font-size: 1.75em;
          background-color: brown;
          text-align: center;
          margin-top:30px;
          margin-bottom: 10px;
          margin-left: 100px;
          margin-right: 100px;
          border-style: inset;
          border-color:#ffff66;
          padding-top: 10px;
          padding-bottom: 10px;}
```

Save your style sheet as "webpage.css." Remember to save it as a plain text file, particularly if you are writing it in a word processor. Once you've saved your style sheet, your next step is to link your XML page to it.

## Link to Your Style Sheet

To link to the style sheet you just created, you will need to add one more line to your XML file. Like the XML declaration mentioned earlier in this chapter, this is a processing instruction, and so it begins with a question mark (?) followed by an instruction that identifies the tag as a "link" to a style sheet: <?xml-stylesheet?>.

Next, add a hypertext reference (href=" ") that points to the location of webpage.css. Finally, define the type of style sheet by adding the type=" " attribute. The value should be text/css. Your style sheet link should look like this:

```
<?xml-stylesheet href="webpage.css" type="text/css"?>.
```

This line should be inserted in your webpage.xml document just below the XML declaration, as in the following listing:

```
<?xml version="1.0"?>
<?xml-stylesheet href="webpage.css" type="text/css"?>
<!DOCTYPE webpage [
<!ELEMENT webpage (heading, para1, logo, para2, closing)>
<!ELEMENT heading (#PCDATA)>
<!ELEMENT para1 (ANY)>
<!ELEMENT logo (ANY)>
<!ELEMENT para2 (ANY)>
<!ELEMENT closing (#PCDATA)> ]>
<webpage>
  <heading>Welcome to my XML page</heading>
  <para1>This is my page of the future.</para1>
  <logo> </logo>
  <para2>It is written in XML.</para2>
  <closing>Good bye!</closing>
</webpage>
```

After you've included the style sheet link, save the page. Make sure that the image you chose for your background image is located in the same directory as your XML page, and you're ready to display it in your browser. When you bring it up, it should look something like this:

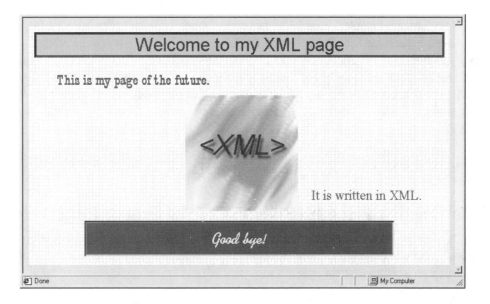

# Learn Good Web Design

Now that you've played with XML a little, you might be wondering why a book on HTML even deals with it. After all, HTML is going to be around a long while. There are even those who question whether XML will be capable of supplanting HTML in the long run. So, why bother learning anything about it? The reason is XHTML.

## Understand XHTML

Although this chapter may not have inspired you to do all your Web authoring in XML, hopefully you began to develop an appreciation for the way XML works and the tougher requirements it imposes. The current recommendation (standard) of the W3C for Web development is no longer HTML, but XHTML. Extensible Hypertext

**18**

Markup Language is *XML-based*. In other words, when you work with XHTML, you still use the familiar HTML elements, attributes, and values, but you avoid the use of "presentational" markup and format your pages with CSS. With XHTML, you also have to adhere to the stricter coding requirements that you find in XML. Sloppy coding is not an option. Unlike HTML, XML is not forgiving of errors in syntax. When the transition to XHTML is complete, and browsers are fully compliant with the new standard, this will be the case with HTML. If you want your pages to be ready for the future, but still backward compatible (HTML), you need to begin to make sure your markup fits the XHTML requirements. (For more on XHTML, see Chapter 17.)

## Web Design Principle: Write XHTML-Compatible Pages

So, how do you write XHTM-compatible pages? For the most part, you have been learning how to do it throughout this book. However, in case you're still fuzzy on the subject, keep these principles in mind:

- **Always include closing tags**   No exceptions. If an element takes an opening tag and a closing tag, always use both. Gone are the days when you could just put a <p> tag at the beginning of every new paragraph and ignore the </p>.

- **Empty elements must always have a closing slash**   If you use an *empty element* (an element that does not enclose content), always make sure that you include a space and a closing slash in the tag, like this: <img />.

- **Always include a value with an attribute**   There are a few instances in HTML where you haven't (till now) had to worry about adding a value to an attribute. Usually this is because the attribute is self-explanatory. For example, using "radio buttons" you could specify an option as preselected by adding the word "checked." Checked was an attribute, but it didn't take a value. Now you need, even in these cases, to include a value with the attribute, as in: checked="checked." Yes, it sounds redundant, but that's the way it goes sometimes.

- **Enclose all attribute values in quotation marks**   In the past, you could get away with leaving these out, but not anymore. When you include an attribute value, put it in quotes, like this: attribute="value". No exceptions.

- **Write your code in lowercase**   XML is case-sensitive; HTML is not. As a result, you will often find code that is a mixture of both. Not a good idea if you want your pages to be compatible in the future. By getting in the habit of writing all your code lowercase, you'll be a long way down the road toward compatibility with the new standard.

■ **Use the id=" " attribute along with name=" "**   The "name" attribute is on the way out, being slowly replaced by "id." Get in the habit of using both, and plan on phasing out your use of name=" ". That way your pages will be ready for the future.

■ **Make sure your tags are all correctly nested**   No overlapping tags, period. Sometimes HTML will let you get away with this, but eventually your pages will crash and burn as a result.

■ **Check your documents to be sure they are well-formed**   With HTML your documents *should be* well-formed (correctly written); with XHTML and XML they *must be* well-formed.

■ **Validate your HTML documents**   Use the W3C's validation service (or somebody else's), and make sure your documents are not only well-formed, but that they conform to the XHTML DTD. You will have three choices when you validate XHTML transitional, XHTML strict, or XHTML frameset. Start with transitional, but work to eventually make your documents conform to the strict standard. The corrections you receive from the validator are great tools to help you learn how to improve your code.

■ **Gradually increase your use of CSS**   Learn to use Cascading Style Sheets. Browser support for CSS is growing, and soon the compatibility issues that have made them a "mixed blessing" will no longer be a problem. In fact, sooner or later you'll *have* to use them anyway. Learn how to do it now.

■ **Gradually decrease your use of presentational elements and attributes**   As you increase your use of CSS, phase out <font>, bgcolor, and so much of the other presentational markup you are using. Define your presentation with style sheets not HTML.

If you make these practices part of your regular coding routine, you will have little or no trouble making the transition to the future of the Web.

## Practice, Practice, Practice

Perhaps as you've read through this chapter, you have enjoyed the freedom of creating your own markup and developing your own "HTML." Or maybe you're just wondering how you can learn more about XHTML and the standards your pages will need to conform to in the future. The online resources in Table 18-1 supply you with plenty of material for research and further practice as you learn XHTML and XML.

| Web Site Name | URL |
|---|---|
| What Is XML? | www.geocities.com/SiliconValley/Peaks/5957/xml.html |
| XML.com | www.xml.com |
| XML Pitstop | www.xmlpitstop.com |
| The Directory of XML Resources | www.xmldir.com |
| Introduction to XHTML with eXamples (Web Developer's Virtual Library) | www.wdvl.com/Authoring/Languages/XML/XHTML |
| XHTML Guru | www.xhtmlguru.com |
| XHTML 1.0: The Extensible Hypertext Markup Language | www.w3.org/TR/xhtml1 |

**TABLE 18-1**    XML and XHTML Resources

# Find the Code Online

To find the code online for this or any of the chapters in this book, go to Osborne's Web site, www.osborne.com, and click the Free Code choice on the navigation bar. From the list of books, select the *How to Do Everything with HTML* option and you will be able to download the book files, which are linked together and organized as an offline "mini" Web site. For more on how to use the "mini" Web site, see Chapter 17.

| Use This Code For... | Look for This Filename |
|---|---|
| XML Web page | webpage.xml |
| Web page style sheet | webpage.css |
| Background image | weavetile2.gif |
| Logo image | xmllogo.gif |

# Appendix A

## Choose Safe Colors for Your Web Page

In Chapter 4 you learned about browser-safe colors and why you need to use them. Although there are many good Web sites and software resources for choosing your colors, you might want to create your own browser-safe colors. However, you'll quickly discover that mixing colors on a keyboard can be a daunting process. Because colors on a video screen don't mix the same way they do with paint, you could waste a great deal of time figuring out how much red, green, and blue you need to create a certain color. Fortunately, the good people at Netscape have done most of the work for you.

# Convert Named Colors to the Nearest Browser-Safe Equivalents

Netscape has developed a list of more than 120 colors that most browsers will recognize by name. With creative names such as aliceblue and lemonchiffon, these colors sound like a Web designer's dream. The advantage of using named colors is that the names (in most cases) give you an idea of how the color will look. The disadvantage is that only a very small percentage of them are browser safe. So, when viewed on a system with limited color display capabilities, your colors will appear mottled or *dithered* (see Chapter 4, "Introducing Color Sensibly into Your Web Pages," to learn more about dithering).

So what do you do if you want to take advantage of the named colors but you also want your colors to look good? The solution is to simply convert a Netscape-named color to its nearest browser-safe equivalent. The only tools you need are the following charts and the calculator you'll find in your Windows accessories folder.

To convert a named color to its browser-safe equivalent, you first must change it from hexadecimal to its decimal value (See Chapter 4 for more on hexadecimal and color values). Then just round the decimal value up or down to the nearest browser-safe value. Finally, convert the value back to hexadecimal (see Table A-1) and you will have a color that will look good on virtually any system.

| Color Amount | Decimal Value | Hexadecimal Value |
|---|---|---|
| 0% | 0 | 00 |
| 20% | 51 | 33 |
| 40% | 102 | 66 |
| 60% | 153 | 99 |
| 80% | 204 | cc |
| 100% | 255 | ff |

**TABLE A-1**    Browser-Safe Conversion Chart

## How Many Colors Are There?

Netscape actually has named a lot more than 120 colors. The number of named colors is more than 400. But the difference between many of these colors is so slight that it's not easy to distinguish between them.

For example, to convert the Netscape-named color *mediumvioletred* to a browser-safe color:

1. Find the name of the color on Table A-2 and note its hex code. The hex code for mediumvioletred is #c71585. This code represents the amount of red, green, and blue (RGB) used to make up that particular color. The values, separated by color, are R=c7, G=15, and B=85.

2. Convert the hexadecimal values to their corresponding decimal values. To do this, open the calculator in your Windows Accessories folder. Select View, Scientific.

3. On the Calculator's top row, you will find four option buttons: Hex, Dec, Oct, and Bin. Select Hex.

4. Type in the Red value; in this case, c7.

5. To convert that to decimal notation, just select the Dec option button. The code c7 should change to 199. The number 199 represents the amount of red in mediumvioletred.

6. Clear the calculator and repeat the procedure with the G and B values. When you're done, you should come up with the following values: R=199, G=21, B=133.

7. All that remains is to round these values up or down to the nearest browser-safe equivalent. A color is browser safe only if it uses color in the following specific quantities: 0%, 20%, 40%, 60%, 80%, or 100%. That's why the following color conversion chart lists only six possibilities. If you check Table A-1, you will find that the nearest decimal value to 199 is 204; so make a note that your red value should be 204. Do the same for green and blue and you will end up rounding green down to 0 and blue up to 153. So, your browser-safe color described in decimal is R= 204, G= 0, and B= 153.

A

8.  Unfortunately, your browser doesn't understand that description. So, we have to convert it all back into hexadecimal. Go back to Table A-1 and look next to the value we chose for red (204); you'll discover the hex equivalent is cc. Repeat the process for the G and B values and you will come up with 00 and 99, respectively.

9.  Now, combine the RGB values you have just arrived at into one code: #cc0099, and you've done it! You have converted Netscape's mediumvioletred (#c71585) to its nearest browser-safe equivalent.

| Color Name | Hex Code | Color Name | Hex Code |
|---|---|---|---|
| aliceblue | #f0f8ff | antiquewhite | #faebd7 |
| aqua | #00ffff | aquamarine | #7fffd4 |
| azure | #f0ffff | beige | #f5f5dc |
| bisque | #ffe4c4 | blanchedalmond | #ffebcd |
| blue | #0000ff | blueviolet | #8a2be2 |
| brown | #a52a2a | burlywood | #deb887 |
| cadetblue | #5f9ea0 | chartreuse | #7fff00 |
| chocolate | #d2691e | coral | #ff7f50 |
| cornflowerblue | #6495ed | cornsilk | #fff8dc |
| crimson | #dc143c | cyan | #00ffff |
| darkblue | #00008b | darkcyan | #008b8b |
| darkgoldenrod | #b8860b | darkgray | #a9a9a9 |
| darkgreen | #006400 | darkkhaki | #bdb76b |
| darkmagenta | #8b008b | darkolivegreen | #556b2f |
| darkorange | #ff8c00 | darkorchid | #9932cc |
| darkred | #8b0000 | darksalmon | #e9967a |
| darkseagreen | #8fbc8f | darkslateblue | #483d8b |
| darkslategray | #2f4f4f | darkturquoise | #00ced1 |
| darkviolet | #9400d3 | deeppink | #ff1493 |
| deepskyblue | #00bfff | dimgray | #696969 |
| dodgerblue | #1e90ff | firebrick | #b22222 |
| floralwhite | #fffaf0 | forestgreen | #228b22 |
| fuchsia | #ff00ff | gainsboro | #dcdcdc |

TABLE A-2    The Netscape Named Colors

| Color Name | Hex Code | Color Name | Hex Code |
|---|---|---|---|
| ghostwhite | #f8f8ff | gold | #ffd700 |
| goldenrod | #daa520 | gray | #808080 |
| green | #008000 | greenyellow | #adff2f |
| honeydew | #f0fff0 | hotpink | #ff69b4 |
| indianred | #cd5c5c | indigo | #4b0082 |
| ivory | #fffff0 | khaki | #f0e68c |
| lavender | #e6e6fa | lavenderblush | #fff0f5 |
| lawngreen | #7cfc00 | lemonchiffon | #fffacd |
| lightblue | #add8e6 | lightcoral | #f08080 |
| lightcyan | #e0ffff | lightgoldenrodyellow | #fafad2 |
| lightgreen | #90ee90 | lightgray | #d3d3d3 |
| lightpink | #ffb6c1 | lightsalmon | #ffa07a |
| lightseagreen | #20b2aa | lightskyblue | #87cefa |
| lightslategray | #778899 | lightsteelblue | #b0c4de |
| lightyellow | #ffffe0 | lime | #00ff00 |
| limegreen | #32cd32 | linen | #faf0e6 |
| magenta | #ff00ff | maroon | #800000 |
| mediumaquamarine | #66cdaa | mediumblue | #0000cd |
| mediumorchid | #ba55d3 | mediumpurple | #9370db |
| mediumseagreen | #3cb371 | mediumslateblue | #7b68ee |
| mediumspringgreen | #00fa9a | mediumturquoise | #48d1cc |
| mediumvioletred | #c71585 | midnightblue | #191970 |
| mintcream | #f5fffa | mistyrose | #ffe4e1 |
| moccasin | #ffe4b5 | navajowhite | #ffdead |
| navy | #000080 | oldlace | #fdf5e6 |
| olive | #808000 | olivedrab | #6b8e23 |
| orange | #ffa500 | orangered | #ff4500 |
| orchid | #da70d6 | palegoldenrod | #eee8aa |
| palegreen | #98fb98 | paleturquoise | #afeeee |
| palevioletred | #db7093 | papayawhip | #ffefd5 |
| peachpuff | #ffdab9 | peru | #cd853f |
| pink | #ffc0cb | plum | #dda0dd |

**TABLE A-2** The Netscape Named Colors *(continued)*

A

| Color Name | Hex Code | Color Name | Hex Code |
|---|---|---|---|
| powderblue | #b0e0e6 | red | #ff0000 |
| rosybrown | #bc8f8f | royalblue | #4169e1 |
| saddlebrown | #8b4513 | salmon | #fa8072 |
| sandybrown | #f4a460 | seagreen | #2e8b57 |
| seashell | #fff5ee | sienna | #a0522d |
| silver | #c0c0c0 | skyblue | #87ceeb |
| slateblue | #6a5acd | slategray | #708090 |
| snow | #fffafa | springgreen | #00ff7f |
| steelblue | #4682b4 | tan | #d2b48c |
| teal | #008080 | thistle | #d8bfd8 |
| tomato | #ff6347 | turquoise | #40e0d0 |
| violet | #ee82ee | wheat | #f5deb3 |
| white | #ffffff | whitesmoke | #f5f5f5 |
| yellow | #ffff00 | yellowgreen | #9acd32 |

**TABLE A-2**    The Netscape Named Colors *(continued)*

# Create Your Own Color Comparison Page

A simple way to view a side-by-side comparison of the two colors in a browser is by creating a two-celled table, with each cell using one of the colors as its background color. Create the HTML document listed in the following to sample the two colors you just worked on. To view new colors, just change the color codes. Better yet, add new cells to your table and build your own, personalized color chart.

```
<html>
<head><title>Color Comparison Chart</title></head>
<body bgcolor="gray">
<h1 align="center">
<font color="white">
Compare Named and Browser-Safe Colors</font></h1>
<table align="center" border="1">
<tr><th bgcolor="silver">Netscape</th>
```

```
<th bgcolor="silver">Browser-Safe</th>
<tr><td bgcolor="mediumvioletred">mediumvioletred</td>
<td bgcolor="#cc0099">#cc0099</td></tr>
</table>
</body>
</html>
```

Of course, if you don't want to go to the trouble of creating your own comparison page, you can visit Osborne's Web site at www.osborne.com. By clicking the Free Code link and choosing the *How to Do Everything with HTML* option, you will be able to download all the code, images, and pages created for this book, as well as an HTML browser-safe color chart page. Also, some excellent color charts and resources can be found at www.visibone.com.

A

# Appendix B

# HTML Practical Reference Guide

Although reading a book on HTML and working through the exercises will give you an understanding of how HTML works and how to use it, you might find that all of those details are hard to keep in mind, particularly if you aren't using HTML every day. This practical reference guide is designed to help you refresh your memory without rereading a whole chapter. It will provide you with a quick reference for many of the HTML elements and attributes you have read about in this book. Keep in mind that this reference guide is designed to be practical, not exhaustive. Not every element and attribute is included here. However, you should find what you need to refresh your memory of how to accomplish some of the most common tasks.

# Create a Web Page

The elements listed in the following table are not all necessary for creating a Web page. However, you will find that most of them come in handy at one time or another.

| To Do This... | Use This... |
|---|---|
| Create an HTML document | <html> </html> |
| Define a Web page's header | <head> </head> |
| Assign a title to your page | <title> </title> |
| Include descriptive information | <meta /> |
| Add an embedded style sheet | <style> </style> |
| Link to an external style sheet or other document | <link /> |
| Add a script | <script> </script> |
| Create a Web page's body | <body> </body> |
| Add comments | <!-- enclose comments here --> |

The elements listed in the preceding table would be arranged in an HTML document as in the following example. Keep in mind that elements such as <meta />, <script>, <link />, and <style> are not required. You use them only when you need them. The following code listing demonstrates how these elements might be arranged in an HTML page:

```
<html>
    <head>
        <title>Title goes here</title>
        <meta Descriptive information and keywords />
```

```
        <style>Embedded style sheet</style>
        <link /> (Linked style sheet or other document)
        <script>Insert script here</script>
    </head>
    <body>Web page body goes here
    <!-- Insert comments between comment tags -->
    </body>
</html>
```

# Work with Text

The elements that enable you to modify and manipulate text are straightforward and easy to use. To cause text to display with the characteristics listed in the following table, simply enclose it between the proper set of tags. For example, to create boldfaced text, place it inside the bold element like this: <b>Boldfaced Text</b>. To cause text to display with multiple characteristics (for example, bold and italic), simply nest one set of tags inside another, like this: <b><i>Boldfaced and Italicized Text</i></b>. The following table lists some basic elements you can use for manipulating the appearance of text.

| To Do This... | Use This... |
|---|---|
| Display boldfaced text | <b> </b> |
| Display italicized text | <i> </i> |
| Underline text | <u> </u> |
| Enlarge text size one step | <big> </big> |
| Reduce text size one step | <small> </small> |
| Display text as superscript | <sup> </sup> |
| Display text as subscript | <sub> </sub> |
| Preserve your spacing and formatting | <pre> </pre> |
| Display text as strikethrough | <del> </del> |

NOTE *Some text effects (italics, for example) have more than one element that will produce the same results. For the sake of simplicity, not all of the elements have been listed in this guide. To explore text elements not listed in the preceding table, see Chapter 2.*

B

# Define Document Structure

HTML was designed for the purpose of structuring hypertext documents. The elements listed here enable you to make the structure of your document clear. With so many ways to create style, display fonts, and so on you might wonder why these elements are even necessary. Keep in mind that nonvisual browsers (braille for the blind, aural, and other alternative browsers) have difficulty with poorly structured pages. The structural elements listed in the following table will assist them in properly interpreting your pages. When constructing your pages, make the best possible use of the structural elements; you will increase your accessibility to those who are using nonvisual browsers.

> NOTE    *Currently, less than one percent of browsers in use are of the nonvisual type. However, although ignoring structural elements might not pose a problem for much of your audience, it's not the only reason for properly defining your document structure. As the new XHTML standard becomes more strictly applied (not to mention XML), having a well-formed document will become increasingly important. Remember: XHTML and XML are not as forgiving as HTML when it comes to poorly defined document structure. So, get into the habit of using these elements the way they were intended, to add a clear structure to your Web page.*

The following table lists the elements that you use to mark off a page's structure:

| To Do This... | Use This... |
|---|---|
| Define a heading (up to six levels) | <h#> </h#> (# can be 1 through 6) |
| Create a paragraph | <p> </p> |
| Assign characteristics to a portion of a page | <div> </div> or <span> </span> |
| Insert a line break | <br /> |
| Draw a horizontal rule | <hr /> |
| Apply attributes to an entire section of a page | <div> </div> |

The <div> and <span> elements are very similar in that they enable you to work with an entire portion of a page. For instance, if you want to center several paragraphs of text, you could align each one separately or you could enclose all the paragraphs inside the <div> or <span> element as in the following code snippet:

```
<div style="text-align:center">
   <p>Paragraph One</p>
   <p>Paragraph Two</p>
   <p>Paragraph Three</p>
</div>
```

Using the <span> element, the code would look like this:

```
<span style="text-align:center">
   <p>Paragraph One</p>
   <p>Paragraph Two</p>
   <p>Paragraph Three</p>
</span>
```

The primary difference between <div> and <span> is that <div> is a "block level" element (marks off a separate division of the page), while <span> is not. In other words, <div> will add a line before and after the content it encloses; <span> formats without marking off divisions.

# Create Lists

Lists are easy to create and provide a useful tool for menus, site directories, lists of links, and outlines. There are three different types of lists to choose from: ordered (numbered), unordered (bulleted), and definition (glossary). The trick to doing lists well is remembering to nest your elements properly. The elements necessary for creating lists are included in the following table:

| To Do This... | Use This... |
| --- | --- |
| Create an ordered (numbered) list | <ol> </ol> |
| Create an unordered (bulleted) list | <ul> </ul> |
| Create a definition list | <dl> </dl> |
| Add a list item | <li> </li> |
| Add a definition term (definition list only) | <dt> </dt> |
| Add a definition description (definition list only) | <dd> </dd> |
| Specify a starting number (ordered list only) | start="#" |
| Specify a bullet type (unordered list only) | type="disc \| circle \| square" |

B

| To Do This... | Use This... |
|---|---|
| Specify a number type (ordered list only) | type="a \| A \| i \| I \| #" |
| Set the value for a particular list item | value="#" (Use Arabic numerals only, no matter what type of numbering is used in the list.) |

Each type of list has its own particular combination of elements. A simple construction of each type of list can be found in the code snippets that follow:

```
<ol>
<li>This is an example</li>
<li>of an ordered list.</li>
</ol>
    <ul>
        <li>This is an example</li>
        <li>of an unordered list.</li>
    </ul>
<dl>
<dt>This is an example</dt>
<dd>of a definition list</dd>
</dl>
```

# Add Images

You can add graphics and photos to your Web site by enclosing them in the image element. When using images, it's good to remember to always specify a height and width for the image. That way the browser will be capable of loading the page faster. A good rule is to use GIF images for art, drawings, and graphics; use JPEG for photos. PNG is an up-and-coming format but is still not as widely supported. The following table lists some of the most common elements and attributes for including images on your page:

| To Do This... | Use This... |
|---|---|
| Include an image | <img /> |
| Tell the browser where to find the image | src="myimage.gif" |
| Provide alternate text | alt="alternate text" |
| Specify an image's height and width | height="#" width="#" (# in pixels) |
| Display a low-resolution image while the higher-resolution image is loading | lowres="filename.gif" |

# Create Hyperlinks

Hyperlinks are what make the Web the "web." You can create links from text, photos, clip art, and so on, by enclosing them inside the anchor element. You also can link to a particular spot on the same page and even a certain spot on a different page. The elements and attributes in this table will help you remember how to create your own links:

| To Do This… | Use This… |
| --- | --- |
| Create a hyperlink | <a> </a> |
| Link to a different page | <a href="webpage.htm">Link</a> |
| Set a named anchor that you can link to (used for linking to a specific spot on the same page or on another page) | <a name="spot"> </a> |
| Link to a different spot on the same page | <a href="#spot">Link</a> |
| Link to a different spot on another page | <a href="webpage.htm" target="#spot">Link</a> |
| Open a link in a new window | <a href="webpage.htm" target="_blank">Link</a> |
| Use an image for a link | <a href="webpage.htm"><img src="image.jpg"></a> |

# Create Tables

Tables often are used to give structure to data, links, images, and so forth on a page. In fact, many Web page layouts are designed around tables. Although the W3C encourages Web authors to use style sheets for layout and element positioning, tables' ease of use still makes them a popular choice of Web authors for layout purposes. Basic table elements and attributes are listed in the following table.

| To Do This… | Use This… |
| --- | --- |
| Create a table | <table> </table> |
| Create a row | <tr> </tr> |
| Create a data cell | <td> </td> |
| Create a heading | <th> </th> |
| Add a caption | <caption> </caption> |
| Turn borders off | <table **border="0"**> |

B

| To Do This... | Use This... |
|---|---|
| Adjust border thickness | <table **border="#"**> (#=thickness in pixels) |
| Add space between cells | <table **cellspacing="#"**> (#=pixels) |
| Add space inside cells | <table **cellpadding="#"**> (#=pixels) |
| Make a data cell span multiple columns | <td **colspan="#"**> (#=number of columns) |
| Make a data cell span multiple rows | <td **rowspan="#"**> (#=number of rows) |

Creating a table can become quite complex if you are planning to have a large number of cells or if you are going to nest tables (place one or more complete tables inside another). However, the basic structure for tables is very simple. Just remember that first you must specify a row; then nest within that row the data cells you want to create. Each data cell will create a separate column. A basic table structure would look like this:

```
<table border="3">
<caption>This is a caption</caption>
<tr><th>Heading 1</th><th>Heading 2</th>
<tr><td>Row 1 Cell 1</td><td>Row 1 Cell 2</td>
<tr><td>Row 2 Cell 1</td><td>Row 2 Cell 2</td>
<tr><td>Row 3 Cell 1</td><td>Row 3 Cell 2</td>
</table>
```

NOTE    *The caption and heading rows are optional.*

# Create Frame-Based Pages

Frames are another example of simple HTML that can become very complex. Complicated framesets with nested frames can be quite confusing to set up. However, a basic frameset really is quite easy to do. The following table lists the necessary elements and attributes. Following the table is an example of how to set up a simple frameset.

| To Do This... | Use This... |
|---|---|
| Create a frameset | <frameset> </frameset> |
| Create a frame | <frame /> |
| Specify a frame's source file | <frame **src="page1.htm"** /> |

| To Do This... | Use This... |
|---|---|
| Assign a name to your frame | &lt;frame **name="frame1"** /&gt; |
| Provide content for noncompatible browsers | &lt;noframes&gt; &lt;/noframes&gt; |
| Specify rows | &lt;frameset **rows="#"**&gt; (Pixels or percentages) |
| Specify columns | &lt;frameset **cols="#"**&gt; (Pixels or percentages) |
| Turn borders off | &lt;frame **frameborder="no"** /&gt; (Default is "yes") |
| Prevent resizing | &lt;frame **noresize** /&gt; |
| Add or remove scroll bar | &lt;frame **scrolling="auto \| yes \| no"** /&gt; (Default is "auto") |
| Control margins | &lt;frame **marginheight="#" marginwidth="#"** /&gt; (# = pixels) |

The code listing that follows will create a simple two-column frameset. Remember that for the frameset to function properly, you need to create at least one HTML document to serve as the source document for each frame. Otherwise, your frames will not display.

```
<html>
<head><title>Simple Frameset</title></head>
<frameset cols="50%, 50%">
<frame src="webpage1.htm" />
<frame src="webpage2.htm" />
</frameset>
</html>
```

# Construct Forms

HTML forms enable you to add interactivity to your page. With a form you can create surveys, guest books, e-mail pages, order forms, and so on. The basic form elements and attributes are included in the following table. Because form construction and design can be very involved, you might want to review Chapter 14 for more detail.

| To Do This... | Use This... |
|---|---|
| Create a form | &lt;form&gt; &lt;/form&gt; |
| Tell the browser how to handle the content | &lt;form **method="post"**&gt; |
| Tell the browser what to do with the content | &lt;form **action=" "**&gt; (You can use the mailto: protocol or refer to a CGI script) |

B

| To Do This... | Use This... |
|---|---|
| Create an input field | &lt;input /&gt; |
| Create a "submit" button | &lt;input type="submit" /&gt; |
| Create a "reset" button | &lt;input type="reset" /&gt; |
| Create a "radio" button | &lt;input type="radio /&gt; |
| Create a check box | &lt;input type="checkbox" /&gt; |
| Create a hidden field | &lt;input type="hidden" /&gt; |
| Create a password field | &lt;input type="password" /&gt; |
| Create a menu | &lt;select&gt; &lt;/select&gt; |
| Add menu options | &lt;option&gt; &lt;/option&gt; |
| Preselect an option | &lt;option **selected**&gt;This is preselected&lt;/option&gt; |
| Add a text input area | &lt;textarea rows="#" cols="#"&gt; &lt;/textarea&gt; |

A form can be as detailed as you need it to be. Take the time to think through your reasons for constructing the form and what you want it to accomplish. You'll save yourself a lot of needless work if you plan it out ahead. The code for a simple form might look like this:

```
<form method="post" action="mailto:me@myemail.com">
<table border="0">
<tr><td>First Name:</td>
<td><input type="text" name="FirstName" size="25" /></td></tr>
<tr><td>Last Name:</td>
<td><input type="text" name="LastName" size="25" /></td></tr>
<tr><td rowspan="3" valign="top">What do you
think of my site?</td>
<td><input type="radio" name="opinion" value="1"
checked="checked" />Great!</td></tr>
<tr><td><input type="radio" name="opinion" value="2" />
Fair</td></tr>
<tr><td><input type="radio" name="opinion" value="3" />
The Pits!</td></tr>
<tr><td><input type="submit" /></td>
<td><input type="reset" /></td></tr>
</table>
</form>
```

TIP

*Use tables to construct your forms, as in the preceding code. This will help you to create a form that looks sharper and more professional.*

NOTE   *You can find an exhaustive reference for all the elements, attributes, and values in the current HTML specification online at www.w3.org/TR/html4. You can even download it free of charge.*

# Add Java Applets

Java applets enable you to add animation and interactivity to your pages with little effort on your part. Once you download the applet, you can embed it on your page with either the deprecated <applet> element or the <object> element. The following table lists some basic elements and attributes you can use with Java applets.

| To Do This. . . | Use This. . . |
|---|---|
| Add an applet | <applet> </applet> or <object> </object> |
| Identify the applet's source code location (for the <applet> element only) | code="www.mysite.com/myapplet.class" |
| Identify the applet's source code location (for the <object> element) | classid="java:myapplet.class" |
| Specify an applet's height and width | height="#" width="#" (#=height/width in pixels) |
| Add space around an applet | hspace="#" vspace="#" (#=hspace/vspace in pixels) |
| Include text for browsers incapable of displaying Java | <applet>Alternative text goes between the tags.</applet> (This also works for <object>.) |

Although the HTML for adding a Java applet can become very complex, depending on the applet, at its most basic it's not much more difficult than adding an image to your page. A simple applet can be added by only using the <applet> or <object> elements along with a few attributes specifying position, size, and so on. The following code shows what the HTML for an applet might look like this:

```
<applet code="www.mysite.com/myapplet.class"
    height="200" width="200" align="right"
    hspace="5" vspace="5">
  Alternative text goes here
</applet>
```

B

# Appendix C

# Insert Special Characters on Your Page

The use of certain characters poses a problem for you as a Web author. For example, you might want to include a copyright symbol at the bottom of your page, but you won't find that character on your keyboard. How do you tell a browser to include it? Let's say you're doing a mathematical formula and you want to place an < or > sign on your page. If you just type in the characters, the Web browser will interpret them as HTML. How can you instruct the browser to display those characters rather than ignoring them or treating them as HTML code? Perhaps you want to include a word from a foreign language and you need a special symbol or accent. What do you do? The way around this and similar problems is through the use of *entities*.

# Understand Entities

Simply put, an entity is a character that either is not accessible through your keyboard or one that will be incorrectly interpreted by the browser. However, these characters are resident in your computer's system, and you can access them through the use of special codes.

The source for entity codes is the ISO-Latin1 character set. ISO stands for the *International Standards Organization*. The rest of the term denotes that this character set is derived from the Latin (or Roman) alphabet. Of course, there are many other character sets, derived from different alphabets. But the one you are most likely to use is ISO Latin-1; this also is the default character set for the Web.

> **NOTE** *Entities described by numbers are called* numeric entities. *Entities described by logical terms are called* character entities. *Many special characters are represented by both types. For example, the copyright symbol © can be written either as a numeric entity, &#169, or as a character entity, &copy; Whichever you use, a Web browser will recognize it as the entity for the copyright symbol and display the symbol in its place.*

An entity must be constructed properly for the browser to recognize it. It always begins with an ampersand (&) and closes with a semicolon (;). In between, you insert either a numeric code or a logical descriptive term. In addition, numeric entities must have the number symbol (#) preceding the entity number. Also, entities are case sensitive; always type them in exactly as you see them on the chart.

> **CAUTION** *Some older browsers might not recognize particular character entities. It's always a good idea to test your page in different browsers to be sure of its compatibility.*

# Insert an Entity in a Web Page

A practical way to experiment with entities is by adding a copyright notice to your Web page. To use the entity for the copyright (©) symbol, follow these steps:

1. Open or create an HTML document.

2. In the <body> section of the document, type **Copyright 2010**.

3. After the word "Copyright," type the ampersand character, **&**.

4. Enter either the numeric or character code. For example, for the copyright symbol you would type **copy** or **#169**.

5. Close out the code by typing a semicolon. Your text should look like this:

   ```
   Copyright &copy; 2010 or Copyright &#169; 2010
   ```

However, on a Web browser it will display this way: Copyright © 2010. Try it out on a sample page. Remember to put the entities in the actual text of your Web page—not in the tags. It would be incorrect to write <h6 &copy;>Copyright 2010</h6>. If you put the entity in the wrong place, the browser will simply ignore it. Type in the following code for a demonstration of how entities work and for a sample of what shows up when they are entered incorrectly:

```
<html>
<head><title>Sample Entity Display</title></head>
<body>
<div align="center">
<h3>Copyright &copy; 2010</h3>
<h3>My Trademark &#174; is a registered trademark</h3>
<h3 &copy;>This line incorrectly puts the entity in a tag</h3>
<h3>This line leaves off &174; a key part of an entity</h3>
</div>
</body>
</html>
```

When you save and display this page, you'll notice, as in Illustration 1, that incorrectly typed entities will be either ignored by the browser or displayed as code in the document.

C

Copyright © 2010

My Trademark ® is a registered trademark

This line incorrectly puts the entity in a tag

This line leaves off &174; a key part of an entity

# Commonly Used Entities

In the following table are some entities you might use. For a more complete list, download the offline "mini" Web site at www.osborne.com.

| Description | Numeric Entity | Character Entity | Character |
|---|---|---|---|
| Exclamation | &#33; | | ! |
| Quotation | &#34; | &quot; | " |
| Number | &#35; | | # |
| Dollar | &#36; | | $ |
| Percent | &#37; | | % |
| Ampersand | &#38; | &amp; | & |
| Apostrophe | &#39; | | ' |
| Asterisk | &#42; | | * |
| Plus Sign | &#43; | | + |
| Comma | &#44; | | , |
| Hyphen | &#45; | | - |
| Period | &#46; | | . |
| Slash | &#47; | | / |
| Colon | &#58; | | : |
| Semicolon | &#59; | | ; |
| Less Than | &#60; | &lt; | < |
| Equal Sign | &#61; | | = |
| Greater Than | &#62; | &gt; | > |
| Question | &#63; | | ? |
| "At" Sign | &#64; | | @ |

| Description | Numeric Entity | Character Entity | Character |
| --- | --- | --- | --- |
| Left Bracket | &#91; | | [ |
| Backslash | &#92; | | \ |
| Right Bracket | &#93; | | ] |
| Left Curly Brace | &#123; | | { |
| Right Curly Brace | &#125; | | } |
| Tilde | &#126; | | ~ |
| Copyright | &#169; | &copy; | © |
| Trademark | &#174; | &reg; | ® |

# Appendix D

## Cascading Style Sheets Practical Reference

Cascading Style Sheets are a largely untapped resource among beginning Web authors. One reason is that CSS's distinctive syntax and terminology appears confusing, particularly when set alongside that of HTML. If you are not working with Web sites all the time, you might find it difficult to keep all the details of CSS straight.

This reference guide is designed to refresh your memory on the basics of CSS syntax and on how to use the various properties to create a special look for your Web site. To use this reference guide, simply think through what you would like to do with CSS; then look at the appropriate chart to find your solution. Remember, the more you use CSS, the more comfortable you will become with it—and the more you will like it.

NOTE     *If you are interested in learning CSS2, you can download the specification free of charge at the W3C's Web site: www.w3.org. Although CSS2 is the current recommendation, browser support for CSS2 is weak at best. CSS2 also is more complex and complicated to use. In the interest of giving you a useful and dependable CSS toolbox, the following charts focus primarily on the properties and values characteristic of CSS1. If you'll stick with the properties in these charts, you shouldn't have many problems with browser compatibility.*

# Understand CSS Terminology

CSS comes with its own unique terminology. Often, beginning Web authors find the new terms daunting, and so avoid using style sheets. However, if you learn what the terms mean and how they relate to HTML, you will find it much easier to master style sheets. The following table contains a list of some of the CSS terms you need to be familiar with.

| Term | Refers To |
| --- | --- |
| Selector | Any part of a Web page to which style rules are to be applied (usually an HTML element) |
| Properties | The characteristics to be modified (corresponds to attributes in HTML) |
| Values | The characteristics assigned to properties |
| Declaration | Combination of a property and value |
| Rule | A selector with one or more declarations assigned to it |
| Inheritance | An element displays the style characteristics of its parent (the element in which it is nested) |

| Term | Refers To |
|------|-----------|
| Parent element | An element that has other elements nested within it. In the following example, &lt;p&gt; &lt;/p&gt; is the parent element: &lt;p&gt;&lt;b&gt; This is bold.&lt;/b&gt;&lt;/p&gt; |
| Child element | An element that is nested inside another element. In the preceding example, &lt;b&gt; &lt;/b&gt; is the child element. |
| Cascade | The way style sheets take precedence over one another *Example:* inline takes precedence over embedded, which has priority over a linked or an external style sheet. |
| Class | A sub-category that you can create and assign to a selector. |
| ID selector | A selector you create by assigning it a special name or number. |
| Contextual selector | A selector whose properties are modified when it occurs in the context of another selector. |
| Pseudo class | A special class created by certain conditions rather than by HTML code. *Example:* links, visited links, and active links |
| Pseudo element | A special application of style that affects only part of the element to which it is applied. *Example:* first-line and first-letter are CSS1's only pseudo elements |
| Inline Style Sheet | Style rules applied inside an HTML element with the style=" " attribute. |
| Embedded Style Sheet | Style rules embedded in a single page with the &lt;style&gt; &lt;/style&gt; element in the document &lt;head&gt; &lt;/head&gt; element. |
| External Style Sheet | Style rules collected in a text document and linked to one or more pages with the &lt;link /&gt; element in the Web page's &lt;head&gt; &lt;/head&gt; element. |

# Review Basic CSS Syntax

To use CSS effectively, you must remember the key elements of style sheet syntax (sentence structure). Keep in mind that a selector is separated from style declarations by a space. In a declaration, the property and value must be separated by a colon (:). Multiple property/value combinations should be separated from one another by semicolons (;). All declarations should be enclosed in curly braces ({ }). A sample style rule will look like this:

```
selector      {property: value;
               property: value;
               property: value; }
```

TIP *Properties and values do not need to be placed on separate lines, but you might find it easier to decipher your style sheet down the line if you do it this way.*

One important exception to the syntax in the preceding example is when you are applying style rules inline with the style=" " attribute. When used inline, style declarations (property: value) are enclosed in quotation marks (" ") rather than curly braces. Thus, applied inline, the previous example would look like this:

```
<p style="property: value; property: value; property: value";>
```

Some of the primary aspects of CSS syntax are listed in the following table.

| To Do This... | Use This... |
| --- | --- |
| Apply an inline style sheet | style=" " <br> (Inside the element you want to modify) |
| Embed a style sheet | <head><style type="text/css">Insert style rules here</style></head> |
| Link to a style sheet | <head><link rel="style sheet" type="text/css" href="filename.css" /> </head> |
| Apply the same style declarations to more than one selector | h1, h2, h3, h4, h5, h6 {color: navy; <br>                 font-style: serif; } <br> (Selectors should be separated by commas.) |
| Use more than one declaration in an embedded or external style sheet | selector  {property: value; <br>         property: value; } |
| Use more than one declaration in an inline style sheet | <element style="property: value; property: value;"> |
| Create a class selector | selector.classname {property: value;} <br> *Example:* p.green {color: green;} <br> (Will cause text to display green when applied) |
| Apply a class selector | <element class="classname"> <br> *Example:* <p class="green">Green text</p> <br> (Applies the preceding example) |
| Create an ID selector | #IDname {property: value;} <br> *Example:* #Myname1 {font-family:cursive; font-size: 8pt; color: maroon;} |
| Apply an ID selector | <element id="IDname"> <br> <p id="Myname1">Applies preceding styles</p> |

| To Do This... | Use This... |
|---|---|
| Create a contextual selector | selector1 selector2 {property: value;}<br>With contextual selectors, the selectors should not be separated by commas.<br>*Example:* p b {color: blue;} (Will cause bold text to display blue when the <b> element is used inside <p>) |
| Apply a contextual selector | <element1><element2>Contextual style applied</element2></element1><br>*Example:* <p><b>Bold text displays as blue</b></p><br>(Based on the preceding example) |

# Understand Measurement Units

Learning to apply measurement units in CSS can be tricky. One thing to keep in mind, particularly when working with length units is the difference between *absolute* and *relative* measurements. Absolute measurements (inches, for example) are fixed and cannot scale or adjust from medium to medium. Whenever possible, use relative measurements (ems, for example). That way, your pages will be capable of adjusting to different types of displays automatically. CSS measurement units are listed in the following table.

| This Unit | Can Be Specified This Way |
|---|---|
| Color | name: (red, blue, black, and so on)<br>hex code: #ffffff<br>hex shorthand: #ff0<br>rgb numeric values: rgb(0, 255, 0)<br>rgb percentages: rgb(20%, 45%, 96%) |
| Percentages | 200%, -14%, +35%<br>(Some selectors cannot take negative values) |
| Lengths (relative measurements) | px (pixels)<br>em (width of the letter "m" for the font in use)<br>ex (height of the letter "x" for the font in use) |
| Lengths (absolute measurements) | pt (points, as in a 10- or 12- point font)<br>pc (picas; 12 points equals 1 pica)<br>in (inches)<br>mm (millimeters)<br>cm (centimeters) |

# Use Font Properties

Using the <font> </font> element is a difficult habit to break. If you begin to experiment with CSS's font properties, you will find yourself using <font> less and less. The font properties, listed in the following table, give you much greater freedom in your page design.

| To Do This | Use This Property | With These Values | Example |
|---|---|---|---|
| Specify a particular font family | font-family | You can use a specific font *Example:* Arial or a generic serif, sans-serif, cursive, fantasy, or monospace | p {font-family: serif;} |
| Choose between normal and italic | font-style | normal \| italic \| oblique | h1 {font-style: italic;} |
| Alternate between normal or small caps | font-variant | normal \| small caps | h2 {font-variant: small caps;} |
| Make a font bolder or lighter | font-weight | normal \| bold \| bolder \| lighter \| 100 - 900 | h3 {font-weight: 500;} |
| Change a font's size | font-size | Absolute: xx-small \| x-small \| small \| medium \| large \| x-large \| xx-large | h3 {font-size: smaller;) |
| | | Relative: larger \| smaller (relative to the parent element) | |
| | | Length: em \| ex | |
| | | Percentage | |

**SHORTCUT**  *A quick way to make multiple font declarations for one selector is by using the font: property. This is a kind of "shorthand" for listing more than one property associated with fonts. It might look something like this: h1 {font: sans-serif 36pt italic lighter}. Just remember that the various properties are separated by spaces and nothing else. The only exception to this is if you are including one or more alternate fonts. Those would be separated by commas. For example, h1{font: Arial, sans-serif 36pt italic lighter}.*

# Apply Text Properties

As with the font properties, text properties greatly increase your ability to specify how the text, word spacing, line spacing, and so on will display when your page is viewed. As much as possible, use relative measurements when you specify these properties. This will allow your page to adjust dynamically. CSS text properties are listed in the following table:

| To Do This | Use This Property | With These Values | Example |
|---|---|---|---|
| Adjust space between words | word-spacing | normal \| by length | h5 {word-spacing: .75 em;} |
| Adjust space between letters | letter-spacing | normal \| by length | div {letter-spacing: 2mm;} |
| Add and remove underlines or other text "decoration" | text-decoration | none \| underline \| overline \| line-through \| blink | a:link {text-decoration: none;} (Removes underlines from links) |
| Control the vertical positioning of an element | vertical-align | top \| text-top \| middle \| bottom \| text-bottom \| baseline \| sub \| super \| (percentage) | p {vertical-align: super;} (Will superscript this element) |
| Convert text from uppercase to lowercase | text-transform | none \| uppercase \| lowercase \| capitalize | span {text-transform: uppercase;} (Will convert all text in this element to uppercase) |
| Justify, center, or align text | text-align | justify \| left \| right \| center | h4 {text-align: center;} (Will center all text in this element) |
| Indent text | text-indent | by length or percentage | p {text-indent: .50in;} (Will indent text 1/2 inch) |
| Adjust line spacing | line-height | normal \| numeric \| by length or percentage | span {line-height: 150%;} (Will set the spacing at 150%, relative to the font size in use) |

# Work with Background and Color Properties

In HTML you are limited to setting background colors and images to the <body> and <table> elements. With CSS you can specify these background properties for virtually any HTML element you choose. That gives you a lot of flexibility in design and makes your job much easier when wanting to create a "look" for your site. The properties for controlling background and color are listed in the following table:

| To Do This | Use This Property | With These Values | Example |
|---|---|---|---|
| Set a foreground color (usually text color) | color | color (name, hex code, rgb) | p {color: #ff0000;} (Sets text color to red for the paragraph element) |
| Specify a background color | background-color | color (name, hex code, rgb) or transparent | body {background-color: white;} (Sets background color to white for an entire Web page) |
| Add a background image | background-image | image url | div {background-image: url(pix.gif);} (Adds a background image to the <div> element) |
| Tell a browser how to repeat an image | background-repeat | repeat (tile) \| repeat-x (horizontally) \| repeat-y (vertically) \| no-repeat (display only one copy of image) | body {background-image: url(pix.gif); background-repeat: repeat-y;} (Causes the image to tile vertically) |
| Turn image scrolling on and off | background-attachment | scroll \| fixed | body {background-image: url(pix.gif); background-repeat: repeat-y; background-attachment: fixed;} (Background image remains fixed while text and other elements scroll) |

| To Do This | Use This Property | With These Values | Example |
|---|---|---|---|
| Position a background image | background-position | percentage or length (value a, value b) \| or top/center/bottom and left/center/right | body: background-image: url(pix.gif); background-position: top, left;} (Positions image in the upper-left corner of the element) |

# Understand and Use Box Properties

If you'll think of every HTML element as being contained inside a rectangular "box," you'll have a pretty good idea of how to use the box properties. With CSS, not only are you able to set margins, borders, and padding for tables (as you can already do with HTML); you now can do it for any element. If you learn to use these properties with class and ID selectors, you will have a virtually limitless array of possible styles at your disposal. The box properties are organized in the following tables: Set Margins, Add Padding, Create Borders, and Specify Size and Float.

## Set Margins

When you think of margins, you probably think of whole pages. Remember to keep in mind the "box" concept. Every element is contained in a box; so when you specify margins with these properties, you are not setting margins for the entire page (unless you are using "body" as a selector). Instead, you are setting the margins for that selector (element). Thus, different selectors can have different margins. Set your margins with the properties listed in the following table.

| To Do This | Use This Property | With These Values | Example |
|---|---|---|---|
| Specify a top margin | margin-top | length, percentage, or auto | blockquote {margin-top: 1em;} |
| Specify a right margin | margin-right | length, percentage, or auto | p {margin-right: .25in;} |
| Specify the bottom margin | margin-bottom | length, percentage, or auto | div {margin-bottom: .3cm;} |
| Specify the left margin | margin-left | length, percentage, or auto | span {margin-left: 5%;} |

| To Do This | Use This Property | With These Values | Example |
|---|---|---|---|
| Use shorthand to specify all four margins to the same size | margin: (value) | length, percentage, or auto | h2 {margin: 10px;} (Sets a 10-pixel margin all the way around) |
| Use shorthand to specify the top and bottom to one value, and the right and left to another | margin: (top/bottom value) (right/left value) | length, percentage, or auto | h6 {margin: .25in .33in;} |
| Use shorthand to set the top margin to one value, the right and left margins to another, and the bottom to a third value | margin: (top value) (right/left value) (bottom value) | length, percentage, or auto | div {margin: 5% 7.5% 3%;} |
| Use shorthand to set all four margins to different values | margin: (top) (right) (bottom) (left) | length, percentage, or auto | p {margin: 2px .3em 4% .27cm;} |

## Add Padding

What is the difference between specifying margins and adding padding? Not a lot, really. Both add extra space around the contents of an element. Think again of the "box" concept. If your element is a box, the margin represents the amount of space between one box and another box. The padding represents the amount of space between the contents of the box and its edge. The idea is similar to cellspacing and cellpadding with HTML tables. The following table shows how to add padding to your elements:

| To Do This | Use This Property | With These Values | Example |
|---|---|---|---|
| Add top padding | padding-top | length, percentage, or auto | span {padding-top: 15px;} |
| Add padding to the right side | padding-right | length, percentage, or auto | p {padding-right: 100mm;} |
| Add bottom padding | padding-bottom | length, percentage, or auto | blockquote {padding-bottom: .50in;} |
| Add left-side padding | padding-left | length, percentage, or auto | td {padding-left: 10%;} |

> **SHORTCUT**  *The shorthand for specifying padding is the same as that used for margins. Remember that the browser starts at the top and moves clockwise when considering multiple values. For example, h3 {padding: 10% 5% 3% 4%;} applies percentage values to the top (10%), right (5%), bottom (3%), and left (4%) sides of the element, respectively.*

## Create Borders

CSS allows you to surround any element (selector) with a border. There are a variety of border styles to choose from (although some browsers will not display the full variety). The following table shows the properties necessary to specify borders.

| To Do This | Use This Property | With These Values | Example |
|---|---|---|---|
| Specify a border style | border-style | inset \| outset \| ridge \| solid \| double \| groove \| dashed \| dotted \| none | table {border-style: double;} (Places a double-lined border around any table elements) |
| Set border colors | border-color | color name, hex code, rgb values | th {border-color: navy;} |
| Set the width of the top border | border-top-width | thick \| medium \| thin or length | td {border-top-width: 5px;} |
| Set the width of the right border | border-right-width | thick \| medium \| thin or length | tr {border-right-width: 1.2em;} |
| Set the width of the bottom border | border-bottom-width | thick \| medium \| thin or length | p {border-bottom-width: thin;} |
| Set the width of the left border | border-left-width | thick \| medium \| thin or length | p {border-left-width: medium;} |
| Use shorthand to set the width of all borders with one declaration | border-width | thick \| medium \| thin or length (multiple values should be written the same as with margins) | h6 {border-width: thin thick; } (Sets the top and bottom border to thin and the side borders to thick) |
| Define all values for a top border with one declaration | border-top | width \| style \| color | span {border-top: thick dashed red;} |
| Define all values for a right border with one declaration | border-right | width \| style \| color | div {border-right: thin groove yellow;} |

| To Do This | Use This Property | With These Values | Example |
|---|---|---|---|
| Define all values for a bottom border with one declaration | border-bottom | width \| style \| color | h3 {border-bottom: medium ridge gold;} |
| Define all values for a left border with one declaration | border-left | width \| style \| color | td {border-left: 5px inset green;} |
| Define identical values for all sides with one declaration | border | width \| style \| color | p {border: thick outset navy;} |

## Specify Image Size and Position

Although the properties in the following table can be used with text elements, more often than not they are used with images. These correspond closely to the HTML attributes that often are applied to the <img /> element. The following table lists the properties related to position and size:

| To Do This | Use This Property | With These Values | Example |
|---|---|---|---|
| Set an element's width (most often used with images) | width | length, percentage, or auto | img.logo {width: 105px;} |
| Set an element's height (most often used with images) | height | length or auto | img.logo {height: 55px;} |
| Position an element with text-wrapping | float | none \| right \| left | image.logo {float: right;} (Positions the image to the right and allows text to wrap to the left) |
| Position an element without text-wrapping | clear | none \| both \| right \| left | image.logo {clear: left;} (Positions the element to the left, below any floating elements) |

# Understand Classification Properties

The properties in the following table can have some strange results if you aren't careful. For example, the display property can be used to prevent certain elements from displaying at all. However, most of these properties listed in the following table are used to tell the browser how to handle various elements, such as lists and list items.

| To Do This | Use This Property | With These Values | Example |
|---|---|---|---|
| Control an element's display characteristics | display | none \| list-item \| block \| inline (Block adds a line before and after the element; inline does not) | img {display: none;} (Turns off image display) |
| Control how a browser handles "white space" | white-space | normal \| pre \| nowrap | p.code {display: pre;} (Preserves your spacing and formatting, just as the <pre> element would) |
| Specify bullets and numbering for lists | list-style-type | disc \| circle \| square \| decimal \| lower-roman \| upper-roman \| lower-alpha \| upper-alpha \| none | ol {list-style-type: lower-alpha;} (Uses lowercase letters) |
| Specify an image for list bullets | list-style-image | image url | ul {list-style-image: url(bullet.gif);} |
| Specify a position for image bullets | list-style-position | outside \| inside | ul {list-style-position: inside;} (Places the bullet inside the list item's content margin, as opposed to outside of it) |
| Use shorthand for specifying a list's characteristics | list-style | (type) (image) (position) | ul.pix {list-style: disc url(px.gif) outside;} |

# Understand Pseudoclasses and Pseudoelements

Pseudoclasses and pseudoelements represent ways of dealing with text that are not present in the actual structure of an HTML document. For example, if you want to specify colors for your links other than those of the HTML default, how do you do it? You must use the pseudoclass designed to address that situation. What if you want to add some drop caps to your text? For that, you use a pseudoelement. Pseudoclasses and pseudoelements are limited in their scope but can be quite useful. The following table lists the pseudoclasses and pseudoelements included in the CSS1 specification:

| To Do This | Use This | Example |
|---|---|---|
| Set a link's characteristics | a:link (pseudoclass) | a:link {color: red;} |
| Set an active link's characteristics | a:active (pseudoclass) | a:active {color: purple;} |
| Set a visited link's characteristics | a:visited (pseudoclass) | a:visited {color: green;} |
| Cause a link to change color when a mouse passes over it | a:hover (CSS2 pseudoclass; might not be supported in all browsers) | a:hover {color: magenta;} |
| Modify the first letter of an element's text | (selector):first-letter | p:first-letter {font-size: 150%; color: red;} <p><p:first-letter>A</p:firstletter>pseudo-element can be very useful in creating special effects</p> |
| Modify the first line of an element's text | (selector):first-line | p:first-line {font-variant: italic; font-size: 1.2em; color: blue;} <p><p:first-line>The first line</p:first-line>of this text will be different.</p> |

This CSS reference guide, although by no means exhaustive, will give you enough material to begin working with style sheets and using them on your site. Once you have mastered CSS1, you might want to begin exploring the new features added in CSS2. Although many of these new features are not well supported yet, in time they will be. If you begin learning them now, you'll be ready to implement them in your Web sites when they are better supported.

# Index

## INTERNATIONAL CONTACT INFORMATION

**AUSTRALIA**
McGraw-Hill Book Company Australia Pty. Ltd.
TEL +61-2-9417-9899
FAX +61-2-9417-5687
http://www.mcgraw-hill.com.au
books-it_sydney@mcgraw-hill.com

**CANADA**
McGraw-Hill Ryerson Ltd.
TEL +905-430-5000
FAX +905-430-5020
http://www.mcgrawhill.ca

**GREECE, MIDDLE EAST,
NORTHERN AFRICA**
McGraw-Hill Hellas
TEL +30-1-656-0990-3-4
FAX +30-1-654-5525

**MEXICO (Also serving Latin America)**
McGraw-Hill Interamericana Editores S.A. de C.V.
TEL +525-117-1583
FAX +525-117-1589
http://www.mcgraw-hill.com.mx
fernando_castellanos@mcgraw-hill.com

**SINGAPORE (Serving Asia)**
McGraw-Hill Book Company
TEL +65-863-1580
FAX +65-862-3354
http://www.mcgraw-hill.com.sg
mghasia@mcgraw-hill.com

**SOUTH AFRICA**
McGraw-Hill South Africa
TEL +27-11-622-7512
FAX +27-11-622-9045
robyn_swanepoel@mcgraw-hill.com

**UNITED KINGDOM & EUROPE
(Excluding Southern Europe)**
McGraw-Hill Education Europe
TEL +44-1-628-502500
FAX +44-1-628-770224
http://www.mcgraw-hill.co.uk
computing_neurope@mcgraw-hill.com

**ALL OTHER INQUIRIES Contact:**
Osborne/McGraw-Hill
TEL +1-510-549-6600
FAX +1-510-883-7600
http://www.osborne.com
omg_international@mcgraw-hill.com